Bruce R. McClelland

Hs 129
PANZERJÄGER!

Hs 129
PANZERJÄGER!

Martin Pegg

[signature]

Colour Artwork and Technical Drawings by
Eddie Creek, Tom Tullis and Arthur Bentley

CLASSIC
PUBLICATIONS

Sun Tzu said: "There are five ways of attacking with fire. The first is to burn soldiers in their camp; the second is to burn stores; the third is to burn baggage-trains; the fourth is to burn arsenals and magazines; the fifth is to hurl dropping fire amongst the enemy."

Sun Tzu: *The Art of War,* 490 B.C.

First published in Great Britain in 1997 by Classic Publications, Quarry Ridge House, 7 Quarry Close, Burgess Hill, West Sussex RH15 0TJ.

© 1996 Colour Illustrations - Eddie J. Creek
© 1996 Colour Illustrations - Thomas Tullis
© 1996 Line Drawings - Arthur Bentley

All rights reserved. No part of this book may be reproduced or transmitted in any form or by any means, electronic or mechanical including photocopying, recording, chemical, optical or otherwise without prior written permission from the Publisher. All enquiries should be addressed to the publisher.

ISBN 0 9526867 1 6

Book design and cover artwork by Colin Woodman Graphic Design

Printed in the UK by: Postprint
                Taverner House
                Harling Road
                East Harling
                Norwich NR16 2QR

CONTENTS

AUTHOR'S INTRODUCTION and ACKNOWLEDGEMENTS 6
FOREWORD By Franz Oswald 9
FROM THE COCKPIT By Gebhard Weber 10
FROM THE GROUND By Willi Tholen 11

PART ONE: **GENESIS** **13 – 59**

    1. **FROM BARBED WIRE TO BLITZKRIEG** The Schlachtflieger: Origins and Development 15
    2. **"A FLYING COFFIN"** Prototypes and the Search for Refinement 1937–1941 25
    3. **"A PLEASURE TO FLY"** The Thoroughbred Emerges 43
    4. **FORTY MACHINES A MONTH** Praise, Condemnation and the Struggle for Production 51

PART TWO: **INTO BATTLE** **61 – 97**

    5. **OSTFRONT - COMBAT DEBUT** Russia 1942 63
    6. **"A QUESTION OF LIFE OR DEATH"** The Cannon Crisis 73
    7. **HIGH HOPES - LOW TEMPERATURES** The MK 101 Cannon in Service 81

PART THREE: **AFRIKA** **99 – 125**

    8. **PANZERFLIEGERSTAFFEL AFRIKA** A Gleam of Hope 101
    9. **"WE HAVE A VERY GOOD NAME HERE…"**
        The Last Phase in North Africa November 1942–April 1943 109

PART FOUR: **PANZERJÄGER!** **127 – 213**

    10. **"SOME SORT OF VISION"** The Battle over the Kuban March–July 1943 129
    11. **"ZITADELLE"** Kursk and the Killing Grounds of Belgorod July–September 1943 143
    12. **FIGHTING RETREAT** The Withdrawal Through the Ukraine October 1943–January 1944 157
    13. **"WHAT SHOULD A TANK-DESTROYER LOOK LIKE?"** A Diversion of Doctrine 161
    14. **"THREE CHEERS FOR THE HENSCHEL LOCOMOTIVE WORKS"**
         Tank-Buster Training and Tactics 171
    15. **"SO LOW, I COULD HAVE SHAKEN HANDS WITH IVAN"**
         Non-Stop Ground-Support January 1944 187
    16. **"INDIANS TO THE RIGHT!"** 10,000 Missions and the Defence of Proskurov 197
    17. **"NOW THE Hs 129 WEARS THE KNIGHT'S CROSS"** Operations in Rumania 1944 209

PART FIVE: **FRIEND AND FOE • TRIALS AND TRIBULATIONS** **215 – 245**

    18. **IN RUMANIAN SERVICE** Operations by the 8. Rumanian Schlachtgruppe 217
    19. **THE Hs 129 FIGHTS THE WEHRMACHT** Rumanian Operations to May 1945 225
    20. **TRIALS AND TRIBULATIONS** Experiments with Special Weapons 229

PART SIX: **BLOOD RED HORIZON** **247 – 301**

    21. **"KEEP YOUR EYES SKINNED AT ALL TIMES"** The Russian Summer Offensives of 1944 249
    22. **"THEY NAILED US TO THE GROUND"** From the Vistula to the Oder January – March 1945 267
    23. **EXTRAORDINARY IMPACT** The Hs 129 B-3 with BK 7.5cm Operations in East Prussia 1945 ... 281
    24. **"WITH PANZERFAUSTEN AND MACHINE PISTOLS"** The Final Ordeal May 1945 295

APPENDIX ONE: ENEMY WITHIN THE CAMP The Captured Hs 129s 305
APPENDIX TWO: CAMOUFLAGE, MARKINGS AND MANUFACTURER'S DATA 311
APPENDIX THREE: LOSS LISTS 317
APPENDIX FOUR: TECHNICAL AND WEAPONS SPECIFICATIONS 327
APPENDIX FIVE: LOGBOOKS AND AWARD CITATIONS 331
GLOSSARY/RANKS 334
BIBLIOGRAPHY 335
SOURCE NOTES 336
INDEX 339

AUTHOR'S INTRODUCTION and ACKNOWLEDGEMENTS

Throughout the history of military aviation, a number of aircraft have emerged as truly outstanding warplanes. Machines such as the Supermarine Spitfire, P-51 Mustang, de Havilland Mosquito and Douglas Dakota gave distinguished service and are remembered with pride by those who flew them. Conversely, and whether justified or not, other aircraft such as the Messerschmitt Me 163 and Fairey Barracuda gained a reputation for being more dangerous to friend than to foe and have been recorded as something of a pilot's nightmare. Between these two extremes are countless other aircraft which, while performing valuable service have, for one reason or another, largely been ignored by aviation historians and, perhaps as a direct result of this, have failed to capture the public imagination. When compared with the best, these machines may be considered satisfactory, yet some deserve more than the few, generally dismissive, lines that they have hitherto been allocated.

One such aircraft was the *Luftwaffe's* Henschel Hs 129, generally described by aviation authors as being "disappointing"; yet for some three years, a handful of these machines together with an equally small number of Junkers Ju 87 Gs, was the only really effective answer to the mass of Russian armour which German ground forces faced on the Eastern front, and it was these machines which pioneered the *Luftwaffe's* use of aircraft as an anti-tank weapon. As such, the Hs 129 is remembered with affection as the *"Panzerknacker"* ("Tank-Cracker") or *"Fliegende Pak"* ("Flying Anti-Tank Gun") by surviving German aircrew and many a German soldier alive today owes his life to the timely intervention of the *Panzerjäger* ("Tank-Hunter") in an otherwise disastrous situation.

However, while the Hs 129 and the members of the units which operated this aircraft have to date been denied their due recognition, extensive research now shows that, with few exceptions, most previously published accounts are both misleading and inaccurate. By presenting new information it is to be hoped that the following pages will at last reveal the achievements of those who flew the Hs 129 and, in doing so, help restore the reputation of this aircraft.

....

During the course of my research, I have been most fortunate in receiving help and encouragement from a large number of individuals and institutions. I would therefore like to record my thanks and appreciation to the following, without whom this history could not have been written:

In the UK, my colleagues in *Staffel* 90, particularly my editor Robert Forsyth, for his belief in this work and his sympathetic and helpful advice; Eddie Creek, who supervised the pictorial content and made his valuable photographic collection available; Arthur Bentley, who painstakingly created the most accurate and comprehensive Hs 129 drawings yet published. Nick Beale, Mike Norton, Jerry Scutts, J.Richard Smith and Tom Willis provided useful advice, documents, photographs or information; Steve Burns sent details of Hs 129 losses and Steve Coates accompanied me on many a research trip and drew my attention to material I would otherwise have missed. Wachek Klepacki also provided photographs. In London, the staff at the Public Record Office and the Imperial War Museum were always helpful, particularly Philip Reed at the IWM's Department of Documents who willingly made available numerous documents and microfilm. Robin Frossard kindly provided many French translations and Ray Cotton and Frank Mattocks gave computer support. Additional help came from Owen Whitefield who expertly read my draft manuscript and from Chris Royston who created the maps. The professional design skills of Colin Woodman and the team at Postprint ensured that this work was produced to the highest possible standard of excellence.

In Germany, Franz Oswald generously gave me his time during a number of interviews, provided a wealth of written information and photographs, was a continual source of inspiration and was instrumental in contacting a number of sources for further information, namely the late Bruno Meyer, Jupp Oehl, Anton Maier, Otto Oeckl, Jutta Nicolaus, Karin Nicolaus and Anne Marie Schneider. I thank him especially for his patience. Equally importantly, this book would have been impossible without the many translations expertly carried out by Hans Obert, whose enthusiasm and wise advice over many years is also greatly appreciated. The late Walter Krause and Georg Dornemann provided first-hand accounts of their operational experiences and I was privileged to be allowed to attend the 10.(Pz)/SG 9's *Staffel Treffen*; Gebhard Weber, Willi Tholen, Willi Scholl and Walter Raufelder subsequently provided me with details of their wartime experiences through numerous letters and I am grateful for the help received from Bernd Barbas, Peter Petrick, Frank Marshall, Jürgen Rosenstock, Alfred W. Krüger, Hans Nawroth, Willy Radinger and Manfred Griehl. *Frau* Busekow at the Deutsch Dienstelle WAst in Berlin provided a friendly and efficient service and I am grateful for the help provided by the staff at the Bundesarchiv-Militararchiv in Freiburg.

In the USA, Tom Tullis created the colour artwork which captures the very essence of the Hs 129; James Crow generously supplied photographs from his superb collection and John Schrenker was also particularly helpful. Henry L de Zeng IV. generously shared with me the fruits of his many years research and I received additional assistance from James H. Kitchens III. and the staff of the Albert F. Simpson Historical Research Centre; help also came from Von D. Hardesty at the National Air and Space Museum's Smithsonian Institution and the staff at the US National Archives.

From Canada, Denés Bernád donated several photographs of Rumanian Hs 129s and helped me to consolidate my thoughts on a number of issues, while David Wadman also supplied photographic material; from Poland, Mariusz Zimney sent data and some excellent photographs while Robert Bock scoured his library for details of Soviet pilots' encounters with the Hs 129. Matti Solonen in Finland provided additional information from his database of *Luftwaffe* losses and from the Czech Republic, Miroslav Bily, M. Balous and Jaroslav Zazvonil provided photographs. In France, Eric Larger offered enthusiastic help. Ken Merrick and David Vincent in Australia provided much useful information. Letters and telephone calls from Martin Mednis, also in Australia, were an inspiration when I encountered particular difficulties.

Finally, I must thank my wife, Shirley, who was most supportive throughout, shouldering my share of the domestic chores while this work was being prepared and sharing my excitement when new photographs or additional information were received in the morning mail.

Martin Pegg
January 1997

One of the Luftwaffe's most experienced anti-tank pilots, Franz Oswald came to II./Sch.G 1 in early 1942 after service during the French campaign with 1(F)./123. With II./Sch.G 1, he flew the Hs 129 in Russia on the central and northern fronts until November 1942 when, as Staffelführer, he led 5./Sch.G 1 in Tunisia. When this Staffel was redesignated 8.(Pz)/Sch.G 2, he became Staffelkapitän on 20.1.1943 and later served again in Russia as Staffelkapitän of 13.(Pz)/SG 9. On occasions he took control of all Hs 129 units on the Eastern Front as Führer der Panzerjäger and was awarded the Ritterkreuz on 24.10.1944. Towards the end of the war, he was appointed Kommandoführer of Erprobungskommando 26.

FOREWORD
by FRANZ OSWALD

It is very pleasing to see that, at long last, a book on the German Hs 129 assault and anti-tank aircraft has been published.

It is a book which tells the story of the development and operational service of the Hs 129 which was designed especially and purely for ground-attack and anti-tank work. It also tells the story of the tremendous achievements of the German anti-tank pilots during the Second World War, especially on the Eastern Front. These achievements were accomplished under frequently extreme climatic conditions, over varying and hostile terrain, with inadequate parts and supplies and whilst fighting against a numerically far superior and uncompromising enemy. With an immeasurable spirit of devotion and sacrifice, the Hs 129 units first provided support for German troops during their sweeping advances and then, from 1943, they desperately attempted to stem the vast avalanche of Soviet manpower and armour. Operating amidst the implacable tide of the war's events, the *Panzerschlachtflieger* and their dedicated ground crews developed a close and vital bond of comradeship which was to outlast even the end of the war. German soldiers fighting on the Russian front held the Hs 129 in fond respect, for more than once the *Panzerschlachtflieger* were their last resort in desperate situations when anti-tank guns were far away and the *Panzerfaust* was not available. Not without good reason did we bear the Infantry Assault Badge on our machines!

The designer of the Hs 129 was Dipl.Ing. Friedrich Nicolaus, chief designer of the Henschel Flugzeugwerke at Berlin-Schönefeld. Coming from the *Reichsluftfahrtministerium* (Reich Air Ministry), he worked there from 1933 until the war's end. Nicolaus had studied German philology before the First World War, but, right at the beginning of that conflict, he volunteered for war service. Impressed by Ernst Udet's successes as a pilot, he became enthusiastic about aviation and after the war he subsequently chose to pursue a technical career. He also learned how to fly gliders.

In the Hs 129, Nicolaus had designed an aircraft eminently suitable for use as a ground-attack aircraft - most notably for anti-tank work. The aircraft was stable in the air and thus was a stable gun platform, allowing efficient aiming and firing. Furthermore, the armoured cockpit provided the pilot with a great sense of security. This became impressively apparent when an aircraft nosed over on landing. While the pilots and crew members of other types of aircraft often suffered severe head injuries or were even killed, generally speaking, Hs 129 pilots escaped free of harm.

A special virtue was the Hs 129's low-level ground hugging attack capabilities which were vital to survival. Taking the aircraft down on the deck was, in many cases, the only way of avoiding being shot down by enemy fighters.

The Hs 129 is criticised only by those who have never flown her or who had no feeling for this sturdy, reliable twin-engined aircraft. Time and again, one hears that the Gnôme-Rhône engines were totally unreliable. That is downright wrong. How else could we have achieved our considerable successes? All those pilots who flew the Hs 129 with success were enthusiastic about her.

We are deeply indebted to Martin Pegg, the author of this book, for his work on the Hs 129. For more than a decade, he has untiringly carried out his comprehensive research, delved into archives in both Great Britain and Germany and contacted various surviving Hs 129 pilots and former ground personnel. Wherever possible, he has interviewed these survivors personally and has also attended two Hs 129 squadron reunions.

This is a book reminiscent of difficult times, during which we did exactly what our opponents claimed for themselves - our duty to our country.

FROM THE COCKPIT
by GEBHARD WEBER

The author has asked me to write an introductory note for his book on the *Panzerjäger* operations from the air and I am delighted to comply. Although a *Staffelkapitän*, I was just one of the many who tried to "kill" Russian tanks which had broken through our lines but I can therefore give an account of the Hs 129 aircraft from the viewpoint of my *Staffel*, the 10.(Pz)/SG 9.

The Battle of Stalingrad late in 1942 marked the turning point of the Second World War. The result was that the German *Wehrmacht* was forced to abandon offensive operations and switch to the defensive. As a means of supporting the Army units, airborne anti-tank work became a dire necessity. Under the control of *Oberstleutnant* Otto Weiss, an experienced *Schlachtflieger*, several types of aircraft were subjected to trials for their suitability as anti-tank aircraft, the best results being achieved with the Ju 87 and the Hs 129. When Operation "*Zitadelle*" - the last great German offensive in the East - was launched in the summer of 1943, there were five Hs 129-equipped anti-tank *Staffeln* which, during the course of the year, were assigned to the *Führer der Panzerjäger*, a newly-formed command later redesignated IV.(Pz)/SG 9 in the autumn of 1943. From 1943, four *Staffeln* operated the Hs 129 B-2 variant, the main advantages of which were its two air-cooled engines and powerful armament; the latter comprised one 20 mm MG 151 and one 7.9 mm MG 17 either side of the fuselage beneath the cockpit and one MK 101 or MK 103 cannon mounted under the fuselage. All weapons were adjusted to converge at a distance of 400 metres and could be fired singly or all at once. In addition, one 50 kg bomb could be carried under each wing.

Another advantage was the excellent field of vision which the pilot enjoyed from his armoured cockpit. This meant that it was possible for us to remain at very low altitude once we had taken off from our airfields. From these airfields, which were usually not far away from our assigned target areas, we made low-level approaches to our targets against which we delivered our ordnance on tanks and supply columns which had broken through our lines. As the situation on the battlefield was frequently confused, we flew early-morning reconnaissance patrols over our main lines with a view to providing the *Fliegerkorps* with the necessary information about the exact position on the ground. The Hs 129 was less suitable for other tasks. Because of its considerable fire-power, enemy fighters showed it great respect but, wherever possible, we avoided air combat as the Hs 129 was too heavy and sluggish for air-to-air fighting and constantly lost height on account of its low-powered 600 hp engines. In short, it was not a "dogfighter" but a "workhorse", not least because its design originated from Henschel, the well-known locomotive manufacturer.

At the war's end, a few examples of the Hs 129 with uprated engines and the very effective 7.5 cm cannon became operational and enjoyed considerable success.

I am pleased to be able to write this introduction because publications on the Hs 129 *Panzerjäger* - which played a vital part in hunting down and destroying enemy tanks - have been conspicuously absent in Germany. On behalf of all anti-tank pilots, I would therefore like to record my sincere thanks to Martin Pegg for his continued and unflagging efforts over the past decade, during which time he has gathered from ex-pilots, technicians and weapons personnel alike, the material from which this book has been compiled.

FROM THE GROUND
by WILLI THOLEN

Although a great deal has already been written describing the events of the Second World War, in my own view, the achievements of aircraft ground crews, known in German as the so-called *"Bodenpersonal"*, have been too briefly referred to. This is especially true of the conditions experienced by the ground crews of the close-support units of the *Luftwaffe's* VIII. *Fliegerkorps*, conditions which, naturally, were completely different from those of the bomber units, night-fighter pilots and, later still, units flying in the defence of the Reich. During our advances in the East in 1941 and 1942, much of our work as ground crews was performed in accordance with official procedures, regulations and the drill-book, but things changed drastically after the catastrophe at Stalingrad.

As members of a *Schlachtgeschwader*, we were equipped with the Hs 129 *Panzerjäger*. We laboured under unimaginable conditions on advanced airfields to keep the machines ready for operations, sometimes in temperatures of minus 30 degrees below zero, sometimes in the 40-50 degree heat of the summer, living only in two-man tents put up over a dug-out in the ground.

The Russians frequently advanced close to our forward landing grounds so that we were compelled to transfer from one place to another almost every day and it was invariably only at the last moment that we mechanics and our essential equipment were airlifted out of a threatened airfield by Ju 52 transports and flown to a new operational airstrip. Once there, we often had to work on the machines late into the night in order to ensure they were ready for operations the next day. Only then could we begin to think of ourselves and our rations and accommodation. Drinking water - not to mention water for washing - was often in short supply. During the summer, we lived in tents close to our aircraft, but on many nights we went without any rest at all; our tents were usually erected over dug-outs which were intended to offer us some protection against the nightly raids by Russian bombers and nuisance aircraft.

In cold weather, or when it was snowing, we were billeted in small Russian farm houses, peasant cottages and huts, very often with the Russians themselves. The aircraft were dispersed as close to these dwellings as possible, for we had to rise very early in the morning to start engines. We had to employ many tricks of the trade; engine heaters and ground starting equipment were rarely available and the engines could only be started by turning them over by hand for a number of revolutions.

Engine changes and all major overhauling work were done in the open air regardless of intense heat or cold, rain or snow. The weapons personnel did not have an easy time either, for it was difficult to work crouched, in the foulest conditions, beneath the aircraft and at the same time, swing down the heavy armour-piercing cannon so that it could be rearmed with fresh ammunition. Sometimes test firing had to be undertaken on the ground to ensure the weapon functioned correctly.

The Chief Aircraft Mechanic, the weapons and bomb personnel were all reliable men and many should have received a decoration of merit in recognition of their service. Not only did a vital bond of comradeship and understanding exist between themselves but there was also a relationship of total trust between them and the pilots, whether officer or NCO, for they recognised the mechanics' skills and had complete faith in their work. I often saw an aircraft technician close to tears when his pilot did not return from a sortie.

Right up to the bitter end, even when our *Staffel* was no longer visited by any *Luftwaffe* technical inspectors, we ground crews did our duty and sometimes much more. Today, in my old age, I often think back to those times and of the many comrades who sacrificed their lives and I am thankful that I had the good fortune to survive.

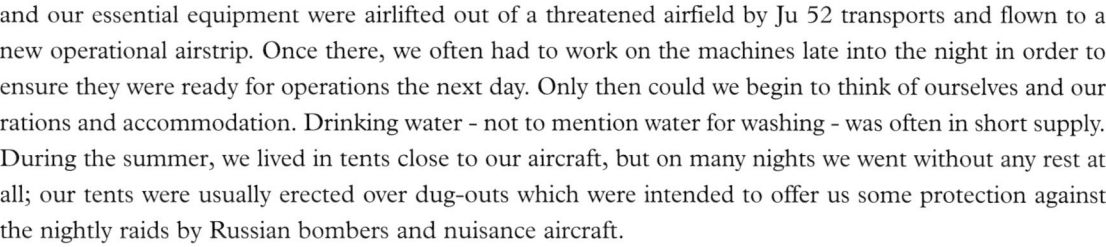

"It had become evident even in World War One, that situations can develop in ground combat in which the only possible way to support the army forces is by means of direct combat action against the enemy forces on the field of battle. Even in those early days, this realisation resulted in the establishment of special air units for such purposes..."

From: *German Air Force Operations in Support of the Army*
General der Flieger a.D. Paul Deichmann
USAF Historical Studies Division Research Studies Institute
June 1962

PART ONE
GENESIS

Der Panzerknacker
MERKBLATT 77/3

ANLEITUNG FÜR DEN PANZERNAHKÄMPFER

ALLE 150 METER EIN PANZER

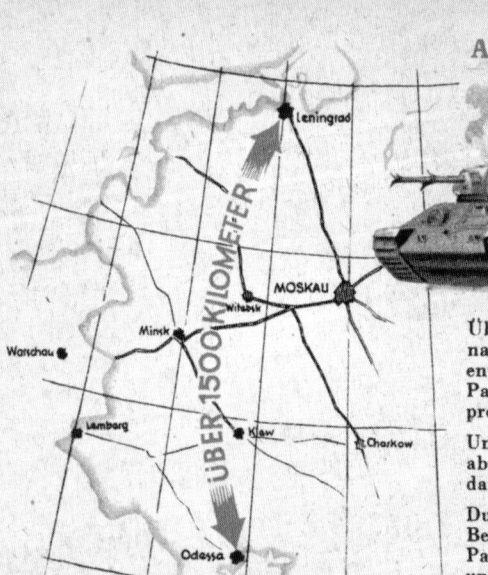

*Was viele andre können täglich,
Das ist für Dich genau so möglich.*

Über 10 000 deutsche Soldaten tragen das Panzernahkampf-Abzeichen. So viele geknackte Panzer entsprechen der Ausrüstung von 200 russischen Panzerbrigaden und der gesamten russischen Panzerproduktion in einem halben Jahr.

Und das alles nur mit den primitivsten Mitteln. Die aber lagen in der Hand von ganzen Kerlen, und darauf kommt's an.

Du fragst Dich, wie das möglich ist bei so ungleichen Bedingungen? Ganz klar: Erst einmal geht doch der Panzer auf gleichwertige Gegner los: Panzer, Pak und Flak. Von Dir will er zunächst gar nichts. Und dann, paß auf:

PANZER KNACKEN KANNST AUCH DU!

From Barbed Wire to *Blitzkrieg*

The *Schlachtflieger*: Origins and development

During the early months of the First World War the official doctrine of most combatant nations was that the aeroplane had no role in war except, possibly, reconnaissance. At that time, aircraft were generally unarmed, but gradually airmen on both sides began to drop darts, grenades or small bombs onto the ground forces they were observing and the aeroplane progressively adopted an offensive role, equipped with guns and bombs specifically for the purpose.

The important effects of deploying low-flying aircraft was recognised by the Imperial German Air Service. At first, the *Fliegerabteilungen, Infanterie* or "Infantry Contact Units" were attached to army divisions and employed for such battlefield tasks as the recognition of friendly advanced positions or the supply of isolated groups of friendly troops with ammunition, food and equipment. During the Battle of the Somme, in 1916, these aircraft were also used to carry out low-level attacks with bombs and weapons fire on enemy trenches, machine-gun positions, artillery batteries, bases and reserves.

The Hannover CL II was a light two-seater aeroplane originally operated by the Schutzstaffeln in an escort role to reconnaissance machines, but was later employed on ground-attack duties.

However, it was not until the Battle of Flanders in 1917 - sometimes called the Third Ypres, or Passchendaele - that organisational and tactical conclusions were drawn from these individual results. In an attack by the German Fourth Army on 10 July 1917, an independent *Staffel* from *Kampfgeschwader* 1 was, for the first time, committed to the low-level direct support of attacking infantry. The results, both in terms of the effect of weapons fire and the impact on enemy morale, showed that the employment of aircraft in the close-support role could have a decisive effect on the outcome of a land offensive. Prisoners confirmed the great effect on morale produced by low-flying aircraft firing at ground targets and the psychological influence on friend and foe alike was so impressive that the German Command decided that, in future, aircraft should intervene in battlefield actions more systematically. As a consequence, the German Air Service's independent *Schutzstaffeln*, or Escort Squadrons, which had been in existence since 1916 and which had been used to provide protection for reconnaissance units, were gradually re-equipped for ground-attack duties and renamed *Schlachtfliegerstaffeln*. A special ground attack school was established to train the flying personnel.

The question of whether a light, fast and manoeuvrable aircraft or a heavy, armoured type should be introduced was settled in favour of a light aircraft at a meeting of *Schlachtflieger* pilots, held in the late autumn of 1917. This resulted in a large number of units being equipped with the Halberstadt CL IV and Hannover CL II and IIIa biplanes with 160 hp engines, a three-hour duration and a maximum speed of 165 kph (103 mph). Being unarmoured, they relied on their manoeuvrability to avoid small-arms fire and were very successful while operating in their intended role of supporting their own infantry at decisive points of attack, but when later used in the defensive role their increasing exposure to small-arms fire resulted in higher losses.

Although not specifically intended for ground-attack work, the aircraft of the *Flieger-abteilungen, Infanterie* which, by the very nature of their duties were compelled to fly low over enemy trenches and positions, frequently found opportunities to employ their machine-guns against ground targets. In these units, armour was preferred instead of speed and manoeuvrability and until purpose-built armoured types became available, the existing two-seat AEG C IV was re-engined and fitted with 390 kg (860 lb.) of armour plate, in which form it was designated the AEG J I. Two Spandau machine-guns, angled to fire forward and downward, were mounted in the rear cockpit floor and the observer attacked ground targets on the main battlefield with a movable 20 mm cannon or small 1 kg fragmentation bombs known as *"Fliegermaus"*. The AEG J I was later replaced by the heavily armoured all-metal Junkers J I aircraft with an armament of two fixed Spandau machine-guns for the pilot, a movable machine-gun for the gunner, six to eight 10 kg bombs with highly sensitive fuzes and, occasionally, mortar bombs. Once the crews adapted to the Junkers J I, they welcomed the high degree of protection afforded by its armour and found the aircraft was well suited to its duties.

By 1917, ground-strafing by both sides had become commonplace and at the Battle of Cambrai during November and December 1917, the British Royal Flying Corps employed hundreds of single- and two-seat scouts which made determined attacks in support of the first British use of the tank, hitting enemy troop concentrations and other targets just ahead of the advancing ground forces.

The Battle of Cambrai also marked the first employment by the Germans of aircraft in a massed ground-attack role. On 30 November 1917, every available *Schlachtstaffel* was committed in support of a successful counter-attack at Cambrai which was carried out with a speed and drive that had never been experienced before on the Western Front. By this time, in an effort to break the trench deadlock and bring mobility to the battlefield, the Germans were again employing new tactics and had formed special battalions of *Stosstruppen* - literally "Storm Troopers". Operating in groups, their favourite weapons were the grenade, (of which each man carried at least one bag), the light machine-gun and the man-pack flame-thrower. The essence of their tactics was infiltration and continual movement; if they encountered opposition they worked their way around it, penetrating the front-line into the enemy's artillery zone, overrunning the batteries and pressing on towards brigade and divisional headquarters. Behind the Storm Troopers came Battle Groups, specially trained to reduce strong-points, which would reinforce and widen the successful penetrations, and then a mass of infantry divisions which would mop up the last pockets of resistance and capture ground.

The task of the *Schlachtstaffeln* was to work in conjunction with the land attack to eliminate centres of resistance and induce fear, the aircraft attacking enemy troops and trenches in the path of the *Stosstruppen* with hand grenades and

The Junkers J I armoured biplane. Powered by a 200 hp Benz engine, this machine featured a completely armoured nose capsule of 5 mm (3/16 inch) chrome-nickel sheet which enclosed the engine and crew compartment. Although heavy, cumbersome and difficult to take off and land on rough ground, the J I was immensely strong and popular with its crews.

The lightly-armed Halberstadt CL II was intended from the outset as an escort fighter for the Schutzstaffeln. Later redesignated Schlachtstaffeln, these units undertook close-support and ground-attack duties with considerable success. In addition to the machine-gun armament, the Halberstadt CL II carried stick grenades which - seen here being loaded into racks by a ground crew of Schlachtstaffel 9 - were dropped by the observer.

The Schlachtstaffeln and Stosstruppen worked hand-in-hand to eliminate centres of resistance and induce fear in the enemy. Here, a member of the Stosstruppen hurls grenades towards enemy trenches.

machine-gun fire, often with devastating effect. Flying at low level, these aircraft machine-gunned and dropped light bombs on the enemy's infantry lines, artillery, and, eventually, the enemy's reserve formations and supply troop columns. In this way aircraft participated in the ground battle to the same extent as the infantry, artillery, and other combatant formations. One British officer writing of this counter-attack on Cambrai recorded that:

> "..the German aeroplanes were very active, flying over our lines in large numbers, very low. They were shooting with machine-guns at the troops on the ground, and I am quite sure this did more to demoralise our men than anything else".

Harried from the air, with Battle Groups and the main weight of the attack widening the gaps in the main trench line created by the Storm Troopers, the British were forced to withdraw in disarray.

The effect of the German Schlachtstaffeln served to demoralise British troops during the Cambrai counter-offensive of November 1917. Here, wary "Tommies" fight to extricate themselves from a mud-filled shell hole near Marcoing, November 1917.

By nightfall on the first day a 40 mile (65 km) gap had been opened in the front line and the British Fifth Army was on the point of disintegration.

The *Schlachtstaffeln* were again used successfully in attack and defence during the subsequent fighting in France early in 1918 and particularly in the last offensive and defensive battles from June to the autumn of 1918. The *Schlachtstaffeln* were especially successful in the heavy fighting during the attempted breakthrough near St. Quentin on 21 March and subsequently against enemy reserves, supplies and columns on the Roman road and against the Somme and canal bridges near Noyan, Ham, Chauny and Peronne. Bridges on the Aisne and Veille were also attacked as well as the airfields around Soissons.

The *Schlachtstaffeln* played a far more offensive role than any other branch of the Imperial German Air Service, being exclusively attack units whereas the *Jagdstaffeln* (fighter squadrons) - although attracting a great deal of publicity and glamour - were used almost exclusively in a defensive role. By March 1918, the conversion of the former *Schutzstaffeln* had been completed and by the end of the First World War, the German Air Service possessed more than thirty-eight *Schlachtfliegerstaffeln*, some being formed into *Schlachtfliegergruppen* of between 4 and 6 *Staffeln*.

Undoubtedly, the German Air Service's ground-attack *Staffeln* had developed into an extremely effective and mobile weapon but, as with many military innovations, a number of problems arose, not the least of which were the questions of effective ground to air communications and the difficulty of providing direct air support to troops once trench warfare gave way to a war of movement. In addition, aircraft losses in the final months of the war grew ever more severe and these facts no doubt helped to diminish the attractiveness of ground-attack units to post-First World War German military planners. As a result, during the period of the reconstruction of the *Luftwaffe* in 1935, no plans were made for the formation of ground-attack units. Despite the success which had been achieved during the First World War, the main emphasis was instead placed on the creation of bomber, fighter and reconnaissance units.

At this time, too, it was not at all clear whether the number of *Schlachtstaffeln* in operation towards the end of the War had, in fact, been necessitated by the conditions of static warfare which had then existed. Thus the General Staff of the new *Luftwaffe* did not consider the creation of units exclusively for the purpose of close-support as being absolutely necessary. Besides, German tacticians such as Heinz Guderian and Erich von Manstein were developing a new concept of modern, motorised warfare based closely on the ideas of Britain's Major-General J.F.C.Fuller and Captain Sir Basil Lidell Hart[1], designed to bring surprise, speed and mobility to the battlefield and thereby avoid the conditions of static warfare which had prevailed during the First World War.

Known as *"Blitzkrieg"* or "Lightning War", the system called for particularly close co-operation between air and armoured forces, with aircraft primarily employed over the enemy's back area - especially against communications - and paving the way for deep armoured thrusts by denying him the ability to organise resistance to counter-attack. But rather than raise and equip ground-attack units specifically for attacks on battlefield targets directly in the line of advance, the prevailing line of thought was that any type of aircraft could be temporarily committed to tactical operations in the battle area as and when the need arose.

There was, however, some controversy over this point in higher *Luftwaffe* circles and a final decision as to whether modern *Schlachtstaffeln* were needed was postponed until the build-up of the *Luftwaffe* had been completed and more experience could be gained. Nevertheless, while these special requirements were kept in mind during the course of technical development, the light dive-bomber was included in the specifications made at that time. It was proposed, however, that the dive-bomber should be used *close to* the front line rather than in *direct support* of ground troops.

In other countries, too, little or nothing had been done to develop a ground-attack air arm after the end of the First World War. As a result, its possibilities had not yet been fully studied or confirmed, and it was this state of affairs which probably led to the air forces of the other great military powers - Great Britain, USA and the Soviet Union - also failing at that time to recognise that a separate ground-attack force was an important aid to land warfare. In Germany, however, the lessons learned during the Spanish Civil War brought about a reversal of previous conceptions regarding the employment of air power in support of the Army. The *"Legion Condor"*, which successfully experimented with ground-attack sorties, acquired much valuable experience and it is interesting to note that this result was brought about only indirectly.

When the Heinkel He 51 was outclassed in the fighter role during the Spanish Civil War, it was employed instead with great success in the ground-attack role.

During the raids on Madrid and other towns in 1936-37, the standard bomber used initially was the Junkers 52/3m and the standard escort fighter, the Heinkel 51. The He 51, operated by 3./J88, soon proved too slow and vulnerable against Russian and American fighters and as a result of this and the consequent losses, it was withdrawn from operations at the beginning of 1937. The German Command was now faced with the choice of either withdrawing the Heinkels from Spain altogether or employing them in another way. The solution was to employ them in the low-level ground-attack role. Refitted with racks to carry six 10 kg bombs, the He 51s

Another type originally employed with success in the Spanish Civil War - but as a dive-bomber as well as a close-support aircraft - was the Henschel Hs 123. Until the creation of a dedicated ground-attack wing in 1942, the Luftwaffe possessed only one Gruppe of such aircraft for close-support duties.

were put back into operation in March of that year. In co-operation with the ground troops and reconnaissance formations, these *Staffeln* were now used in direct support of the Army on the battlefield. Methods and tactics were quickly improved and offensive and defensive operations were soon being carried out by Franco's troops solely with the assistance of the ground-attack units.

At first, co-operation with ground forces was of the most primitive kind and there was no ground-to-air radio/telephone or even an effective method of signalling, yet the pioneering efforts and enthusiasm of the men in Spain proved remarkably successful. The He 51s, joined later by Hs 123s, Ju 87s and Bf 109s, were used with decisive results in the ground-attack role. Initially at least, these aircraft were able to undertake bombing and strafing sorties with complete freedom directly over the battle zones, and although improvements in the enemy's anti-aircraft defences led eventually to correspondingly higher losses, the ground-attack aircraft played a decisive part in ground operations.

The importance of this innovative use of aircraft in the ground support role was recognised by the *Luftwaffe* General Staff and in the early Spring of 1937, the *Reichsluftfahrtministerium* (RLM) - the German Air Ministry - issued a specification calling for a new *Schlachtflugzeug*, or "ground-attack aircraft". This specification was subsequently met by the Henschel 129.

The successes achieved in Spain also resulted in the activation of five so-called *Schlachtfliegergruppen* (SFG) - intended for the pure ground-attack role - immediately prior to the occupation of the Sudetenland, when the possibility of armed conflict had to be taken into consideration. These units were designated SFG 10, 20, 30, 40 and 50, and between 1 July and 1 September 1938, previously inexperienced pilots had to be trained as operational pilots, those serving with SFG 10 and 50 operating the Hs 123 while the other three *Gruppen* flew the Ar 68, He 46 and He 51. However, these *Schlachtfliegergruppen* were only temporary units created solely for the occupation of the Sudetenland and the belief that the *dive-bomber* would be the decisive weapon of the future led to all but one of the *Schlachtfliegergruppen* being subsequently disbanded and re-equipped with the Junkers Ju 87.

The Ju 87 formations, however, were neither bomber nor ground-attack units but formed an independent arm in the *Luftwaffe* as dive-bombers. Their task at this time did not consist of ground-attack but the attacking of strategic targets within their range, (i.e. for the bombing of small military targets in the area immediately behind the enemy lines) and the introduction of the Ju 87 dive-bomber in strength therefore amounted to a reverse suffered by the supporters of pure ground-attack. Nevertheless, a small number of enthusiasts in the RLM who advocated the philosophy of ground-attack succeeded in keeping the concept alive and one *Schlachtfliegergruppe*, the former SFG 20, was retained. Subsequently redesignated the II.*(Schlacht)/Lehrgeschwader* 2 on 1 November 1938, this *Gruppe*, the *Luftwaffe's* only ground-attack unit, continued to operate the Hs 123 until early 1942 and, once absorbed into the first *Schlachtgeschwader*, the aircraft remained in front-line service until 1944.

During the Polish and French campaigns of 1939 and 1940, operational experience yet again reinforced the need for a specialised ground-attack aircraft to replace the obsolete Hs 123 biplanes and supplement the Ju 87 dive-bomber units. However, the General Staff, while appreciating the importance of ground-attack, also believed that the Ju 87, which had emerged from these campaigns with a legendary reputation, possessed a general purpose value which would enable it to undertake the task of helping the Army forward step by step through direct support *as well as* providing close support for the Army by means of softening-up attacks on communications and vital rear areas. In the event, the course of the Second World War brought about a considerable change in the duties of the dive-bomber units which, in order to survive in the face of improved anti-aircraft defences, were eventually forced to abandon dive attacks and operate instead in the ground-attack role. The Ju 87 was also later equipped with 37 mm cannon for anti-tank work and although a few far-sighted individuals fought the tendency to rely entirely on this aircraft, it nevertheless had a profoundly adverse influence on the creation and subsequent development of specialised *Schlachtflieger*.

As well as the demand for dedicated ground-attack units, the first battles of the Russian campaign also gave rise to the first service requirement for armour-piercing weapons to destroy tanks from the air. Since the earliest days in Poland and France the elderly Hs 123 biplanes of II.(*Schlacht*)/LG 2 had met with some success against tanks, most notably during the French campaign when the unit had assisted in the destruction of a French armoured attack on the city of Cambrai. At the start of the Russian campaign, too, aerial anti-tank fighting was largely undertaken by *Luftwaffe* dive-bomber and ground-attack units operating the Ju 87, Messerschmitt Bf 109 and Hs 123. Again there was the occasional success as, for example, when a *Staffel* of Hs 123s led by *Hauptmann* Bruno Meyer, succeeded in driving no less than 48 Russian T-34 and KV 1 tanks into an area of

A Schwarm of Hs 123 A-1s at rest. By September 1943, only Lt Günther Müller's 7./Sch.G 1 continued to operate the type. It originally entered service in the autumn of 1935.

marshland to the south-west of Vitebsk where they became bogged down, sank and were abandoned. What made this achievement particularly remarkable was that the Hs 123 pilots, having already exhausted their bombs and ammunition, relied solely on their engine noise and aggressive mock-attacks to panic the tank drivers! But successes such as these were obviously due more to luck than to any German technical or tactical superiority and there now developed a continually increasing demand not only for a more advanced ground-attack aircraft but one with an anti-tank capability too.

The *Luftwaffe* General Staff had also come to realise that as the war progressed, the division of existing *Luftwaffe* strength between a number of theatres was inevitably causing its striking power in each sector to be reduced. Moreover, the almost continuous employment of the *Luftwaffe's* bomber units to help the step-by-step movement forward of the army was leading to the point where any form of *strategic* air warfare was being abandoned in favour of close-support operations. In order to release the bomber units for their

During the early war years, the Ju 87 was employed against back-area targets as a dive bomber, only later becoming a ground-attack aircraft.

strategic missions, there was a corresponding shift in policy which at last resulted in firm operational plans being laid down for the provision of support for the Army by specialised ground-attack units. *General der Flieger* Hans Jeschonnek, *Luftwaffe* Chief of Staff and a keen proponent of close air support, now issued orders for the creation of two such *Schlachtgeschwader* which were to be properly trained and equipped for the ground-attack task and would implement the tactical lessons which had been learned from the previous employment of the *Luftwaffe's* sole *Schlachtgruppe*, the II.*(Schlacht)/Lehrgeschwader* 2. This creation of the first *Schlachtgeschwader*, although overdue, was undoubtedly a step in the right direction and all Germany's enemies eventually followed suit and created units solely for close tactical air support.

At the same time, however, the opportunity to create a unified close-support force was lost, for with the creation of the *Schlachtflieger* it would have been logical to have combined them with the *Stuka* force and placed them both under a single controlling authority responsible for their proper development and inspection. However, because of the difficulties under which the dive-bomber formations had to fight in all theatres of the war, the ever increasing enemy defences, the specialisation of day and night operations and the special tactics required to combat tanks, so new technical developments and the replacement of obsolete aircraft became essential. Instead, the *Stukas* remained under the control of the inspector responsible for bombers and the *Schlachtflieger* were placed under the inspector for fighters. One separate inspectorate would have looked after the interests of a single dive-bomber and ground-attack arm quite differently and with more vigour than two Air Officers who still had to contend with their main tasks - the fighter arm in one case and the bomber arm in the other. In the event, these Officers were so much concerned with the development of their own specialist arms that the interests of ground-attack could only be considered to a very small extent.

From early 1942 to October 1943, the officer responsible for all fighter, destroyer and ground-attack aircraft was the fighter expert *Generalmajor* Adolf Galland who, unfortunately, had little time for ground-attack aviation. During the Spanish Civil War, the young *Oblt.* Galland had flown as *Staffelkapitän* of the *Legion Condor's* 3./J88. After 250 missions in Spain, Galland returned to Germany and was posted to Berlin where his

General der Flieger Hans Jeschonnek, Luftwaffe Chief-of-Staff and a keen proponent of close air support.

considerable experience in low-level attacks with the He 51 undoubtedly made him the ideal man to evaluate the tactical employment of ground-attack units in that campaign. However, this work proved so distasteful to him that he rushed through it and then intentionally forgot all the results of his investigation!

Galland was then posted to various fighter units, but a month before the beginning of the Polish campaign in September 1939, he was infuriated to find himself returned to a ground-attack unit; a *Staffelkapitän* of II.*(Schlacht)*/LG 2 had fallen out and a replacement was needed. The Polish campaign was a busy time for this unit and in 21 days Galland flew 87 missions in the Hs 123. Later, an attack of rheumatism, contracted while flying half-naked in open cockpit aircraft in Spain, forced Galland to seek medical attention and he managed to convince the medical officer that because of his condition he could no longer fly such aircraft. In this way he succeeded in securing a posting back to a fighter unit flying closed cockpit Messerschmitt Bf 109s.

After a brilliantly successful career as a fighter pilot, Galland was appointed *General der Jagdflieger* in November 1941 and as such became responsible for introducing and applying new technical and tactical knowledge for the day fighters, night fighters and *Schlachtflieger*. In this position he at first found himself handicapped by his own inexperience in getting things done at

Generalmajor Adolf Galland, the General der Jagdflieger, showed little interest in ground-attack matters.

high level, his lack of knowledge of staff work and the fact that no one could give him any clear direction as to exactly what he was to do. Although he learned rapidly, the wasted months of inactivity held up some technical and organisational developments and, due to the gross incompetence of most of his predecessors in office, he had to make up for the accumulated laziness of many uninspired people.

With such difficulties lying in the path of his main responsibility to fighters, it is not surprising that his problems left him with little time to devote proper attention to the ground-attack component of his command. The *Schlachtflieger* were not only of little interest to him but also had to be formed at the expense of the fighter arm which, as Galland complained, "had to supply the ground-attack units with everything" and depleted the fighter-arm's personnel and material resources. Even once established, the ground-attack units continued to be neglected and although the fighter arm continued to have a priority claim on materials, as far as personnel were concerned the ground-attack units soon began to attract very able men of the highest calibre.

Only after a year and a half, on 7 September 1943, was the separate post of *General der Nahkampfflieger* (Close-Support) created. On 7 October 1943, this command was redesignated *General der Schlachtflieger* and at last embraced all day and night ground-attack, dive-bomber and anti-tank formations under a single autonomous command. With the removal of the ground-attack units from his domain, Galland was glad that the Fighter Arm had rid itself of a valuable but anomalous appendage whose only similarity to fighters was that some units used the same type of aircraft. From this point on *Schlachtflieger* tactics and training enjoyed some uniformity and the interests of the ground-attack arm, particularly in the field of tactical and technical development, were followed with the greatest care and energy.

---

1 Major-General J.F.C. Fuller was an intellectual soldier who had served with the Oxfordshire and Buckinghamshire Light Infantry and later became a distinguished military historian. Captain Sir Basil Lidell Hart had served with the King's Own Yorkshire Light Infantry but became an enthusiastic advocate of the tank.

"A Flying Coffin"

Prototypes and the Search for Refinement 1937-1941

2

In the early Spring of 1937 the RLM's *Technisches Amt* (Technical Office) issued its specification for a *Schlachtflugzeug*, a ground-attack aircraft specifically intended for the direct support of ground forces. Based on the experiences gained during the First World War, which seemed to indicate that any aircraft operating at low level against enemy ground forces would require protection against ground fire, the specification called for a relatively small but heavily armoured aircraft. It also stipulated that the design should include a forward firing armament of at least two 20 mm MG/FF cannon plus 7.9 mm machine-guns.

The specification was issued to four aircraft companies: Hamburger Flugzeugbau (later Blohm and Voss), Focke-Wulf Flugzeugbau GmbH, Gotha Waggonfabrik AG and Henschel Flugzeugwerke AG. Of these companies, Gotha did not respond and the Hamburger Flugzeugbau offered their P.40 project, a DB 600 powered development of their two-seat Ha 141 asymmetrical reconnaissance aircraft already under construction. This contender was eliminated as a ground-attack aircraft at an early stage but work continued on the reconnaissance version, the BV141, until, in the spring of 1942 the General Staff finally cancelled any plans to introduce the aircraft to front-line service.

Focke-Wulf's proposal was for a close support adaptation of their two-seat twin-boom Fw 189 reconnaissance aircraft. With a special, heavily-armoured central nacelle accommodating the pilot and rear gunner, the Focke-Wulf proposal first became the Fw 189 V1b and, following further modifications, the Fw 189 V6. The forward firing armament consisted of the two obligatory 20 mm MG/FF cannon plus four 7.9 mm MG 17 machine-guns, in addition to which a pair of 7.9 mm MG 81 machine-guns was provided for rear defence. Although not mentioned in the specification, the RLM had intended that the new *Schlachtflugzeug* should be a single-seater and for this reason the two-seat Fw 189 proposal was not viewed favourably.

In this respect, the Henschel entry - the only original design to be submitted - met the *Technisches Amt's* requirement and, on 1 October 1937, after an assessment of the available proposals, the RLM took the decision to accept both the Henschel *and* Focke-Wulf submissions. Although the *Technisches Amt* preferred the Henschel design, it was also interested in the possibility of using all the main components of the existing Fw 189 and design development contracts were awarded accordingly.

The firm of Henschel und Sohn was founded in Kassel in 1848. During the second half of the 19th century the company became one of the world's largest manufacturers of railway locomotives, products which became so well known on account of their robust construction that they were popularly regarded as exemplifying the epitome of sound workmanship, strength and reliability in much the same way as Rolls Royce came to be identified with its luxury cars in Great Britain. By the early 1930s, by which time Henschel und Sohn was also producing buses, heavy lorries and machine tools, the board of directors was seriously considering adding aircraft manufacture to the company's range of activities and, in 1931, it tried to purchase the near bankrupt firm of Junkers. When it became clear that negotiations were unlikely to produce the

Two views of the early wooden mock-up of the proposed armoured cockpit for the Fw 189. This preliminary design was scrapped in favour of the Fw 189 V1a. Below, the rear gunner's position.

Above: The original Fw 189 V1a prototype, D-OPVN, was rebuilt as the Fw 189 V1b to compete with the Hs 129 for the contract for a heavily armed and armoured ground-support aircraft. This early adaptation first flew in the spring of 1939 with Argus As 410 engines and fixed pitch propellers, but results were disappointing.

Above left: The completed Fw 189 V1b after modification to the crew compartment. This version was written off in an accident due to the poor visibility from the cockpit. Fixed pitch propellers are still in evidence. Note the two yellow fuselage bands denoting modification.

desired result, Oskar Henschel broke off further talks and, in February 1932, ordered instead the founding of his own aircraft company.

By 30 March 1933, Henschel Flugzeugwerke GmbH had been established in Kassel under the direction of *Dipl. Ing.* Erich Koch. A second plant, *Werk* II, the factory of Ambi-Budd Waggon- und Apparatebau AG, then standing empty at Berlin-Johannisthal, was added in July. A further factory at Schönefeld near Berlin, later to become *Werk* I, or the main plant, was dedicated with ground-breaking ceremonies on 15 October 1934 and went into production on 22 December 1935.

Henschel's intrusion into the aviation field was resented by *Reichsmarschall* Göring's deputy, the State Secretary, *Generalleutnant* Erhard Milch and the established aircraft companies. Complaints were frequently heard that Henschel managed its affairs without proper guidance from the RLM and obtained its staff by luring technical personnel from other companies. As with other newcomers to the aircraft industry, the company - which had since become Henschel Flugzeugwerke AG - was at first only considered as a potential source of licence-built aircraft from other, more experienced aircraft companies, so that when *Werk* I opened at Schönefeld, it immediately started production of Ju 86Ds, followed later by Do 17s and Ju 88s. Once Henschel's own designs were accepted by the RLM for series production, *Werk* II at Johannisthal began manufacture of the Hs 123 close-support biplane. This was later followed by the Hs 126 tactical reconnaissance aircraft which was produced at *Werk* I and II and, later still, production lines were set up at Werk II for the Hs 129 and Ju 88. A third factory, *Werk* III at Berlin-Schöneweide, later made the Hs 293 and Hs 294 guided missiles and a new aero-engine subsidiary, Henschel Flugmotoren GmbH at Kassel-Altenbauna, produced Daimler-Benz engines under licence.

Henschel Flugzeugwerke began preliminary design work on the required *Schlachtflugzeug* in January 1938, the project receiving the designation P.46. During February and March, various discussions were held with the *Technisches Amt* as Henschel's project was refined to meet the *Luftwaffe's* requirements and, in April, final development began and the P.46 received the official designation "Hs 129". Designed by Henschel's chief designer, *Dipl. Ing.* Friedrich Nicolaus, the Hs 129 was a cantilever low-wing monoplane developed entirely for attacking ground targets including armoured fighting vehicles. Except for the fabric covered control surfaces, the airframe was to be of all metal construction and the aircraft was designed from the outset with a view to ease of production, being composed largely of rolled and pressed work with almost complete elimination of extrusions. The wings, which had very few ribs and large detachable panels on the undersurfaces, were of two-spar construction in order to best arrange the disposable load of fuel and ammunition, and to keep the centre of gravity within the necessary limits. The whole design was

One of Henschel Flugzeugwerke's large, modern factories and design offices during the 1930s. The influence of the Bauhaus "modern movement" is clearly evident in the architecture. Trees, large areas of lawn and park benches all provided a pleasant working environment for employees.

Generalfeldmarschall Erhard Milch, from February 1939, Inspector General of the Luftwaffe and Secretary of State for Air, took over as Director-General of Equipment on Udet's death in November 1941. Outstandingly capable as an organiser, Milch understood little about close-support aviation and was sceptical about the Hs 129.

based upon a number of firm requirements, as *Dipl. Ing.* Nicolaus himself explained: "The Hs 129 was designed to replace the Hs 123 as a ground-attack and, later, as an anti-tank aircraft. The requirements which we proposed in the construction of the Hs 129 included heavy armour protection for the pilot against defensive fire and when making heavy crash-landings; a most powerful armament against ground targets, including tanks, and optimum operability and serviceability when operating from makeshift forward landing strips. According to reports we later received from the front, these requirements were well satisfied and the aircraft was liked in much the same way as the earlier Hs 123".

A visual mock-up of the Hs 129 was completed in May. Duly inspected by representatives from the *Technisches Amt*, a completion date for the final construction mock-up was set for July, at which time delivery of the raw materials required to build the first two of three prototypes was expected to begin. On 20 July 1938, the construction mock-up was ready for viewing and in August the design was finalised to that of a single-seat, low-wing aircraft, powered by two Argus As 410 twelve-cylinder inverted-vee air-cooled engines. Delivery of additional materials commenced in November 1938, when work started on the first prototype, the Hs 129 V1, W.Nr. 3001, and a start date for the flight testing programme was set for April 1939.

Further deliveries of raw materials were received during December and January, during which months work on the Hs 129 V1 progressed well and it seemed the aircraft would start its flight testing as planned. By February, however, although construction of the airframe was still progressing to schedule, it became clear that delivery of the first pre-production Argus As 410A-0 engines would not be in time to meet the forecasted April flight date. Although one engine was received in March, the second was not delivered until a month later and the first flight of the Hs 129 V1 was consequently delayed until 26 May 1939. The flight test programme soon revealed that various changes were required and work on these progressed until 20 June. Four days later, on 24 June, the V1's variable pitch mechanism on the left hand propeller failed during a test flight and the aircraft crash-landed at Schönefeld.

In July, a special display was held at the *Erprobungsstelle* Rechlin at which Hitler was shown the *Luftwaffe's* most advanced weaponry. This display had been suggested by Milch to Göring in April and was duly arranged for 3 July when it was planned that the exhibition of equipment - certainly at that time the most advanced in the

Ernst Udet (left) with Hitler, Göring and other visitors at the Erprobungsstelle Rechlin on 3 July 1939. In the firing butts in the background is Bf 110, D-AAPY, belonging to Rheinmetall which was equipped with the MK 101 30 mm cannon. Hitler showed great interest in this cannon and Göring immediately ordered it into production but, Udet seeing no need for it prohibited its further development.

world - would include a demonstration by the Hs 129. Fortunately, the damage sustained by the V1 prototype in the crash-landing of 24 June was only slight and the necessary repairs were carried out in preparation for the transfer flight to Rechlin where the machine was to be demonstrated before the *Führer*.

The display took place as planned on the fine summer afternoon of July 3rd. As well as the Hs 129, the *Führer* saw the He 100 and Bf 109 fighters, prototypes of which had broken the world speed record, the He 176 rocket-propelled interceptor, and a number of bomber aircraft including an He 111 which made a rocket-assisted take-off. Also on show was the new MK 101 aircraft cannon which was mounted in a Bf 110 B-0 (coded D-AAPY) jacked up in the firing butts; this weapon, in which Hitler showed great interest, would later play a significant part in the Hs 129's service career.

After the exhibition, the Hs 129 V1 was returned to Schönefeld where the engines were removed, quickly overhauled by Argus, and re-installed by 13 July. Meanwhile, modifications were carried out to the trimming tabs, ailerons and rudder, and by 19 July the machine was ready for further test flights to evaluate the vision panels for forward visibility, as well as the aircraft's speed, landing flaps, general performance and handling. Such testing continued to the end of the year and revealed the need for further modifications including the installation of strengthened engine bearers, strengthening of the front and rear wing spars and changes to the rudder trim tabs. However, testing was dogged by a requirement for further development of the Argus variable pitch gear following evaluation at Rechlin in mid-August.

By September it had become clear that the Fw 189-based proposal had fallen short of expectations and was found lacking in a number of technical respects, test pilots commenting that forward vision was inadequate, performance was sluggish and handling characteristics were generally poor. Although there was in fact little to choose between the Fw 189 and the Hs 129 in terms of performance and general characteristics, the RLM had nevertheless concluded that production of the Hs 129 was justified on the grounds that various further improvements were proposed and that, being smaller than the Fw 189, the Hs 129 would be less vulnerable to ground defences and, at two-thirds the cost,

cheaper to produce. As a result of these considerations, Henschel Flugzeugwerke received an order to build twelve Hs 129 A-0 series machines.

The Hs 129 A-0 retained the two 7.9 mm MG 17 machine-guns of the original proposal but the Oerlikon MG/FF cannon were replaced. At the time of the original design, the MG/FF, then being manufactured under licence in Germany, was the only 20 mm weapon available which met the original armament specification but it had the disadvantage of a low rate of fire and a drum magazine of only 45 or 60 rounds capacity. By the time work started on the Hs 129 A-0 series, Mauser-Werke A.G. had developed their faster-firing, high-velocity, belt-fed MG 151/20 and all A-0s completed had these weapons installed in place of the obsolescent MG/FF.

A flight test programme for the second and third prototypes, the Hs 129 V2, W.Nr. 3002 and the V3, W.Nr. 3003, was originally agreed with the RLM to start in September but testing of both was delayed. In the case of the V2, this was at first due to a shortage of one variable pitch

Dipl.Ing. Friedrich Nicolaus, the creator of the Hs 129, photographed in 1938. Nicolaus was born in Darmstadt on 15 July 1893 and studied German philology before volunteering for service in the First World War. Later, he learned to fly gliders and after a technical education, became a certificated engineer, rising to become Henschel's chief designer. In 1945, he served with the Volksturm civil defence force and in 1949 joined GHH in Dusseldorf. He retired in 1958 and died in 1973.

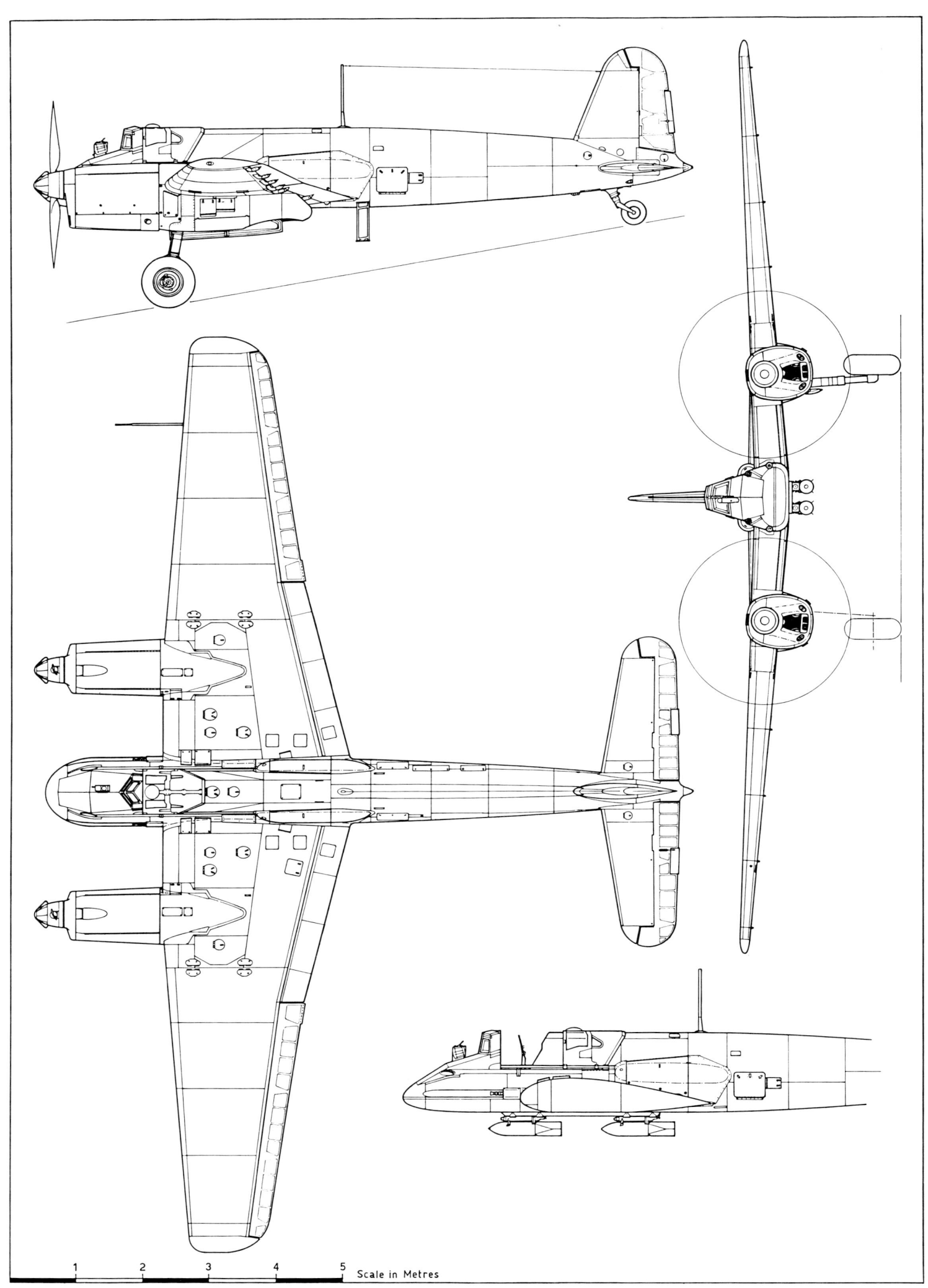

Scale in Metres

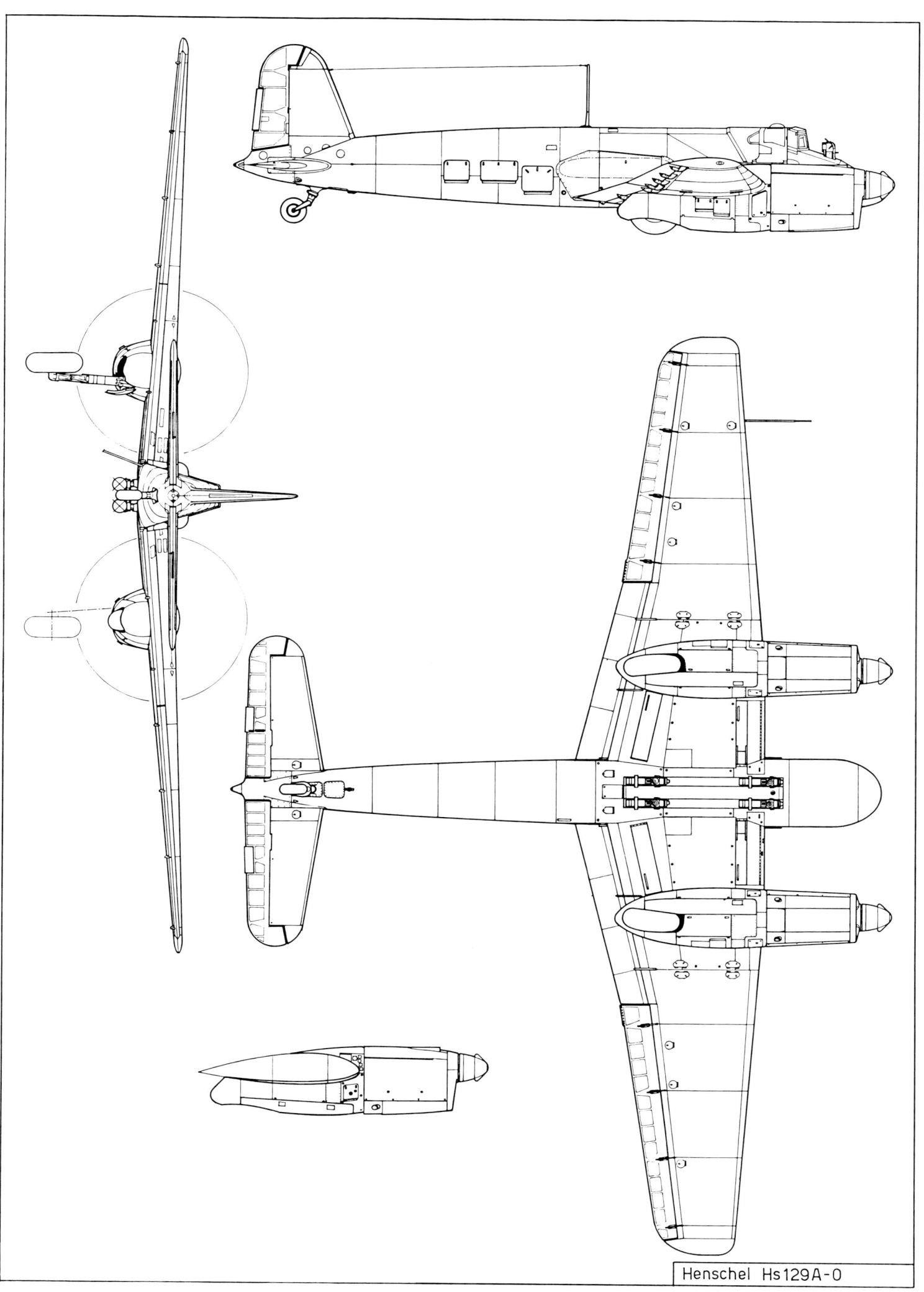

Henschel Hs 129A-0

without ammunition and with fuel only in the fuselage tank, the Hs 129 prototypes were unable to attain the speed and rate of climb originally calculated for a fully laden machine. Trials also showed that the take-off run was long, acceleration and rate of climb poor, and considerable physical effort was required by the pilot to recover from even a shallow dive. With increased speed, forces on the control surfaces grew until, in a 45 degree dive, they became almost solid. Indeed, during flight testing on 5 January 1940, the Hs 129 V2 failed to recover from a dive and was totally destroyed.

The Hs 129 V3 prototype was required to test the improved Argus As 410A-1 engines but delivery of these was late and, due to a lack of engines, propellers and variable pitch mechanisms, the V3 did not fly until 2 April 1940. Speed and general performance trials in May were further disrupted by engine problems and the loss of engine oil, but the machine was nevertheless flown to Rechlin on 31 May for engine tests. The following month the aircraft's undercarriage was damaged during a landing and it was returned to *Werk* II at Johannisthal at the end of June for repairs. Since it did not fly again until March 1941, further flight testing of the type could only be continued with just one aircraft, the Hs 129 V1. Equipped with bomb release equipment specifically intended for ground attack operations and revised cockpit armour, the V1 was duly transferred to the *Erprobungsstelle* Rechlin on 31 July 1940.

The completed Fw 189 V6 with Argus As 410-A1 engines and variable-pitch propellers, was the prototype for the proposed Fw 189 C series and first flew in early 1940. A new armoured central nacelle based on the second V1b provided a modified hood and a new wing centre section housed two forward-firing 20 mm MG-FF cannon and four 7.9 mm MG 17 machine-guns. The design of the crew compartment was very similar to that of the Hs 129, including the external mounting of the gunsight. All proposals for production of the Fw 189 C were abandoned when the V6 was found lacking and the Hs 129 was selected.

mechanism but while the machine lay idle, a requirement arose for a starboard engine to replace that on the V1 which had been damaged during its flight tests. The starboard engine was therefore removed from the V2 and at the same time the fin and rudder assembly from the V1 - which was then undergoing trials with a new canopy since visibility from the cockpit was considered to be poor - was exchanged with that from the V2. With no other replacement engines available, the V2 remained grounded until 30 November 1939, when it finally took to the air for the first time. Even then there were continuous problems with the Argus variable pitch propellers throughout December.

Flight testing and works trials of the V1 and V2 prototypes were affected by the poor performance and reliability of the engines which developed only 430 hp each instead of the expected 465 hp. Furthermore, the promised improvements and progressive development of the aircraft resulted in a serious twelve per cent increase in empty equipped weight and even

Meanwhile, in June 1940, Henschel had all but completed the manufacture of the twelve pre-production Hs 129 A-0 aircraft and work had already begun on the proposed operational production version, the Hs 129 A-1 in order to satisfy an initial order for 12 aircraft which was subsequently increased to 16 machines. However, unforeseen problems with the cockpit canopy actuation and hydraulic system of the A-0s prevented final delivery and further problems with the carburettor and Argus engine and cowling assembly continued until December 1940. Even then delivery could still not be completed until the following month due to further changes requested by Rechlin.

Staff from the *Inspizient für Schlachtflieger* and pilots from *Erprobungskommando* 129, the unit formed at Rechlin to test the aircraft under operational conditions and smooth the service introduction of the type, as well as some pilots from *Major* Weiss's II.(*Schlacht*)/LG 2, carried out

Official handbook drawing showing Hs 129 A-0 standard armament of 2 MG 17s and 2 MG 151/20s.

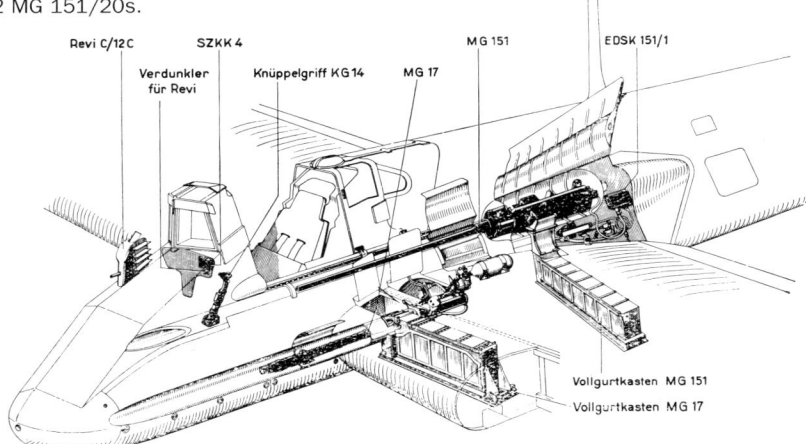

a works inspection on 19 November. All were agreed that even with the two 465 hp Argus As 410A-1 in-line engines, the pre-production Hs 129 A-0 was still seriously underpowered and they criticised the poor visibility from the aircraft's very small and heavily armoured cockpit.

The completed Hs 129 A-0s were later issued to various training units where some survived until 1944, but again they were so universally disliked by both pilots and ground-crews that this sub-type became known as *"der fliegende Sarg"* - the "Flying Coffin". Gebhard Weber, later a *Staffelkapitän* decorated with the German Cross in Gold, flew the Hs 129 A-0 while training in 1943 and described the cockpit as "... very cramped and the visibility was correspondingly poor". Franz Oswald, later a *Staffelkapitän* and holder of the *Ritterkreuz*, awarded for the impressive number of tanks he and his unit destroyed with a later model of the aircraft, summed up the A-0 as "... impossible".

Following the critical reports received from test and service pilots alike, the *Luftwaffe* flatly refused to accept the proposed production model, the Hs 129 A-1, even though work on the 16 machines started in June was well advanced but behind schedule due to a shortage of parts for the armament and hydraulic system. Although still far from satisfactory, the Hs 129 A-1 was to have featured all the modifications required as a result of the prototype test programme including a self-centring tail wheel, a new canopy, revised cockpit armour, electrically actuated trim tabs on the elevator and rudder, together with the Argus As 410A-1 engines first tested on the V3. These engines were more powerful than the original As

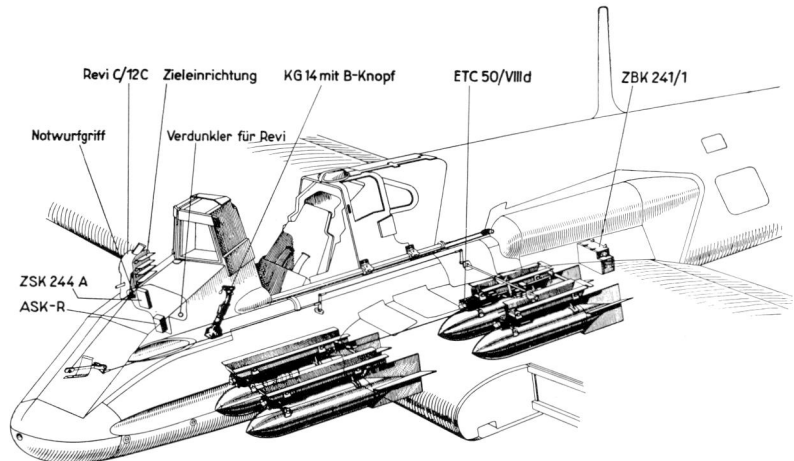

410A-0s and each provided the expected 465 hp at 3,100 rpm. However, given the Hs 129 A-0's disappointing performance, Henschel's design team had already anticipated the *Luftwaffe's* refusal to accept the A-1 production aircraft and had projected a slightly larger version of the basic design, designated the P.76.

This new project, which had a wingspan of 15.5 m (50.85ft), a height to the top of the airscrew arc of 3.5 m (11.48ft) and a length of 10.16 m (33.33ft), was to take advantage of the more powerful Gnôme-Rhône 14M radial engine which became available to the German aircraft industry following the fall of France. However, anxiety on the part of the General Staff regarding the unacceptable production delays which would inevitably result from the tooling up and manufacture of the P.76 called for an alternative solution and the RLM ordered Henschel to investigate the possibility of marrying the newly-available Gnôme-Rhône engine to the partly

Hs 129 A-0 showing standard bomb payload hung from the ETC 50/VIIId racks.

The Gnôme-Rhône 14M engine, front, right rear and left rear views.

(See page 330 for key to numbers).

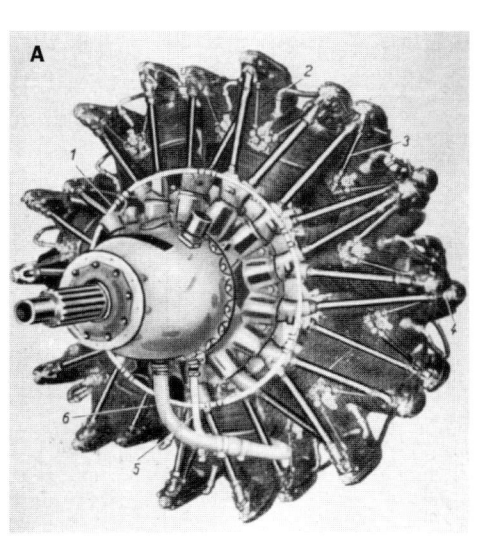
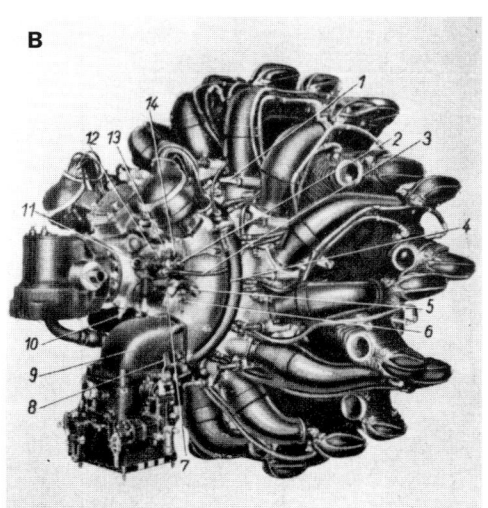
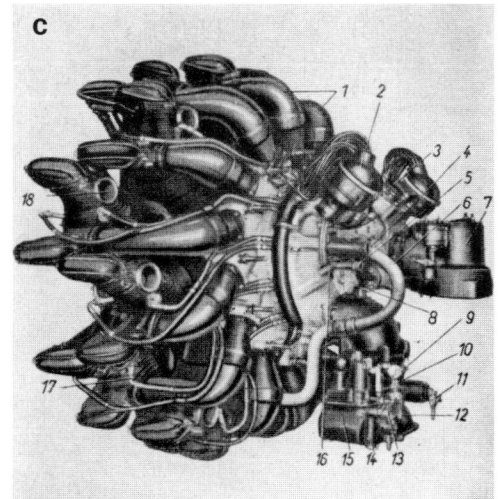

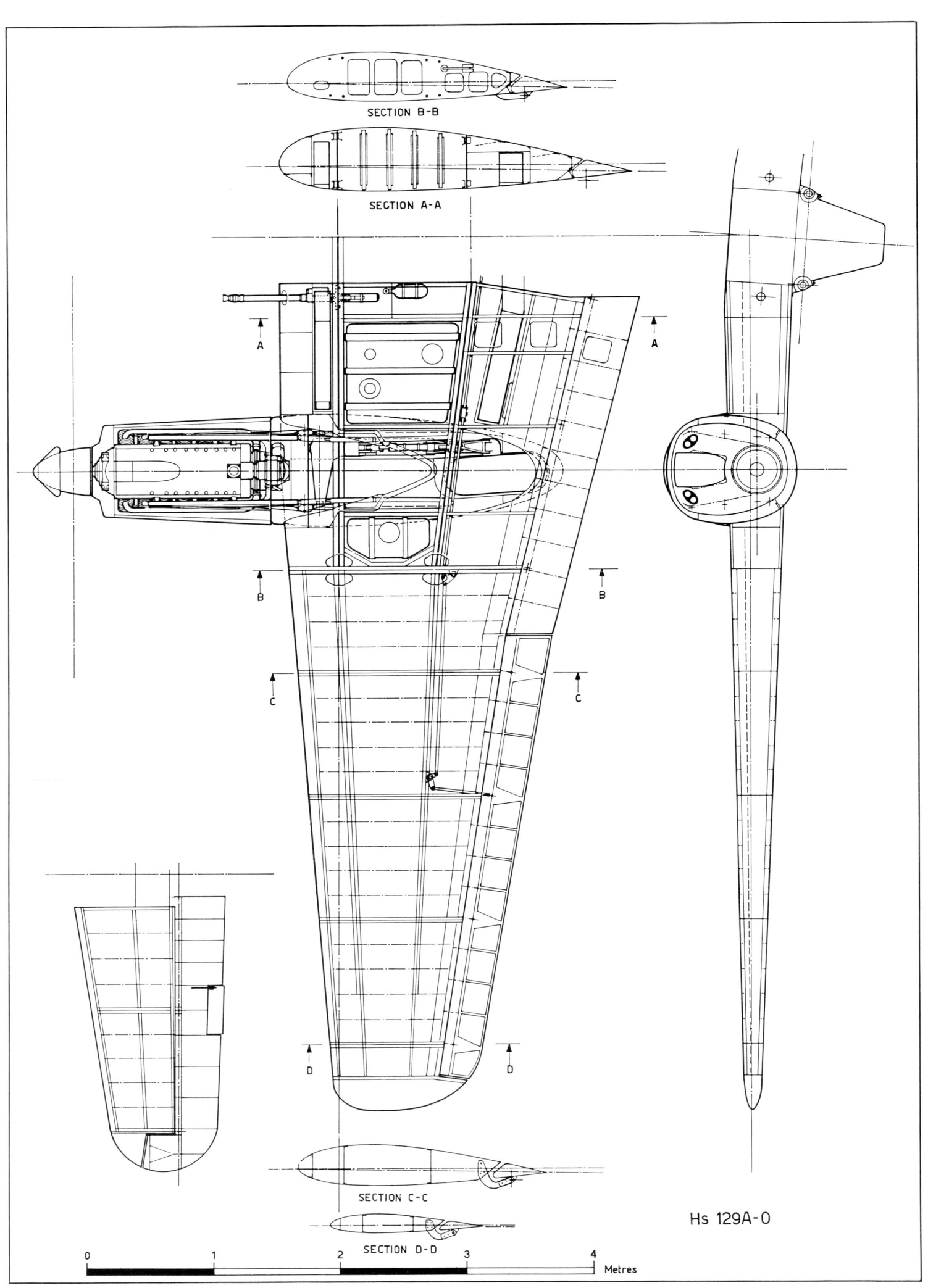

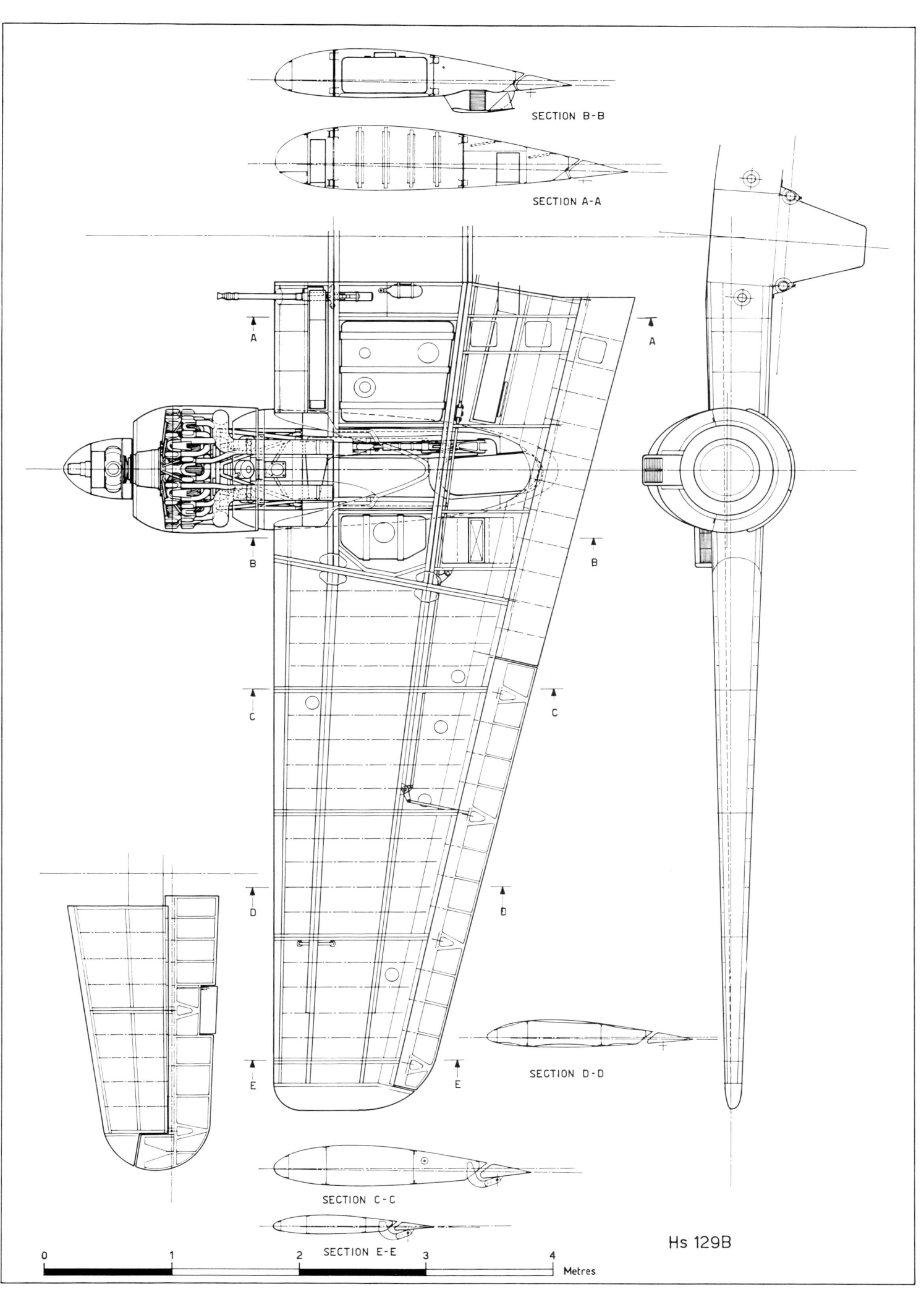

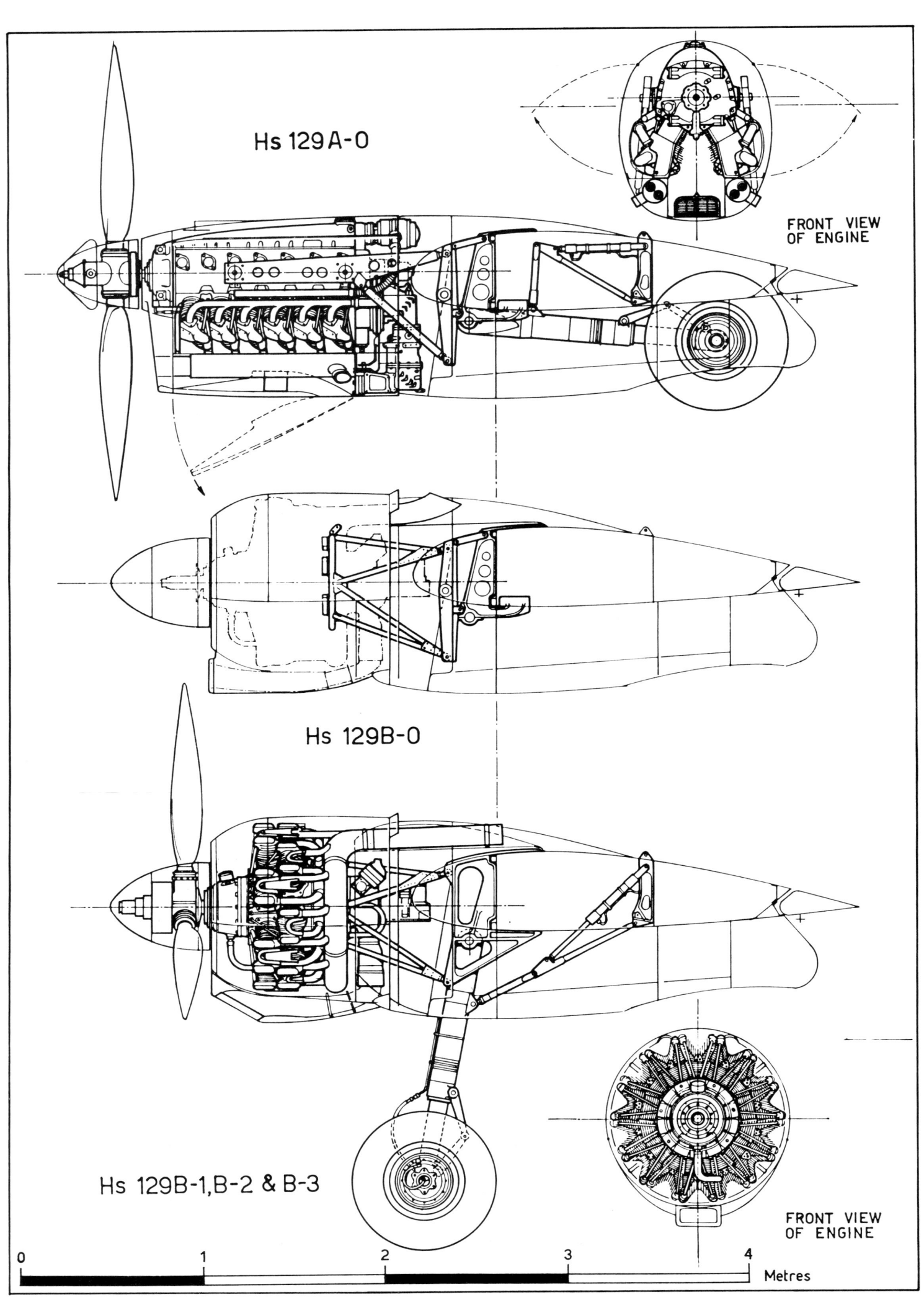

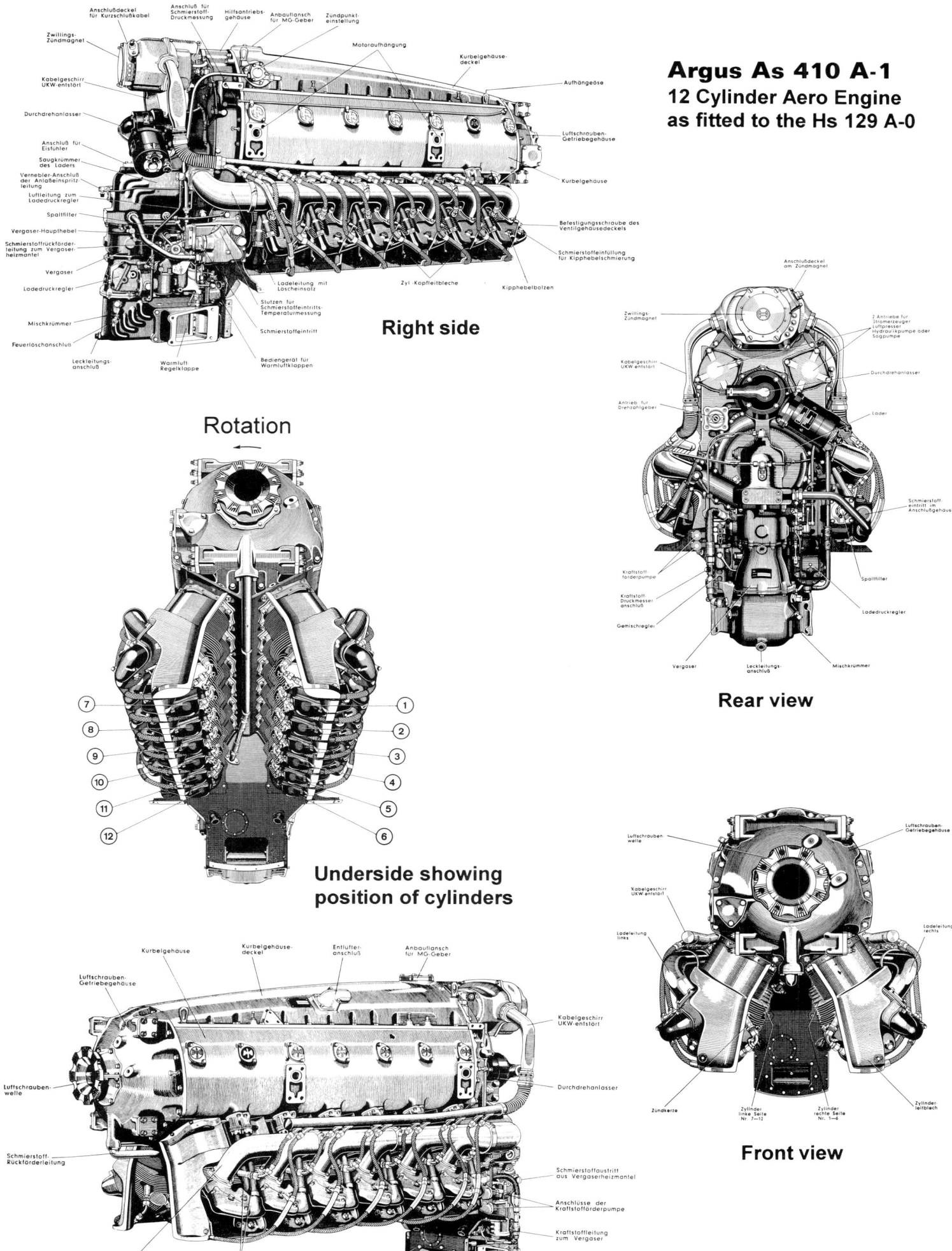

Happy faces after a flight-test. From left to right: Dipl.Ing. Carl Frydag, Henschel Works Director; Flugkapitän.Ing Hans Wilhelm Kaempf, Chief Test Pilot; Herr Regelin, Head of the Design Office and Dipl.Ing. Friedrich Nicolaus, Chief Design Engineer. Kaempf was later killed while testing the Hs 130 E-0 V2, which crashed due to an engine fire.

Feldwebel Willi Tholen. Already a skilled civilian engine fitter in the automotive trade, Tholen was drafted into the Luftwaffe in 1939 and sent to a Luftwaffe Aviation School where he received a high level of technical training and became an aero-engine fitter and flight mechanic of extraordinary ability. He served throughout the war, seeing service with II.(Schlacht)/LG 2, 4./Sch.G 1 and 10.(Pz) SG 9.

completed Hs 129 A-1 airframes. Detailed investigations into this conversion began in September 1940 when it was also decided that production of the 16 aircraft already being built as A-1s would be stopped and that, provided the outcome of the conversion investigation proved satisfactory, the aircraft would instead be built as B-0s with Gnôme-Rhône engines.

Unteroffizier Willi Tholen, a highly skilled engine fitter then serving with *Lehrgeschwader* 2, remembers: "There were many pilots in LG 2 who had previous combat experience and now worked as instructors with the replacement training *Staffel* of the II.(*Schlacht*)/LG 2. In mid-August 1940, the replacement training *Staffel* transferred to Cognac where we heard rumours that we would receive a new ground-attack aircraft, the Hs 129 and that it would be fitted with the Gnôme-Rhône engine. We were already familiar with this power-plant because there were large stocks available from the French Potez 63. When we returned to Lippstadt, I, together with two other *Unteroffiziere*, dismantled a Gnôme-Rhône engine in order to study its constructional layout but when the first Hs 129s arrived, they were fitted with the Argus 410 engine which was much too weak for the armoured aircraft."

"Soon afterwards, a group of us was detailed to the Henschel works near Berlin where we were to assist in the conversion of the existing airframe to accept the French engines. We were allowed to inspect the new aircraft and its Gnôme-Rhône engines down to the last detail. We were also allowed to watch the whole production process and were invited to give our opinions. One feature of the engines new to the *Luftwaffe* was that they were left and right-handed. The whole installation process had to be hurried through against time and we were hard pressed. The original engine mountings had to be modified, of course, together with the engine oil lines and electrics, and there were other changes to enable the engines to be replaced quickly in the field".

The Gnôme-Rhône 14M engine had originally been designed for fast, twin-engined fighters and light bombers and, as was common Gnôme et Rhône practice, two engines of each sub-type were produced, one turning anti-clockwise and the other clockwise, the object being to have a pair of engines for fitting into twin-engined aircraft. These pairs of sub-types were numbered consecutively; the 14M4 and 14M5 were installed in the Hs 129. The 14M4 engine was mounted on the port wing coupled to a Ratier three-bladed variable-pitch propeller which rotated in an anti-clockwise direction while the starboard propeller was driven by a 14M5 engine which rotated clockwise to balance the effect of engine torque. At 964 mm (3ft 2in) diameter, the 14M engine was a particularly small and compact design in relation to its output and was a 14-cylinder twin-row radial with two valves and two sparking-plugs per cylinder. Each engine provided 700 hp for take-off and a nominal power of 650 hp at 3,993 m (13,100 ft) and 3,030 rpm with 900 mm Hg boost.

When first produced, the 14M engine held great promise but had given serious troubles during early development and a French engineering officer who had almost exclusive dealings with this type remarked that they were a "... disgrace to French manufacture". Although in service with the French Air Force in 1939/40, not all the engine's faults had been cured when the Henschel design team began to consider it as an alternative to the Argus engine. As is usually the case with high-duty air-cooled engines, a great deal of trouble was experienced with the cooling and the *Erprobungsstelle* Rechlin called in particular for lower cylinder head temperatures. Despite repeated attempts to improve cooling by fitting modified cowlings and cowling gills, no entirely satisfactory solution was found and as test flights had shown that the engine would in any case withstand higher operating temperatures, the RLM raised the allowable cylinder head temperatures in order that the engines could be passed off as acceptable.

In time, German aero-engine experts modified and improved the French engine until it became as reliable as any German engine, but the myth persists that the Gnôme-Rhône engines were in some way sub-standard. A number of possible explanations exist for this. Firstly, it is known that Gnôme et Rhône suffered from a tendency to exaggerate the power output of their new models. It may be, therefore, that end users were disappointed to find that, as a rule, production engines were almost invariably down on performance. Another possibility is that RAF Intelligence obtained information about the engines from engineers and workers who had either left France to join Allied forces at the very time when the 14M was still in its early development stages or who may have felt obliged, for patriotic reasons, to disparage the products the French aircraft and aero-engine industry was producing for the German war effort. There was, however, a delivery problem, and this will be examined in detail later.

According to *Dipl. Ing.* Nicolaus, the Gnôme-Rhône engines were in fact only intended as a temporary solution to the problem of insufficient power and were to have been replaced either by new As 411 or As 403 engines under development by Argus, or an unspecified type from BMW, possibly the 9-cylinder BMW 800. In the event, due to restrictions later imposed on the

Two views of the Hs 129 A-0 W.Nr.3010, GM+OG. These photographs were used in an official German recognition publication which mentioned the aircraft's double-trapezoid wings, "sugar loaf" rudder and likened the cockpit area to "a pike's jaw". To enhance this latter feature as a recognition aid, the forward fuselage of the A-0 series was painted to resemble a pike's head, complete with eyes, nostrils and rows of sharp teeth.

Below left, spinner and variable pitch mechanism; centre, Gnôme-Rhône 14M installed; right, engine bearer.

1 Motortragring (Engine Carrier Ring)
2 Rohrstreben (Main Bearers)
3 Elastiche Aufhängung (Elastic Attachment)
4 Gummielement (Rubber Element)

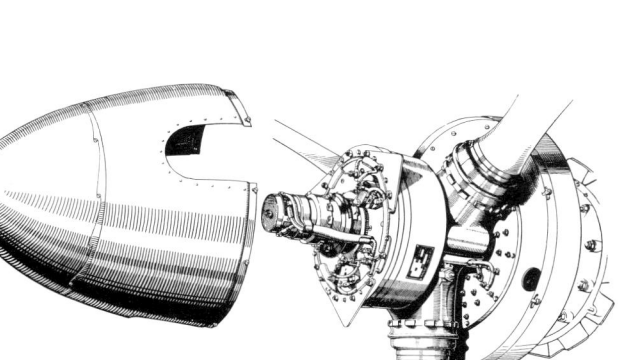

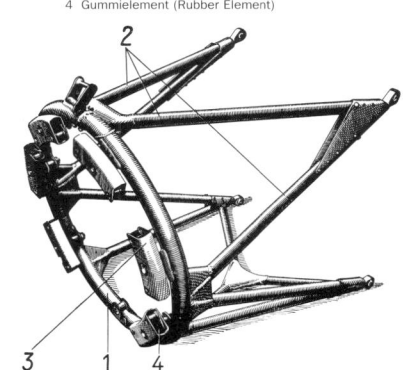

Hs 129 A-0 White '10' W.Nr. 3010
SG 101, France 1944.

All Henschel Hs 129s were finished in a standard factory-applied splinter pattern, comprising **Black-Green** 70/**Dark Green** 71 upper surfaces and **Light-Blue** 65 undersides. This machine carried the last two figures of the *Werk Nummer* in **white** on the outboard faces of the engine nacelles. The full W.Nr. was painted in **white** on the rear fuselage with the factory call sign, 'GM+OG' being applied in **black** on the fuselage sides and beneath the wings. A large pike's mouth marking was painted in **red**, **black** and **white** on the nose. The latter feature was intended to enhance the shape of the nose as a recognition aid and a German recognition publication of the period describes the nose area as '... like a pike's head'. All surviving Hs 129 A-0s later served with the *Luftwaffe's* ground-attack schools and although most went to Deblin-Irena in Poland, this example also served in France with SG 101 based at Clermont-Ferrand where it was eventually 65% damaged in an Allied bombing attack on 30 April 1944. This aircraft carried the standard under-fuselage bomb racks. The National insignia were: B2 crosses on the wing undersides, B1 crosses on wing upper-surfaces and fuselage sides and H2 *Hakenkreuze*.

German war economy, these new engines did not become available and Nicolaus was forced to consider other alternatives. The Italian Issota-Fraschini Delta and the Gnôme-Rhône 14 M38 are among the engine types known to have been flight tested in connection with the Hs 129 C, and although one C-1 was built and flown, it was not adopted for series manufacture. Progressive improvement of the Hs 129 was therefore mainly restricted to changes in the aircraft's armament.

In October, 1940, it was decided that the Hs 129 V3 would be the test aircraft for the new engines and this machine, which had since been repaired following its earlier crash-landing, was converted to accept the French Gnôme-Rhône radial engines. Installation was begun at Schönefeld in January 1941, and in this new configuration the machine was redesignated Hs 129 V3/U1. Flight testing began on 19 March 1941, and continued until May when, following one flight, its undercarriage again collapsed and the aircraft was damaged in the subsequent belly-landing. However, enough data had already been gathered to show that the installation of the more powerful engines had improved the aircraft's most serious performance deficiencies and it was decided that the 16 Hs 129 A-1s then under construction would be converted to accept the new engines under the designation Hs 129 B-0. Converting these airframes to accept the French radial engines and their associated equipment presented no insurmountable difficulties, the main alteration being the replacement of the earlier wing centre section with one designed around the new power plants and the installation of their oil coolers which were situated under the wings outboard of the nacelles and in front of the flaps.

The typically French engine bearers were modified to conform more closely with standard German practice by fitting German mountings which located on the fireproof bulkhead. All oil lines were changed to ones of German manufacture which ran through a new German oil collector fitted in front of the fireproof bulkhead. This collector was mounted on four Silentbloc rubber bearings which, in the early days of the machine's service life, were the cause of some trouble. During take-off and landing, the bearings were subjected to severe vibration and came away from the oil collector causing a sudden and dangerous loss of oil. If such a failure occurred on take-off, the pilot had to land immediately or risk an engine seizure. The fault was cleared by mounting better rubber bearings.

Other modifications included the outer wing sections, which were given a straight leading edge, the repositioning of the electrically-actuated trim tabs, and the relocation of some internal equipment in order to compensate for the change in centre of gravity caused by the heavier French engines. Although due to have been completed in November, it is believed the first 15 machines were converted at Berlin-Johannisthal late in December, the remaining one following in January, in which month the C-1 was also completed.

In addition to the Hs 129 V3/U1, further flight trials at Rechlin were continued with at least three

The grotesque armoured cockpit of the Hs 129 V1 exhibited all the faults inherent in the RLM's specification. This photograph shows the so-called "vision panels" which provided forward visibility and the externally mounted gun/bombsight.

View of the Hs 129 A-0 showing the Revi 12 sight and the enclosed blast-tubes for the fuselage-mounted MG 151. The "vision panels" were retained but the addition of side windows did little to improve visibility.

A unique air-to-air shot showing three Hs 129 A-0 pre-production aircraft in formation. Note that the Werk Nummern have been applied to the rear fuselage, a practice also seen on some early Hs 129 Bs.

Movement of the 6 mm armoured steel rear-sliding cockpit canopy of the Hs 129 A-0 was controlled by a chain guided by sprockets, the mechanism being mounted externally on the fuselage side. Here, a member of the ground crew demonstrates how to crank open the canopy. Note the small, spring-loaded footholds provided in the wing.

Hs 129 B-0s, W.Nr. 0016, 0017 and 3007, acting as trials and development aircraft. One aircraft was used to test the aerodynamic refinements of the airframe which were to be incorporated in the B-1 series to be built against Delivery Plan 19/11 which the RLM had issued in April calling for 30 machines. W.Nr. 3007 made its first test flight on 19 March 1941 with no known problems. In the A-0 and proposed A-1, the pilot's cockpit armour had been constructed from flat or only slightly curved armour plating which formed an armoured box which was then clad in light metal sheeting. The same feature was incorporated in the Hs 129 B-0, but with the B-1 this practice was discontinued and by drawing on the experience gained in the stamping of aerodynamically shaped armour plating, it was possible to dispense with the additional light metal sheeting as the armour plate itself now formed the fuselage shape. In this way, the forward fuselage lost its flat, angular appearance and the fuselage cross-section could be replaced with a more rounded, streamlined design which further improved the pilot's view forward and downward and the more elegant curves blended better with the wing. The Hs 129 B-1 also differed from the B-0 in that, following several requests by the RLM for improvements, important modifications were made to the cockpit glazing and engine cowlings. The canopy was, at last, completely redesigned so that the earlier V-shaped windscreen on preceding versions was replaced by a single piece of curved

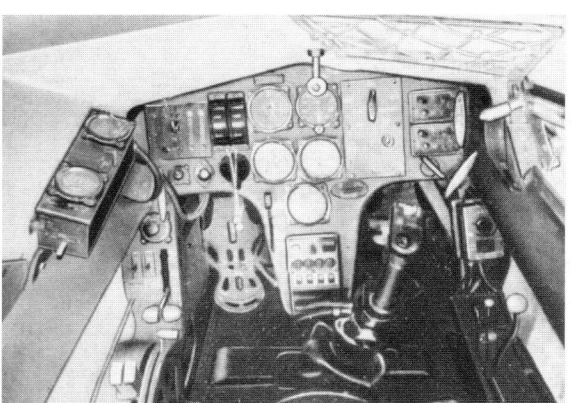

Instrument panel and cockpit layout of the Hs 129 A-0

armoured glass and the canopy side and top replaced by Plexiglass panels. This new arrangement had been first flight tested on the Hs 129 V3 and although the glazed areas were still small and reinforced by heavy cockpit framing, the new canopy completely cured the earlier visibility problems. Other, more minor, alterations were made to the enclosed gun blast tubes which, on some aircraft, were replaced with open troughs which became standard on subsequent production models.

Eventually, by 3 January 1942, the first Hs 129 B-0 and B-1 aircraft had begun to reach service units, two Hs 129 B-0s being delivered to the *Ergänzungs-Schlachtgruppe* of *Lehrgeschwader* 2 for pilot conversion training, together with three aircraft from the Hs 129 B-1 production series. The first loss of an Hs 129 B-0 occurred on 6 January 1942, when *Fw.* Konrad Bewermeyer crashed and was killed at Rechlin in W.Nr. 0017.

"A Pleasure to Fly"

The Thoroughbred Emerges

3

Installation of MG 17 machine gun.

A sequence of photographs from a training manual showing the installation and removal of MG 17 machine gun and MG 151 cannon.

Removing the MG 151 from an Hs 129 B-1.

with front-line units and the optional bomb rack was by far the most commonly used conversion set employed on operations, at least until the MK 101 became available. This rack could carry either a single 250 kg bomb, four 50 kg bombs, or ninety-six 2 kg SD 2 anti-personnel bombs.

Additional bomb racks were mounted as standard under each wing outboard of the engines and the loads most frequently carried on operations consisted of two 50 kg SC 50 bombs or two bundles each containing twenty-four 2 kg SD 2 anti-personnel bombs.

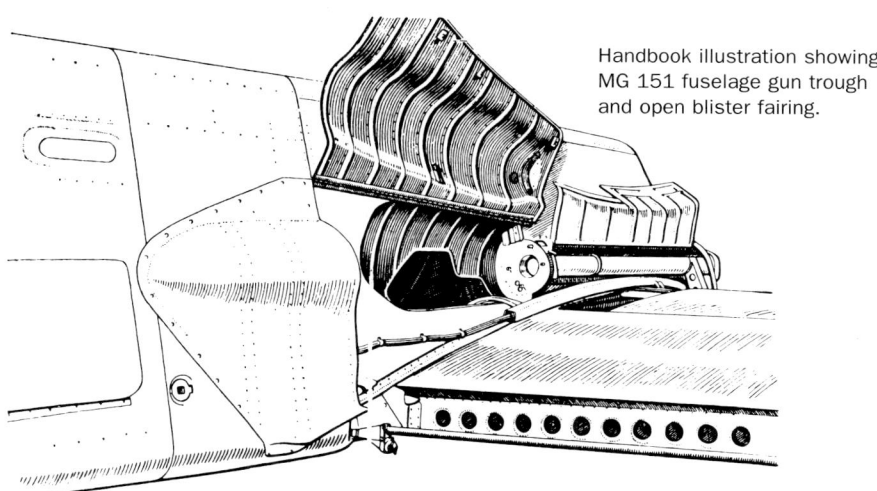

Handbook illustration showing MG 151 fuselage gun trough and open blister fairing.

A feature of the Hs 129 already mentioned was its most comprehensive armour plating. The pilot sat in a completely armoured box, the vertical plates fore and aft being 8 mm (.315 in) to 12 mm (.473 in) thick and the sides, bottom and top being 6 mm (.236 in). The engines had only a semi-circular 5 mm (.197 in) thick plate which protected their lower halves and carburettors from astern and slightly below. The oil coolers were similarly protected by 5 mm (.197 in) plate in the sides, bottom and shutters. The armour protection for the nose section in particular called for some complicated production work; some of the sheets were bent in more than one plane, especially the side sheets which were formed to incorporate the blast channels for the guns. In this respect, Henschel gained experience in the shaping of armour plate which the German steel industry itself did not possess and in January 1942 the RLM ordered Henschel to commence manufacture of shaped armour plate for the Me 210, Bf 110, Bf 109 and Ju 87.

In front of the pilot and fitted in a 6 mm (.236 in) pressed armoured steel frame, was a curved, laminated, bullet-proof windscreen some 56 mm (2.206 in) thick. Behind this was a similarly shaped piece of 6 mm (.236 in) "Triplex" type glass with a 10 mm (.394 in) air-space between the two, through which hot air could be passed for de-misting purposes. The cockpit canopy on production machines completely cured the visibility problems of the preceding sub-types to an extent that the same *Ritterkreuzträger* who condemned the Hs 129 A-0 as "impossible" was later to describe the view from the new canopy as "excellent".

The cockpit interior was well laid out, though small and somewhat cramped. As with some other types of German twin and multi-engined aircraft, some of the instruments, notably the rev-counter, fuel gauge, oil temperature and combined fuel and oil pressure gauges, were

An Hs 129 B fitted with an under-fuselage 4 x MG 17 conversion pack. Each weapon was installed with 1,000 rounds of ammunition.

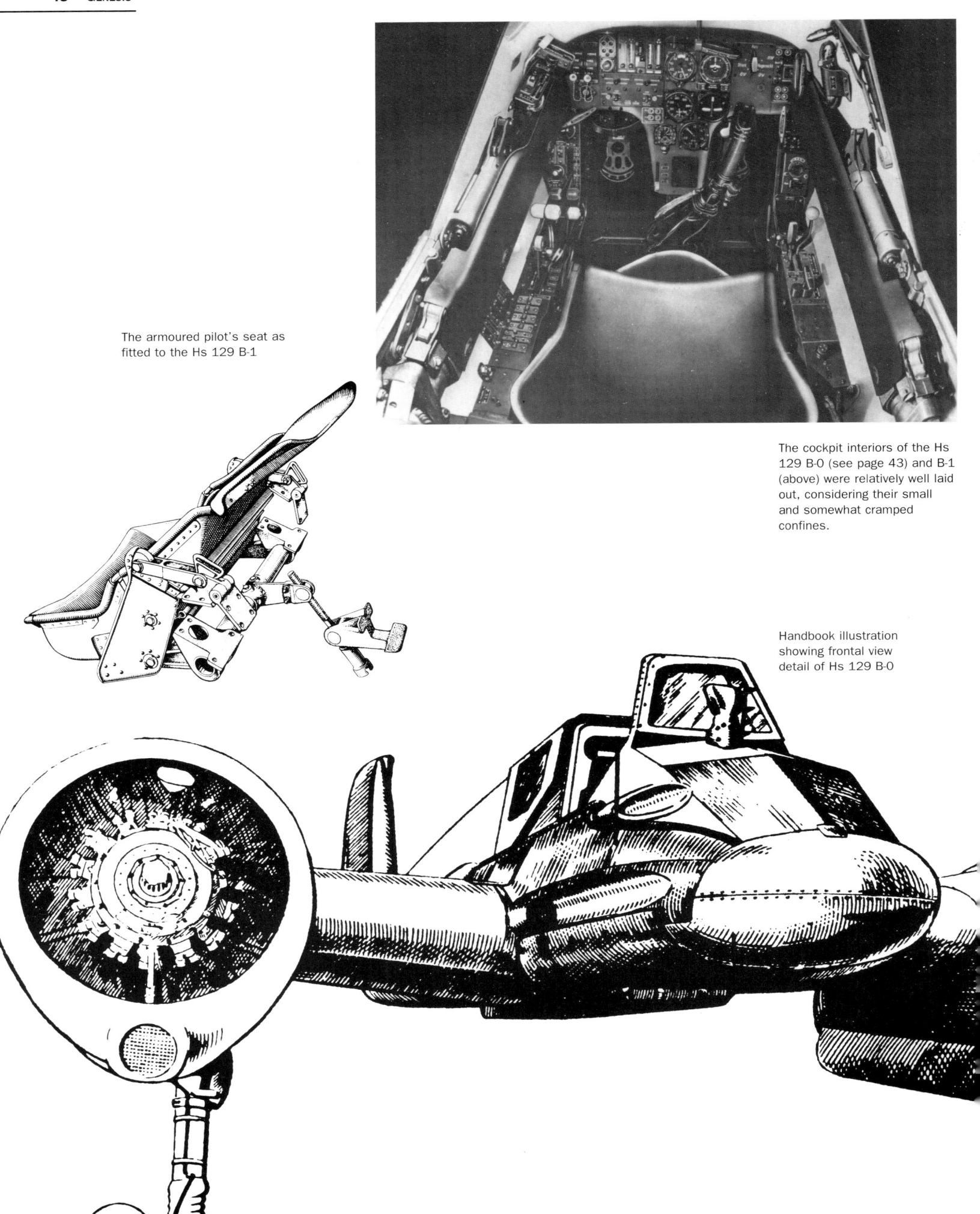

The armoured pilot's seat as fitted to the Hs 129 B-1

The cockpit interiors of the Hs 129 B-0 (see page 43) and B-1 (above) were relatively well laid out, considering their small and somewhat cramped confines.

Handbook illustration showing frontal view detail of Hs 129 B-0

Early Henschel photographs showing an Hs 129 B-0, coded KK+VP, making low-level passes for the benefit of the camera.

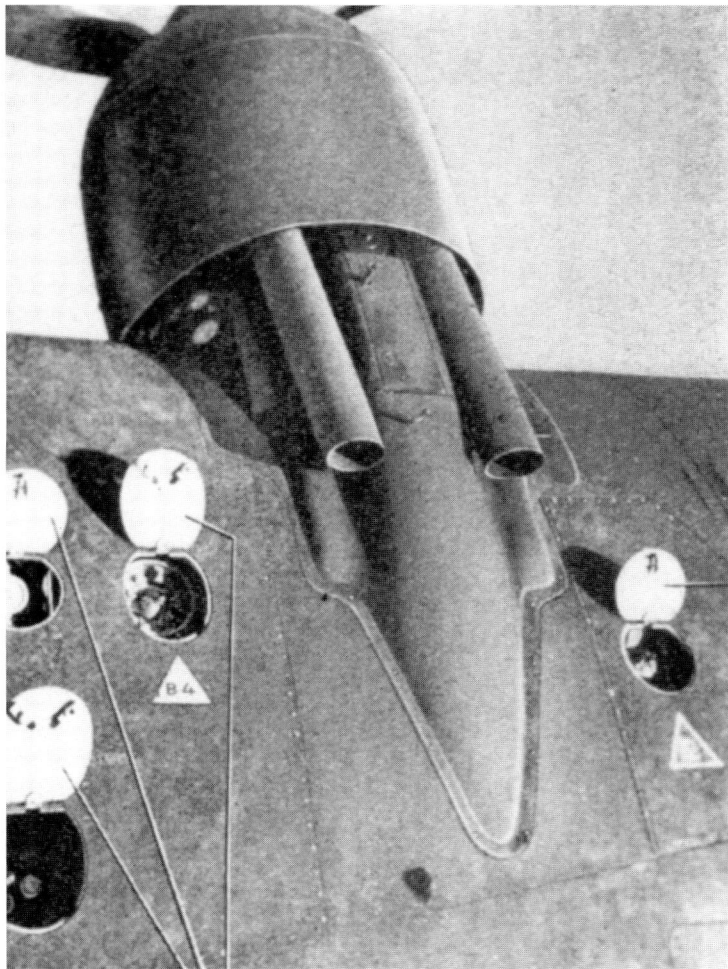

The closely cowled Gnôme-Rhône 14M engine with long exhaust pipes of an early Hs 129 B. As a result of concerns associated with engine overheating, later cowlings featured additional louvres.

A rare view of four early production Hs 129 Bs in formation.

mounted outside the cockpit and positioned on the inboard faces of the engine nacelles where they were readily visible. On account of the thick, curved glass windscreen and the parallax effect arising from it, the combined bomb and gunsight was likewise positioned outside the cockpit. This consisted of a Revi C12/C or C12/D sight, on the side of which was mounted a crude form of bombsight comprising four horizontal vanes with vertical wires passing through them. Release heights of 10, 50, 100 or 200 m (33, 164, 328 or 656 ft) were marked on the vanes and the pilot aimed his bombs by aligning the target with the particular vane appropriate for release altitude.

The aircraft's handling characteristics were by now, as most operational pilots later commented, excellent. There was no tendency to swing while landing or during take-off and the aircraft has been described as "a pleasure to fly" and an "extremely stable gun platform". No heavy pressure was required on the control column except when pulling out of a dive but this, of course, would be experienced with any type of aircraft. Stalling was harmless; the aircraft went into a dive from any position of stall and responded immediately to the controls. In fact, the only criticism pilots had of the aircraft was that despite the conversion to the more powerful Gnôme-Rhône engines, it was still somewhat under-powered. Consequently, take-off runs with a fully loaded Hs 129 were extraordinarily long and while climbing ability was slow, this was of no great concern to the pilots since their ground-attack sorties were in any case always carried out at low and extra-low level. This lack of engine power also restricted the speed of a loaded Hs 129 to around 324 kph (200 mph), and although this meant that the pilots were within range of enemy ground defences for longer than would have been the case with a faster aircraft, a greater speed, particularly at low levels, would have made it very difficult for them to quickly and accurately identify small battlefield targets. In an emergency, extra power could be applied via a lever mounted on the left-hand side of the cockpit which increased engine performance to 110 percent.

In the opinion of pilots interviewed for this work, all agreed that they were prepared to trade increased speed for accurate target identification and weapons aiming, particularly as the machine was sufficiently well-armoured to afford a high degree of protection for the pilot and, to a lesser extent, the engines. Nevertheless, even pilots who flew sorties during the later stages of the war when Russian anti-aircraft defences had become most formidable, could not be shaken from their belief that the Hs 129 was an ideal machine for their purposes.

---

1 CONTRARY TO ASSERTIONS IN EARLIER PUBLICATIONS ON THE Hs 129, LITTLE INFORMATION HAS COME TO LIGHT REGARDING THE DESIGNATION OF THE RÜSTSATZ BEYOND THE FOLLOWING WHICH ARE CONTAINED IN THE Hs 129 AIRCRAFT TECHNICAL HANDBOOKS:

RÜSTSATZ I - STANDARD BUILT-IN ARMAMENT OF 2 x MG 17 AND 2 x MG 151
RÜSTSATZ II - PACK OF 4 x MG 17s UNDER THE FUSELAGE
RÜSTSATZ III - MK 101
R8 - MK 103

Forty Machines a Month

Praise, Condemnation and the Struggle for Production

4

In early January 1941, manufacture of the pre-production Hs 129 B-0 series was discussed by the *Luftwaffe* General Staff. At that time, the Henschel plants in Berlin, as elsewhere, were already engaged in the sub-contract manufacture of the Ju 88, Ju 188 and other bomber types. Insufficient works capacity remained for the manufacture of large numbers of Hs 129s and as the *Luftwaffe* was not prepared to accept any reduction in the planned number of bomber aircraft which might result from large-scale Hs 129 production, it was decided that Henschel would carry out the specialised operations and final assembly but that the manufacture of most major Hs 129 components and sub-assemblies would be sub-contracted to various factories in occupied France.

An order from the General Staff to establish two *Geschwader* specifically for ground-attack duties resulted in the Hs 129 programme being suddenly allocated top priority status. As the previously assigned industry priority level "S" had caused delays in delivery from sub-contractors and disrupted the delivery schedule, the programme was allocated the highest priority classification "SS". In February, it was decided to stockpile tail assemblies, undercarriages and wings as a contingency against delays in series production, a move which proved prudent as starting-up difficulties were indeed experienced by the French sub-contractors. In April 1941, it was decided that finishing of the Gnôme-Rhône engines for series production would be undertaken by SNCA du Nord in Paris, and by November 1941, the main sources of supply for other airframe parts and assemblies had been established although each of these relied, of course, on a number of further sub-contractors. Henschel Flugzeugwerke would manufacture the armoured cockpit and equipment and also be responsible for final airframe assembly, equipment installation and flight testing while sub-contract work would be allocated as follows:

Fuselage: Rölz in Graslitz, Sudetenland.
Wing centre section: Ambi, Berlin-Johannisthal.
Undercarriage, tail assembly and outer wing section: Chausson, Paris.
Engine mountings and outer cowling: SNCAN, Paris.
Inner engine cowling and individual items of equipment: AEG, Wildau.

As well as the 16 Hs 129 B-0 conversions, the RLM's Production Plan No. 21/Ü, called for the completion of 50 Hs 129 B-1s by April 1942, and a further 200 machines of the improved B-2 sub-type with greater load carrying capacity to be delivered by April 1943. In the event, production of both the B-1 and B-2 sub-types was delayed because of raw material shortages and the need to implement modifications resulting from operational experience. In particular, the aircraft's hydraulic equipment and the propeller's variable-pitch mechanism continued to give trouble and there were also numerous fractures of the brake drums. More seriously, a number of aircraft were lost due to problems with the fuel system and the engines were found to be easily contaminated with the dust and sand from operational airfields. Because of the great number of modifications which had to relieve these difficulties, it was not possible to adhere to the planned delivery programme.

From a very early stage Henschel Flugzeugwerke had planned that the Hs 129 should possess an anti-tank capability and the manufacturers carried out a number of investigations into the possibility of installing large-calibre weapons in the aircraft. However, production of the MK 101 cannon was also delayed and it proved impossible to keep to the original intention which called for the first aircraft to be sent to the front equipped with the cannon.

Deliveries against the RLM's first order for fifty Hs 129 B-1s began in January, 1942, when the Johannisthal factory completed three

An Allied aerial photograph of Johannisthal airfield taken on 19 February 1942 showing the Henschel Werk II factory buildings at bottom left. The factory consisted of two very large hangars and one medium sized hangar plus a number of workshops off the north boundary. There were no runways, take-offs and landings being made on a large area of grass. The factory had been covered photographically twice previously on 29.9.1941 and 30.1.1943 but although medium-sized aircraft were present, in both cases photographic quality prevented positive identification. This photograph is therefore the first in which Hs 129s had been identified on a German aerodrome. Sixteen Hs 129s can be seen (there was one more on the field which was not completely covered), the majority with light-coloured noses. Also visible is an Fw 189 and an Fw 190; the Focke-Wulf factory is the group of buildings to the right.
Opposite: a corresponding British Air Ministry map of Johannisthal.

Carl Frydag (left), director of Henschel Flugzeugwerke AG and Dir.Dipl.Ing. Otto Oeckl, the leader of the Sonderausschuss – or Special Committee – F8, which was responsible to the Reichsminister for Equipment and War Production for matters concerning Henschel affairs. Oeckl's offices were situated at the Berlin-Schönefeld factory.

Hs 129 B-2 clearly showing the later filters under the engine cowlings and the yellow nose. The landing light was a feature not usually seen on the B-2.

machines against a plan of six, the shortfall being attributed to material procurement difficulties and problems with the aircraft's hydraulic system. In February, when ten machines plus three to make good the January shortfall should have been completed, only another three aircraft were finished, Henschel management explaining that adherence to the delivery plan was again not possible due to the many modifications necessary. In April, production rose to 31 but monthly output did not reach this figure again until October when 33 Hs 129 B-2s, which had begun to replace the B-1 in May, were delivered. At the end of 1942, total Hs 129 production amounted to 219 aircraft of the B-1 and B-2 variants plus one B-0 and one C-1. In addition 17 aircraft damaged in service had been repaired and re-delivered.

Although initial difficulties in starting up series production delayed delivery of completed aircraft to service units, and although there were other occasional difficulties in Henschel Flugzeugwerke meeting delivery targets - mainly due to sudden increases in the delivery plan ordered by the RLM and the general German mismanagement of the French aircraft industry - there was nevertheless always an adequate number of factory-fresh machines available to meet demand. By August 1942, 100 series aircraft had been delivered to the front, of which, according to factory records, 16 had been lost. New aircraft were ferried to Aircraft Forwarding Stations established on German-held airfields away from the front lines in Russia, where they were held until required to replace combat losses within the operational units.

Defective or damaged aircraft were taken to Front Repair Stations (*Frontreparaturbetriebe*), while extensively damaged machines were transferred to the Home Repair Station (*Heimatreparaturbetrieb*), in effect the factory where the type was first built. It was found that because of the Hs 129's excellent flying characteristics and stability, even quite seriously damaged aircraft could be patched up and readied for transfer by even the most simple means. Operational units were pleased with the Hs 129 and the RLM also considered the type a successful addition to the *Luftwaffe's* inventory. At the end of May 1942 the RLM confirmed its faith in the aircraft by allocating materials for a further 200 aircraft to be delivered against Aircraft Delivery Programme 20/d and on 1 July 1942 *Gen. Ing.* Walter Hertel, the head of *Amtsgruppe Beschaffung* in the *Technisches Amt* confirmed that production of a further 400 Hs 129s would be authorised. On 3 July, Programme 21 was officially amended to bring total orders to 650 aircraft and by September, the number increased to 758.

Despite early enthusiasm and increased orders for the type, some indication of the indecision which was to feature in all future Hs 129 manufacturing programmes may be seen in the minutes of Milch's conferences at the RLM during 1942. Because of the need to rationalise the number of different aircraft types already in production and to save on critical strategic raw materials there was already a tendency to draw up provisional plans to phase out Hs 129 production. When it later became clear that the role of this aircraft was so specialised that it could not be met by any other type, production plans were again increased but at a conference on 30 December 1942 attended by Göring, Milch and Galland, it was suggested that either the strategic raw-material content would have to be reduced or the type could perhaps be replaced completely by the Focke-Wulf 190[1]. This would certainly have brought about a reduction in the variety of operational aircraft types and manufacture of spare parts, but the performance of the Fw 190 in the ground-attack role was then unknown. *Reichsmarschall* Göring decided this matter, at least temporarily, by calling for an investigation to determine the Fw 190's suitability as a future ground-attack aircraft, but until such investigations had been completed, Hs 129 production was to continue only at a level sufficient to replace combat losses in the units already equipped with the type.

Continued production of the Hs 129 was eventually set accordingly at 40 machines a month, but with the ambivalent Milch praising the Hs 129 one minute and condemning it the next, its future position was still uncertain. In April, 1943, Milch confirmed that in his view there was indeed a need for an armoured aircraft able to operate over the battlefield, yet later the same month he wanted the whole Hs 129 programme stopped completely. In May he was lamenting the lack of a suitable tank-buster and complaining about delays in equipping the Hs 129 as an anti-tank aircraft, yet he would later disparage the Hs 129 as a "... lame duck".

Although monthly Hs 129 production figures rose during 1943, the required number of 40 machines per month was not achieved until June, a month which saw total output of all Hs 129 types reach 440, of which 253 had been lost.[2]

It was accepted that while the Gnôme-Rhône

engines were now technically very good, the engine *supply* situation was "catastrophic". Following the fall of France in June 1940, an attempt was made by the French to evacuate the Gnôme-Rhône factory in the Boulevard Kellermann in Paris as a result of which, several trainloads of completed engines and various components were removed from the premises. When the Germans arrived, they found the factory virtually deserted and in July they soon began to dismantle the machinery for storage. However, in September 1940, the factory was re-opened and during the next two months both the machinery and a number of workers returned, together with some new Swiss machine tools. At the same time,

In this view of an Hs 129 B-2 at Johannisthal, Luftwaffe personnel are seen receiving instruction from Henschel factory staff. The Fw 190 in the background is taxiing back to the adjacent Focke-Wulf works.

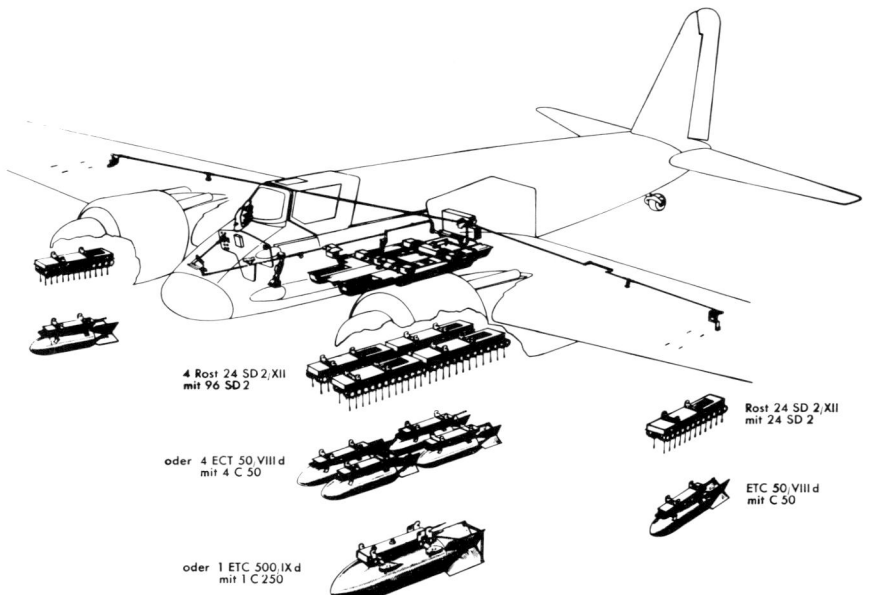

View of bomb release and weapons control panel in the Hs 129 B-1.

Drawing showing various bomb-load configurations applicable to the Hs 129 B-1 and B-2.

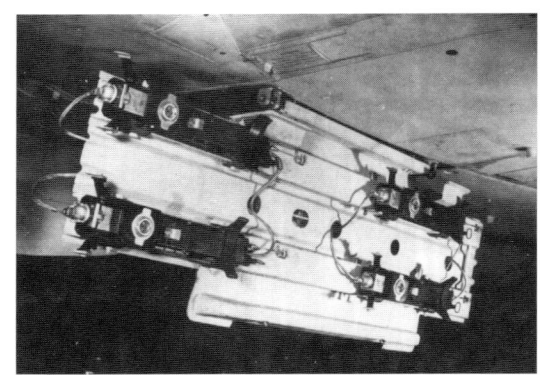

Standard Bomb Carrier tray fitted with 4 ETC/VIII d Bomb Carriers.

Standard ETC Bomb Carrier tray as fitted to Hs 129 B-1 and B-2.

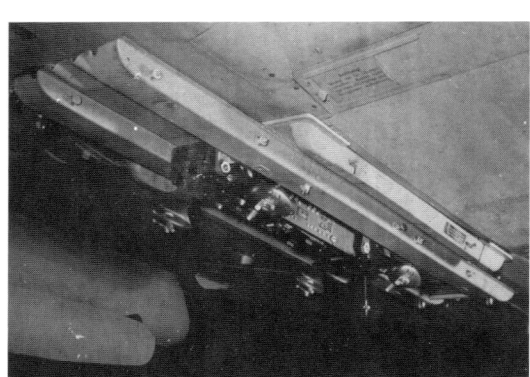

It was possible to mount a single SC250 on the fuselage rack but this configuration was rarely, if ever, used operationally by the Luftwaffe. The 250kg bomb option was however widely used by Rumanian units operating the Hs 129.

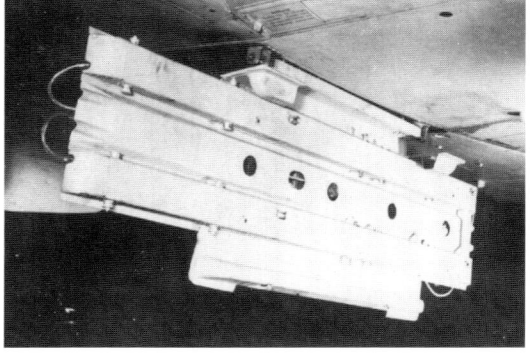

The standard under-fuselage tray carrying four SC50 bombs as fitted to the Hs 129 B-1 and early Hs 129 B-2s.

the whole of occupied Europe was scoured for Gnôme-Rhône engines in order to send them to Boulevard Kellermann for testing.

Following an intense programme of testing during the first six months of 1941, production of new engines began in May of that year under close security, as the Germans were sensitive about possible sabotage. However, since no repair work was undertaken at Boulevard Kellermann, the entire testing, repairing and completion process was somewhat laborious. After testing, engines requiring work were sent to the Voisin factory at Issy-les-Moulineaux where they were repaired. They were then returned to Paris for testing, sent back to Voisin for strip examination and then moved again to Boulevard Kellermann for further testing. Nevertheless, some 200-250 engines of various types were processed every month, although this number fell towards the end of 1941 when fewer engines were received at the factory. Simultaneously however, the production of both new and reconditioned Gnôme-Rhône 14Ms was increased to around 60 per month, although this varied according to German requirements. By February 1943, the requirement was for 80 M-4 and M-5 sub-types, an amount corresponding exactly to Henschel's 40 aircraft monthly production plan.

All completed 14Ms were delivered to C.A.M.S. at St. Denis. Shortly before the war, C.A.M.S. had been acquired by S.N.C.A. du Nord in Paris and when S.N.C.A.N. became the main contractor for preparing the 14Ms for installation in the Hs 129, C.A.M.S. - under S.N.C.A.N. direction - fitted the engines with cowlings, gills, fuel and oil pipe connections, engine controls and starters. During 1942, output averaged 20 fitted engines per week and although the Germans continually pressed for an increase, this was not possible. One reason for this was the dire labour policies of Fritz Sauckel;[3] as Henschel reported in February 1943, the number of workers drawn from the French aircraft industry and reassigned to the Reich was so large that French sub-contractors were unable to meet their delivery commitments to such an extent that the entire delivery schedule for finished Hs 129s was placed in jeopardy. The RLM was even forced to resort to the black market in order to obtain the required numbers of engines and investigations were made regarding the possibility of replacing them altogether with German BMW or Argus As 403 engines. Despite delays in deliveries of engines and equipment, completion of 40

An Hs 129 B-1 is prepared for a test flight by factory ground staff. This aircraft is connected to a ground starter battery but service aircraft operating in the field would be started by hand employing an inertia starter.

machines per month was maintained until November, but just when it looked as if production might be brought back on target, December's aircraft building programme was disrupted by three RAF air raids on 2nd, 24th and 29th of the month. All three Henschel factories were hit and *Werk* II at Johannisthal sustained considerable damage. Although only three aircraft were completely destroyed, a further 35 machines in various stages of production were damaged and the delays which resulted from clearing up bomb damage and repairing these aircraft reduced production to 24 machines. At year end, of an all-type total of 664 aircraft, Hs 129 B-2 output amounted to 414, total value (RM.45,689,040) merely 16 short against a target of 430. Although more Hs 129s were produced at Johannisthal in 1943 than in any other year, production still occupied only 13.56% of total capacity, the remaining 86.44% being devoted to the building of bomber aircraft.

The year 1944 was particularly difficult as far as maintaining aircraft deliveries was concerned.

The minimal area of the Hs 129 fuselage is well illustrated in this close-up which also shows the truncated triangular section of the fuselage.

By this time, 3,000 workers were employed at Johannisthal and in most sections of the plant a single 11-hour shift was worked seven days a week, though some departments also worked a night shift. By March 1944, total Hs 129 output of all types had crept up to 754 aircraft of which 510 (68%) had been lost. On 2 May 1944, Henschel pointed out to the *Technisches Amt* that as Gnôme-Rhône had fallen behind by two months in its delivery of engines to the Henschel assembly plant in Paris, disruption to production of the new Hs 129 B-3 could not be avoided. A revised production plan was drawn up to allow for this disruption but on 10 May the aluminium and bronze foundry at Gnôme-Rhône was shattered in a raid and in July, Henschel again wrote to the RLM explaining that difficulties with the electricity supply and transportation system in France were also causing frequent delays to the Paris suppliers. The delivery of engines again fell behind and Chaussons, the supplier of tail units, was in arrears.

By mid-1944 the most important aspect of German industrial effort was the production of fighter aircraft. By using all available resources, it was hoped that fighter production could be raised to such a level that the enemy would be forced to abandon his bombing plans which were destroying German industry. A so-called *Jägerstab*, or "Fighter Staff", was formed on the suggestion of *Feldmarschall* Milch under the energetic Karl-Otto Saur of the Armaments Ministry in order to rationalise aircraft production generally and increase the output of fighter aircraft to the highest possible degree. Members of the *Jägerstab* were empowered to visit factories and make suggestions which would enable difficulties to be overcome, and they would recommend methods by which the production level of fighter aircraft could be maximised. Subordinate technical divisions dealt with transport, machinery, buildings and power, and as the *Jägerstab* had direct access to the *Führer*, the highest authority could be available to implement decisions taken. By the end of May the total number of aircraft types in production had been reduced to 32 and the production of fighter aircraft significantly increased, but again policy regarding the Hs 129 was confused. At a *Jägerstab* conference on 3 July 1944, Saur stated that as part of the rationalisation programme designed to cut production to 16 types by the year 1946, the Hs 129 was to be phased out. However, at a conference just three days later, he called for the Hs 129's continued manufacture as a matter of extreme priority, pointing out that June production had amounted only to 27 aircraft against the 40 planned and demanding that future production should increase to 48 machines per month. By this time, however, it was too late for any further vacillation. Henschel had earlier warned that the existing contract was coming to an end and had pleaded in vain for something to be done to resolve the worsening supply problems in France if production was to continue.

In Germany, too, the demand to replace men lost at the front meant that industrial manpower was at a premium and Milch's conference minutes show that arguments frequently broke out regarding the allocation and employment of the remaining workforce. The shortage of skilled labour in particular was so acute that sometimes the success or failure of an aircraft or particular weapons programme depended on the availability of as few as six or ten men; when shortages of parts from France disrupted Hs 129 production, the German labour affected was transferred to work elsewhere, but some difficulty was experienced in effecting their return once the French delivery arrived and production could be resumed. Such a situation had arisen on 10 July when Henschel wrote to the RLM pointing out that although production of the Hs 129 B-3 with large-calibre cannon had been allocated top priority in accordance with a *Jägerstab* order of 7 July, it needed the manpower taken from Ambi Budd and requested that it should be returned as *Werk* II was already 16 wing centre-sections behind schedule.

In August 1944, the *Luftwaffe General Stab* finally agreed to terminate Hs 129 manufacture in favour of fighter production and instead of the 40 aircraft called for that month, only three could be completed, plus two repairs. Shortly afterwards, the French factories were in any case lost as a result of the Allied advances on the invasion front and in September 1944 the remaining stocks of finished parts and assemblies already in Germany were used up in the manufacture of the last seven Hs 129 B-3s.

As well as new aircraft, damaged Hs 129s continued to be delivered to Johannisthal for repair direct from operational units. Between February and September 1944, when production was finally terminated, a total of 60 Hs 129s was repaired and 225 new aircraft produced. The total figure of 859 Hs 129s produced at *Werk* II is probably correct, but by using loss reports, pilots' log-books, photographic evidence and only such other reliable material, the author has attempted to reconstruct the blocks of *Werk Nummern* allocated to the Hs 129. The results are shown in the accompanying table and exceed 1,200 machines. Clearly, the discrepancy between the two figures cannot be solely due to the loss of completed airframes during Allied bombing raids on the factories and although it has been suggested that production took place at some "shadow" factory in addition to Johannisthal, no evidence of this has come to light and the differing figures cannot yet be explained.

Hs 129 Werk Nummer Block and Production Ratio		
Werk Nummer	**Type**	**Quantity**
3001 - 3003	V1 - V3	3
3004 - 3017	A-0	14
0016 - 0031	B-0	16
0151 - 0200	B-1	50
0201 - 0450 (1)	B-2	250
140491 - 140890 (2)	B-2	400
141111 - 141130	B-2	20
141201 - 141300	B-2	100
141371 - 141410	B-2	40
141501 - 141590	B-2	90
141651 - 141760	B-2	110
141831 - 141880	B-2	50
141961 - 142005	B-2	45
142031 - 142100	B-2	70
162031 - 162050	B-3	20
		1278

1 Production order for first 250 B-2s against Program 20/d.
2 Additional 400 B-2s ordered 3/7/42 against program 21/Ü and confirmed in new Programme 22 of 1/9/42.

---

1 Tests were later carried out with components manufactured in less critically important raw materials. W.Nr. 0016, for example, was used to test the variable pitch propeller mechanism gears in which the bronze was replaced by an aluminium silicon alloy substitute.
2 By comparison, Henschel had, by this time, produced 255 Hs 123s and 910 Hs 126s.
3 Fritz Sauckel was the Plenipotentiary General for Slave Labour Mobilization 1942-45. He conducted "slave raids" into Soviet Russia and other occupied territories deporting five million people from their homes with ruthless efficiency. He was hanged in October 1946.

"As soon as the Hs 129 appears, the entire front will cry out for more…"

Gen.Ing. Gottfried Reidenbach
Head of Abteilung GL/C-E2 (Airframes) Technisches Amt
14th April 1942

PART TWO
INTO BATTLE

An early Hs 129 B-1 casualty was W.Nr.0191 of 5./Sch.G 1 shot down by AA fire near Konstatinovka on 23 May 1942. The aircraft was subsequently repaired but was destroyed on 21 February 1944 during a bombing raid on Diepholz airfield while on transfer with Fl.ÜG 1.

Hs 129 B-1 of Sch.G 1 with bombs mounted on wing and fuselage racks. The segmented spinner tip is a feature often seen on early Hs 129s. The demarcation line between upper and under-surface colours on the cowling is unusual as are the cowling louvres which appear to consist of a single slot and recess rather than the two separate exits of later models.

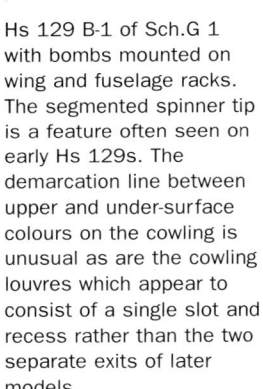

Left: A carrier tray with four racks fitted for SD 2 anti-personnel bombs.
Right: SD 2s mounted on the racks. A configuration of 96 bombs could be loaded under the fuselage, while a further 24 bombs could be loaded to each wing. Due to their tendency to hang-up on the rack, these were not a popular weapon with pilots or ground crews.

Ostfront
Combat Debut

Russia
1942

5

At the end of 1941, the *Luftwaffe's* only existing ground-attack *Gruppe*, II.*(Schlacht)/Lehrgeschwader* 2 was withdrawn from operations on the Eastern Front and disbanded. In accordance with orders issued by *General der Flieger* Hans Jeschonnek, its aircraft and personnel were used to form the first dedicated ground-attack wing, *Schlachtgeschwader* 1. This new unit was formed on 13 January 1942 and consisted of a *Geschwaderstab* and two *Gruppen*. The *Geschwaderstab* and I. *Gruppe Stab* were formed from senior personnel from the former II.*(Schlacht)*/LG 2, while members of the *Erprobungskommando* Hs 129 and personnel from Erg.Sta.II./LG 2 were transferred to form a cadré of II./Sch.G 1. The original 5.*(Schlacht)*/LG 2, which had since been redesignated 10./LG 2, now became 8./Sch.G 1 and retained its Hs 123s, while the remaining personnel of Erg.Sta./LG 2 were posted to form the so-called *"Ergänzungsjagdgruppe Ost"* (Replacement Fighter *Gruppe* East), which was to be the training and replacement unit for the new *Schlachtflieger*.

The three *Staffeln* of the I. *Gruppe* were based at Werl and equipped with Bf 109Es. The II. *Gruppe* formed at Lippstadt with the 4., 5., 6. and 7. *Staffeln* equipped with Hs 129s. The 8. *Staffel* received Hs 123s but, in order to provide each *Gruppe* with four *Staffeln* and to enable all the Hs 129 *Staffeln* to be controlled by one *Gruppenstab*, 8./Sch.G 1 was attached to the I. *Gruppe*.

Once formed, *Schlachtgeschwader* 1 began a five-month working-up period during which time the various *Staffeln* were brought up to strength. As the ground and flying personnel familiarised themselves with their new equipment, so the Hs 129 pilots practised bombing and strafing attacks in conjunction with the Werl-based Bf 109 *Gruppe* and battlefield tactics were worked out. Pilots were mildly surprised after flying their first training sorties to discover that the Hs 129 B possessed pleasing handling characteristics, one writing: "... it is a very stable machine in the air and I have the impression that it will be very good for ground-strafing."

SCHLACHTGESCHWADER 1
ADMINISTRATIVE AND OPERATIONAL COMPOSITION JANUARY 1942

I. GRUPPE (WERL)	II. GRUPPE (LIPPSTADT)
1. Staffel (Bf 109)	4. Staffel (Hs 129)
2. Staffel (Bf 109)	5. Staffel (Hs 129)
3. Staffel (Bf 109)	6. Staffel (Hs 129)
8. Staffel (Hs 123)	7. Staffel (Hs 129)

Within the *Geschwader* there was a great deal of activity and certain key personnel made factory and training visits. On 13 January, Henschel's Schönefeld offices were visited by three experienced ground-attack pilots who had earlier served with II.*(Schlacht)*/LG 2: *Major* Otto Weiss, the first *Schlachtflieger* to have been decorated with the *Ritterkreuz* on 18 May 1940 and, on 31 December 1941, the first also to receive the Oak Leaves; *Oblt.* Bruno Meyer, who had been awarded the Knight's Cross on 21 August 1941, and *Lt.* Ritter. *Major* Weiss made a short test flight in an Hs 129 before going on leave. On 23 February, *Oblt.* Siegfried Steinhoff arrived at Lippstadt to head the 5. *Staffel*, only to leave again almost immediately for Rechlin where he was to attend a course on Hs 129 operating procedures. Three days later, Otto Weiss returned after having been promoted to *Oberstleutnant* on 1 February and appointed *Geschwaderkommodore*. Bruno Meyer arrived amid speculation that he was to be given command of the II. *Gruppe* but this position was given instead to *Hptm.* Paul-Friedrich Darjes and Meyer was instead appointed *Staffelkapitän* of the 4. *Staffel*. Following completion of his course at Rechlin, *Oblt.*

In April 1942, Hs 129 B-1, W.Nr.0166 was based at Lippstadt with 4./Sch.G 1 when it was coded "A". Here, the same aircraft is seen in the summer of 1942 on the eastern front, repainted as Blue "K". Note the yellow identification markings, the unit badge and the black triangle of the Schlachtflieger. Barely visible on the upper nose panel is the Infantry Assault Badge.

This early Hs 129 B-2 W.Nr.0226 displays typical camouflage and markings, although the black centres to the crosses were deleted on later production machines. This aircraft belly-landed on 4 August 1942 in poor visibility and was 35% damaged. The bulge of the MK 101 cannon fairing may be seen under the fuselage.

Steinhoff returned to the unit accompanied by the entire remaining staff of the *Erprobungskommando* Hs 129.

Training was apparently completed at Lippstadt with only three accidents. The first occurred on 12 April when an Hs 129 B-1, W.Nr. 0177 belonging to the 6. *Staffel* crashed, killing its pilot, *Uffz*. Willi Elbers. Henschel immediately despatched Wilhelm Kaempf, the company test pilot and engineer, to investigate the exact cause of the crash which was finally traced to engine failure. On 22 April, W.Nr. 0161 from the *Geschwaderstab* was slightly damaged while taking-off and on 23 April, W.Nr. 0175 of 6./Sch.G 1 crashed due to engine trouble. Although the aircraft was seriously damaged, the pilot escaped uninjured due to the sturdy construction of the cockpit area.

At the end of April, the various *Staffeln* of *Obstlt*. Otto Weiss's *Schlachtgeschwader* 1 began to leave their training bases in Germany and, one after the other, set out for the Southern Sector of the Eastern Front where the *Geschwader* was to operate under *Luftflotte* 4. There, the Spring thaw which had severely disrupted *Luftwaffe* flying operations was over, the aerodromes in Russia had begun to dry out, and the Germans were preparing themselves for their 1942 campaign. The original plan was to break through the Russian Front between Kursk and Rostov, capture the oilfields in the northern part of the Caucasus and establish a line along the River Don from Voronezh to Stalingrad. Later, the capture of Stalingrad itself was added to the plan as a secondary objective.

A prerequisite for the launching of this plan was to cover the German flank by the complete occupation of the Crimea and *Generaloberst* Wolfram von Richthofen's VIII. *Fliegerkorps* was moved from the central front in order to provide the necessary close air support. While parts of Sch.G 1 were ordered to the Crimea to join VIII. *Fliegerkorps* and support the German drive towards Kerch, elements were assigned to IV. *Fliegerkorps* to support the main offensive towards the Caucasus. The 4./Sch.G 1 left for the Eastern Front on 26 April, making intermediate stops at Leipzig, Breslau, Crakow, Zitomir and Nikolayev, arriving at Grammatikovo in the Crimea on 6 May. About 15 Hs 129s were ferried to the Crimea and, since servicing crews on the intermediate airfields were unfamiliar with the new type and

Paul Friedrich Darjes was Gruppenkommandeur of II./Sch.G 1 from 1 March to 1 October 1942. During this time, the Gruppe flew many successful operations in the East for which Darjes was awarded the Ritterkreuz on 14 October 1942.

A characteristic of the aircraft of Stab.II./Sch.G 1 was the segmented spinner tips. Also visible is the triangle marking of the Schlachtverbände.

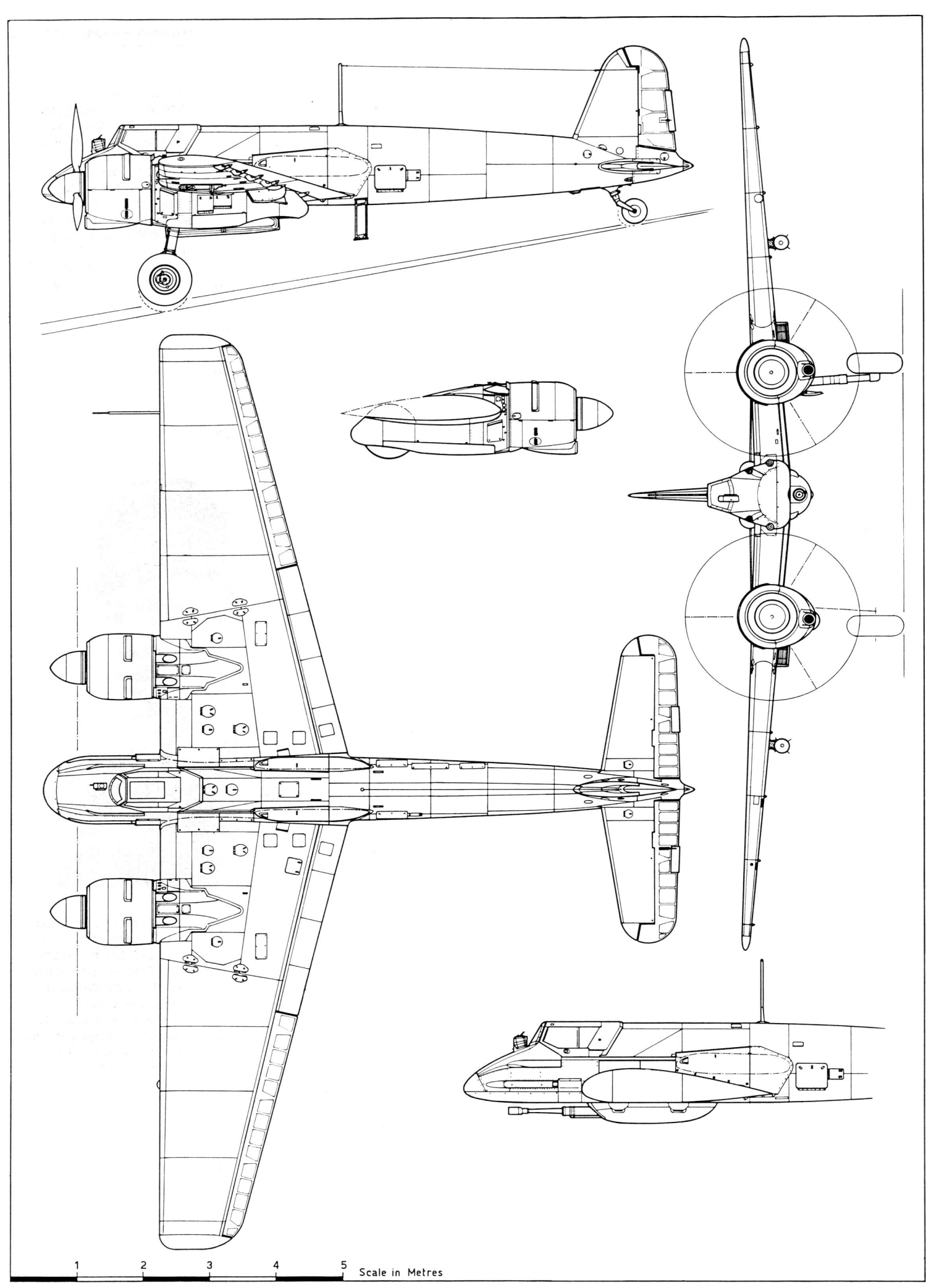

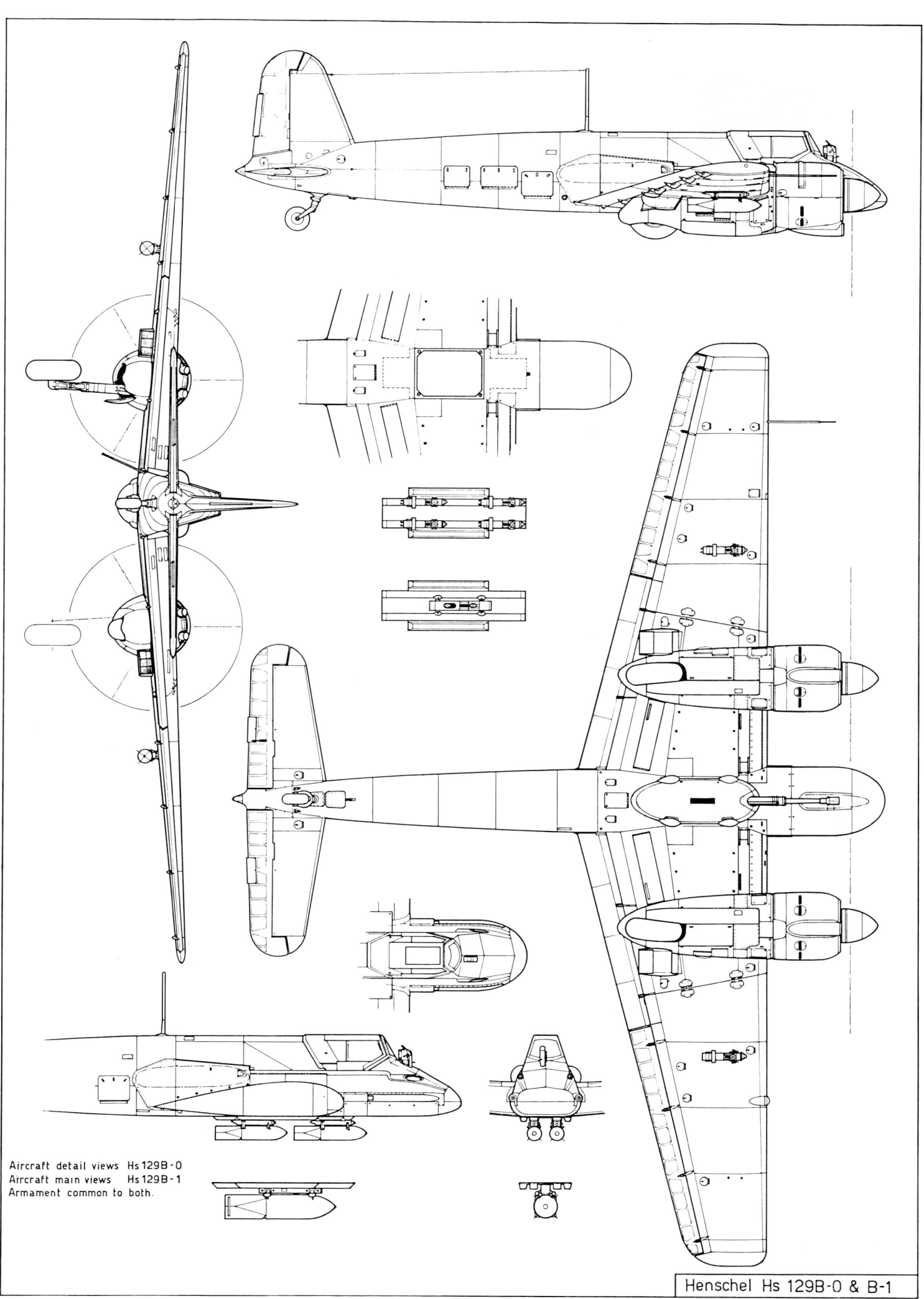

Hs 129 B-1 Blue 'K' W.Nr. 0166

5./Sch.G 1, Eastern Front, June 1942.

This aircraft was camouflaged in the standard RLM 70/71/65 splinter pattern. The markings show a **white** lined triangle painted on the **green** fuselage sides. The machine carried the standard **yellow** theatre markings of the Eastern Front on the nose, underside wing tips and fuselage band with the Berlin Bear *Staffel* badge painted behind the cockpit. The position of the W.Nr.0166 in **white** is unusual. Also, contrary to popular belief, little evidence has come to hand to confirm the widespread use of the colour **blue** for *Staffel* identity codes in Hs 129 units. However, evidence suggests that this is one such aircraft which, in addition, also had its spinner tips painted **blue.** The aircraft carried the infantry assault badge on its nose. The aircraft was fitted with an MK 101 cannon. The national insignia were: B2 crosses on wing undersides, B6 crosses on wing upper-surfaces, B5 crosses on fuselage sides and H2a style *Hakenkreuze*.

Hs 129 B-1 Chevron – White 'O'

5./Sch.G 1, Eastern Front, Summer 1942.

This aircraft carried a large **black** triangle – the marking of the Schlachtflieger units – outlined in **white** behind the fuselage cross and **yellow** theatre markings on the nose, wing tip undersides and fuselage band. An unknown four-figure *Werk Nummer* was carried in **white** at the base of the fin and the spinner tips were also painted **white**. The Berlin Bear *Staffel* badge was applied behind the cockpit and the camouflage was the standard RLM splinter pattern 70/71/65. The aircraft was fitted with an MK 101 cannon. The national insignia were: B2 crosses on wing undersides, B1a crosses on wing upper-surfaces, B3 crosses on fuselage sides and H2a style *Hakenkreuze*.

Standing on the wing of an Hs 129, Bruno Meyer describes flying procedure to Generaloberst Wolfram von Richthofen, CO of Luftflotte 4. Commander of VIII. Fliegerkorps during the Polish, Flanders, Balkan and Russian campaigns, von Richthofen acquired a reputation as the foremost exponent of intensive close-support operations.

its engines, some 15 ground personnel accompanied the Hs 129s in a Ju 52. Joining up with other parts of the *Staffel* which had left for the Crimea by land transport three weeks earlier, flying operations began the day after the aircraft arrived.

Pilots of 5./Sch.G 1 still awaiting orders to transfer to the front followed the fortunes of the *Staffeln* already in action with great interest and were encouraged by a report that an Hs 129 belonging to the 4. *Staffel* returned safely despite receiving two direct flak hits. The 5. *Staffel* started its journey to the front at 17:00 on 18 May, making its first intermediate stop at Leipzig before continuing to the Eastern Front where it flew its first sorties from Konstantinovka in the main breakthrough sector a few days after arriving. The *Geschwader's* first Hs 129 combat loss, however, occurred near Kerch on 9 May during a low-level attack against enemy motor transport which had been observed directly in front of the German lines. Hs 129 W.Nr. 0168 was seen to receive a direct flak hit and the pilot, *Hptm.* Max Eck of *Stab* II./Sch.G 1, was reported missing in action.

Air operations were intense and personnel were on duty from morning to night - from 03:00 to 21:00. A feature of the airfields in southern Russia was the severe dust clouds caused by large numbers of aircraft taking off and landing. During the day, the horizon was often black with dust and this caused problems with the Hs 129's engines which lacked adequate dust filters. There was also trouble with the variable pitch mechanism in the airscrew hub but this was cured later that summer by fitting improved electric motors. Accommodation, consisting of tents erected on the airfield, was permanently subjected to the sight and sound of battle; the thunder of the guns, Russian bombs dropping on advancing troops, German flak firing in reply, prisoners marching to the rear, Russian reconnaissance aircraft circling overhead. In the combat area, the sky was full of German aircraft of all types; so many ground-attack machines, fighters, *Stukas* and bombers, all passing within a hair's breadth of one another meant that German pilots had to fly with their eyes wide open if they were to avoid a collision!

Most Hs 129 sorties carried out in IV. and VIII. *Fliegerkorps'* areas of operations were close-support attacks with bombs and guns directed against enemy positions, infantry, artillery, motor transport and tanks. Already the support rendered by the *Schlachtgeschwader* over the front lines was winning great appreciation from the ground forces. Divisional commanders praised the activities of the *Schlachtflieger* and the Commander-in-Chief of Army Group South, *Generalfeldmarschall* Fedor von Bock, stated that his infantry always received a large boost to their morale when the ground-attack aircraft appeared.

In addition to its ground-attack duties, a *Schwarm* of four aircraft from 4./Sch.G 1 also carried out an attack against a Russian airfield in the Crimea which was occupied by about 70 Soviet fighters. The *Staffelkapitän*, *Hptm.* Bruno Meyer, later recalled: "Our low-level strafing attacks left about forty aircraft blazing wrecks. One Hs 129 was even victorious in aerial combat when for the first time an Hs 129 shot down an I-16. The remaining Soviet fighters, about thirty in all,

"Ferntrauung": a simple table with flowers, the Reich war flag, a steel helmet, rifles and an Hs 129 serving as a backdrop as Oblt. Meyer and Lt. Plümer conduct a marriage ceremony by proxy for three members of II./Sch.G 1.

were unable to get away before they were overrun by an advance party from a motorised brigade which had made a surprise push forward deep into enemy territory. The brigade's vehicles were extremely short of fuel and the soldiers, being unfamiliar with aircraft fuel systems and being unable to find the fuel cocks, simply bayoneted the aircraft to get at the precious fuel".

The intended clearing of the Crimea was still unfinished when the Russians opened an unexpected offensive in the Kharkov sector of the front. During the previous January, Soviet attacks had resulted in a large salient being formed which jutted into German-held territory from Izyum to Barvenkovo. It was the German High Command's intention to eliminate this Soviet salient, which represented a permanent threat to Kharkov, with a pincer operation, but the attention of the Russians was also focused on this area. On 12 May the Russians struck with overwhelming force to the north of Izyum and also mounted an offensive to the south with even more concentrated power. German and Rumanian divisions in the area found themselves being attacked by a vastly superior enemy possessing colossal armoured support and the Germans were now compelled to transfer the greater part of their close-support forces in the Crimea north-eastwards to meet this threat. The reunited Sch.G 1 mounted intensive air operations in order to help save the situation and, operating from airfields close to the Barvenkovo salient, was conveniently placed to participate in the vital battles of encirclement which took place in this area.

Soviet forces around Izyum were well supported by the Red Air Force which maintained a heavy scale of attack against German-occupied airfields in Southern Russia causing substantial damage to aircraft and ground establishments. At Konstantinovka, II./Sch.G 1 was bombed several times but thanks to the Henschel's rugged construction, these particular attacks were not successful. On one occasion, four Boston bombers appeared at around 2,438 m (8,000 ft) over Konstantinovka airfield and although bombs exploded in the middle of the *Gruppe's* dispersal area and steel splinters riddled two Hs 129s, it was found that the shrapnel had passed through the airframes without causing any internal damage. Once the tyres had been changed, the two aircraft were restored to operational condition and the many small holes in the aircraft did not affect their flying characteristics.

By 17 May, the Soviets were within 18 km (11 miles) of Kharkov but German ground and air action had successfully contained the attack and German forces were able to launch a counter-offensive. Now the Russians themselves faced encirclement. By 23 May the Barvenkovo salient had been cut off. One of the pilots flying with 4./Sch.G 1 at this time was *Uffz.* Anton Maier, already a veteran ground-attack pilot who had earlier flown 150 missions in Russia with the Hs 123. Maier flew thirteen operational sorties from Grammatikovo before 4./Sch.G 1 moved out of the Crimea as a result of the Russian attack around Izyum. He completed another eight sorties in the Hs 129 but on 22 May, owing to a fuel feed fault, he crash-landed at Grishina, south-west of Barvenkovo. His aircraft was a write-off, and although Maier was lucky to escape

Bruno Meyer was already an extremely experienced Schlachtflieger before flying the Hs 129. After missions flown in Poland, Belgium, France and central and northern Russia with the Hs 123 biplane, he was awarded the Ritterkreuz on 21 August 1941 after 540 missions. In early 1942, he was posted to II./Sch.G 1 leading 4./Sch.G 1 in Russia and the newly created 4./Sch.G 2 in North Africa before returning to the Eastern front to become Führer der Panzerjäger and Kommandeur of IV./SG 9.

Anton Maier was one of the Luftwaffe's most experienced ground-attack pilots, flying 150 missions with the Hs 123 equipped II.(Schlacht)/LG 2 before joining the Hs 129 Staffel, 4./Sch.G 1 at Lippstadt in March 1942. After flying 308 Hs 129 sorties with 4./Sch.G 1, 4./Sch.G 2 and 12.(Pz)/SG 9, during which time he destroyed 29 tanks, Fw Maier was awarded the German Cross in Gold on 26.11.1943. Shown here as a Leutnant after receiving his commission, "Toni" Maier is wearing the Frontflugspänge in Gold with the Schlachtflieger pendant.

from the wreckage alive, he was badly injured and did not return to operations until February 1943.

On 23 May 1942, three more Hs 129 B-1s were shot down by flak in operations around Izyum. *Fw.* Alfred Katzberg flying with *Stab* II./Sch.G 1 baled out of his W.Nr. 0186 when it was hit and caught fire. Although Katzberg made a clean exit 9 km (5.6 miles) south-west of Petrovskaya and his parachute was seen to open, a strong wind carried him over the Russian lines and he was never seen again. The 5. *Staffel's Uffz.* Heinz Lammel was posted missing after his aircraft, W.Nr. 0157 coded B+, took a direct hit in one engine. Lammel tried to crash-land his burning machine 11 km (6.8 miles) west of Petrovskaya, but it hit the ground and exploded. The third loss that day was W.Nr. 0173, also from 5./Sch.G 1, which crashed near Petrovskaya. It is believed the pilot survived.

On 24 and 25 May, II./Sch.G 1 participated in what was to be one of the bloodiest actions of the whole war in the East as the Russians tried to break out of their encirclement. For two days they launched themselves against the German Army and during the late evening on 26 May the *Gruppe* helped prevent a breakout attempt by heavy cavalry forces of the Russian I, V and VI Cavalry Corps and armour of the Sixth and Fifty-Seventh Armies. These most successful operations were conducted without a single Hs 129 being lost although W.Nr. 0172 was

A slightly blurred but dramatic air-to-air photograph showing an Hs 129 B-1 of Stab., II./Sch.G 1 in flight over southern Russia, 1942. This aircraft carried the Staffel emblem behind the cockpit and the black triangle of the assault units on the fuselage sides.

damaged by enemy ground fire on 26 May. On the Soviet side, only remnants escaped and when the fighting ended on 28 May, the Germans had taken 240,000 prisoners and captured more than 1,200 tanks and 2,000 guns.

Sch.G 1 was also engaged against the Soviet Thirty-Eighth Army which attacked Kupyansk to the north of Izyum. *Oblt.* Bruno Meyer, who flew his 500th mission on 31 May, later recalled: "Our infantry fought bitter defensive battles against a numerically superior enemy, the main Soviet thrust being directed against the Chuguyev-Kupyansk railway line using strong tank forces. All the Hs 129 *Staffeln* were thrown into the battle to stop the enemy but, fond of night and bad weather fighting, the Russians succeeded time and again in making local breakthroughs with the result that our infantry was hard pressed all the time".

But here, too, the Russian attacks were halted and eventually turned back, enabling Army Group South to straighten and stabilize its front line along the western banks of the Donets and Oskol to the east of Kharkov in preparation for the German summer offensive.

An Hs 129 B-1 on a grass strip somewhere in Russia during the summer of 1942. Typically for this period, the aircraft is fitted with a fuselage bomb rack.

"A Question of Life or Death"

THE CANNON CRISIS

6

At the start of Operation *"Barbarossa"*, the German invasion of Russia in July 1941, there were two Russian armoured vehicle designs of which the Germans knew nothing; the KV Heavy tank and the T-34 Medium tank, both of which mounted a 76.2 mm cannon which was far more powerful than the armament of any German tank. The KVs, named after Marshal Kliment Voroshilov, the People's Commissar for Defence at the time of their approval in 1940, were protected by 75 mm to 130 mm (3-5 ins) armour, depending on the particular model, and were almost impervious to German anti-tank guns.

In view of the *Luftwaffe* General Staff's failure to ensure that an airborne anti-tank cannon reached the front in adequate numbers, it was fortunate that although Russian attacks were frequently supported by strong armoured forces, the tank units themselves had not been employed as effectively as they might have been. Russian theories regarding the employment of tanks had centred around the erroneous and outdated view that armour was best used in support of infantry. This restricted the T-34's superb cross-country performance and reduced the use of armour to the pedestrian pace of the infantry. In addition, instead of employing their T-34 and super heavy KV-1 and KV-2 tanks in bulk formations at selected points, the Russians committed them piecemeal, with the result that in spite of the terror they originally caused, the superior Soviet tanks were frequently outnumbered and destroyed by German tank companies and anti-tank guns. A sudden and necessarily hurried attempt to reorganise the Soviet tank arm into armoured formations only resulted in further exceptionally heavy losses since they had to be led by infantry officers and other officers lacking the necessary experience in armour.

Later, in the autumn of 1942, more experienced tank commanders succeeded in establishing wholly armoured formations and laid down firm principles for their employment. By the end of 1942, "Tank Armies" were formed, each consisting of one or two tank corps and a mechanised corps consisting largely of infantry with tanks in support. In order to overcome a shortage of lorries in the Soviet Army, and because difficult terrain, or ground rendered impassable to wheeled vehicles by bad weather, often prevented the infantry from moving up with the tanks, the infantry were organised into "special landing troops" which rode into battle on the sides and backs of the tanks themselves.

Accounting for 68% of total Soviet tank production, the T-34 medium tank was, without doubt, the best in the Red Army, if not the world, at this time and was of such basic excellence in design and performance that it lasted the war without major modification. Its most noteworthy feature was the admirable design of the hull armour with its well-sloped plates offering maximum resistance to attack. In armoured fighting vehicle design, the slope of the armour is critical and protects the tank in two ways; it is likely to make a shot fired at it from ground level bounce off, and it presents a greater thickness to the attacking shot. For example, the T-34's 45 mm (1 1/2 in) glacis was angled back at 30 degrees, so affording the equivalent ballistic protection of 90 mm (3 1/4 in) plate.

The Russian KV-1 heavy tank was armed with a 76.2 mm gun, carrying 111 rounds and was managed by a crew of five.

The superiority of the T-34 had first become apparent during the battle of Mtsensk, near Tula in October 1941, when German gunners noticed that their 30 and 50 mm shells had no effect on its frontal armour. The T-34 outstripped all its contemporaries in armour, armament and mobility and unless it was engaged at extremely close range or a lucky shot hit its tracks or some other relatively soft spot, German anti-tank shells simply bounced off. On one occasion in 1941, a single T-34 charged the German lines and despite being engaged by tanks and anti-tank guns of the 17. Panzer Division, was able to penetrate the German lines for a distance of some 14 km (9 miles) before it became stuck in marshy ground. Even then, it required heavy artillery to destroy it.

Broadly speaking, there are three ways to defeat the protection offered by the armour on a tank or other armoured fighting vehicle: setting the vehicle on fire; shattering the armour by detonating a large explosive charge on the side of the vehicle; or by punching a hole through the armour plate.

Setting fire to a tank is not particularly easy and as a general method of attack was impossible in 1942 due to a lack of suitable incendiary devices. As for the explosive charge, by the beginning of the Russian campaign, the *Luftwaffe* General Staff had become aware that attacks against tanks with bombs were largely ineffective. Although this had soon become very obvious to the leaders of operational units it was only slowly appreciated by the policy-forming staffs. The most promising method then in use of delivering a bomb against tanks was known as the "*Steckrübenwurf*" or "Turnip Lob". In this method the tank was always attacked at right angles to its side in an extremely low-level run-in. Just before reaching its target, the aircraft would climb to between 20 and 30 m (66 to 98 ft), then dive down on its target to deliver its bomb squarely against the tank's sloping side. In order to be effective, the bomb had to actually hit and explode against the side of a tank or hit the ground within 1-2 m (3-6 ft) of it and ricochet into its side before exploding. This method of attack was different from that used by the dive-bomber units, the *Stukageschwader*. The dive-bombers attacked by diving steeply towards the target, but the probability of scoring a hit by dive-bombing was lower. During the course of the first winter campaign in the East, II.(*Schlacht*)/LG 2 in particular had many opportunities of destroying all types of fighting vehicles using bombs delivered in shallow angle attacks, most notably at

The Soviet KV-2. Although little used after 1941, this massive and cumbersome tank was still a formidable vehicle. It featured a 122 mm or 152 mm howitzer and was protected by armour up to 110 mm thick.

"Prinadlezhit-Chetverki" - Russian tank crew slang for the ubiquitous T-34/76. These frontal and rear views of the classic medium tank clearly illustrate the well-designed sloping turret and hull armour which offered maximum resistance to attack. Despite a degree of inconvenience caused to the crew through cramped internal conditions and somewhat primitive controls, such disadvantages were far outweighed by the T-34's high speed and excellent power-to-weight ratio.

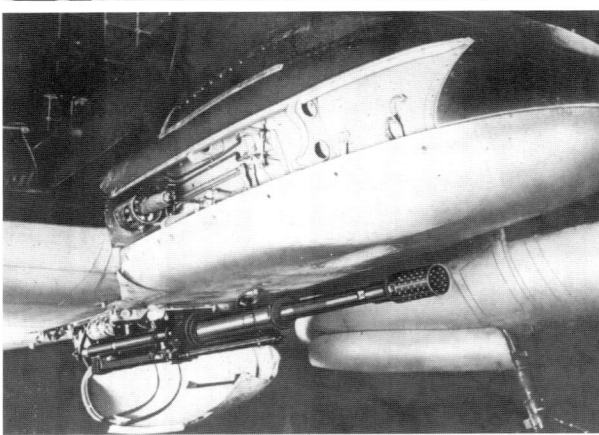

Right and far right: A sequence taken from official RLM handbooks showing the MK 101 cannon in various stages of installation and maintenance. The entire gun pack comprising MK 101 and fairing could be swung down for reloading and servicing. The weapon can be seen here on its purpose-built light metal maintenance cradle beneath the centre section of an Hs 129. The cradle was designed to facilitate the ease of handling.

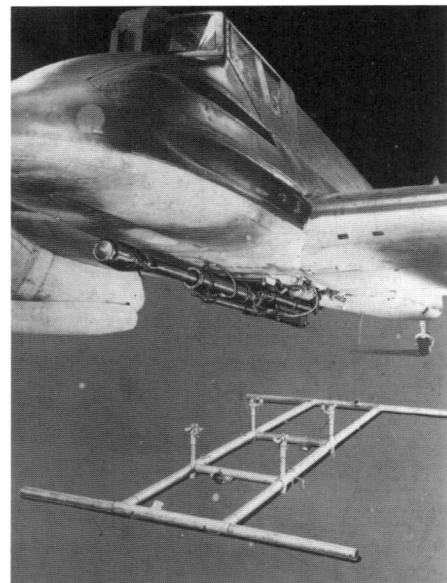

Smolensk, Viasma and Kalinin. On occasions, considerable successes had been achieved but, overall, only a handful of pilots fully mastered the technique of bombing tanks and that they did so at all only delayed the development of specialised tank-busters armed with heavy cannon.

The most successful method of making holes in armour plate was (and still is) to fire a solid lump of very hard metal which, by sheer energy and momentum, punches its way through armour. This is achieved by firing a projectile, which should be as hard and as heavy as possible - hence the use of tungsten-carbide cored ammunition, which also flies very accurately to long ranges - from a high-velocity gun, so that the projectile travels very fast. Clearly, the success rate of aircraft against armour could be increased if, instead of bombing tanks, they could be destroyed by aircraft cannon but, in order for this to be successful, the projectile had to strike the target at the correct angle or it would simply bounce off. In attack and defence, tank crews naturally chose to present their thicker frontal armour to enemy ground positions, but the pilot of an anti-tank aircraft equipped with an armour-piercing cannon would be able to manoeuvre to attack the more vulnerable parts of the tank. The most favourable approach would be directed against the more thinly armoured sides and rear areas where, by diving at right angles to the armour plating, the chances of shells penetrating to the inside of the tank would be greatly increased; as well as reducing the probability of ricochets, a shell striking the tank's armour at an angle of ninety degrees has a shorter distance to travel in order to pierce it. Such favourable angles of attack were only possible from the air.

Slowly the *Luftwaffe* General Staff came to the realisation that the provision of such an airborne anti-tank gun was a matter of the greatest urgency, particularly as the German Army possessed far too few anti-tank guns and these were dispersed throughout the entire length of the Eastern Front. Concentrating suitable ground weapons in time and in sufficient force at the point of an armoured attack was often impossible owing to the distances involved, poor roads and weather, whereas properly equipped aircraft could be quickly flown up to a point of crisis.

The requirement for a "flying anti-tank gun" had also been recognised by *Dipl. Ing.* Nicolaus's design team, which had made provision for the Hs 129 to carry an anti-tank gun at a very early stage of the aircraft's development. The service use of such a weapon was, however, delayed. At first, this was due to the *Luftwaffe* General Staff's failure to realise its potential. Later however, although some officials at the RLM gave their support to the Hs 129 as a *Panzerjäger* - a "tank hunter" - and the idea also had the enthusiastic backing of Hitler and Göring, there was a complete lack of any co-ordinated driving force possessing the enthusiasm and authority necessary to overcome production difficulties and ensure the weapon reached the front in suitable quantities and in the shortest possible time.

As early as 1939, the *E-stelle* Rechlin had carried out a series of very promising trials with the 30 mm MK 101 cannon which Rheinmetall-Borsig had been developing since 1936 for aircraft use. The MK 101 was essentially a scaled-up version of the earlier 20 mm S-18-1100 anti-tank rifle (an infantry defence weapon) produced by the Waffenfabrik Solothurn A.G., a Swiss company owned by Rheinmetall. It was originally intended for installation in such aircraft as the unsuccessful Focke-Wulf Fw 57 *Kampfzerstörer*[1] which did not progress beyond the prototype stage. After witnessing a demonstration of the cannon's impressive fire-power during the exhibition at Rechlin in July 1939, Göring had ordered it into production, calling for the rapid manufacture of 3,000 weapons. Although a small number of Messerschmitt Bf 110 C-6s had been equipped with hand-made MK 101s and used operationally by *Erprobungskommando* 210 against tanks and other ground targets during the French campaign of 1940, Udet had prevented - indeed forbidden - its further development, apparently because he could see no logical reason why such a cannon would be required.[2] Due to this lack of official interest, and also due perhaps to reports from *Erp.Kdo.* 210 which complained that early examples of the cannon had a tendency to jam after firing only a few rounds, Göring's order for the series production of the cannon was not properly followed up.

Further difficulties were caused by a lack of manpower and industrial capacity. Visiting the Rheinmetall-Borsig weapons plant in Berlin late one evening in March 1942, the newly appointed Minister of Armaments, Albert Speer, discovered that although the workshops were equipped with valuable machine tools, they were standing idle as there were simply not enough workers to man a second shift. In the area of weapons manufacture, RLM conference reports repeatedly mention the critical shortage of suitable labour without which

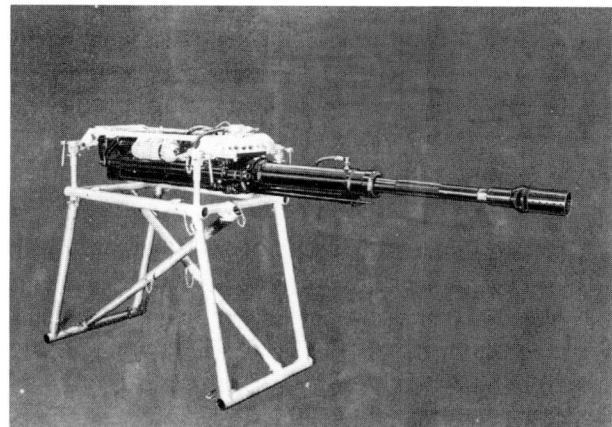

a particular project could not be completed and disputes frequently arose over the allocation of perhaps just thirty men.

In any event, no tooling had been laid down for

the mass production of the MK 101. Weighing an exceptionally heavy 180 kgs (367 lbs), the MK 101 was originally intended to be only an experimental design pending the availability of the improved MK 103. Consequently, the manufacture of expensive tooling for mass production could not be justified and each weapon completed was virtually handmade. The MK 101 was therefore expensive, labour intensive and difficult to manufacture, which only exacerbated the demands being made on the already limited resources available. Although the decision to manufacture the cannon manually was intended to free machine tool capacity for the mass production of the similar but lighter and faster firing MK 103, by May 1942, when it was needed for the Hs 129, only ten pre-production MK 103s had been built, no firing trials had been carried out and mass production was at least another year away.

The minutes of conferences held in April and May 1942 show the enthusiasm many individuals then felt for the Hs 129 and the MK 101 and MK 103 cannon. At a conference on 14 April, *Gen.Ing.* Gottfried Reidenbach, head of airframe development in the *Technisches Amt*, said that although the *Generalstab* had called for only 250 of these aircraft, he was "... convinced that as soon as the Hs 129 appears, the entire front line will cry out for more". *Obslt.* Edgar Petersen, *Kommandeur der Erprobungsstellen* reported that six Hs 129s were then serving with a trials unit at Rechlin where the serviceability rate was extremely high for the aircraft including its weapons and airframe. It was expected that even in winter, the serviceability rate would be around 70 to 80 per cent but, said Petersen, "... unfortunately, the machine cannon are still in storage at Rechlin."

Two weeks later, *Obst. i.G. Dipl-Ing* Wolfgang Vorwald, Chief of the *Technisches Amt*, confirmed that his office considered the Hs 129 "... a very important weapon. Time and again we hear from the Front that the infantry insists on the *Luftwaffe* warding off tanks because they themselves cannot ...". Referring to the installation of the cannon, he went on to say that "... the *C-Amt* of the *Technisches Amt* has suggested that the MK 101 equipment be provided for the entire '129 *Gruppe* to permit it to use the MK 101 for all missions."

Frontal view of Hs 129 showing the MK 101 cannon fairing swung down for maintenance.

In answer to a query about production of the aircraft itself, Henschel director and Chairman of the *Hauptausschuss Zellen* (Main Committee for Airframes) Carl Frydag explained that the Hs 129 was behind schedule because the General Staff had not intended to use the aircraft, a reference to the earlier refusal to accept the Hs 129 A-1. As for the cannon, production delays had been due to the huge numbers of work hours which were required but which were simply not available.

On 13 May 1942, *Reichsmarschall* Göring presided over a mid-day conference at Carinhall, his large country estate on the Schorfheide, some 80 km (50 miles) north-east of Berlin. Attending were *Feldmarschall* Milch, *Generaloberst* Jeschonnek and Göring's Chief Adjutant, *Major i.G.* von Brauchitsch. At Rechlin, Göring said, it had been shown that tungsten-carbide shells fired from an MK 101 in a standing position had easily pierced 80 mm (3 ins) of armour plate from a distance of 100 m (328 ft). Moreover, he had been told that if fired from the air at a more favourable angle, 100 mm (4 ins) thick armour could be pierced. The only disadvantage was the capacity of the MK 101's six-round magazine which had, Göring said, to be "... increased at all costs". Similarly, the production of the special ammunition was to be sped up and at the same time Göring also called for investigations into the possibility of installing a larger cannon of 50 mm calibre in the Hs 129.

"These machines," Göring observed, "are especially suitable for use against tanks which have broken through the front line. A procedure must be adopted to ensure that these aircraft are distributed over the whole front. It would be most practical to assign them to fighter *Gruppen* and to use them exclusively against tank penetrations". Then, with regard to the newly operational Hs 129 *Schlachtgruppe* already assigned to *Luftflotte* 4, he asked Jeschonnek, Chief of the *Luftwaffe* General Staff, to make arrangements for all the existing aircraft to be issued with 30 mm anti-tank cannon and appropriate ammunition as soon as possible.

Yet despite such optimism, when II./Sch.G 1 left for the Eastern Front it is believed that only three of its aircraft had been fitted with 30 mm cannon. The minutes of Milch's conference for 26 May show that despite efforts made to equip the front-line Henschel 129 *Staffeln* with the cannon, *Generaloberst* von Richthofen, officer commanding VIII. *Fliegerkorps*, was reluctant to accept the weapon. Referring to the delays and the lack of cannon at the front, an angry Milch

An Hs 129 pulls up after a practice attack against a dummy target. Note how close the aircraft would pass over its victim.

found reason to complain to *Major i.G.* Storp, the head of the *Luftwaffe's* Tactical/Technical Requirements Group:

Milch: *"What has happened is a scandal! You gave me three cannon whilst the others lay around somewhere. I have not reported this to the Reichsmarschall although he wants to know about it. We've pulled the last test pieces out of Rechlin and even taken four cannon off aircraft there. All the others are laying around at Lippstadt or wherever. Why didn't you send them forward? Why are some still at Lippstadt?"*

Storp: *"VIII. Fliegerkorps didn't want them."*

Milch: *"So, they never arrived at the front! To the Reichsmarschall it's a question of life or death which he's fretted about day and night. He and the Führer are worried that we won't have anything to counter successful tank breakthroughs. An 88 mm isn't always at the right place at the right time. With the 30 mm tungsten ammunition one has something for defence against any armoured attack, both in the main battle areas and at other breakthrough points. It's a dreadful thought that we have all given our best energy to this day and night in order to emphasise the situation and then the cannon are not used."*

Meanwhile, on 19 May, *Dipl. Ing.* Nicolaus had been called to the RLM to discuss the whole question of large calibre weapons for the Hs 129 and later that month he spent a further three days in discussion with Rheinmetall-Borsig. Henschel had already prepared drawings showing the 50 mm Flak 41 in the Hs 129 and by July consideration had been given not only to the installation of the 30 mm MK 103, but also the 37 mm Flak 18 with twelve rounds and the 50 mm Pak 38 which,

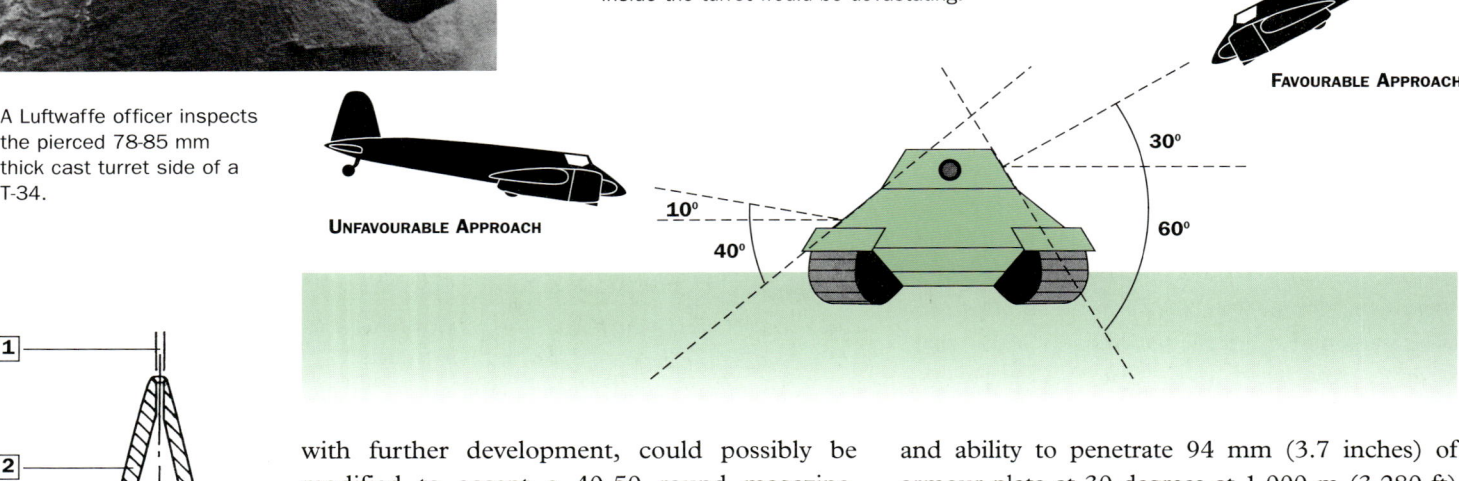

EFFECT OF 30MM ARMOUR-PIERCING SHELL ON SLOPING ARMOUR PLATE

A) The slim pointed shape and the high density of the tungsten-carbide core enables the anti-tank shell to travel at very high velocity.

B) The core punches through sloping armour. Externally unimpressive, the effect inside the turret would be devastating.

Upon entering, the 30 mm tungsten-carbide shell broke up into hundreds of jagged pieces which, together with fragments of the turret armour ricocheted around the interior of the turret and crew compartment.

FAVOURABLE APPROACH

UNFAVOURABLE APPROACH

A Luftwaffe officer inspects the pierced 78-85 mm thick cast turret side of a T-34.

30 MM SOLOTHURN TUNGSTEN CARBIDE SHELL

1. VENT HOLE
2. LIGHT ALLOY BALLISTIC CAP
3. 2 VENT HOLES
4. TUNGSTEN-CARBIDE CORE
5. LIGHT ALLOY ENVELOPE

with further development, could possibly be modified to accept a 40-50 round magazine. These investigations showed, however, that while the MK 103, Flak 18 and Pak 38 were all feasible options, the Flak 41 was too heavy.

At the beginning of 1942, instructions had been issued to investigate the use of the Army's new 75 mm Pak 40 anti-tank gun as an aircraft weapon which could be suitably adapted and despatched to the front without delay. Contracts calling for this gun for Army use had been placed in 1939 but, due to the pressures of other work, it was not ready for production by the opening of the Russian campaign. Once the limitations of the existing equipment were seen, the Pak 40 contracts were sped up and the gun went into full-scale production. It was used with considerable success throughout the rest of the war and its performance and ability to penetrate 94 mm (3.7 inches) of armour plate at 30 degrees at 1,000 m (3,280 ft) was considered entirely satisfactory.

Rather than develop a fully automatic loading mechanism for the Pak 40 it was thought that a semi-automatic mechanism would present fewer difficulties and could therefore be in service earlier. However, as a semi-automatic cannon would require a member of the crew to assist with the loading operation, a single-seat aircraft was out of the question and the robustly constructed Ju 88 with its crew of four and general good strength was a natural choice. As will be related later, the results of the Ju 88 trials, although disappointing from an operational viewpoint, would eventually benefit the development of a 75 mm fully-automatic cannon for use in the Hs 129 and a version so equipped did see service in the autumn of 1944.

---

1 KAMPFZERSTÖRER: LITERALLY "BATTLE DESTROYER" OR HEAVY-FIGHTER, BUT BASICALLY A MULTI-PURPOSE AIRCRAFT COMBINING THE ROLES OF HEAVY FIGHTER, LIGHT BOMBER, RECONNAISSANCE AND GROUND-ATTACK.

2 IN AN ALLIED COMBINED SERVICES DETAILED INTERROGATION REPORT DATED 24.5.43., GEN.MAJOR BASSENGE, AT THE TIME OF HIS CAPTURE GERMAN AIR DEFENCE COMMANDER OF TUNIS AND BIZERTA BUT WHO SERVED AS A GROUP LEADER IN THE TECHNISCHES AMT UNTIL EARLY 1938, STATED: "THIS 30MM GUN WAS READY FOR USE IN SPRING '37 AND UDET FORBADE ITS FURTHER DEVELOPMENT. HE SAID TO ME PERSONALLY, "YOU MUST KNOW YOURSELF I DON'T NEED SUCH A GUN AT 50 METRES. I BLAZE AWAY WITH A MACHINE-GUN OR WITH 2 OR 4 MACHINE GUNS.""

High Hopes – Low Temperatures

The MK 101 Cannon in Service

7

The appearance of the Hs 129 at the front had already caused the Russians some considerable concern and, although only three cannon-armed aircraft were available for operations in May, news of their introduction was soon reported. On 26 May 1942, an article appeared in a Swedish newspaper, stating:

"It is learned that the Germans employed at Kerch and Kharkov a new armoured fighter 'plane described as a "flying anti-tank gun". This new aircraft is equipped with a gun using special ammunition with high armour-piercing potential which can penetrate the armour of Russian super-tanks".

With just three Hs 129 cannon aircraft operational, results were bound to be limited and it was as a ground-attack, not anti-tank, aircraft that the machine had made its greatest impression on the enemy to date. Now, however, the aircraft's anti-armour capability was to be greatly enhanced through the delivery to front-line units of further MK 101 cannon. With a barrel length of 1.35 m (4.4ft), the MK 101 complete with breech was some 2.44 m (8 feet) long and the entire installation was carried under the Hs 129 by means of a detachable mounting beneath the fuselage, the cannon extending from the rear wing spar to within 610 mm (2 feet) of the nose of the aircraft. The breech mechanism was enclosed within a streamlined fairing and the whole installation could be quickly detached by

Oblt. Franz Oswald, 5./Sch.G 1's Technical Officer photographed in the summer of 1942 in front of a communications lorry adorned with the Staffel emblem.

withdrawing four spring-loaded pins, one from each corner of the mounting, from lugs on the bottom flange of each wing spar. Similarly, by withdrawing only two of the pins, the entire gun and mounting could be swung down for loading and servicing.

Instead of the earlier 6-round drum, the cannon was fed by a drum magazine containing 30 rounds of ammunition, either high-explosive

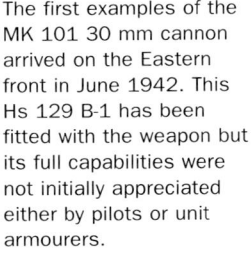

The first examples of the MK 101 30 mm cannon arrived on the Eastern front in June 1942. This Hs 129 B-1 has been fitted with the weapon but its full capabilities were not initially appreciated either by pilots or unit armourers.

tracer with a nose fuze or, for anti-tank work, special tungsten carbide armour-piercing high-explosive rounds. These were very long and pointed projectiles with a light aluminium alloy envelope and a hard tungsten carbide core. The shell cases were made of steel and were coated with a brown protective lacquer during manufacture to inhibit corrosion. The weapon itself was capable of both single-shot and automatic fire, and a selector switch was fitted to the aircraft's control column so that the MK 101 could be fired independently of the built-in fuselage armament or, if required, all weapons could be fired together. Bomb release was controlled by a separate thumb lever mounted on the side of the stick.

A batch of these weapons was eventually delivered to the front in June 1942, when Ju 52 transport aircraft loaded with MK 101 cannon, special tungsten-carbide hard-core ammunition and a number of engineers from the *E-stelle* Rechlin, landed at Kharkov-Rogan. The cannon were assigned to the Hs 129s of 4./Sch.G 1 which immediately went into action with them against tanks. This was the period of the renewed Russian offensive against Kharkov in the defeat of which the Hs 129 played a successful part. Russian prisoners-of-war captured at this time stated on interrogation that Hs 129s had not only put many tanks out of action during the battle of Kharkov, but also caused panic among Soviet troops. Excellent results were also achieved during the subsequent Russian retreat from Kharkov to Voronezh, when attacks were made by waves of up to 21 aircraft against the tanks of Marshal Timoshenko's South West Front.

This successful debut was of great interest to Hitler who was later to say that the *Panzerjägerstaffeln* would form the backbone of the *Ostfront* during the coming winter. *General* Galland also confirmed that the Hs 129 and MK 101 combination was a suitable new weapon for future employment, but the pilots themselves began to express doubts and to question the effectiveness of the armour-piercing ammunition, pointing out that, when German ground forces advanced and occupied the scene of fighting, no tanks were found which had been hit by aircraft cannon. The majority of pilots disliked the cannon and as a consequence gun mountings were dismantled and replaced by bomb-racks. As a result of this, when German forces burst through the Russian lines between Kursk and Rostov towards Voronezh and the River Don in July, II./Sch.G 1 flew many missions in pursuit of the retreating enemy using bombs as the main offensive weapon.

With this shift in the direction of German main effort to the Kursk area and, at the end of June and early July 1942, eastwards towards Voronezh, the entire *Gruppe* was operating on the central sector of the southern front but with its various

Close-up of the 5./Sch.G 1 Berlin Bear emblem on a flak-damaged Hs 129 B-1. Note also the proximity of the yellow octane triangle to the emblem.

An Hs 129 B-1 of II./Sch.G 1 taking off and landing. The weapon configuration seen here consists of an MK 101 cannon under the fuselage and containers for SC10 bombs under each wing.

Two photos of Hs 129 B-2, W.Nr.0350, of Pz.Jä.St./JG 51 in the early spring of 1943 including a close-up of the cockpit showing the construction of the seat and cockpit area which were composed almost entirely of armour plate. The aircraft, seen here still with traces of winter camouflage on the wings, was later transferred to the 8./Rumanian Schlachtgruppe.

Staffeln operating from Kharkov, Volchansk, Shatalovka, Orel and Kursk. The 5. *Staffel* flew from Kharkov-Rogan for most of June, mounting its 100th sortie from there on 12 June. During his 11th mission on the 13th, *Oblt.* Franz Oswald discovered that the variable pitch motor on his right airscrew had stopped working. On returning to Kharkov-Rogan, his mechanic found that a fist-sized hole had burned through the exhaust collector ring. Remarkably, the engine itself did not catch fire although exhaust flames had spurted out of the hole the whole time the engine had been running.

The 6. *Staffel* lost two Hs 129 Bs to flak on 28 June, one of these belonging to *Lt.* Hans-Hermann Steinkamp, the armaments officer of II./Sch.G 1 *Gruppenstab*. Now operating from Frolov-West against retreating Russian troops, his aircraft, W.Nr.0208 coded N+, was hit by enemy infantry fire. With his left engine burning, Steinkamp was forced to make an emergency landing in enemy territory and came down some 3-4 km (2-2½ miles) north-east of a railway bridge over the River Tim. Fortunately, he was able to avoid capture and returned to his unit, later becoming one of the most successful and highly decorated Hs 129 pilots.

On the evening of 29 June, the *Kommandeur* of II./Sch.G 1 (*Maj.* Darjes), the *Gruppenadjutant* (*Oblt.* Kent) and *Oblt.* Oswald took part in a particularly frustrating and unsuccessful mission. Just before their take-off, Darjes discovered that he had forgotten to bring his map and asked Oswald to give him his. Shortly after the three aircraft had become airborne, however, Darjes radioed that his engines were giving trouble and that he was returning to the airfield. The other two aircraft continued with the mission, Kent leading, until the weather deteriorated to such an extent that it was decided that they, too, would have to return. Kent then announced over the R/T that his compass had failed and that he was lost. Oswald, without a map, assumed command and decided to fly in a north-westerly direction. Then, two fighters appeared, approaching the Henschels from the left. Oswald saw them first and, radioing Kent, turned towards them. After some defensive manoeuvres, both pilots realised

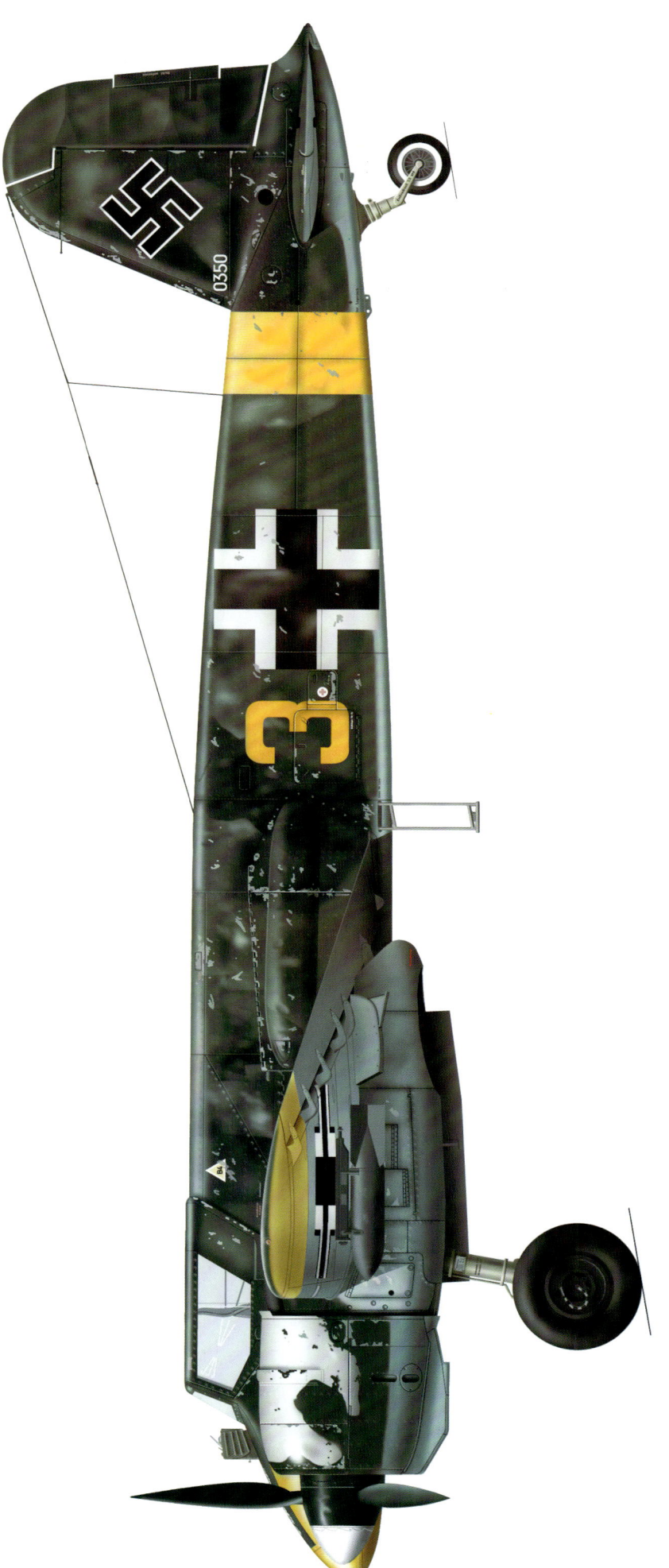

Hs 129 B-2 Yellow '3' W.Nr. 0350
Pz.Jä.St./JG 51, Eastern Front, Spring 1943.

While aircraft of the *Schlachtgeschwadern* were marked with coloured numbers as used by standard *Jagdgeschwader* (Fighter Units), the machines of *Panzerjäger Staffel 'Mölders'* were marked with code letters. The aircraft shown here is camouflaged in the standard 70/71/65 RLM splinter pattern and still bears traces of a temporary **white** washable winter paint. In particular, the wings, from the tips to the outside of the engine nacelles still retained some of the temporary **white** finish and irregular **white** patches can also still be seen on the cowlings. However, only residue traces of **white** were left on the rest of the machine where the temporary paint had not been completely washed off. Heavy exhaust staining marked the wing upper-surfaces **white** paint. The Eastern Front **yellow** theatre markings were applied to the nose, underside wing tips and fuselage band. The aircraft was fitted with an MK 101 cannon. The national insignia were: B2 crosses on wing undersides, B1a crosses on wing upper-surfaces, B3 crosses on fuselage sides and H2a style *Hakenkreuze*.

To allow Panzerjäger Staffeln to rapidly move to a new location complete with supporting ground personnel, Hs 129s were fitted with a rigid glider-towing attachment, similar to that seen here on a Ju 87 B towing a DFS 230 during the air transfer of 4./Sch.G 1's ground personnel. Although used to a limited extent, the attachment was not popular with all Hs 129 Staffeln and the Henschel factories ceased incorporating the towing device in January 1944.

A snow camouflaged Hs 129 B-2, W.Nr.0334, still wearing factory codes. Ironically, this machine has the modified cowlings for improved cooling.

that the fighters were friendly Bf 109s, but in the meanwhile, both Oswald and Kent had lost sight of one another.

Oswald flew around firing flares in an attempt to find Kent but the two were unable to locate each other and eventually each set course for home alone. With the aid of his map, Kent was at last able to re-orientate himself and returned to his airfield on the last drops of his fuel. Meanwhile, Oswald, with his fuel also running low and with dusk falling, decided to set a straight course to the west: "There was no airfield to be seen anywhere, so I decided to set my machine down on a field alongside which was a road along which our own troops were advancing. I put my wheels down and made a smooth landing, after which I ordered a tank man to stand guard while I rode in a truck to the nearest village. There I organised six men from a baker's company to stand night-guard and called up my *Staffel*. They had almost decided to place my name on the loss list and were very pleased to hear from me, especially Kent, who had a bad conscience."

"During the night, I requested a supply of fuel from a fighter airfield about 15 km away and, early next morning, while I was inspecting my machine and pacing off the distance I would require for taking off, a tanker arrived to fuel up my aircraft. The tanker people helped me to start up my engines and I took off without a hitch, arriving back with my *Staffel* by 08:00".

From mid-July the *Gruppe* concentrated on supporting the Sixth and Fourth Panzer Armies' drive towards Stalingrad. During July and August 1942, enough 30 mm MK 101 cannon had been scraped together to equip 5./Sch.G 1, but the lack of suitable tank targets resulted in this *Staffel* too continuing to fly a large number of conventional ground-attack sorties. The whole *Gruppe* and its *Stab* flew with great success against a variety of ground targets. Sometimes the speed of the armoured divisions' advance was such that an airfield in Russian hands one day was so far in the rear a few days later that aircraft using it were unable to reach the front lines. On other occasions the Army easily advanced with little direct air support, though a maximum effort was laid on if a particularly worthwhile target was found. Other times were very busy and the

Henschels took off day after day to bomb and strafe the enemy, returning only to refuel and rearm. The sortie rate was punishing and pilots began to write of:

> "... *the severe strain put on our mental and physical strength, our Geschwader always following the tank spearheads, transferring from one airfield to the next every few days. Haven't even time to build a tent. We are so tired we just fall asleep through exhaustion. In obedience to Stalin's order not to give up a single centimetre of their territory, the Russians no longer withdraw but put up fierce resistance. Engine hits, full penetration of the fuel tanks and holes in the wings, all are daily bread to the Schlachtflieger and, in most cases, do not bother us*".

Although it was very cold at night, the days were hot. In June, the weather had been very changeable, bright sunshine sometimes turning to downpours which, as the soil was unable to absorb the rain, made dirt roads and parts of the airfields very muddy. By September, the weather was more settled and sometimes mid-afternoon temperatures reached 29 degrees in the shade. Again the landing grounds sweltered in the summer heat beneath a permanent cloud of dust which hung in the air as a result of the constant take-offs and which settled in a thick layer everywhere. Although take-off schedules were delayed as pilots waited for the long dust trails to settle, the sortie rate was so high that although the Hs 129 had only been operational since May, by 17 August, the *Gruppenkommandeur*, *Major* Darjes, was able to report that his *Gruppe* had flown more than 2,500 operational missions with the aircraft.

Oblt. Franz Oswald, since 26 June Technical Officer of the *Gruppenstab*, entered in his log book details of the operations flown and the variety of targets attacked. At this time the 30 mm cannon was still in short supply and all the following were bombing sorties:

24.7.42 Destroyed AA gun with bombs
28.7.42 Attacks against flak positions
01.8.42 Attacks against artillery positions and a fuel train
02.8.42 My 100th operational sortie against Russian field positions
03.8.42. Destroyed artillery positions as confirmed by radio message from the 297th Infantry Division
07.8.42 Attacked artillery positions
09.8.42 Destroyed an armoured train. Operations discontinued due to the heat (62 degrees in the sun). Aircraft became too hot to touch
10.8.42 Several attacks against artillery positions
14.8.42 Attacks in support of advancing ground forces

From personal letters made available to the author, it is possible to expand on the operation of 3 August. A German division was running low on ammunition and Oswald, Kent and another pilot were ordered to fly over the area to maintain

Top: An Hs 129 "+ N" on a frozen Russian airfield. Hangar facilities were rare and aircraft were often exposed to the terrible cold of the winter.
Centre: An Hs 129 B-1 of 13.(Pz)/JG 51, a unit which used identification numbers instead of letters. Normally, the white of the national insignia soon became grimy so that the application of fresh white snow camouflage paint created a considerable contrast.
Bottom: Mechanics and ground personnel laboured under the most extreme conditions to maintain aircraft in flying condition.

Above: Personnel from 4.(Pz)/Sch.G 1 gaze across the frozen Russian plain at an enemy aircraft shot down by German flak. The bus was the Staffel's mobile Gefechtstand (Command Post) and is adorned with the "Panzerbär" emblem.
Above Right: A close-up of the "Panzerbär" emblem of 4.(Pz)/Sch.G 1. A less warlike bear is featured on the coat-of-arms of the city of Berlin - home of the Henschel aircraft factories - and it is believed that the emblem of 4. and 5./Sch.G 1, both of which featured a bear, were designed by Henschel works personnel.

the soldiers' morale. As *Oblt*. Oswald wrote:

"We flew up to the front in search of targets and dropped some bombs onto enemy vehicles. I was flying as No. 2 in the section and when pulling up from a strafing run I discovered there was an enemy artillery position right below us. I radioed Kent and immediately made a strafing attack on this new target. I could see the effect my shells were having and soon two artillery emplacements were burning. Shortly afterwards, two ammunition stores exploded with a brilliant display of fireworks. We destroyed the remaining guns, shot up a lorry and set it on fire and destroyed a horse-drawn cart before heading home. Hardly had we landed when our own division radioed to thank and praise us for our good work."

Besides combat losses, further casualties in personnel and the loss or damage to aircraft were attributable to a number of airfield accidents. On 12 July, the 6. *Staffel* had two of its aircraft damaged when they were rammed by a Ju 87 at Kartnishevka. A number of aircraft were also damaged by overtired and overstrained pilots making bad landings and on 3 August one of 5. *Staffel's* own bombs exploded in the dispersal area at Frolov-West, to the west of Stalingrad, damaging Hs 129 W.Nr.0211 and an Hs 123.

On 15 August, *Uffz*. Karl Wultsch from the 5. *Staffel* was shot down by flak near Rshev in an Hs 129 B-1 which had been fitted with a 30 mm MK 101 cannon. This aircraft came down virtually intact behind the enemy lines and *Uffz*. Wultsch was captured for interrogation. For the first time the Russians were able to examine an almost undamaged Hs 129 and, equally significantly, were now able to obtain full details of the cannon and its special armour-piercing ammunition.

On 17 August, *Oblt*. Oswald took off from Frolov-West on an anti-tank operation with *Lt*. Arnold Plümer as his wingman, but the day turned out to be a "crash-day", as Franz Oswald recounted: "My wingman, *Lt*. Plümer, was knocked down with his aircraft in flames. We were flying over a Russian field emplacement when anti-aircraft guns or a quadruple machine-gun opened fire, hitting both of us and setting the right engine of Plümer's aircraft alight. I immediately told him the direction in which he should fly and advised him to make a wheels-up landing. He got down with his fiercely burning machine and belly-landed on very rough ground, suffering a complicated fracture of his right upper arm and, presumably, concussion of the brain. I flew over the forced-landed aircraft and circled over it at low altitude to see whether Plümer had managed to climb out and was told later that, despite the heat and the flames, he was pulled out of the burning machine by two Croatian soldiers. Suddenly, my own right engine stopped, obviously as a result of the hits I had received. When my engine cut, I was flying eastwards, towards the enemy. I tried to pull round and head for friendly territory, but the aircraft flew a great radius because of its slow speed and low altitude and I decided to make a belly landing. The ground was very rough and my landing was anything but smooth; there was a loud bang and my aircraft left a big trail of dust behind it as it careered over the uneven surface and I was thankful that I only sprained my back and hit my shin. How I got out of the cockpit I don't know, but I found myself out of the aircraft and drawing my pistol all in one short action before running to our lines as fast as I could. German soldiers told me later that I came down only half a kilometre from three Russian tanks."

"I walked to where Plümer's aircraft had come to rest and found it a blazing wreck only 1.5 km away from where I had crashed. The Croats, who had pulled Plümer from the cockpit had already put him aboard a truck and he looked pale and only half conscious. He recognised me but could not remember anything."

"I took a car and drove to a field dressing station to fetch a doctor and an ambulance. On my way back I called at the Croatians' command post where they were all very kind to me and treated me to cognac, cigarettes, food and drink".

Night was falling as the ambulance set out for the nearest clearing station and it was completely dark when, at 02:00 the next morning, the ambulance arrived at the main dressing station where Plümer was bandaged. The Croatian soldiers were later each awarded an Iron Cross in recognition for their endeavours, but Plümer had been severely injured in the crash. Although he later rejoined the *Gruppe*, Plümer did not fly again but served until the end of the of the war as *Gruppenadjutant* of IV.(Pz)/SG 9.

As previously mentioned, the 30 mm cannon was not much used by II./Sch.G 1 during this period and, as the aircraft of the 4. *Staffel* were not fitted with the type of fuselage carrier required for 250 kg bombs, it instead used up old stocks of 10 kg bombs. Five 10 kg bombs were bundled together using a tensioning tape and attached to the aircraft's ejector racks using the normal attachment eye. An Hs 129 could carry up to 40 of these bombs; two bundles were mounted under each wing and four carried on the fuselage rack. When the bundle was dropped, the retaining tape was cut by the ejector rack and the bombs, fitted only with impact fuzes, burst over a wide area. Understandably, because the bombs were already live when they were mounted under the aircraft, this makeshift arrangement was not popular and it sometimes happened that while an aircraft was taxiing to the take-off position, a bomb slid out of the cluster and exploded on impact. If a pilot had to make an emergency landing, he first had to release the bombs, but since they could not be dropped "safe", this had to be done from a reasonable altitude.

It was also possible to replace the four bomb carriers under the fuselage with two racks carrying some 100 x 2 kg SD 2 bombs. These bombs had blades which opened on release and acted like a propeller on a threaded rod, so that after a specific number of revolutions the bomb became live. The SD 2s were mounted on the aircraft using the threaded rod and released row by row from the front backwards. Sometimes, the slipstream caused the rods to jam in their guides and the last two or three would hang up and

The mess room of 4.(Pz)/Sch.G 1 somewhere in the East. The Führer's portrait hangs over the door and the wall is decorated with a mural depicting an Hs 129 attacking a Russian tank. Note also the propeller blade (right) marked with the Staffel designation.

Above and Right: Ground crews braved the elements and carried out maintenance, servicing and front-line repairs regardless of the weather. Note the remaining residue of the temporary white winter camouflage on the wings and fuselage of the aircraft shown.

become live on the rack. When the aircraft touched down, however, the bombs were shaken off the rack and exploded immediately. Due to the danger to the carrying aircraft the use of these bombs was soon discontinued but other types continued to be used and, in the words of *Hptm.* Bruno Meyer: "... tank killing by means of cannon sunk into oblivion". It was under these circumstances that the RLM sent an expert on 15 mm and 30 mm armour-piercing ammunition to II./Sch.G 1 charged with the task of convincing flying personnel of the effectiveness of cannon attacks on tanks if properly carried out.

Meanwhile, in accordance with Göring's instruction of 13 May concerning the creation of an anti-tank *Staffel* for the fighter units, cannon equipped Hs 129s had been issued to the special anti-tank *Staffel*, 13.(*Panzer*)/*Jagdgeschwader* 51 "*Mölders*". Serving with this unit were several pilots who would later become expert tank killers and in time the *Staffel* went on to achieve a number of notable successes, but as far as the conduct of operations was concerned, it was found that the Hs 129 pilots had little in common with the *Geschwader's* fighter pilots and as a result relations between the anti-tank *Staffel* and the rest of the unit became strained. Although the 13. *Staffel* was administratively subordinate to JG 51's Staff, most of the *Geschwader's* fighter personnel were not even aware of its existence as it flew its own specialised sorties on other sectors of the front.

After completing its training at Deblin-Irena in Poland, 13.(Pz)/JG 51 set out for the Eastern Front under the command of *Oberleutnant* Eggers. On 5 August the *Staffel* was ordered to Kharkov-Rogan, south-east of Kharkov, but it was soon transferred and first went into action at Rzhev on the Moscow Front in the Central Sector. Between 14 August and 26 September, this unit, operating with 8 Hs 129s, carried out 16 operations in the Rshev area against tanks. In 73 sorties they claimed to have hit 29 tanks for the loss of three aircraft, plus one slightly damaged.

At the end of September, the situation on the Dugino sector of the front (between Rshev and Vyasma) where the *Panzerjäger Staffel* of JG 51 was based, was quiet and good use was made of this lull in active operations to carry out a period of intensive training in cannon attacks against dummy tanks under the personal direction of the RLM expert. The whole *Staffel* reached a 60 per cent average of hits and successful firing practice against the heaviest types of Soviet tanks increased the confidence of the crews in the cannon. At the same time, combined exercises in R/T were carried out with the Army in order to make sure that air support would arrive as required at the scene of fighting. By the end of November, this training was considered to have reached a satisfactory level and the Pz.Jä.St./JG 51 was ready to return to operations.

Meanwhile, in the South, where II./Sch.G 1 had been left to convert to the armour-piercing cannon in the field, the Hs 129 pilots had formed the erroneous impression that a tank was only effectively hit if it was set on fire. In order to achieve this they followed the wrong tactics of using up all their ammunition on a single tank even though hits, indicated by flashes produced by the impact of the magnesium-pointed shells, had been observed. In fact, it was not necessary to set tanks on fire; what mattered was that shells, on penetrating the tank, should kill or disable the crew. However, instances had been reported of enemy tanks continuing to fight even after receiving direct hits and it was to be expected, therefore, that in order to ensure that tanks were positively put out of action they should be repeatedly attacked until some visible evidence of their destruction could be observed. In all fairness to the pilots, it should also be pointed out that there is evidence to show that they were instructed by higher authorities to consider tanks destroyed only if they were seen to give off great clouds of smoke, to be on fire or to explode. In any event, this lack of proper training or direction extended from aircrews to armourers, who not only considered the introduction of cannon an additional burden but, like the pilots, had little or no experience of the new weapon. As a result, II./Sch.G 1 experienced defects in armament.

Just as the armourers were unfamiliar and therefore unqualified to maintain the cannon, so also the technical personnel were now experiencing difficulties with the Gnôme-Rhône engines. Under normal conditions, a well maintained engine was considered very reliable and continued to run even after light battle damage, but due to the high sortie rate there was frequently insufficient time to devote to engine

maintenance. Piston troubles were common and the design of the engine made even changing spark plugs difficult. This, together with a shortage of spare parts in the field workshops and the consequent inability to get repairs carried out quickly and efficiently, rapidly led to a steady decline in serviceability.

To help overcome this problem it was suggested that each Hs 129 should be equipped with towing gear so that during movements from one airfield to another, each pilot could tow a glider carrying the necessary equipment and maintenance personnel for his aircraft. In view of motor transport difficulties and the poor state of the roads which prevented the rapid transfer of ground personnel to airfields nearest to a point of crisis, this was considered the only feasible method of securing the high degree of mobility essential to throw the Hs 129s into battle against threatening concentrations of Soviet tanks at any point of the front and thus meet the Russians on equal terms. This proposal was in fact adopted with remarkable success and as early as March 1942, tests had been carried out at Rechlin with Hs 129 KG+GM towing a DFS 230 cargo glider. Trials went so well that it was possible to complete all tests in one flight lasting barely an hour. As a result of the renewed suggestion that operational effectiveness would be improved if the Hs 129s towed their spares and maintenance personnel, the test flights were resumed in October 1942 with Hs 129 KG+GI towing DFS 230s to measure take-offs with heavier loads. By mid-April 1943, a tail hook of the same type as used

Above: In almost all cases where temporary white camouflage paint was applied, care was taken to avoid overpainting the yellow recognition markings on the nose. The poor quality of this photograph is due to the effect of frost on the original film.

on the He 111 was being employed by Hs 129 aircraft on the aerodrome at Deblin and, eventually, glider towing during unit movements from airfield to airfield was a viable option, each unit having its own gliders specifically for this purpose.

However, the extent to which glider towing was actually used is still not known. Willi Tholen remembers that he made several flights in a DFS transport glider, which could carry up to six other men, but in each case the towing aircraft was a Ju 87, not an Hs 129. He confirms there were some Hs 129s fitted with a towing hook, but that in 4./Sch.G 1 at least, not a single towed flight was made with the Hs 129. Tholen also remembers that being towed by a Ju 87 was not a pleasant experience; in the summer of 1943 especially, thunderstorms were guaranteed to give a rough ride. On the other hand, use was made of the Hs 129's baggage compartment situated in the centre of the port fuselage. This was sometimes used to transport a member of the ground crew though he had to be of small build!

In November 1942, the weather consisted largely of fog which, while generally lifting by 09:00, sometimes lingered all day. The Russian muddy season had arrived again; roads were impassable and flying conditions all but impossible. With a cloud base of between 100 and 200 m (approx. 300-600 ft) and only a few kilometres visibility, it is doubtful if even pilots in the First World War would have flown, but the

Hard-pressed German infantry in grimy winter snow-smocks take cover in a slit trench somewhere in Russia. With the extreme cold and appalling weather conditions hampering logistics and armoured advances, German Army units fighting on the Eastern front relied heavily upon, and were grateful for, the support rendered by the Panzerjagdflieger.

Left and Far Left: A good impression of the freezing, bleak Russian winter is given here in these two photographs depicting Hs 129s taxiing to their take-off points. The presence of factory codes on the fuselages is of note. Note ground sheet marking the runway to assist pilots while taking-off and landing.

Final salute: The funeral of Oblt. Eduard Kent, Staffelkapitän of 4./Sch.G 1 at Tatsinskaya, January 1943. The ground was frozen so hard that explosives had to be used to blast a hole for the coffin. Kent, notorious for his dare-devil flying, pioneered anti-tank work using cannon but was killed on 5 January 1943 while demonstrating a cannon attack.

Henschels took to the air just the same. By now, II./Sch.G 1 had virtually abandoned all use of the MK 101 and in late November, while based at Millerovo, north-west of Rostov, the *Gruppe* was heavily engaged on bombing operations with 20 Hs 129s and 10 Bf 109E aircraft against the Russian advance from the Don bend towards the Donetz. On 28 November, after his work with 13./JG 51, the RLM's ammunition specialist now arrived at II./Sch.G 1's headquarters and, on discovering that no use was being made of the cannon, immediately communicated with the *General der Jagdflieger's* Inspector of Ground-Attack Forces obtaining orders that the fuselage bomb-racks be removed and the aircraft re-equipped with cannon. Owing to the rapid development of the Soviet offensive, however, there was no time for training and a number of pilots went into action without any experience of cannon or any instruction in attacking tanks.

It was this lack of training, together with the extreme cold, which prevented the Hs 129s from being more successful on the morning of 16 December 1942. That day, a powerful force of some 250 Soviet infantry tanks from the newly formed First Guards Tank Army broke through the lines in a fierce counter-move against von Manstein's flagging relief offensive directed at Stalingrad, and drove deep into the Rumanian Third and Italian Eighth Armies in the Don bend where they "...roamed around as if in peacetime behind the fleeing Italians". Bomber and dive-bomber units failed to achieve any success, but in two days of operations, six cannon aircraft from 4./Sch.G 1 succeeded in destroying ten tanks and hit others with measurable results without loss to themselves. This achievement, although a valuable indication of what the Hs 129 could accomplish, was on too small a scale to affect ground operations and *Hptm.* Frank Neubert, who had replaced Darjes as *Gruppenkommandeur* in October, later wrote of the MK 101 during this engagement: *"Owing to the great cold, the MK 101 failed when anti-tank ammunition was used. When*

tried on the ground, the weapon fired perfectly, but in the air it was beset with troubles. Even the engineer sent by the RLM was unable to remedy the situation".

Apart from technical faults, cannon stoppages were also caused by snow and slush. Running up the engines on the ground caused any loose snow or slush to be thrown back along the centre line of the fuselage by the counter-rotating propellers where it entered the cannon fairing and adhered to the mechanism. Pilots frequently took off with between 50 and 100 kgs (approx. 100-200 lbs) of snow stuck on their aircraft's undersurfaces. This not only considerably increased the aircraft's take-off weight but, once airborne, the icy slipstream caused the wet snow to freeze solid and jam the ammunition feed.

On 22 December, unable to hold up the Soviet advance, II./Sch.G 1 was compelled to fall back to Voroshilovgrad. By now, the strength of the unit had been greatly reduced by anti-aircraft and infantry fire; none of the Bf 109s were left and as a temporary means of restoring strength, the anti-tank *Staffel* of JG 51 was transferred from the Moscow Front and subordinated to II./Sch.G 1. The arrival of the trained pilots of this unit had a good effect on the personnel of the *Gruppe* and the anti-tank *Staffel* of JG 51 benefited by receiving full facilities in the *Gruppe* workshops. On one occasion a single Hs 129 was able to set four tanks on fire with its MK 101 cannon and badly damaged two more with direct hits. The strained situation was relieved at the beginning of January 1943 by the arrival of a few replacement aircraft and it was again possible to detach the anti-tank *Staffel* of JG 51 from II./Sch.G 1. On 27 January the former was withdrawn with only six serviceable aircraft to Kursk, where it was re-equipped. While operating together between 1 and 16 January, II./Sch.G 1 and the anti-tank *Staffel* of JG 51 each claimed to have destroyed 13 tanks, despite the fact that enemy action and the weather had reduced the average daily serviceability to only two cannon aircraft.

Meanwhile, 4./Sch.G 1, which had been operating over the encircled Stalingrad area, had withdrawn to Tatsinskaya. The *Staffel* was now under the command of *Oblt.* Kent, a pilot who had acquired a reputation for dare-devil flying. Anti-tank work by 4./Sch.G 1 using the 30 mm cannon had started under his command and Kent, himself one of the first pilots to succeed in destroying tanks by cannon attacks, was keen to demonstrate to the whole *Staffel* how tanks could be easily knocked out by this new weapon. Close

Hptm. Alfred Druschel, Gruppenkommandeur of I./Sch.G 1, Oblt. Georg Dörffel (then a Staffelkapitän with I./Sch.G 1) and Willy Scholl who bore the unusual rank of Hauptfeldwebel of 4.(Pz)/Sch.G 1 on Tatsinskaya airfield for Oblt. Kent's funeral. When Druschel became Geschwaderkommodore in June 1943, Dörffel took over as Kommandeur of I. Gruppe.

to the airfield was an abandoned T-34, a victim of the recent fighting, and on 5 January, the *Staffel* was assembled on both sides of Kent's planned approach path. Everyone was excited to witness the demonstration and watched intently as Kent made a low run-in at the tank and, when in range, fired his cannon. The tank was hit and the Henschel, W.Nr. 0275, pulled up from its strafing pass and circled round for another run-in. Kent made his second low approach and the tank was hit again; but as the Henschel pulled up, its rear fuselage struck the tank's turret and broke away. The aircraft reared into the air and travelled some 100 m (300 ft) before plunging to the ground. The two engines and the armoured cockpit were wrenched from the airframe as the machine completely disintegrated, throwing the pilot's broken body out of the cockpit. Engine mechanic Willi Tholen described the event as "...a show with a terrible ending. The only thing we could do was to gather the pilot's dismembered remains, put them into a wooden case, blast a shallow hole in the hard-frozen ground and bury them in the snow".

The 4./Sch.G 1's new *Staffelkapitän*, *Hptm.* Dietrich Gerhardt, was forced down in an aircraft marked F + △ on 20 January and although his machine was a total loss, Gerhardt escaped without injury. Ten days later, *Hptm.* Frank Neubert, the *Gruppenkommandeur*, was shot

Willi Tholen (to right) and Heini Kelber servicing the BMW 132 engine of an Hs 123 in sub-zero temperatures during the winter of 1942-43

down and wounded by flak near Skurbiy and his W.Nr. 0306 written off.

All *Luftwaffe* flying units operating in the depths of the fearsome Russian winter experienced great difficulty in maintaining any degree of serviceability. As the temperature dropped, lubricants froze, and tyres became so brittle that they lost their air pressure or cracked and broke up. Oil lines froze, with the result that there was a high incidence of eroded pistons. On average, engines could only withstand 40 hours of flight time between overhauls as against 200 hours under normal circumstances. As engine wear and tear on this scale was completely unknown before, even the most generous estimates regarding spares were inadequate and, due to the effects of extreme cold on metals, valves had to be adjusted and this, too, resulted in additional difficulties in starting engines.

The terrible cold of the Russian winter brought particular privation and hard work to the ground personnel, many of whom lacked proper, warm clothing. If lucky, they were accommodated in Russian huts and cottages. When no buildings were available, holes were dug in the ground and covered with a tent or logs. Sometimes, however, the ground was frozen so hard that explosives had to be used to make a hole which was then deepened by digging. Despite such primitive accommodation, they nevertheless did everything in their power to keep aircraft serviceable. With their continued and untiring efforts, they were successful, even though aircraft were always parked in the open and all maintenance work had to be carried out in the open air. This called for special dedication and skills, as Willi Tholen describes: "Our *Staffel* had many personnel who, rather than being professional soldiers, were skilled workmen with a special talent for improvisation. In winter, when we had especially low temperatures, we had difficulties with our French engines, but it must be emphasised that any other type of engine operating under these conditions presented the same problems. There was virtually no difference between the French and German engines and although an engine fitter could change the spark plugs of a BMW more quickly, the BMW had only nine cylinders compared with the 14-cylinder Gnôme-Rhônes."

"My speciality was to start up the engines outdoors in temperatures as low as -20 to -30 degrees Centigrade by using acetylene gas which, unlike the normal petrol/air mixture, ignited at low temperatures. When the aircraft returned from a mission, we prevented the engines from cooling down by starting them up several times during the night. Some Hs 129s were delivered to us with an oil dilution system installed which was based on the "cold-start" method learned from the Russians. By adding 2.5 per cent of petrol to the engine oil via a special petrol cock, the viscosity was greatly reduced and facilitated starting up an engine even if it was icy cold. As the engine became hot, the petrol evaporated and the proper oil viscosity was soon restored."

The engine mechanics also reported that in very cold conditions the lubricating grease in the planetary gears of the already sensitive variable-pitch mechanism was transformed into a hard resin which prevented the airscrew pitch from easily changing. Until a liquid grease became available, a successful method of softening the existing lubricant was to inject petrol into the spinner or run it down the propeller blades. Although this had the desired effect, it made sense to have a fire extinguisher close to hand when starting up as some of the petrol in the spinner was drawn into the engine. Even in summer, ground fires on starting up the engines were quite frequent and the aircraft's operating manual warned: *"If the engine stops after a few revolutions, check immediately for an air intake fire. If the air intake is on fire, switch off ignition, close throttle and extinguish fire with fire extinguisher"*.

In temperatures as low as -30 degrees, instruments either took a long time to work properly or functioned inaccurately and inaccurate engine instruments led to more serious damage or to total engine failure. Oil, freezing in the oil lines, led to burst oil tanks, hydraulic oil pumps lost pressure and therefore their effectiveness, and water in transformers, batteries, radio equipment and other sensitive instruments condensed and froze. Combat losses had already greatly reduced unit strength and, despite the outstanding efforts of the ground crews, the severe winter conditions prevented adequate repair and maintenance of the surviving aircraft. As a result, the average number serviceable from a *Gruppe* of 36 machines was six, the equivalent of half a *Staffel* and these were frequently grounded by snow, ice and fog.

On 20 February 1943, Pz.Jä.St./JG 51 recorded four aircraft on hand, of which just two were operational. Only part of Sch.G 1 was operational at this time and possessed 40 aircraft of which only 28 were ready for operations. It should be noted that among Sch.G 1's aircraft were a number of Fw 190s; a Bf 109 *Staffel* and a Staff flight had been ordered to give up their aircraft in November prior to conversion to the Fw 190 at Deblin-Irena. In February 1943 the *Geschwader* was still in the process of a change which was to result in most *Staffeln* completing conversion to the Fw 190A-5 by the first week of March. The Hs 123s continued to be flown by 7. *Staffel* and the Hs 129 equipped only the 4. and 8. *Staffeln*, though these were strengthened or oversize units with an establishment increased from 12 to 16 machines.

II./SCHLACHTGESCHWADER 1
SUMMARY OF OPERATIONS – 1942

Hs 129	3,138 sorties
Hs 123	1,532 sorties
Bf 109	1,938 sorties
Bombs released:	1,386.5 tonnes
Soviet aircraft destroyed:	
	52 shot down
	55 destroyed on ground
Gruppe casualties:	20 Hs 129
	5 Hs 123
	16 Bf 109
Tank claims & M/T destroyed:	
	91 tanks
	1,081 light M/T
	273 other vehicles

Two Hs 129s captured by the Russians share a hangar with three Bf 109s. The tail plane on the extreme right is in the colours of the Hungarian Air Force. Both Henschels appear to have been in the middle of a major overhaul and lack engines. The nearest Henschel, W.Nr.0288, carries Stab markings and is fitted with replacement outer wings and flaps from a snow-camouflaged machine.

"We carried out our first operation on 17 November 1942. I led a formation of three Hs 129s in a freelance sweep near Bir El Abd, destroying two British armoured cars... On the return flight we encountered for the first time British Crusader tanks at a road junction. Our joy to get western enemies before our guns after so many months of fighting on the Eastern front was so great that we gave vent to our feelings and could not refrain from demonstrating to the British exactly how a text-book attack should be carried out."

Hptm. Bruno Meyer
Staffelkapitän 4.(Pz)/Sch.G 2

PART THREE
AFRIKA

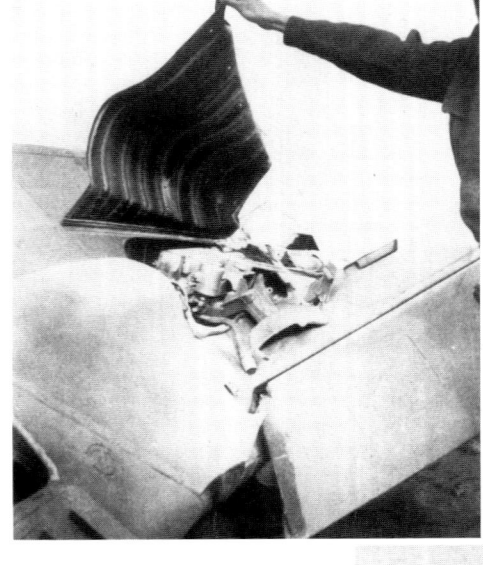

Hs 129 B-1, W.Nr.0296, Blue "A" of 4.(Pz)/Sch.G 2, was the first aircraft of this type to be examined by the RAF. The aircraft made a bad landing at El Adem due to the waterlogged state of the airfield during which the port undercarriage leg collapsed. An attempt was made to destroy the aircraft by placing demolition charges on the engines and fuel tanks but the remains provided valuable information to RAF Air Intelligence. The white spinner tips were painted with a 1/3rd blue segment. Note the original dark green finish on the lowered flaps.

The 30 mm MK 101 cannon found in the wreckage of Blue "A" was salvaged for examination. Here, as an RAF Intelligence team study the burnt remains of the Henschel, the size of the cannon is shown to advantage.

Panzerfliegerstaffel Afrika

A Gleam of Hope

8

Soon after its first operations, Meyer's "Schlacht- und Panzerfliegerstaffel Afrika" was caught in two sandstorms which rendered its aircraft unserviceable. With MK 101 weapons and ammunition removed, the aircraft were moved back from one airfield to another as the German retreat from El Alamein continued and the Staffel subsequently took no further part in the North African theatre.

single Hs 129 was totally inadequate for tank-hunting and, before any more of the unit's machines could be fitted with this filter, higher authorities had become aware of the conversion and totally disallowed any operational missions on the grounds that they were too dangerous and that flight safety would be jeopardised! At the same time, it was extremely difficult for the *Staffel* to obtain spares from the European supply depots or lay hands on the engines at Cognac since all available transport aircraft were still heavily committed to flying in the vital and desperately needed fuel for the *Panzerarmee Afrika*. Eventually, when a Gotha transport glider was loaded with spares and assigned to the *Staffel* as a flying repair and maintenance station, it was prematurely released in all haste north of Derna by the towing He 111. Apparently, the Heinkel pilot had incorrectly believed that an enemy fighter attack was imminent and the jettisoned workshop glider, together with all the essential spares, crashed into the sea. It was the last straw.

On 31 December the remaining seven machines of the *Staffel* limped further back to Castel Benito airfield near Tripoli but by 10 January 1943, not a single one of these seven aircraft was operational. Oil consumption for a flight of only some 200 km (125 miles) had risen to 24 litres (5.5 gal.) per engine, i.e., about 70 per cent of the total oil tank capacity, whereas normal consumption over this distance should have been between four and six litres (1-1.3 gal.).

On 13 January 1943, Allied air forces mounted a bombing raid against Castel Benito airfield, during which the aircraft dropped a new kind of fragmentation bomb consisting of bundles of six 10 lb. (4.5 kg) bombs wired together. Most of the bombs fell on the German workshop hangar, damaging 11 Axis aircraft and destroying 23, of which three were Hs 129s belonging to 4.(Pz)/Sch.G 2. Of the surviving Henschels, only a single extensively damaged Hs 129 could be patched up and this machine was able to struggle back to Tunis, though it had to make a lengthy stop at Gabes on the way for further repairs. At the same time the flying and ground personnel were transferred by air to the *Staffel's* supply station at Comiso, on Sicily, the intention being to refit the unit at Bari in southern Italy, after which it was thought that the *Staffel* would return to operations in the Tunisian area. But events took a different turn; instead, the ground personnel were transferred to Russia by rail and the pilots went to the Henschel works delivery station at Berlin-Johannisthal to collect new machines before following the ground crews to the Eastern Front. This was not, however, the end of Hs 129 operations in North Africa.

"We have a very good name here..."

The Last Phase in North Africa
November 1942 – April 1943

9

On 14 September 1942, *Oblt.* Franz Oswald was given command of 5./*Schlachtgeschwader* 1, at that time still operating on the Eastern Front, and appointed its *Staffelführer*[1]. Very soon afterwards however and acting upon the express order of no less than Adolf Hitler, the *Luftwaffenführungsstab* instructed Oswald to transfer nine of his pilots and ten cannon aircraft to another unit, leaving the young *Oberleutnant* with just twelve pilots under his now somewhat depleted command. Happily though, the following month, Oswald and his pilots journeyed to the Henschel factory in Berlin where they refitted with new Hs 129 B-2s complete with newly applied desert camouflage and tropical equipment.

Although potential tropical equipment for the Hs 129 had already been tested in December 1941, the Hs 129 B-2 variant resulted from discussions which had taken place in February 1942 between Henschel and the *E-Stelle* Rechlin on proposed Hs 129 B-1 tropical operations. Subsequently, in March of that year, Hs 129 B-0 W.Nr. 0016, which had been specially converted, made various temperature test flights with BMW air-filters and a new oil filter. By May, when W.Nr. 0016 made a number of further flights to test a tropicalised cylinder cover, it had been decided that delivery of the Hs 129 B-1 would be terminated at 50 machines and that production would then switch to aircraft with tropical equipment, this tropicalised version being designated Hs 129 B-2.

After receiving its Hs 129 B-2s, 5./Sch.G 1 was based at Jesau in East Prussia since it was originally intended that the *Staffel* would return to operations on the Russian Front, but the Allied advance from El Alamein demanded that the unit should be despatched instead to North Africa. Indeed, 5./Sch.G 1 had no sooner left Jesau on 5 November when, on the 8th, four days after the Allied victory at El Alamein, co-ordinated amphibious landings by British and American forces - conceived to complete the destruction of Axis forces in North Africa - were made along the coasts of French Morocco and Algeria. German reaction to the invasion was both swift and vigorous and as early as 9 November troops and *Luftwaffe* units began to arrive from Sicily to hold Tunisia, which was vital to Rommel's retreat. By 10 November, the Germans had established a strong bridgehead with a short, defensible perimeter and situated at an adequate distance from the main ports of Tunis and Bizerta which was then expanded to form a front from which they were able to resist attacks by numerically superior Allied forces.

The 5./Sch.G 1's transfer to the Tunisian bridgehead was continually delayed by bad weather. On 17 November, the *Staffel* was due to arrive at Erfurt but because of a completely incorrect weather forecast on 16 November, the formation flew into extensive fog and, in the Grossenhain area, low cloud. As the pilots

Ground crew prepare an Hs 129 B-2 Trop for a sortie. This aircraft, belonging to 5./Sch.G 1, is fitted with four ETC 50/VIII bomb carriers under the fuselage and the intake for the redundant cockpit heater has been covered with a piece of doped fabric. Details of further tropicalisation are obscure, the aircraft otherwise appearing identical to a normal B-2. A tropical version of the ETC 50 was produced, this having a fairing in front of the carrier to provide protection from dust.

had no blind-flying experience and the Hs 129 lacked the necessary instruments, this could have spelt disaster. In the event, the formation separated and landed at different airfields. This was a testing time and as Franz Oswald remembers: "I made it to Cottbus where I landed alone. I was convinced that all the others had crashed and were dead. I was so worried that I felt if I had looked at myself in a mirror I would have seen that my hair had turned grey! Then, to my profound relief, reports began to come in that the rest of the formation had landed safely at scattered German airfields. It had been a risk but it went well."

In fact, the only casualty was *Fw.* Otto Kiefer, who flew into the ground near the Dresden-Gera *Autobahn* but survived although his aircraft was 95% destroyed.

On 17th, the *Staffel* assembled again at Grossenhain and took off for Erfurt at 14:35 where they landed safely at 15:40. But again the weather delayed any further progress until 21 November. Oswald was growing more and more anxious about the delay, especially as he knew how urgently the *Staffel* was required in Tunis and had been ordered to telephone *General* Galland every night to report his position. Although air-traffic control were correct to forbid the flight, Oswald was determined to press on and after investigating the weather conditions for himself, found that although Erfurt was almost entirely covered by cloud, conditions on the flight-path south of the Thüringian Forest were good: "Although flying control still refused to give permission for us to take off, I ordered my pilots to their aircraft and instructed them to start engines. The noise immediately attracted the attention of a member of the airfield's ground staff who came running up, waving furiously at us that take-off was forbidden, but we left him standing alone behind us as we continued to taxi out."

"Then red flares started coming up from all over the place. I pretended not to have seen them but finally in one last but unsuccessful attempt to stop us, someone ran right up to my aircraft and fired a flare directly at my cockpit. There was no ignoring that, but I was furious and as we sailed past I shouted out to this man that, in the words of Goethe's "*Götz von Berlichingen*", his CO could kiss my arse!"

"Eventually, on 25 November, we took off from München-Riem in clear weather and set course for Vicenza in Italy. The scenery was beautiful but shortly after we'd crossed the Alps, my red fuel warning light came on and when I

landed I was down to the very last drops of my fuel. At last, on 29 November, *Obgfr.* Hesse and I touched down at El Aouina, the first arrivals. The rest of the *Staffel* followed us in shortly afterwards. In Tunis I had to present myself before *Oberst* Harlinghausen, *Fliegerführer Tunisia*, as someone had reported my unauthorised take-off from Erfurt. Although he was very grim at first, I was able to justify my actions and was dismissed on friendly terms."

Although airfield conditions in Tunisia were less harsh than in Libya, the Winter of 1942-43 was one of the worst on record. Numerous torrential rainstorms turned the ground into seas of mud, but at least there were no sandstorms and 5./Sch.G 1 was able to report a high degree of operational readiness. Unlike the desert landing

An Hs 129 B-2 during an engine change. Note that the removed wing in the background shows a variation of the sand over green camouflage overspray.

Camouflage finish on this shrouded Hs 129 is clearly a green overspray on a light base, this contrasting to other known desert schemes.

Two frames from a cine film, one showing an Hs 129 of 8.(Pz)/Sch.G 2 banking at low-level during an attack against Allied armour and supply transport in Tunisia, while the other shows two Hs 129s, one diving steeply towards the ground. Curiously, although the film was shot by an Allied cameraman, both pictures appeared in the German *Berliner Illustrierte Zeitung* of 25 February 1942 which stated that the diving machine was attacking enemy vehicles. In fact, the "diving" Hs 129 is spinning completely out of control and, a few seconds later, it plunged into the ground.

grounds where, quite apart from enemy air opposition, the heat, abrasive dust and sand had ruined Bruno Meyer's prospects of success, El Aouina was a large, long-established and well maintained airfield situated on the coastal plain north-west of Tunis. However, the terrain inland of Tunis itself consists of barren mountainous slopes, crags and precipitous gorges. So rough was this country that the Allies could usually only move their supplies overland on the relatively few available roads which led through the mountain passes. This of course, made them very vulnerable to air attack.

By late November, attacks and counter-attacks by both sides had resulted in a front line being established from Bou Arada in the south through Medjez el Bab and Sidi Nsir past Sedjenane. The 5./Sch.G 1 flew its first operational sortie in Tunisia on 30 November, the day after its arrival, when *Oblt.* Oswald accompanied by *Ogfr.* Hesse took off from El Aouina and destroyed one Allied tank. Two days later, on 2 December, a total of nine sorties was made in two separate operations against British tanks and vehicle concentrations belonging to the 5th Northamptonshire Regiment and 1st East Surrey Regiment which had advanced close to Tebourba. Here the overall results of *Luftwaffe* attacks against tank concentrations and motorised columns were excellent, particularly as road congestion had led to the enemy's forces being massed in one area. The next day, three Henschels took off at 17:30 to attack gun batteries and troop positions near Tebourba and on 4 December, three of the *Staffel's* Hs 129s again took off to attack tanks and vehicles south-west of there and reported scoring hits on some of the vehicles.

Operating in the same area on 5 December against vehicles and troop concentrations, the unit carried out two bombing and strafing operations but, although the bombs were seen to explode in the target area, very dense light flak prevented any positive results from being observed. One of the attacking aircraft was damaged by ground fire, but the pilot escaped unhurt and made a safe landing at his home airfield.

So far, *Oblt.* Oswald was fairly happy with the results achieved, as the following extract from a letter dated 4 December, 1942, reflects:

"Up to now I have flown four operations. We ourselves do not have any contact with enemy fighters which seem mainly to be Lightnings, twin-fuselage American aircraft which are very good but which are regularly shot down by our own fighters."

On 9 December, Oswald again wrote home:

"The day before yesterday and again today we have had very good successes, eight tanks, armoured cars or transport vehicles being shot up in flames without any loss to ourselves."

That day, rain had so softened the local airfields that the regular morning reconnaissance carried out by a Ju 88 from an *Aufklärungsgruppe* had to be delayed as the aircraft was unable to take off from the waterlogged runway. However, it was decided to despatch two Hs 129s to attack enemy tanks and armoured vehicles in the Goubellat - Pont-du-Fahs - Bou Arada area. Here, they found a variety of suitable targets and despite machine-gun and rifle fire from the ground they attacked and set on fire three vehicles. Clouds of dust and smoke prevented accurate identification and these vehicles were claimed as either tanks or lorries. In addition, five Bren-gun carriers were set on fire and, as some of these were seen to explode, it was thought that they must have been carrying fuel up to the front line.

Nevertheless, the vulnerability of armoured vehicles to anti-tank measures varies and different vehicles respond to attack in different ways. Armoured cars were normally thinly armoured and, being driven by petrol engines, were easily set on fire. Each of the principal Allied tanks used in the Tunisian theatre possessed its own characteristics. The British Valentines were tough

Oblt. Oswald awarding the Iron Cross 2nd Class to two of his pilots; Uffz. Lelanz (left) and Fw. Heisel (right). Later in the Tunisian campaign, Lelanz shot down a Spitfire and damaged another while flying an Hs 129.

and usually gave their crews time to get out. The Churchill burnt slowly, again giving plenty of time to escape. The American Shermans had a reputation of being fire-bombs, nicknamed "Ronsons" by their own crews and "Tommy Cookers" by the Germans. It was said that the crew had five seconds to jump out of a penetrated Sherman before the flames were sucked into the crew compartment.

On 12 December, all ten of the *Staffel's* Hs 129s took off to attack enemy activity reported south east of Goubellat. Although three of the aircraft were damaged by machine-gun fire from the ground, five tanks, an armoured car, five gun tractors and two lorries were set on fire and destroyed, while two further tanks and a four-barrelled anti-aircraft gun mounted on the back of a lorry were also shot up and damaged.

On 18 December, the pilots of two Hs 129s reported sighting a submarine south of Hammamet. Two days later, two of 5./Sch.G 1's aircraft were sent out on the unit's one and only anti-submarine patrol when it was hoped that the aircraft's heavy armament would prove devastating to any such vessel seen, but in the event, it was not sighted again. Later, that same day, three aircraft set out to attack enemy columns on the road near Pont-du-Fahs, but this, too, proved unsuccessful and the flight had to be abandoned due to bad weather.

After two weeks of operating without loss, unit morale was high and on 14 December a war correspondent visited the *Staffel* to interview its pilots and learn something of its operations. Writing home, Oswald proudly stated that: "*We have a very good name with the Army here on account of our work.*" Indeed, during a short visit to Rome some months later, Oswald overheard a conversation in which some Army officers were describing Hs 129 attacks they had witnessed in Tunisia. According to these officers, observers on the ground were taken completely by surprise. Approaching the target at a height of only 1-2 m (3-6 ft) above the ground - the normal altitude for their ground-attack operations, especially later when Allied fighters had to be avoided - the Hs 129s appeared without warning, attacked with devastating results for the enemy, and were gone again as suddenly as they had appeared. Nothing, however, is more dangerous than low-level flying - the breakneck speeding over the ground which seems to act as a magnet. A fraction of a second's inattention, a mere glance to one side meant a crash and the machine hitting even a slight rise in the ground or, on road-strafing sorties, hurtling into a telegraph pole. The pilots had to remember, too, that in no circumstances could they gain height after an attack but had to remain close to the ground to avoid flak. Flying at extra-low altitude was also an effective way of avoiding enemy fighters and on or about the 12 December, four Hs 129s successfully bombed Le Goulat while, 1,000 m (3,000 ft) above, a patrolling formation of Spitfires was completely unaware of the Henschels' presence.

During the Henschels' attacks, only a single

Oblt. Franz Oswald (right) inspects a captured American M3 medium tank. A detailed knowledge of the construction of enemy AFVs was essential for successful anti-tank work.

The characteristic silhouette of the Hs 129 was not well known to the Allies in North Africa and in both US and British combat reports, the type was confused with the Ju 88. The aircraft shown here flew with 5./Sch.G 1 in Tunisia.

pass was made before the anti-aircraft gunners could take proper aim. If the aircraft returned to make a second attack on the same target the flak would be ready and waiting, putting up such a barrage that it was almost impossible to fly through it unscathed. All the pilots knew this; it was elementary in a *Staffel* which specialised in low-level attacks and the British, as Oswald later recalled, always brought up mobile heavy flak to protect their convoys. This was a new experience for, in Russia, Oswald had observed that the enemy had been slow to appreciate that targets unprotected by anti-aircraft guns were practically inviting air attack.

By 22 December the Allied air forces had increased in strength and 5./Sch.G 1 suffered its first loss in Africa. This was a particularly hectic day for the *Staffel*. Thirteen Hs 129 sorties were carried out in three separate missions against road traffic and enemy troop concentrations near Djebel Chakeur. One armoured and eight motor vehicles were destroyed and a further ten motor vehicles were shot up and damaged. In addition, cavalry and horse-drawn wagons were bombed and an ammunition dump set on fire. The Henschels were escorted on each mission by Bf 109s from II./JG 51 and these fighters also claimed 11 motor vehicles destroyed and another four damaged. During one of these attacks, the Henschels were spotted by P-38 Lightnings from the American 58th Fighter Squadron, which incorrectly identified them as Ju 88s. Although the American pilots claimed two "Ju 88s" shot down, in fact only one Hs 129 was lost, W.Nr. 0315, piloted by *Uffz.* Gustav Fröhlich which crashed in no-man's-land. In a sad Christmas Day letter home, *Oblt.* Oswald mourned the loss of his friend and comrade:

> *"Yesterday it was Christmas Eve. I would be untruthful if I were to say that it was a happy evening, for two days earlier one of my pilots, Uffz. Fröhlich, was lost. He was on his 105th operational mission when he was shot down by enemy fighters. He was only just 22 years old, a dear, kind boy who was very well liked by all. His loss has hit us all very hard."*

On 23 December, three Henschel 129s on an armed reconnaissance mission destroyed one medium tank and a motor vehicle, claiming one more of each as damaged. The four Bf 109s from II./JG 51 flying as fighter escort also claimed a vehicle destroyed, but bad weather prevented any further success. Similarly, although two Hs 129s, again escorted by II./JG 51, took off on an armed reconnaissance mission on the 25th, the operation had to be aborted due to poor weather conditions.

During the morning of 27 December, *Oblt.* Oswald led eight Hs 129s on an armed reconnaissance mission in an area 25 km (16 miles) south-west of Pont-du-Fahs. A *Schwarm* of II./JG 51's Bf 109s flew with the Henschels as fighter escort. When the formation had flown some 40-50 km (25-30 miles) behind the front lines, they discovered a number of armoured cars dispersed in a farm and bombed them with good results. Although not all the armoured cars had been destroyed and the remaining vehicles presented an excellent target, Oswald gave way to what he later described as a "... funny feeling" - a

Arab tribesmen gather at the scene of the crash-landed Hs 129 coded "Z+" also shown on page 109. A team of Luftwaffe technicians work in the background to strip the machine of useful spares.

kind of presentiment, an unhealthy intuition - and decided not to carry out any strafing attacks on the farm, especially as there were bound to be other targets worth shooting up on the roads they would fly over on the way back home. This they did, strafing more armoured cars, setting some on fire and severely damaging a good many more. Oswald then decided to lead the *Staffel* straight back home and was flying relatively slowly over a grass-covered hilly area when he passed over what he believed to be a fairly heavy machine-gun or flak position. Without any warning, the wing behind his aircraft's left engine suddenly erupted into a sheet of flame and in seconds the aircraft was trailing a stream of fire almost twice its own length.

In the same instant, Oswald's Number Three in the *Schwarm* called over the radio: "Uhlan One, (Oswald's call-sign) your left engine is on fire!" With remarkable coolness Oswald replied, "Victor, Victor - Thanks, but I've already noticed!"

Now came the problem of finding a suitable place to make a crash-landing, for it was obvious that the blazing Henschel was not going to make it home. The ground below was still uneven and too rough for a successful crash-landing but, fortunately, a reservoir not marked on any maps of the area, appeared ahead of him. Oswald immediately steered towards it and set the machine, now burning like a torch, down on the surface. The water extinguished the flames and, jettisoning the cockpit canopy, he got out and into the water. It was deep, and he had to swim to the shore, but his saturated fur flying boots made his feet feel like lead and he had to abandon them in order to keep afloat. As he recalls: "The speed of my emergency landing had carried me far out into the lake and now my waterlogged clothes made it very difficult to swim to the shore. I eventually reached firm ground, though, and started to run, but that was difficult, too, because my wet clothing was heavy with water and stuck to my body. I continued running until I reached a clump of trees and at this time I thought I could reach my own lines quite easily. However, I soon realised that I was wrong and that I was, in fact, still some 12 to 15 km from them. Suddenly, only about ten metres away, I saw a French soldier leading a donkey by its reins. We both stared at one another for a few seconds before I ran off. He obviously didn't recognise me as a German, for he didn't do anything. He probably thought I was an Arab."

"After running for a safe distance, I hid under a bush and stayed there for ten hours until it was dark. I couldn't move much without showing myself and it soon became quite uncomfortable. Then some more French soldiers came by and although they passed only 2 to 2.5 metres from where I hid, they didn't see me and in fact didn't even appear to be a search party out looking for me. Although the countryside was full of French soldiers, the other Hs 129s had forced them to keep their heads down and they did not see me swim to the shore. This was confirmed when I heard one of the soldiers say that he thought the pilot of the German aircraft which had crashed

When an aircraft made an emergency landing in a remote area, a salvage team would first remove the weapons and anything else of value. If the airframe could not be saved, it was usually destroyed by demolition charges.

The camouflage of this crash-landed Hs 129 B-2 of 8.(Pz)/Sch.G 2 appears to consist of two darker colours applied in a light mottle over the sand-coloured base.

into the lake had probably drowned. Obviously the Frenchman with the donkey hadn't reported seeing me either."

"I finally reached the German lines after slogging up and down hills for thirteen hours in my bare feet. During the time I had hidden, the water in my socks had caused the skin on my feet to soften and wrinkle up, just like when you have spent too long in a hot bath, and they soon became very painful. Hobbling on, at one point I came across a French outpost, but again I was not recognised as a German airman for the soldier who saw me didn't raise the alarm."

"The first German soldiers I saw belonged to a flak unit. They had been warned that a German airman had been shot down behind the enemy lines and were almost expecting me. They sat me down by their fire and brought me a flask of cognac, buttered bread and hot coffee. It was the best meal I had ever tasted! Eventually, they put me on the back of a lorry and I was returned to my comrades."

The day Franz Oswald returned to his unit, 28 December, eight Hs 129s under the command of *Lt.* Jurck, together with a fighter escort provided by II./JG 51, carried out an attack on French tanks and vehicles south-west of Pont-du-Fahs. Although five enemy vehicles were destroyed and two more vehicles and a tank damaged, the German aircraft were intercepted by nine RAF Spitfires from 111 and 152 Squadrons which had taken off to escort three Hurricanes from 225 Squadron on a ground strafe in support of the French troops. At the same time, American P-38 Lightnings from the 14th Fighter Group appeared on the scene and a tremendous air battle developed. That evening, Oswald, who had not flown that day as he was resting his lacerated feet, wrote:

"...three of my machines have been lost due to enemy fighters. One of my pilots [Fw. Otto Siems in W.Nr.0307] was killed, but the other two returned safe and sound. They were attacked by 36 Lightnings and Spitfires but together with their fighter escort they fought like lions. Obergefreiter Lelanz shot down one Spitfire and slightly damaged a second. The '109 escort lost an aircraft and although they succeeded in shooting down more of the enemy, I'm afraid the superior forces were just too great."

"We fight here generally against overwhelming superiority but the tremendous spirit of the German soldiers in Tunisia is a real delight. It is no rarity that a single German fighter will dive onto 18 enemy four-engined bombers, or two German fighters will take on an enemy escort of 12 machines. If the enemy fighters are not at least three times as strong as we are, they avoid combat. It is exactly the same with all the other units."

With the start of the new year 5./Sch.G 1 was redesignated and became 8.(Pz)/Sch.G 2. By this time, *Luftflotte* 2 had already recorded its first misgivings about Hs 129 operations in a theatre where the enemy was rapidly gaining air superiority. On 28 December the Air Fleet's war diary stated that:

"Operations by Schlachtflieger are only possible when accompanied by strong fighter escort since the Hs 129 is completely helpless against enemy fighters and cannot defend itself."

Five Hs 129s attacked enemy vehicles near Fondouk on 2 January, one of the aircraft belly-landing on the way home south of Tunis for reasons unknown.

Although most Hs 129 attacks at this stage were made with aircraft fitted with the 30 mm cannon under the fuselage and a bomb rack under each wing, some of 8.(Pz)/Sch.G 2's aircraft were equipped for employment as pure bomb carriers to be used against

At the beginning of 1943, 5.Sch.G 1 was redesignated 8.(Pz)/Sch.G 2. This photograph of an Hs 129 B-2 from that Staffel clearly shows the camouflage scheme which was specially developed at Rechlin to provide the most effective finish for aircraft which had to operate over water and also over land where vegetation and desert sand were a feature.

Destroyed British motor transport litters the desert.

such targets as soft-skin vehicles where the use of valuable tungsten ammunition was not necessary. A typical bomb load for such sorties consisted of four SD 50s mounted on the fuselage rack and an AB 23 container on each of the wing racks. The AB 23 was also widely used at this time by the Ju 87s of St.G 3, and one of this unit's pilots has given a clear account of a sortie flown in Tunisia during which he delivered the weapon in the same low-level horizontal attack as employed by the Henschel 129:

> "The AB 23 consists of fifteen 2-kg SD 2 bombs all packed together in one container. It looks a bit like a 250-kg bomb but a bit thinner. It is dropped like an ordinary bomb but opens up as soon as it is clear and bursts open so that the fifteen SD 2 bombs come tumbling out. These SD 2s have a kind of windmill vane on them which revolves, and after two or three turns the bomb becomes live. They explode at the slightest touch, scattering very, very small, sharp, and above all, very hot fragments in all directions. It has a terrific dispersal effect. The whole thing flies to bits. They come down very slowly and continue turning like lime-leaves as they fall. And then, by the time you're past, you see everything going up in short sharp explosions below. The AB 23 is a hell of a thing against infantry, motor cars and lorries on the roads. It tears everything to pieces."

> "We flew an attack at very low level along the road near Pont-du-Fahs. We were three aircraft carrying SD 23s only - five of them each - and as we approached the target area we put on speed. One aircraft flew just above the road, just over the tree tops, and the others to the left and right, lower than the tree tops. And then we scattered our bombs, dropping the containers one by one, pressing the release button all the time. When the people in the lorries heard us, they leapt out and ran in all directions into the fields, but they didn't notice that on each side of the road there was another '87 also dropping the things. What a blaze there was. All the lorries were on fire. The people were all killed and the vehicles which weren't set on fire all had splinters in the engine or the fuel tank and so on. It's a hell of a thing with a terrific dispersal."

Early on the morning of 3 January a co-ordinated attack by two Hs 129s, five Ju 87s from II./St.G 3

Pilots of 8.(Pz)/Sch.G 2 from l. to r.: Lt. Jürk, Uffz. Lelanz, Staffelkapitän Oblt. Oswald, Uffz. Krause, Fw. Heisel and Lt. Petz.

and eleven Bf 109s was carried out against enemy vehicles immediately west of Fondouk. While the Bf 109s provided fighter cover, the Ju 87s dived to drop SD 250 bombs on anti-aircraft batteries, allowing the two Hs 129s to approach fast and low to attack the vehicles with SD 50s and the deadly AB 23s. The Stukas found their targets to be extremely well camouflaged and difficult to spot but claimed to have scored hits in their general area. Since there was no sign of enemy fighter activity, the Bf 109s descended to ground level and proceeded to shoot up enemy emplacements, but without achieving any noticeable results. Meanwhile, under cover of the diversion created by these attacks, the pair of Henschels streaked in at low level. Their attack set fire to two vehicles and badly mauled a tank and four other vehicles. Of the five Ju 87s which had taken part, four were hit by ground fire, three being so badly damaged that on their return they were declared total losses, while the fourth returned to its base with both its crew members wounded. Both Hs 129s returned safely.

Later that day, 3 Hs 129s with 9 Bf 109 *Jabos* and an escort *Schwarm* from JG 53 attacked a convoy at a cross-roads 8 km (5 miles) north-east of Ousseltia. One tanker and four lorries were set on fire and five more badly shot up.

On 18 January, *Oblt.* Oswald had another narrow escape. That morning, a reconnaissance aircraft had reported that a good deal of enemy traffic, almost certainly from the British 1st and 6th Armoured Divisions, had been observed on the roads around Bou Arada. Two convoys each of 15 vehicles had been sighted, while 30 tanks had been observed moving across country in the fields 1-2 km (1/2-1 mile) west of Bou Arada. An initial attack by five Fw 190s from III./SKG 10 and six Fw 190s from II./JG 2 had already met with some success in this area, destroying two tanks, immobilising one, bombing others and strafing the tank crews, but this attack had also alerted the ground defences. Thus, when *Oblt.* Oswald took off at 12:30 with three Henschels and an escort of eight Bf 109s from II./JG 53 to attack the tanks and motor transport, it was inevitable that they would run into trouble.

In the target area, British anti-aircraft gunners saw the three Henschels come out of low cloud

and make their surprise attack, the aircraft flying at about 240 m (800 ft) with intervals of approximately 365 m (400 yds) between each machine. The British gunners immediately opened fire with Bofors and Bren guns. Everywhere gun muzzles flashed and tracers criss-crossed the air. Franz Oswald recalled: "This was our first sortie in about fourteen days; myself (in W.Nr. 0322), *Oblt*. Krause and *Lt*. Petz. During my first strafing run I shot up a British heavy tank and set it on fire, but the defences were immensely strong. A rain of fire from machine-guns and flak. My machine received many hits, and the radio and compass were put out of action. One round passed through the cockpit just ahead of the armour plate, grazed the back of my head, and went out again through the perspex panel on the other side. I was bleeding pretty heavily."

The second aircraft, W.Nr. 0292, flown by *Oblt*. Fritz Krause, was hit by even more withering fire. The British troops observed a number of .303 strikes on the port side of the fuselage from nose to amidships and saw Krause's aircraft drop its nose before it slowly half-rolled onto its back, dived inverted into the ground and burst into flames.

Oswald had no time to see what had happened to Krause. He had troubles of his own. In an attempt to get clear of the ground fire, his aircraft flew so low that British soldiers later reported that it had hit the ground with its tail. It was then seen to make a flat turn to avoid a hill, during which the soldiers again thought it hit the ground with its wing tip. However, Oswald is adamant that at no time did his aircraft come into contact with the ground. In fact, what the soldiers probably saw was dust thrown up by the aircraft's slipstream for, miraculously, the aircraft flew on: "I flew away and made contact with the escort fighters. Since my radio was out of action, I had to rely on sign language in order to tell the Messerschmitts that I was wounded and, since my compass was also u/s, that I needed to be guided home. I flew up close to one of the fighters, put my finger in the bullet hole in the canopy and then, after touching the back of my head with my hand, held my blood-smeared fingers up for the pilot to see. The Messerschmitt pilot understood immediately and escorted me home so that I was able to put my machine down in a normal landing. It was my thirtieth operation in Tunisia. I didn't see it myself, but both Krause and Petz were shot down, too, though Petz later reported in, having made a successful belly-landing."

Fortunately, Oswald's head wound was not as bad as it looked, and a few days later he was back in the cockpit of his aircraft, only to have another lucky escape when it suffered a double engine failure: "On 20 January I had to make an emergency landing in the desert due to the failure of both engines. They searched for me for ten hours a day over two days with two *Storch* aircraft, but they couldn't locate the spot where I had

Far Left and Left: The lower engine cowlings have been removed from this Hs 129 B-2 of 8.(Pz)/Sch.G 2 being towed to a maintenance area for a change of air filters. Despite its appearance in the photograph far left, the basic finish was, in fact, an overall green oversprayed with a sand colour which was particularly densely applied around the nose and forward fuselage.

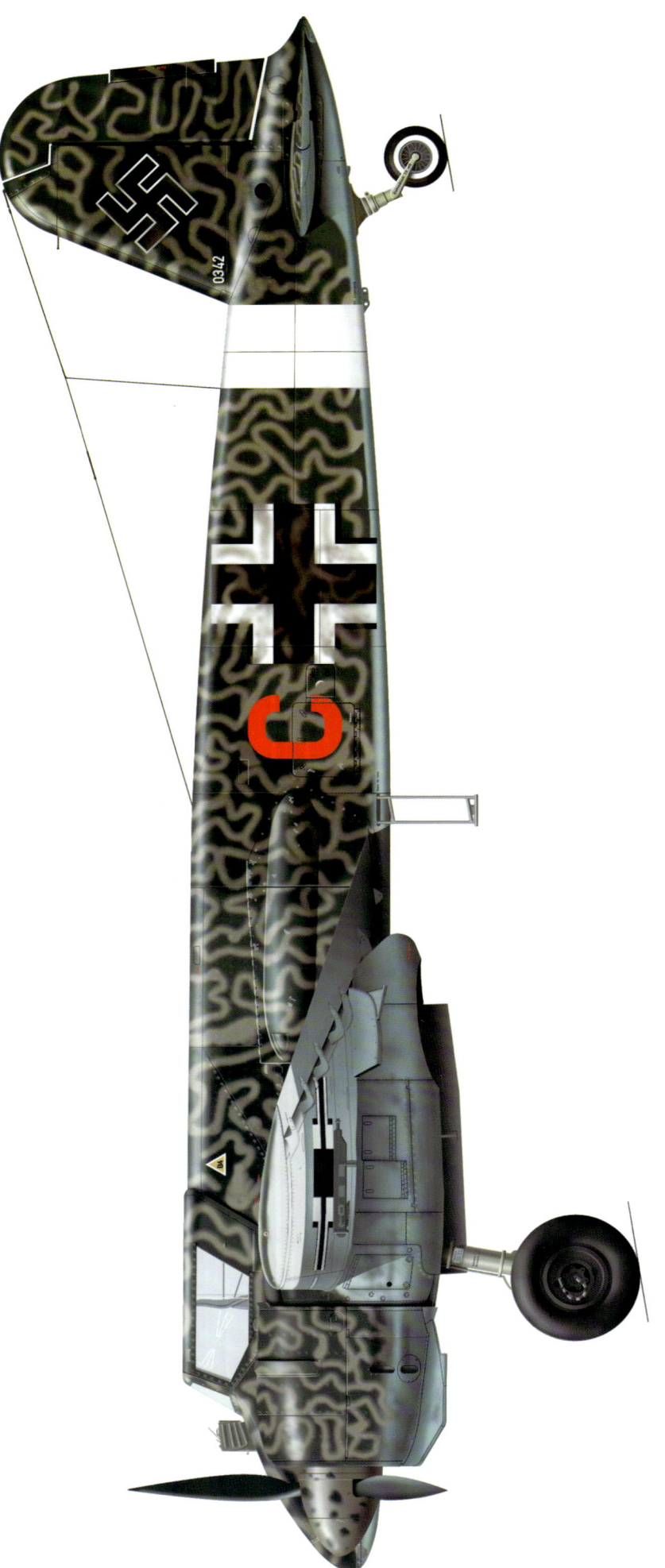

Hs 129 B-2 Red 'C'

8.(Pz)/Sch.G 2, El Aouina, Tunisia, early 1943.

The camouflage on this aircraft consisted of an almost continuous wavy line sprayed in a **sand** colour over the standard splinter pattern 70/71 **green** upper-surfaces with the undersides in **light blue** 65. This overspray, known as 'Wellenmuster', is believed to have been developed by the *Erprobungsstelle* Rechlin as the most suitable camouflage for aircraft operating over both land and sea in the Middle East. On this machine, the **tan** overspray on the port-side spinner has been so densely applied that it gives the impression of **green** mottles on a sand background. The starboard spinner of this aircraft was a replacement in plain **Black-Green** 70 and an oversprayed **white** *Werk Nummer* appeared at the base of the fin. The aircraft was fitted with an MK 101 cannon. The National insignia were: B2 crosses on wing undersides and fuselage, B1a crosses to upper-surfaces and H2a *Hakenkreuze*.

crash-landed. After waiting by my aircraft for three and a half hours I decided to make a move and spent the night with some Nomads in their tents. After a total absence of twenty-six hours I made contact with German troops at 2 o'clock on the second day and was returned to my unit. The next day we flew out to the wreck of my machine in the two *Storch* aircraft. We stripped it of anything useful and then blew it up using two mines."

Early in 1943, *Luftwaffe* units in Tunisia were visited by *General* Galland who had been sent to Italy on an extended tour of duty to boost morale and learn at first hand just what conditions were like in *Luftflotte* 2's area of operations. *Oblt.* Oswald who, since 20 January 1943, had been officially appointed *Staffelkapitän* of 8.(Pz)/Sch.G 2, was determined to speak to him. Spares and replacements for the *Staffel* had been requisitioned but they had simply failed to arrive and this had a correspondingly adverse effect on the unit's ability to continue operations. Oswald resolved to tell Galland in no uncertain terms that the unit should either be sent to Russia, where he felt it could operate more effectively, or it should be re-equipped entirely with new aircraft, ideally the Fw 190.

In the event, something quite unexpected occurred. Almost immediately following Galland's visit, during which he promised to intervene on Oswald's behalf, the replacement Hs 129s and pilots which Galland had personally ordered arrived - together with the replacements Oswald had *originally* requested. As the recently-appointed *Staffelkapitän* later joked, "Almost overnight I suddenly found myself a "*Gruppenkommandeur*" with over thirty aircraft on strength!"

As already mentioned, a number of *Luftwaffe* units in Tunisia at this time were operating the Fw 190. This magnificent aircraft had first appeared in the area in mid-November, when the fighter *Gruppe*, II./JG 2, arrived as part of the German reinforcements. In addition, III./ZG 2's ground-attack fighter-bomber version was now operating in Tunisia, as well as the similarly equipped SKG 10. When *Hptm.* Werner Dörnbrack, *Gruppenkommandeur* of II./Sch.G 2 arrived in Tunisia with his *Gruppe* of Fw 190s and expressed his poor opinion of the Hs 129, Oswald hoped that his *Staffel* too would be retrained and converted to the Fw 190, but instead the Oswald *Staffel* received a new operational directive. Experiences in Russia had shown that the Hs 129 was most effective if its attacks were directed only against tanks which had broken through the German front line and were without organised anti-aircraft defences. Henceforth, all Hs 129 units, whether in Russia or Tunisia, were therefore ordered only to attack such targets as

Allied reports list a total of ten Hs 129s on El Aouina airfield. This photograph is of Red "C". However, no report mentions that this aircraft was found there.

had actually broken through. Naturally, this had the effect of reducing the number of sorties flown and resulted in a period of enforced idleness. Oswald fumed: *"No operations for a week. This is no good at all. Galland should either send us to Russia or give us different machines, preferably the Fw 190."*

Operations were also hampered by high winds and driving rain. On 10 January, *Fliegerführer Afrika* reported his forces had been able to mount only limited operations on account of the bad weather and soft airfields.

February and March 1943 were also months of especially heavy *Luftwaffe* losses due to anti-aircraft fire and the successful continued build-up of Allied air forces. Now British and American fighters swarmed everywhere and *Luftwaffe* airfields were increasingly the subject of particularly heavy Allied bombing, some of which gave *Oblt.* Oswald some rather unusual and dangerous experiences. On one occasion he had been flown from Gabes to Tunis as a passenger in a *Storch*. As Oswald's pilot prepared to leave Tunis, a formation of Allied bombers appeared overhead and proceeded to rain splinter bombs - designed to cause maximum damage to parked aircraft - onto the airfield. It was obviously high time to make a hasty departure and the *Storch* took off amid the torrent of exploding bombs. Fortunately, the aircraft was not seriously damaged, but a splinter from a nearby explosion entered the cockpit and, barely missing the pilot's hand, sliced the top off the control column. The pilot was so alarmed that he let go of the stick and drew back his hands. Only Oswald's prompt action in grabbing the stick prevented the machine from crashing! Then on 22 March, one of Oswald's engines failed while he was flying from La Fauconnerie to Mozzoura-North in an Hs 129. Using only his one good engine he set the machine down on Mozzoura-North airfield and taxied in, but as he did so one wheel ran into a slit trench and the aircraft flipped onto its back. At the same time, a formation of enemy bombers attacked the airfield and Oswald had to sit out the raid trapped upside down in his cockpit!

Towards the end of March it became evident that in view of the enemy's numerical strength in fighters, technically outmoded types such as the Hs 129 and particularly the Ju 87 dive-bomber, were absorbing so many friendly fighters for escort purposes that other duties allocated to the fighters were suffering. These types were frequently no longer able to hold their own against the enemy's defence and application was therefore made for these formations to be relieved. This measure was not, however, put into effect until the middle of April.

A sortie representative of Allied air superiority and typical of the less than satisfactory results now being achieved, occurred on 23 March when a single Hs 129 escorted by two Bf 109Gs from 8./JG 77 took off from La Fauconnerie on a tactical reconnaissance flight over Maknassy. Whilst flying towards the objective at 1,000 m (3,000 ft), they encountered a formation of six or seven Douglas Boston medium bombers, escorted by some 30 Spitfires. The two greatly outnumbered Bf 109Gs prepared to attack the bombers but were themselves engaged by the fighter cover and one of the Bf 109s received hits in the engine and in the starboard cannon which forced the pilot to make a wheels-up landing. The Hs 129 had, meanwhile, headed for home at the first sign of this trouble.

By 10 April, repeated Allied bombing and an acute shortage of fuel, supplies and spares had reduced the strength of 8.(Pz)/Sch.G 2 to 16 Henschels, of which only two were operational. At this stage, the number of *Luftwaffe* flying formations in Tunisia was reduced since they could no longer be adequately supplied as a result of the Allied sea blockade and attacks against the supply flights which battled haplessly to get through from Sicily. The first units to be moved from Africa to Italy were the Ju 87 and Hs 129 *Staffeln* which, for all practical purposes could no longer be employed operationally as their

Another Hs 129 B-2 at El Aouina. Clearly under repair when found, it was later pushed out of the hangar and scrapped.

performances were inferior to an excessive degree when compared with those of contemporary Allied types. On 20 April, therefore, with the end of Axis resistance in Africa in sight, 8.(Pz)/Sch.G 2 began its evacuation to Trapani on Sicily and then on to Decimomannu on Sardinia. During the flight to Sicily the surviving aircraft flew at very low level to avoid interception and although no enemy aircraft were encountered, Allied air superiority in the area was now so complete that the *Staffel* was ordered to avoid all contact and, if attacked, to land on water and get out of their aircraft at once.

By 25 April, an advance detachment of 8.(Pz)/Sch.G 2 had landed at Decimomannu and by the 28th, eight of the *Staffel's* aircraft were established there to be rested and held in readiness until transferred again to Bari on the Italian mainland. However, the *Staffel* had arrived at their Sardinian base without their *Staffelkapitän*, since *Oblt.* Oswald had become lost in fog during the transfer flight and had been forced to make a landing on an airfield at Ajaccio, the birthplace of Napoleon Bonaparte, on the island of Corsica. His aircraft refuelled by hand-pump, Oswald took off once the weather had cleared and soon rejoined his *Staffel* at Decimomannu.

At the beginning of May it was obvious that the struggle for Tunis would soon come to an end. All personnel who could possibly be spared were now being evacuated to Sicily in night transport flights. By the afternoon of the 8th, the moment had come when there was no more aircraft fuel available for operations. With the agreement of Army Group Africa, C-in-C South issued orders for the remaining flying formations to be withdrawn to Sicily, bringing to an end all *Luftwaffe* operations carried out from bases in Tunisia. In a post-war report on the battle for Tunisia, *General* Seideman wrote of Hs 129 operations there:

"The use of the aircraft which could have influenced the course of operations a great deal in our favour was hampered by technical defects, such as faulty carburettors, so that the favourable results hoped for did not materialise".

When the Allies occupied El Aouina and its satellites, they discovered among the many abandoned *Luftwaffe* and Italian aircraft the machines which Meyer and Oswald had been forced to leave behind. As for the pilots of the Hs 129 *Staffeln*, a fitting tribute was provided by *General* Galland when he said: "I sent two '129 *Panzerjägerstaffeln* down to Africa when Tunis was gradually being encircled. Their crews consisted of well-trained, excellent men, but they could do nothing against the enemy's superiority".

In late June, the unit was recalled to Deblin-Irena for subsequent employment on the Eastern Front. It was at this time that *Oblt.* Oswald - refreshed from a period of leave in Munich, during which time his *Staffel* had been under the temporary command of *Lt.* Jurck - suffered a dramatic and extremely unpleasant injury. After setting out on a route which would take them across northern Italy, over the Alps to Munich, the *Staffel* made an intermediate stop at an Italian airfield to refuel. Having survived the hazards of so many operational sorties and a number of emergency landings, Oswald was severely burned when his flare pistol was accidentally discharged in the cockpit of his aircraft. As already described, the cockpit of the Hs 129 was extremely small and the stowage area for the pilot's flare pistol on the right-hand wall of the cockpit was not satisfactory. Instead, the pilots carried the pistol

The same aircraft as opposite after being moved into the open. The remains of an Me 323 transport may be seen in the background.

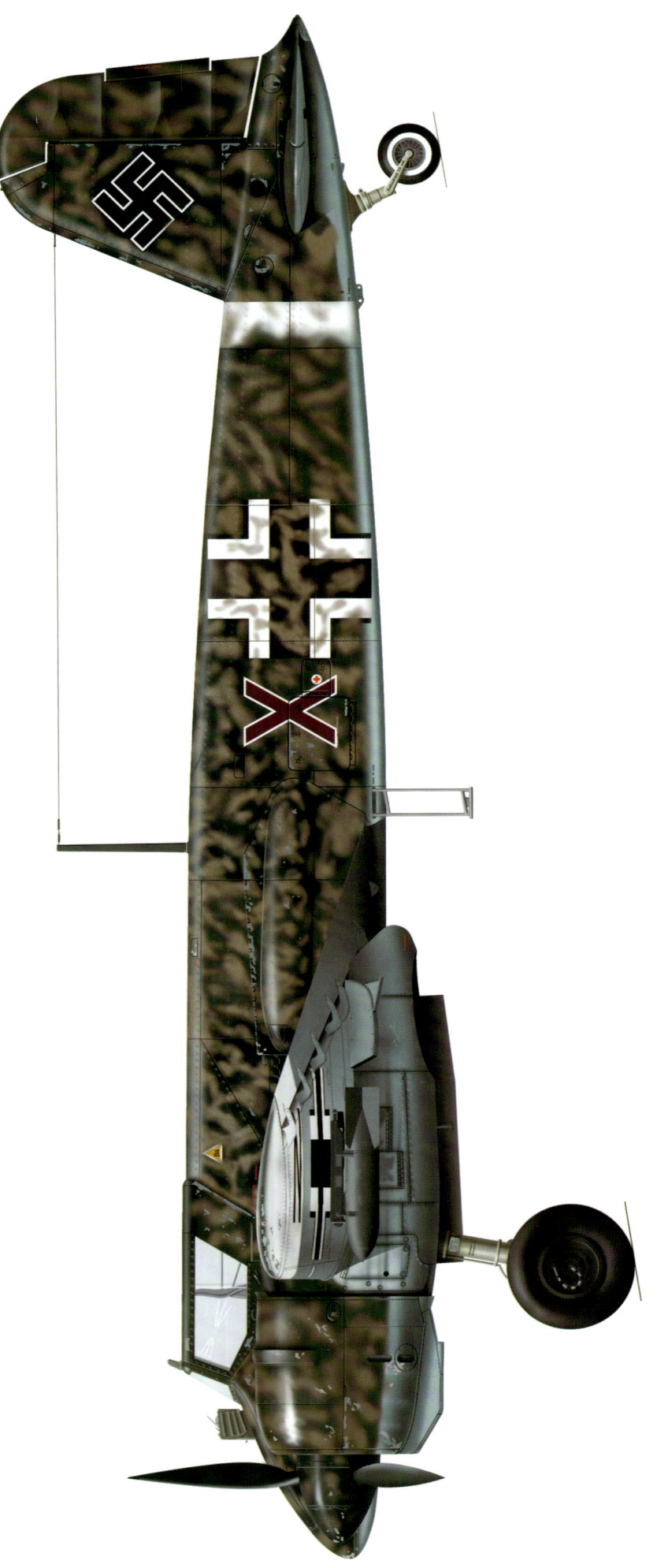

Hs 129 B-2 Purple 'X' W.Nr. 0278
8.(Pz)/Sch.G 2, El Aouina, Tunisia, early 1943.

Found abandoned at El Aouina, this machine had an upper-surface camouflage consisting of the standard splinter **green** 70/71 scheme with a **faded sand-coloured** overspray on all upper-surfaces. This was also applied to tone down the **white** of the fuselage African Theatre markings. The wing tips had **white** undersides but this aircraft did not have the **white** nose and brightly coloured spinners seen on other Hs 129s operating in the Middle East. The factory call-sign, 'DQ+ZN' in **black**, appeared on the wing undersides with the W.Nr. 0278 in **white** being slightly obscured by over spray paint. Although the RAF A.I.2(g) report on this aircraft describes the colour of the identification letter as 'purple', this was probably the result of either **red** being applied over an earlier **blue** 'X' and bright sun causing severe bleaching and discolouration. The aircraft was fitted with an MK 101 cannon. The National insignia were: B2 crosses on wing undersides and fuselage, B1a crosses wing upper-surfaces and H2a *Hakenkreuze*.

loaded, but broken, in some other, more convenient part of the cockpit, ready for instant retrieval should it become necessary to signal the colours of the day to any friendly flak which might inadvertently open fire on the German aircraft.

As was usual, a mechanic was standing on the wing to assist the pilot in strapping in, but on this occasion, as the mechanic closed the canopy it accidentally fired the flare pistol. The flare bounced around the cockpit like an uncontrollable firework, burning Oswald's hands, face and thighs. The cockpit filled with dense smoke making it difficult for him to locate the canopy release handle. The mechanic, rooted to the spot, was too shocked and distressed to do anything but watch in helpless horror. Eventually, Oswald managed to wrench open the canopy himself but his hands and thighs were very badly burned. Following initial treatment in a local military hospital, he was later flown to Munich-Riem in a Ju 52 from a meteorological unit where he received further medical attention at Oberföhring hospital. At one point during his six week incarceration there, an officer from the local air-control detachment visited him to present him with the *Deutsches Kreuz* in Gold as he lay on a stretcher![2]

Meanwhile, the remainder of the *Staffel* went on to Deblin-Irena once again under the command of *Lt*. Jurck. Here it was re-equipped for operations in Russia though it did not see action again until August, 1943.

An American serviceman seated in Purple "X", W.Nr.0278, at El Aouina. The factory code of this aircraft, "DQ+ZN", was painted on the underside of the wings, which - by the time the aircraft was examined by Allied Air Intelligence - had been removed.

HS 129 B-2s FOUND ABANDONED BY ALLIES IN TUNISIA		
Werk Nr.	**Markings**	**Remarks**
0277	"+ I" Factory code DQ + Z (probably M) Stencil lettering on fin "Fernruf Mirow 231". (Telephone number of E-stelle Rechlin.)	Crashed and partly burnt out.
0278	"+ Purple X" Factory code DQ + ZN	Wings removed, otherwise fair.
0317	"+ Red L" Factory code CH + SJ	Fair.
0324	N/A	Scrap. Fuselage only
0326	"+ Red K" outlined white.	Good condition - flyable.
0327	None	Scrap
0342	"+ Red C"	Fair
0381	N/A	Scrap. Fuselage only
0385	"Blue G +"	Wings removed, otherwise fair.
0408	"+ Red T"	Fair condition
N/A	N/A	Scrap. Fuselage only

---

1 Each officer assigned to lead a Staffel first became a Staffelführer, but after some time had elapsed and the officer had shown that he was able to lead the Staffel, he was proposed as Staffelkapitän, the nomination being made by the RLM.

2 Later Oswald erroneously received the Deutsches Kreuz in Gold a second time and after the war, while a POW of the British in Hamburg, he presented his duplicate medal to an Oberleutnant who had lost his.

"My Staffel, together with other Staffeln, attacked in relays and the enemy suffered heavy losses. Our pilots could see the panic-stricken response of the Russian tank crews and the retreating armour presented splendid targets for us. Each pilot made his run-in at low level and fired his armour-piercing shell at just the right instant, just like on a firing range. When we went in for the kill, a steady approach and a well aimed shot were vital to knock out a tank - I would say that it was a real art..."

Oblt. Georg "Drops" Dornemann
Staffelkapitän 4./Sch.G 1 & 10.(Pz)/SG 9

PART FOUR
PANZERJÄGER!

Red, white and green spinners and yellow identification markings made the Hs 129 a colourful machine, further enhanced by the application of the Infantry Assault Badge and "kill" markings. This sequence illustrates the diminutive cockpit of the Hs 129 and also shows the MK 101 cannon and the nose features. In the background is Red "G", showing that "kill" markings were only applied to the port-side of the rudder.

"Some Sort of Vision"

The Battle Over the Kuban
March – July 1943

10

Throughout the early months of 1943, the *Luftwaffe's* ground-attack units were reorganised and restructured. By February, 1943, all the remaining Hs 123 biplanes had been concentrated within 7./Sch.G 1 and 7./Sch.G 2 and, with the exception of 4. and 8./Sch.G 1 and 4. and 8. (Pz)/Sch.G 2 equipped with Hs 129s, all other

Obstlt. Otto Weiss (left), the General der Jagdflieger's Inspector for Ground-Attack operations was transferred from Berlin in February 1943 to take command of all Hs 129 units under the title "Panzerjagdkommando Weiss" at Zaparozhe. In mid-April, when Weiss was returned to the staff of the General der Jagdflieger, Hptm. Bruno Meyer (centre) took command of the Panzerjagdkommando as the "Führer der Panzerjäger". This photograph is believed to show the handing-over ceremony.

Staffeln, together with the *Gruppen-* and *Geschwaderstab* flights, had already converted to the Focke-Wulf 190 fighter-bomber. At the same time, all Hs 129 units on the Eastern Front were placed under the command of *Oberstleutnant* Otto Weiss, the Inspector for Ground-Attack Operations for the *General der Jagdflieger*, who was specially transferred from Berlin to take command of these units. Known as *Panzerjagdkommando Weiss*, this purely anti-tank command had its headquarters and support airfield at Zaporozhe, all Hs 129s being concentrated there at the end of February.

Panzerjagdkommando Weiss was purely a command and control unit and its staff did not at this time fly operational missions. Instead, the *Panzerjagdkommando's* main task was to concentrate and direct all Hs 129 *Staffeln* in critical areas where the weight of enemy attack was greatest and also to supervise their orientation, training, and increase operational readiness. The wasteful use of the anti-tank *Staffeln* for operations other than tank-killing, e.g. reconnaissance, was ruled out and except in the case of a sudden Russian armoured breakthrough, the individual *Staffeln* had strict orders not to mount anti-tank operations on their own initiative.

However, co-operation between the *Panzerjagdflieger* and the army proved vital to the overall effect of German strategy in southern Russia as was the case on 19 March 1943 when the Army's elite Infantry Division *Grossdeutschland* attacked the village of Tomarovka. Responding to a call by the Division for anti-tank support, a number of Hs 129s attacked enemy armour around the village, but soon the Henschels themselves came under attack from Soviet Polikarpov I-16 fighters. An air battle ensued, in which the Hs 129s shot down at least one fighter which crashed only 100 m (109 yds) from the half-track belonging to the commander of *Grossdeutschland's* reconnaissance battalion. Resuming their attacks on the enemy tanks, the Henschels destroyed all but two of them and these were finished off by *Grossdeutschland's* own self-propelled guns. When Tomarovka was taken, the German infantrymen counted 29 knocked-out Russian tanks.

In early April, the aircraft and flying personnel of Meyer's 4./Sch.G 2 arrived in Russia from Africa and, pending its complete restoration to operational readiness, the *Staffel* was based at Zaporozhe. In mid-April, the flying component was joined by the ground personnel who arrived by rail. Upon his arrival, *Hptm*. Meyer himself was transferred to take over command of the *Panzerjagdkommando Weiss* which was then renamed *Führer der Panzerjäger*. At the same time, *Obstlt*. Weiss was transferred back to the staff of the *General der Jagdflieger* and Meyer's position as *Staffelkapitän* of 4./Sch.G 2 was taken over by the newly-arrived *Major* Matuschek.

In his new capacity, Meyer immediately tried out some Bf 110s, Ju 87s and Ju

UNITS UNDER THE COMMAND OF FÜHRER DER PANZERJÄGER, April 1943
COMMANDER: HAUPTMANN BRUNO MEYER

Anti-Tank Staffel	Commander	Airfield	Front Sector	Assigned
8.Sch.G/1	Ruffer	Kerch V	Kuban	I. Fliegerkorps
4.Sch.G/1	Dornemann	Stalino	Donets Bend	IV. Fliegerkorps
Pz.Jä.St./JG 51	Eggers	Kharkov	Oskjoll Bend	VIII. Fliegerkorps
4.Sch.G/2	Matuschek	Zaporozhe	–	In reserve

88s which had been experimentally fitted with various anti-tank cannon. The Bf 110s were not successful in this role as they were large aircraft which, lacking the extensive armour protection of the Hs 129, proved extremely vulnerable to ground fire. Trials were also carried out with Ju 87s fitted with two 37 mm *Flak* 18 cannon modified for aircraft use and mounted adjacent to the aircraft's fixed undercarriage, but pilots assigned to the trials unit were at first reluctant to fly low-level anti-tank missions. Torn away from the duties for which they had been specifically trained, the former dive-bomber pilots now had to operate single-handedly instead of flying as part of a thickly-packed formation at higher altitude. This dislike of operating at low level was due, wrote Meyer, not to any lack of good will on the part of the *Stuka* pilots but to the fact that the water-cooled engine of the Ju 87 was much more vulnerable to small-arms ground fire than the air-cooled engines of the Hs 129. Eventually, however, new tactics were worked out and in due course the Ju 87 tank-buster became an important component in the *Luftwaffe's* anti-tank arm, the dive-bomber units St.G 1 and St.G 2 being the first to operate with a special Ju 87 G anti-tank *Staffel* attached.[1]

Far less successful were the experiments conducted by *Staffel* 92 with a number of Ju 88s fitted with a 75 mm anti-tank gun and magazines of armour-piercing high-explosive ammunition. As the cannon was not at this time a fully-automatic weapon, a member of the Ju 88 crew was specifically required to perform the loading process but, like the rest of the crew, had been trained to carry out quite different tasks. Crews which had previously distinguished themselves on bomber operations now had to make a radical switch to anti-tank work which called for quite different skills. Needless to say, this was quite impossible, all the more so since the Ju 88 crews frankly expressed a hearty dislike for this particular kind of mission.

These Ju 88 trials were also plagued with many armament and engine problems. On one occasion, it took four Ju 88s 75 minutes to become airborne after an alarm and, of these, only one or two succeeded in reaching the front sector some 60 km (37 miles) from the airfield. The others were forced to turn back before reaching the target and after four sorties from Poltava against such excellent targets as KV 1 tanks moving across open fields, the Ju 88 *Staffel's* activities ground to a halt and the unit was moved back to Germany.

Red "S+ –", W.Nr.140508, carried two victory markings.

Despite this disappointment, the OKL continued to believe that the Ju 88 had a place as an anti-tank aircraft. When, in March 1943, a proposal was put forward for an entire anti-tank *Geschwader* of three *Gruppen* to be ready for action in the winter of 1943/44, the Ju 88s from III./KG 51 were to form part of the unit. This new anti-tank *Geschwader* was to be raised from existing units as follows:

UNITS PRESENTLY AVAILABLE

4.(Pz)/Sch.G 1	Hs 129
8.(Pz)/Sch.G 1	Hs 129
4.(Pz)/Sch.G 2	Hs 129
8.(Pz)/Sch.G 2	Hs 129
Pz.Ja.Staffel JG 51	Hs 129
Pz.Ja.Staffel St.G 1	Ju 87
Pz.Ja.Staffel St.G 2	Ju 87
Erprobungskommando Ju 88 (Pz. Jäg)	Ju 88

PLANNED FOR THE WINTER 1943/44

1 Panzerjäger-Geschwader of 3 Gruppen:

I. Gruppe	5 Staffeln Hs 129 (currently as above)
II. Gruppe	2 Staffeln Ju 87 (currently as above)
III. Gruppe	2-3 Staffeln Ju 88 Pz. Jäger (to be formed from the disbanded III./KG 51)

In the event, these plans were never fully realised and the closest OKL came to achieving its aims came in October 1943 when the Hs 129 units, which had in any case been operating together under the command of the *Führer der Panzerjäger*,

Hs 129 B-2 Red 'J' W.Nr. 0364

8.(Pz)/Sch.G 1, Kuban, Russia, May 1943.

This machine was camouflaged in the standard 70/71/65 **green** splinter pattern which appears very faded and dusty, particularly around the rear fuselage and tail area. Eastern Front **yellow** theatre markings appeared on the rear fuselage band, nose and undersides of the wing tips. A thin **white** band separates the **red** tip from the basic **black-green** 70 spinner colour. The W.Nr. 0364 appeared in **white** on the fin. The Infantry Assault Badge was stencilled in **white** on each side high in the centre of the fuselage and on the upper nose panel which had added details in **black** separately stencilled over the **white**. The additional fuselage badges were, like the *II.Gruppe* bar, features seen only in the Spring of 1943. The tank 'kill' markings in **white**, vary in outline and detail and were seen only on the port side of the rudder and may have been applied solely for propaganda photographic reasons as the photos show the aircraft with different numbers of kills. In any event, the display of victory symbols was not a feature many *Schlachtflieger* carried into action for fear of Russian reaction should the pilot crash-land in enemy territory. This aircraft was shot down by ground fire on 27 May 1943. The aircraft was fitted with an MK 101 cannon. The National insignia were: B2 crosses on wing undersides, B6 crosses on wing upper-surfaces, B5 crosses on fuselage sides and H2a *Hakenkreuze*.

The much photographed Hs 129 B-2, W.Nr.0364, Red "J" was an aircraft operated by 8.(Pz)/Sch.G 1 in the Kuban. Here the aircraft is shown both being refuelled and in its dispersal with a single column of eight tank "kill" markings on the rudder. However, these markings and also the application of the additional Infanterie Sturmabzeichen applied to the fuselage sides were probably used simply for the benefit of the camera. The aircraft has a II. Gruppe bar aft of the fuselage cross and displays an overall dusty and worn appearance. Note also that the fuselage cross lacks the black centre seen on the Hakenkreuz. Red "J" was shot down by ground defences on 27 May 1943.

were formed into a single *Gruppe*, the IV./SG 9. A further *Gruppe*, the I./SG 9, formed from the anti-tank Ju 87 G *Staffeln*, was added in 1945, at which time some progress had been made towards re-equipping both *Gruppen* with rocket-firing Fw 190s. As for the proposed third *Gruppe*, trials meanwhile continued well into 1944 with the Ju 88 fitted with various cannon installations, even though by this time it had become obvious that the Ju 88 was unsuitable for employment in the anti-tank role. Rather than any conviction that the Ju 88 was a suitable anti-tank aircraft, however, the need for these continued trials was dictated by shortages of tungsten. This forced the *Luftwaffe* High Command to consider destroying Russian armour with heavy calibre high-velocity weapons rather than tungsten-cored armour-piercing shells.

With the German recapture of Kharkov in mid-March 1943, the position in Southern Russia stabilised. For a short time it appeared that active *Luftwaffe* operations were at an end and it seemed the flying units might obtain a respite of about two months in which to restore strength and serviceability. From the end of March until early July there was indeed a relative lull on the Eastern Front while both sides prepared for the summer campaign, but this situation was quickly transformed by increasing Soviet pressure on the precariously isolated Seventeenth Army in the Kuban, threatening the whole German hold on the Taman bridgehead. To meet this threat, the bulk of the *Luftwaffe's* long-range bomber and close-support units, previously operating in the Donets sector, was concentrated in the Crimea and the Taman peninsula.

The scale of German air operations in the Kuban and the battle for the Taman bridgehead was a struggle on the same scale as the battle for Tunisia, and the possibility of a German defeat was viewed as scarcely less significant than the loss of North Africa. The *Luftwaffe* could not therefore afford to neglect the Kuban.

Following Fourth Panzer Army's success in clearing the right bank of the Donets north to Belgorod, Hitler turned his attention to the river line south-east of Kharkov. In this sector, due to the tell-tale signs of Russian activity, there was opportunity for a quick, relatively easy thrust across the Donets offering attractive tactical advantages. Such a move would straighten and shorten the front south-east of Kharkov and, by pushing it further east, block the Russians from

Ground crews from 8.(Pz)/Sch.G 1 watch a formation of Ju 87 Ds taking off. All the Ju 87s have had their wheel spats removed.

Three yellow-nosed Hs 129 B-2s flash past the camera in a low-level pass over their airfield. As large formations of anti-tank aircraft used simultaneously over the battlefield hindered and confused each other, anti-tank units usually fought in Rotten (pairs) or Schwärme (four aircraft elements).

attempting another assault on the right flank of von Manstein's Army Group South.

At first, bad weather at the beginning of April held up German operations until a heavy blow by massed forces was launched on 17 April. Although operations were maintained at a high level during the days that followed, they did not meet with the success expected and in spite of a remarkable concentration of forces the *Luftwaffe* did not achieve unchallenged air superiority. Indeed, the delay enforced by the bad weather, during which a large proportion of the *Luftwaffe* in Southern Russia was concentrated on Crimean airfields, had taken away the element of surprise and given the Soviet Air Force the necessary opportunity to assemble a force adequate to meet the German threat. In addition, air attacks were made particularly difficult by the heavy defensive fire of a permanent front.

It was during these operations in the Kuban that increased publicity began to be given to the *Luftwaffe's* anti-tank *Staffeln*. The number of German press reports covering the *Panzerjäger* began to grow and to emphasise the importance and the exploits of individual pilots. *Oblt.* Rudolf-Heinz Ruffer and his *Staffel*, 8./Sch.G 1, became the subject of particular attention. Ruffer, who had earlier flown the Hs 129 with the *Panzerjäger Staffel* of JG 51, transferred in March 1943, to 8.(Pz)/Sch.G 1 where, on 8 April he was

Pilots of 8.(Pz)/Sch.G 1 pose with W.Nr.0364. The aircraft carries 13 "kill" markings but, inexplicably, only 7 appear in the first column, whereas there are 8 to be seen in other photographs in this chapter. A former member of Sch.G 1 states that for a short time pilot's "kill" markings were painted on the vertical tail surfaces. This practice was discontinued when it was found that obviously successful pilots brought down behind enemy lines were badly treated and sometimes shot. Ninth from right in this line up is Lt. Hans-Hermann Steinkamp, later Staffelkapitän of 14.(Pz)/SG 9.

The Infantry Assault Badge proved a popular emblem with the Schlachtflieger. As well as appearing on the Hs 129, it was also used on the Hs 123, Fi 156, Bf 109 and Fw 190.

appointed *Staffelführer* and led his unit in remarkably successful operations in support of German troops in the Kuban bridgehead.

In view of the weight of repeated Russian assaults against the German positions, the order restricting Hs 129 operations to sorties only against Soviet armoured breakthroughs was suspended and attacks were successfully carried out to break up concentrations of Russian tanks as they regrouped in preparation for an attack.

A close-up of the armoured nose of an Hs 129 B-2. This machine carried an MK 101 cannon under the fuselage and has had the Infantry Assault Badge stencilled on the nose panel. The intake and exhaust stub for the petrol-driven cockpit heater may be seen to the right while the bulge and circular orifice closer to the centre are believed to show the position of the gun camera.

The Russians had always fully understood and appreciated the art and value of camouflage, yet despite their most skilful efforts to hide their tanks, armoured concentrations were observed and immediately came under attack by the "*fliegende Panzerjäger*" or, as the German press now began to call the Hs 129s, "*fliegende Pak*" - "Flying Anti-Tank Guns".

As a symbol of the common fighting spirit and close bonds between the *Schlachtflieger* and the Army, *Luftwaffe* personnel stencilled the *Infanteriesturmabzeichen* - Infantry Assault Badge - on the fuselage sides and nose panels of their aircraft. While this was by far the most common adornment, other emblems had also been used. In Africa, some machines belonging to Meyer's 4./Sch.G 2 are known to have carried on their nose panel a silver-painted representation of the *Luftwaffe's Panzer* Assault Badge showing a tank advancing through a laurel wreath. In addition, some members of the *Schlachtflieger* were presented with a small, enamel, shield-shaped lapel badge to wear on their uniforms. This featured a miniature Infantry Assault Badge in silver on a green background and these highly-prized mementoes were worn with great pride. When interviewed during the preparation of this work, Franz Oswald showed the author his Knight's Cross - considered to be Germany's most coveted wartime military decoration - but commented that the presentation of the small, unofficial lapel badge, which he regretted having long since lost, was of more significance and importance to him than his *Ritterkreuz*!

But there was more than a common spirit uniting these two arms of the *Wehrmacht*. Above all they were both fighting against the same enemy tank formations and this bond between airman and soldier was nowhere stronger than with the German grenadiers who, from their battle lines in the swamps and marshes of the Kuban, shared in the success of the attacks by the flying tank-hunters against Soviet armour. A war correspondent's report from this period describes how, on one occasion, the enemy had just launched an armoured assault against German positions when the tanks were spotted by a *Schwarm* of anti-tank aircraft led by *Oblt*. Ruffer, at that time his *Staffel's* highest scorer with thirteen confirmed tank kills. In their dug-outs and foxholes, the German infantry listened intently to the drone of aircraft engines as the *"fliegende Pak"* flew out towards the enemy and, apparently heedless of the Soviet ground defences, immediately attacked the advancing armour. Before long, tanks could be seen on fire and columns of thick black smoke rose into the air as a signal of the enemy's destruction. Vehicles which escaped the first attacks were ruthlessly hunted down and destroyed until the battlefield was littered with Russian tanks knocked out before they could engage the German ground forces. All during the battle the grenadiers cheered wildly at every success of their airborne comrades; each tank destroyed was one less they would have to face later.

Also participating in this action was an Army battalion commander, *Ritterkreuzträger Oblt*. Jacob who, although wounded in the fighting, refused to leave the area for medical attention until he had personally thanked Ruffer and the other pilots of the anti-tank *Staffel* for their support. Although the ground fighting had been very bitter and required the utmost from each and every soldier, Jacob said, they had all been greatly encouraged by the actions of their flying comrades and, as a result, the grenadiers had not only forced the Soviets to retreat but made important territorial gains.

A sight to cheer the heart of many a battle-weary and exhausted Panzergrenadier pinned down by enemy armour; an Hs 129 searching for targets.

It is clear from this and other similar accounts that quite apart from the material damage the *Panzerjagdflieger* inflicted on the enemy, their low-level attacks had a great morale-boosting effect on friendly troops. A report from the files of the *General der Jagdflieger* dated March 1943, particularly mentions the numerous messages and telegrams received from the infantry in which they expressed their gratitude for the support given by the *Panzerjäger*. This appreciation is again well illustrated by a report on an incident which occurred on 2 January 1943, when a *Schwarm* of Hs 129s on a "free hunt" in and around Voroshilovgrad-Millerovo noticed that Russian tanks, supported by infantry equipped with flame-throwers and grenade launchers, were threatening to annihilate a small group of German troops from the 575. *Panzergrenadier Regiment* enclosed in the village of Antonovka.

As part of the 384. *Panzergrenadier Division*, the 575. *Panzergrenadier Regiment* had been rushed to the Eastern Front in December 1942 from

A close comradeship developed between the German Panzergrenadiers fighting amidst the swamps and marshes of the Kuban in mid-1943 and the pilots of the Hs 129 Staffeln which supported them against the hordes of Russian tanks they faced.

peaceful garrison duties in Belgium to bolster the collapsing southern sector, but during its first action it behaved badly and panic broke out in its ranks. Now, a month later, it had still not recovered from the shock of being transferred to face a powerful and ruthless enemy and until the arrival of the *Luftwaffe's Panzerjäger*, the future had looked so hopeless that the grenadiers had destroyed everything apart from weapons and ammunition to prevent them falling into enemy hands. Finally, the remaining ammunition had been equally distributed; each grenadier was given ten rifle bullets and ordered to open fire only at the closest possible range.

Once they had released their bombs on the enemy infantry, the Henschels set to and attacked the tanks with their cannon. Two T-34s were destroyed and the remainder, together with the surviving infantry, were forced to flee, but one of the Hs 129s was hit by ground fire and forced to make an emergency landing close by. The pilot managed to stagger across to the relieved German soldiers and the reception he received is described in the following report:

"Still unable to believe that thanks to the timely intervention of the Schlachtflieger they had actually routed the Russians at the last minute, the grenadiers thought that the appearance of the pilot was some sort of vision. Everyone wanted to see him, to touch him and to talk to him. Men with wounds dressed only with makeshift bandages dragged themselves over to give him their hand in thanks. The leader of the grenadiers, an old Oberst, wanted to give him something, but the whole group did not have a single cigarette between them".

Such valuable support, both in terms of firepower and the effect on morale was not achieved without losses. Operations flown from Anapa in support of Seventeenth Army, cut off in the constantly shrinking Kuban bridgehead, were intense and costly. The Soviet Air Force outnumbered the *Luftwaffe* four to one in this sector, and the unusually large number of anti-aircraft guns had been reinforced. The 4.(Pz)/Sch.G 1 lost an Hs 129 B-2 around Krymskaya on the 8th and another on 13 May while 8./Sch.G 1, operating from the over-crowded airfield at Kerch V in the Crimea and from Anapa in North Caucasia, lost one Hs 129 B-2 to ground fire on 5 April; two Hs 129 B-2s were shot down on 15th; two more in the Krymskaya-Bakanskaya area next day; one on 3 May; two to flak on 5th; two more on 27 May and one to flak and fighters on 29th. In most cases the pilots were able to

Lt. Otto Mostböck of 4.(Pz)/Sch.G 1 and his Hs 129 B-2. Mostböck was killed on the airfield at Stalino-North on 12 April 1943 when his aircraft, W.Nr.0423 coded "M+", crashed and burned after developing engine trouble. The photographs below show the funeral procession and grave of Otto Mostböck.

escape with their lives due to the sturdy protection of the aircraft's armoured cockpit and returned, some unhurt, to their unit. Here they paid tribute to their aircraft and many a glass was raised in a toast to the long life of the Henschel locomotive works' robust design. But on 29 May, the *Panzerjäger* lost one of their best anti-tank pilots, *Oblt*. Seuken of the Pz.Jä.St./JG 51. While making a firing pass against a T-34 to the west of Krymskaya, his machine, W.Nr. 4046, was hit by light machine-gun fire which originated from a point at right angles to his line of flight. The aircraft crashed, killing the pilot instantly. Another pilot from Pz.Jä.St./JG 51 was lost and two aircraft from 4.(Pz)/Sch.G 2 were shot down at Krymskaya on 1 June.

In addition to sorties flown in direct support of the Army, operations were also laid on against small boats which were being used in great numbers by the Russians to ferry troops behind the German lines in an attempt to bring about the collapse of the Kuban front. In dealing with these small craft, anti-tank ammunition was not required and cannon were loaded instead with shells fitted with specially sensitive fuzes to ensure they exploded on contact with the soft wooden sides of the boats. During one such mission, on 3 May, *Hptm*. Ruffer himself was brought down by ground fire in W.Nr. 0392, crash-landing "... like Robinson Crusoe on an island in the middle of the lagoons." He was eventually rescued by a company of German assault troops and taken back to his unit in a Fieseler *Storch* piloted by Meyer's adjutant, *Lt*. Gebhard Weber. Remarkably, Ruffer survived being shot down three times in succession though, as the contemporary account on the next page so graphically shows, not without a considerable strain on his nerves.

Although Ruffer's account of his ordeal mentions the appearance of Russian fighters, some months were yet to elapse before they were to become any real threat in terms of both quantity and quality. By far the larger number of Hs 129 losses at this time - some seventy-five per cent - was due to the fearsome and intense anti-aircraft and infantry fire which the *Panzerjagdflieger* invariably encountered whenever they attacked. By the summer of 1943, the Russians had developed counter-measures to the Henschels' low-level attacks, as Bruno Meyer explained: "With our fixed forward-firing armament, it was impossible to attack tanks other than by diving at them at an approach angle of between 30 and 40 degrees. The run in was never made at a steeper or shallower angle or else it would have been impossible for the pilot to take aim at his target without the aircraft hitting the ground. As we always had to make our approach in exactly the same way, this was therefore the time of greatest danger. This was exactly the most critical point in anti-tank work and the Russians were very quick to realise this weak point."

"Since there was no other twin-engined aircraft type with forward-angled wings being used for tank busting, the Russian tank crews were soon able to recognise the Hs 129 and realised that if they came under attack, it would be carried out along the somewhat rigid lines described. So, the Russian tank crews just got out of their tanks, stood beside them under cover and took careful aim with their sub-machine guns. Immediately after firing his guns, the pilot had to

The 8.(Pz)/Sch.G 1 suffered very heavy losses in the bitter fighting over the Kuban and during April and May, lost 11 aircraft to ground defences and fighters and another 4 damaged due to enemy action or airfield accidents.

The Ordeal of Hauptmann Rudolf-Heinz Ruffer

My Staffel was flying over the wide, swampy lagoons on the edge of the Sea of Azov. This endless area consists only of reeds, and the monotony is interrupted merely by countless small ponds and lakes. From the air it doesn't look at all dangerous, but no one escapes from these swamps. They are without bottom and only the local people know of the few safe paths through them.

At a forward position on the edge of the lagoons was a German strongpoint. The German soldiers there were sunbathing and they waved to us as our patrolling Hs 129s flew overhead. All seemed to be pretty quiet until, one day, a Ju 87 discovered some boats in this lonely area. When the pilot dived down to investigate further, he drew heavy fire. Further observation revealed that perfectly camouflaged Soviet boats had infiltrated the area in small groups and the Russians were evidently trying to find ground firm enough to launch a surprise offensive.

But they had overlooked one vital factor – German air power. The boats were attacked first by Ju 87s which succeeded in sinking a number of them but, as the Stukas were unable to carry out the job by themselves, they were soon joined by our Hs 129s. Learning a lesson from the damage they had already suffered, the Russians quickly brought up their flak which, at some newly-established strongpoints, included emplacements equipped with four-barrelled machine-guns. These made things very difficult so, initially, we circled around suspicious areas at some distance to be sure that we were outside the range of these machine-guns. Then we dived down to attack. A large ammunition boat blew up with a violent explosion and others were holed in their sides and sank amid clouds of black smoke. Inexplicably, the defences did not open up while we made another pass, nor the next, nor even during our fourth pass against a large number of boats in a channel. Once more I flew in low and blazed away with all I had, but then the flak suddenly opened up with a terrific barrage. There were tracers and smoke trails everywhere and it was impossible to take any evasive action. I had to continue with my attack, flying down into the enemy fire and shooting with all my weapons at the places where the tracers originated. I registered some good hits but, naturally, I couldn't silence all the positions. Then things really began to happen. A flak hit tore a large part of my left wing open. The panels opened up like petals and the entire left-hand engine came off and cartwheeled away! The aircraft wallowed like mad but, remarkably, it remained in the air. At 20 metres (60 ft), and then down to 10 metres (30 ft), I flew away from the still firing enemy positions and, with only one coughing and faltering engine, made off as best I could with the aircraft banked right over. It struggled on but clearly wouldn't fly far, so I set course for the German positions in the south-west.

The lower wing was brushing the reeds. I gripped the stick and pulled with all my strength. An island appeared before me. Will I make it? Sweat was running into my eyes. I took the precaution of jettisoning the canopy hood because if the aircraft overturned on landing it would have been impossible for me to get out and I would have drowned in the swamp. I reached the island and the aircraft smacked down amid a torrent of water. Black mud shot up and into the cockpit. Landed! I was soaked through with mud and filthy water.

I clambered out of the cockpit and took stock of my situation, fully expecting the Russians to appear at any moment, for they had certainly seen my emergency landing. I jumped off the aircraft and onto the ground, only to sink deep into the morass. It took an almighty effort to pull myself out again. I tried the ground at other places, but it was no good; some seven eighths of my immediate vicinity was surrounded with swamps and dirty water. In an emergency, the remaining one eighth would perhaps enable me to swim, but where was I to swim to? On my right there was a lake, but I doubted that the edges would be firm enough for walking. And if I could reach the lake's edge but had to return to my aircraft, I'd have lost too much body heat and that would be dangerous. On the other hand, there was some advantage in remaining where I was in that I was surrounded by swampy marshland and the Russians couldn't approach unobserved. Sitting in safe cover in my armoured cockpit, I could see any approaching boats and fire at them with my pistol. I had 18 cartridges. I also knew some Russian. Perhaps I could capture any approaching boat, steal a Russian uniform, and get away?

I smelled horribly from the filthy mud all over me, so I found a pool of cleaner water and washed my clothes. I only had lightweight summer clothes on, which would be warm enough while I sat in the cockpit during the heat of the day, but they wouldn't afford much protection against the cold of the night.

Wanting to have a look around, I climbed up onto the tailplane so that I could see further. I was startled to see that not far away there was a boat, but it disappeared again before I could make out whether or not it was the Russians looking for me. I listened, but heard only the lonely sound of the wind in the rushes. Then there was the roar of aircraft engines overhead. I pressed myself against the fuselage and looked up into the sky. Hurrah! It was my comrades, flying overhead and waggling their wings. Then I thought… the radio! I ran to the cockpit and found that it still worked. Via the radio they told me that a German boat was already searching for me and with a final wave of their wings they flew away again. The hours passed slowly. There was only the sound of the wind in the reeds for company and I was both hungry and thirsty. I had only had some coffee and a little dry bread for breakfast before our hurried take-off.

Late afternoon. Once, I heard Russian voices carried on the wind as they desperately tried to find me. Some time later, a flare was fired close by, but I couldn't respond because all my own flares were wet. I thought that perhaps it could be my comrades looking for me and I was furious I couldn't answer them. Now I was getting desperate. Perhaps I should try walking south-west, towards our own positions? I made a reed mat to walk on and set out, step by step and sometimes crawling. But the mat only supported my weight for about five seconds, by which time I had sunk up to my knees. I struggled on. Every movement became long and painful. My muscles became weaker and weaker, but I struggled forward a metre at a time until I eventually reached firmer ground. Somehow I summoned new strength to go forward, but I only ran into more swamps. Again the laborious fight with the swamp and the razor-sharp reeds. My hands were bleeding and sweat ran in small rivers over my whole body. After I had covered about 550 metres (1,804 ft) I came to a ditch, about 2-3 metres (6-9 ft) wide. Now my will-power was exhausted. It was impossible for me to cross. There was a dark red film before my eyes. My knees gave way, and I sank to the ground.

I was awakened from my state of exhaustion by the roar of aircraft engines. Though my comrades had come to look for me again, I knew they wouldn't find me near my aircraft and perhaps would think that I had already been saved. I shouted and waved, but they banked away and disappeared into the distance. At that moment I almost lost all hope of ever being rescued.

The only thing to do was to return to my aircraft. Once more I began the agonising, excruciating fight with the reeds and the swamp. I was bleeding from my scratches and sweating profusely. It took me three times as long to return to the aircraft. Sometimes I almost gave up; the distance seemed endless. Then I saw the wings of my machine and with the last of my strength, clambered up onto one wing and collapsed. I recovered quickly though and washed and wrung out my underclothes. I pulled off my thick socks, too, and tried to dry them. After I'd cleaned them, I put my clothes back on again, but they were still pretty wet. Darkness had fallen during my struggle back and now the wind died down. It was a cold, starry night, filled with the sounds of birds and frogs. Tired and aching all over, I climbed into the armoured cockpit. Hunger gnawed at my stomach. Earlier, I had pulled some loose panels from the damaged wing, and now I positioned them over my head. Then I opened my parachute and snugly wrapped up in the warm silk, fell asleep in seconds.

Some time later I suddenly woke up with a start, most likely because the frogs had stopped their croaking. Was it a sign of danger? I was too tired to care and, through sheer exhaustion, fell asleep again.

I woke up early the next morning and then dozed while I waited for the sun to rise. I got out of the cockpit when the sun became too hot. It was a beautiful day. Perhaps today I would be rescued. I lay on one of the wings and sunbathed to warm up. Once again some Hs 129s appeared overhead. I stood up and waved. The pilots waved back and told me over the radio that a boat would come soon. They dropped some food, but it fell too far away. I felt depressed and disappointed. I would have given anything for something to eat. They dropped a dinghy, too, but it fell about 25 metres (75 ft) away on the edge of an open area. I fought my way to it, half running, half swimming, but when I finally reached it I was dismayed to discover that it had been punctured by the sharp reeds. I kept it to drape over the cockpit as a cover for the night.

Then I was startled when someone called out. I threw myself onto a wing. A boat was approaching. "How many are you?", a voice asked. It was a strange question, but at least the language was German. "One!", I replied, only to regret it an instant later when a voice said in Russian "Karoch!" ("Good!"). Was this a trap? In two bounds I was back in my armoured cockpit. I gripped my pistol and watched carefully. From what I could see, it appeared that one man in the boat carried a long, typically Russian style rifle. I decided to wait for them to draw closer and then I would fire. But as they came nearer I was able to see more and more of them until it became clear that they must be Germans for the man in the bows was wearing a German medic's uniform. It was the rescue boat which had been sent out to find me, in which were some German soldiers and some Russian volunteers.

At last I was able to have something to eat. When I got back to my unit, my men found it hard to believe that this dirty, sweaty, blood-encrusted figure before them was their Staffelkapitän. I learned that they hadn't been able to locate me at first and it was only after a reconnaissance aircraft had taken some aerial photographs of the area that they were able to find me.

My rescue naturally called for some kind of celebration and this turned out to be a pretty "wet" affair. The next day, although I had been ordered to convalesce and spend the day resting, I was soon woken up and told that the Kommandeur had ordered a mission. Naturally I was included. Of course, had I insisted, someone else could have taken my place, but as Staffelkapitän and out of loyalty to my comrades I felt it was my duty to go. So I collected my flying gear and went to the briefing with the rest of the Staffel. We learned that some of our Grenadiers had been surrounded by a strong ring of enemy tanks and we were ordered off to attack this armoured force. Once over the target area we were fired on by the light, medium and heavy flak which protected the masses of tanks. Nevertheless, we waded in, diving down onto the target. Above us, too, there were Russian fighters and, with one eye on them and the other on my target, I twisted and turned to left and right at low level. Because of these manoeuvres, the fighters could not get a good shot at me and I continued to close in on my tank. It exploded after my fourth shot. A cloud of dark smoke and bright flames came out of the turret cupola. Then, suddenly, there was a "click-click" as my machine was hit. Splinters flew around the cockpit. I looked around to both sides but I couldn't see anything. My low level flying had shaken the Russians off, but the instruments on the left engine nacelle were all registering zero. In the same instant, the engine failed, spluttering into silence.

Now I was down in the valleys and gullies at the foothills of the Caucasus mountains, flying only on the right engine. With the steep sides rising up on both sides, such flying would have been dangerous enough with two good engines, and I had to wrestle with the machine in the confined spaces, my one good engine at full throttle and the machine banked right over to avoid hitting the valley sides. It was an absolutely hellish experience, yet I somehow managed to control the stricken aircraft and succeeded in getting back to Anapa. I was very relieved to be back in one piece and I had certainly learned something about flying.

Yet I knew full well that sooner or later I would have to take off again on another operational sortie. Needless to say, I wasn't looking forward to it at all. Having already narrowly survived two hazardous missions in succession I was full of apprehension and was suffering from a severe attack of nerves. The weather grounded us for two days, but then I had to take off for the third time. Again our target was to be enemy armour. Would I survive this next mission? I had a heavy feeling in the pit of my stomach and felt very tensed up.

When we passed over the front, the enemy flak was unusually silent. Why? Were they trying to lure us into a false sense of security? During my first attack I hit three tanks and set them on fire. Second attack. Still the flak doesn't open up, and another enemy tank is destroyed. Then, on our third pass, all hell is let loose. We are surrounded by a wall of shells. As I lead the Staffel through it, my aircraft is hit. A 5 cm anti-aircraft shell exploded beneath the cockpit. Splinters fly all around, but I escape being wounded as the explosion occurred behind my armoured backplate. I report my situation to the rest of the unit and the "Kettenhund" flying on my right tells me that the right engine is trailing smoke. I notice, however, that the instruments are normal for the moment and I am toying with the idea of making another pass when all the needles drop to zero and flames burst from the damaged engine. I try to feather the propeller, but it is no use. It's high time I went home. My machine is losing height and, because the pump for the hydraulic installation is dependent on my failed engine for power, the undercarriage will not lower normally.

Will I be able to make it back to Taman? I must decide whether to belly-land here or press on and try to use the hydraulic hand-pump to get the undercarriage down. I decide to try and make it home, but now the aircraft is flying even more slowly and losing height. During the final bank in to land, because I have to pump the lever twenty times in order to get the undercarriage down, I am controlling the aircraft with only my right hand on the stick and all while flying on one engine. Perhaps it would have been better to have made a belly-landing after all, for as soon as I had the undercarriage down, it began to look as if I didn't stand a chance of getting home. The Henschel was sinking lower and lower, and then the other good engine began to splutter. I was completely bathed in sweat, but I battled on to the airfield. As I put the aircraft down on the ground, I noticed immediately that in addition to all the other damage, one tyre was punctured, too.

Once the machine had rolled to a stop, I released my safety straps, stood up in the cockpit and then climbed down to the ground. My knees were knocking like mad, and I just flopped down beside my wrecked aircraft. Now I could see that the tail, too, was badly damaged and was literally hanging on by a thread. I fished about in my pocket for my pipe, but I felt too dazed even to light it. I stayed there, just sitting beside my aircraft for a whole hour, completely indifferent and drained of all emotion. I was utterly worn out and suffering from an apathetic numbness induced by nervous exhaustion.

Oblt. Rudolf-Heinz Albert Ruffer posing for the camera on the tail of Red "G" displaying 13 victory markings. These kill markings were applied to the port-side rudder surfaces only.

had to pass through their hail of fire. As the splinters from our anti-tank shells' aluminium cases hardly posed any danger to the Russians and the hard tungsten core penetrated into the tank's interior, and since we were always sure to hit our target, it made sense for the Russians not to remain sitting in the tank but to climb out and stand beside it."

In fact, all Russian soldiers were trained to fire at attacking aircraft with whatever weapons were to hand and the concentrated fire of many rifles, pistols and sub-machine guns was frequently successful. In the case of the Hs 129, despite the aircraft's armoured undersurfaces the engines were relatively lightly protected and although they would sometimes continue to run after being hit, many aircraft were brought down by small-arms fire. Even more dangerous to aircraft, however, was the deadly Russian flak which was well respected by all German flyers. Relying on density of firepower rather than accuracy, Russian anti-aircraft gunners could quickly put up a ferocious protective barrage of shells. Stationary targets were surrounded by anti-aircraft protection of all calibres and when German anti-tank aircraft began to concentrate their attacks on moving tanks, the Russians quickly responded by providing their armoured

pass over the tank at a height of between three and six metres (10 and 20 ft), and it was at precisely this moment, when our aircraft presented an excellent target for the dismounted tank crews, that they would blaze away at us with all they had, knowing full well that our aircraft

formations with the protection of special anti-aircraft units which rode into battle alongside the tanks. Sometimes the anti-aircraft guns were towed by the tanks themselves and the gun crews were expert at quickly unlimbering and making their weapons ready to meet any prowling aircraft.

---

1 ONE PILOT ASSIGNED TO THE TRIALS UNIT WAS HPTM. HANS-ULRICH RUDEL, LATER TO RISE TO THE RANK OF OBERST. HE, TOO, WAS AT FIRST UNENTHUSIASTIC ABOUT ATTACKING TANKS AT LOW-LEVEL WITH THE CANNON-ARMED JU 87, BUT LATER DEVISED TACTICS WHICH ENABLED THE AIRCRAFT TO BECOME A VERY EFFECTIVE TANK DESTROYER. BY MAY 1945, RUDEL HAD SUCCEEDED IN DESTROYING OVER 500 TANKS WHILE FLYING THE JU 87.

"Zitadelle"

Kursk and the Killing Grounds of Belgorod   July – September 1943

11

Early in June 1943, all *Luftwaffe* Hs 129 *Staffeln* on the Eastern Front, with the exception of the Pz.Jä.St./JG 51, were completely withdrawn from operations and moved back to the *Führer der Panzerjäger's* support airfield at Zaporozhe where they were restored to full operational strength. While operating under the command of *Oblt.* Eggers, Pz.Jä.St./JG 51 had escaped heavy losses and, now under the command of *Oblt.* Hans Jentsch, it was up to full establishment strength. It was therefore able to remain at its airfield near Kharkov. Information from *Luftwaffe* records clearly shows that Hs 129 wastage increased as operations were resumed after the winter battles and subsequent spring thaws, but that losses dropped to zero in June when the *Panzerjäger Staffeln* were withdrawn from action and strict orders were issued that these units were to be held in readiness for a forthcoming operation, code name *"Zitadelle"*. Until this was launched, the Hs 129 *Staffeln* were available for combat only in the most critical circumstances.

During the previous winter, the Russians had captured a large salient between Orel in the north and Belgorod in the south with the city of Kursk at the centre. Operation *"Zitadelle"* was intended to eliminate this bulge in the front line with a double enveloping attack against the Russian salient. If successful, such an operation would destroy a large number of Russian divisions, would decisively weaken the offensive strength of the Russian Army, and would place the German High Command in a more favourable position for continuing the war in the east.

The German plan of attack, scheduled to open in the first week of July, involved the Ninth and Fourth Panzer Armies, both enormously strong in armour, striking north and south of the salient respectively. However, the Russians were well aware of the German intentions and had prepared deep and exceptionally strong defensive positions in exactly those areas where the two attacks were to go in. The resulting battle, the Battle of Kursk, was the largest tank battle fought during the Second World War and involved over two million men, 6,000 tanks and 4,000 aircraft.

In the south, Fourth Panzer Army was to strike from the area north of Kharkov towards Kursk with a total of 15 divisions forming two *Panzerkorps*. One of these, the II. SS *Panzerkorps* under SS-*Obergruppenführer* Paul Hausser, contained the three élite *Waffen-SS* divisions, 1. SS Panzer-Grenadier Division *"Leibstandarte Adolf Hitler"* (SS-LAH), 2. SS Panzer-Grenadier Division *"Das Reich"* and 3. SS Panzer-Grenadier Division *"Totenkopf"*.

Shortly before the German offensive was due to start, all *Luftwaffe* senior officers and unit commanders were ordered to their *Luftflotte* or *Fliegerkorps'* headquarters where they were briefed on the current situation and given details of the forthcoming operation. It was stated that the breakthrough of German troops essentially depended on the effect of the *Luftwaffe's* first attacks. Each crew was to be made aware of the decisive importance of their effort, for the army units had to rely completely on the support provided by the air force and expected every crew to do its best. After his briefing, Bruno Meyer

The MK 103 cannon.

contacted the officers and tank crews of Fourth Panzer Army and the commanders of the SS-LAH. Pilots were given the opportunity of taking a look at the new Tiger tank from the air in order to familiarise themselves with the formidable fighting vehicle now equipping the German divisions, and the *Waffen-SS* gave demonstrations of its anti-tank weapons. The Hs 129 pilots reciprocated by making dummy attacks against captured tanks.

During the preparations for the attack, each Hs 129 *Staffel's* establishment was increased from 12 to 16 aircraft and with all units up to full strength, a total of 68 combat-ready Hs 129s was available for the coming offensive. Moreover, in June, 4.(Pz)/Sch.G 1 had been sent to Germany where it was equipped with aircraft fitted with the new MK 103 cannon. This weapon was of the same 30 mm calibre as the original MK 101 but its main advantage was a higher rate of fire. "*Zitadelle*" was to mark the operational debut of the MK 103 as an anti-tank weapon but it was at first to prove disappointing in service as early models were susceptible to jamming.

Anxious to play an active part in the battle, Meyer disregarded the Ob.d.L's order that he should continue to operate in a purely command capacity and on the eve of the battle he flew to Mikoyanovka, about 8 km (4 miles) south-west of Belgorod, in order to join his units. Here, *Staffel* after *Staffel* landed at fifteen minute intervals, followed by Ju 52 transport aircraft bringing in the ground personnel. By now the Hs 129 units had become accustomed to making such moves only by air and had dispensed with all superfluous personnel. In addition, only those vehicles which were absolutely necessary were kept and this heavier material was transported close to the new airfield by rail. At the same time, an officer in charge of a railway munitions and material supply train brought Meyer the welcome news that he had spare Hs 129 parts, spares for the MK 101 and supplies of special anti-tank ammunition.

As a final part of his preparations, Meyer made contact with *Major* Alfred Druschel, a very experienced ground attack pilot and holder of the Knight's Cross with Oakleaves and Swords, then the *Kommodore* of Sch.G 1 based with the neighbouring Fw 190-equipped *Staffeln* of I./Sch.G 1. Meyer ensured that each would be kept well informed of the situation at the front, particularly in those areas where the main thrust was to be made.

Operation "*Zitadelle*" opened on 5 July.

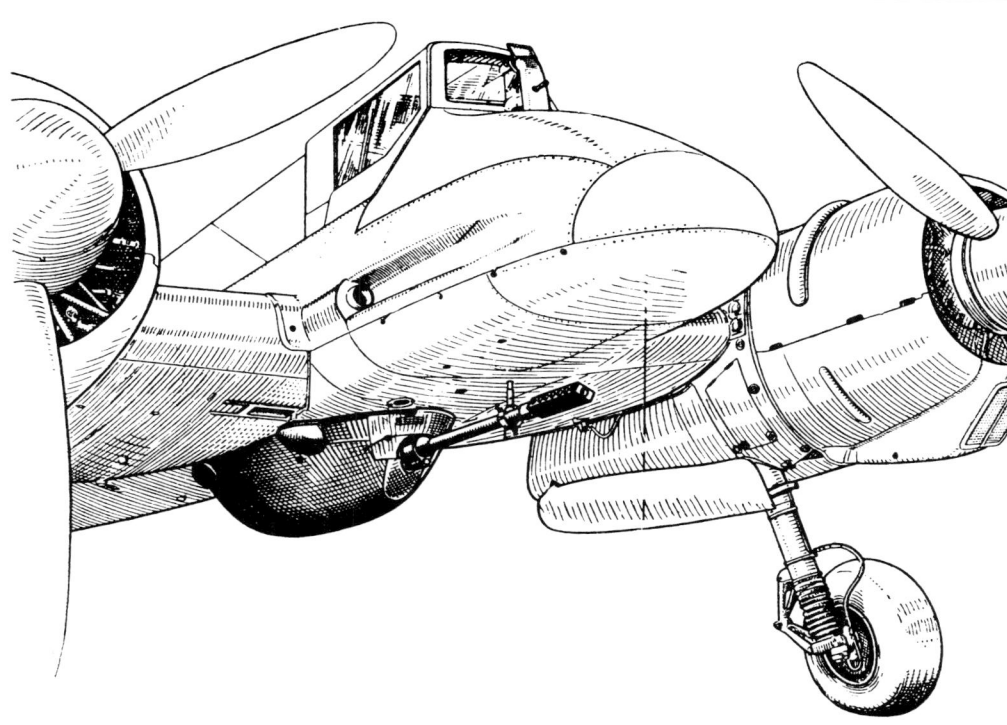

Official handbook drawing showing MK 103 Rüstsatz under an Hs 129 B-2.

Following an overnight thunderstorm which helped to relieve the uncomfortable pall of heat hanging over the region, the day dawned bright and warm, a typical languid summer's day in Central Russia. On the southern wing of the salient, Fourth Panzer Army initially made good progress though the cost was high. Enemy opposition was strong, but as the Russians had withdrawn the mass of their mobile formations, little armour was encountered and, lacking suitable targets, the Henschels flew no missions of any great importance during these first two days. The pilots were sent out to fly one sortie each in four-aircraft sections (*Schwärme*) against a few stray tanks, but this was more for the purpose of orientation and familiarisation than to relieve any great danger to the ground forces. Then, on 7 July, units of the SS-LAH advancing on the roads towards Korocha encountered a strong force of T-34 and KV 1 tanks some 15 km (9 miles) east of Belgorod and a fierce encounter developed. Fortunately, Meyer's command post was situated next to that of the SS-LAH and after familiarising himself with the situation, he took off with one of his *Staffeln* and headed for the battle area. A radio message was sent via a Ju 52 communications aircraft so that 4./Sch.G 1 and Pz.Jä.St./JG 51 were also alerted and these too headed for the battle area where they were joined by Sch.G 1's Fw 190s. After a two-hour contest fought in co-operation with the army's flak, the aircraft succeeded in beating off the Russian attack and when the last pilot left the battlefield for home, dusk was falling.

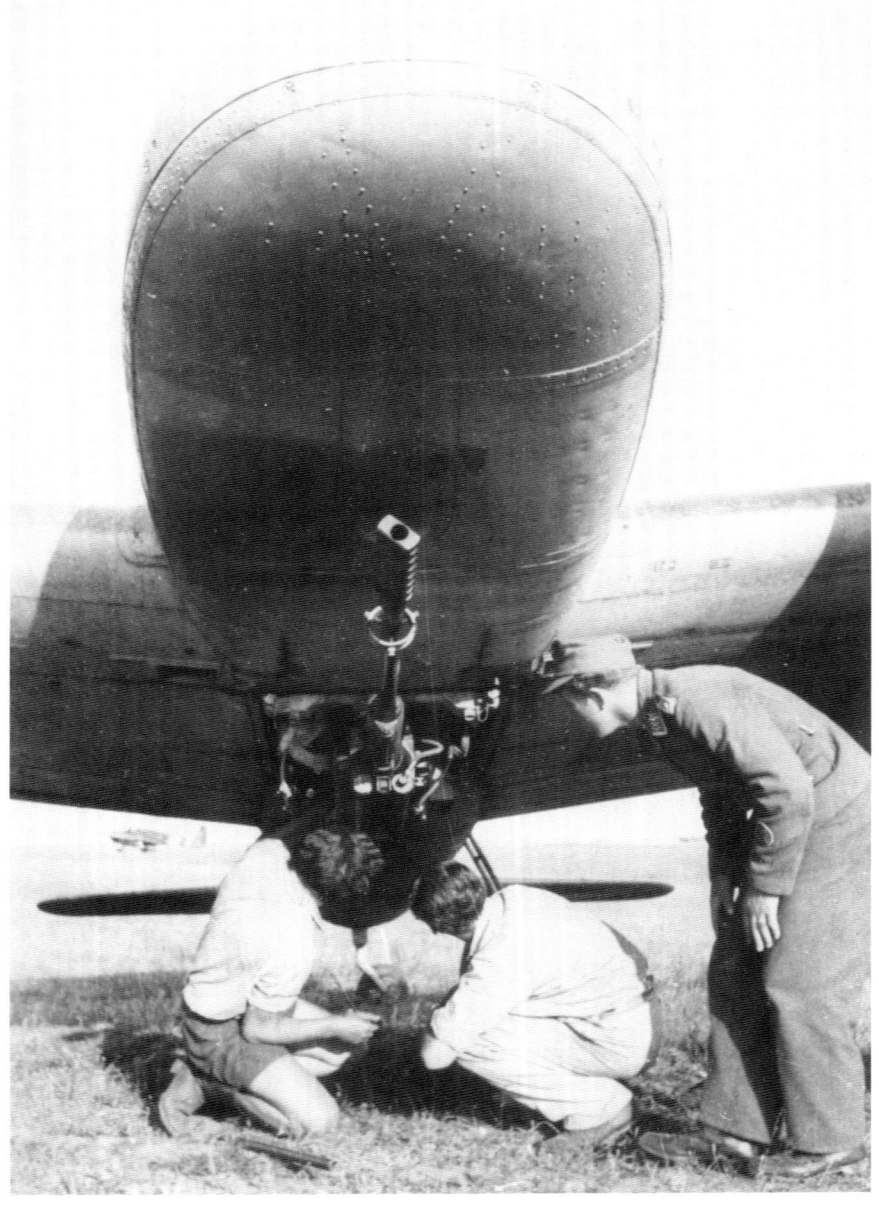

With barrel clamp in position, armourers make final adjustments to an MK 103 cannon. The screws on the clamp ensured precise final alignment.

MK 103 cannon ammunition box.

As Meyer later recalled: "The countryside presented a weird sight with its smouldering and fiercely burning tanks. From time to time a tank exploded and a heavy pall of smoke curled upwards into the air. There had been virtually no losses on our side, though some machines had been slightly damaged on their undersides by debris hurled up by exploding tanks. Emergency repairs were hurriedly carried out during the night so that our aircraft were fully serviceable again in the morning and ready for operations. It was impossible for us to count exactly how many tanks we had knocked out since the whole success was shared with army units. However, the satisfaction of having helped to rectify an extremely awkward situation was sufficient for the anti-tank fliers, and it was they who had carried the main burden of the fighting."

On the morning of 8 July, Meyer sent a *Schwarm* of his aircraft to search for any hostile armour in the area, but none were to be found. Flying low over the German positions, the Henschel pilots saw their own troops waving handkerchiefs to them in greeting, but, as they did not lay out any of their emergency ground markers or recognition strips to signify they required aid or aerial support, the Henschels flew on to patrol the front line to the north and north-west of Belgorod. Here the *Schwarm* found and attacked a weak force of Red Army tanks and, as some battle noises had been heard directly to the east during the previous night, the standing patrols were extended to cover this area also.

Here again they knocked out a few tanks which had broken through into weakly occupied infantry positions and, said Meyer: "Our close-support work ahead of these units was a great pleasure. The men in the foremost positions laid out their ground strips or emergency markers in almost textbook fashion as if on the drill ground. We found that these ground-to-air communications functioned far better in the less important areas of the front. In the area of the main thrust, the *Waffen*-SS were inclined to rely too much on their own strength and were reluctant to ask for close air support for fear of revealing a weakness. Incidentally, some of the soldiers' ground markers were put together from their old bed sheets and underwear, but they always served their purpose well. If an enemy tank penetrated into our positions, where perhaps it might not be easily seen from the air, then we found violet smoke markers were the best means of ensuring that the pilot could identify the target".

In the early hours of the afternoon, the situation in this sector seemed to calm down too, and the anti-tank *Schwarm* extended the surveillance area by flying in a north-easterly direction where the ground seemed to be occupied only by weak Russian and German forces. The aircraft then flew on to the SS-LAH, whose men were concentrating on the hills north-east of Belgorod in order to defend advancing troops from enemy armoured columns reported to be pushing from the Morotchka area. From there, they continued their surveillance flights in an easterly direction past Belgorod and returned to the airfield. So, by sending out a *Schwarm* at set intervals to relieve the one already on patrol, and with each relieved *Schwarm* returning by the same route, it was possible to ensure that the entire front line was regularly covered.

To the east and north-east of Belgorod, there were several staggered woods stretching from north to south. From here, the country was difficult to observe and any enemy advance would be hard to spot. That afternoon, Meyer had been out on one of the surveillance flights himself without seeing anything unusual, but as he was returning home at tree-top height he saw in the fields to the west of the woods, a mass of Soviet soldiers which had certainly not been there when he had made his outward flight to the SS-LAH. Meyer immediately gave the alarm over the radio, for he realised at once that an entire infantry brigade supported by a strong tank force was intent on attacking the flanks and rear of the II. SS *Panzerkorps* and the SS-LAH.

Back at the airfield, Meyer's pilots sprinted to their machines and quickly took off. Besides arousing his own anti-tank *Staffeln*, his alarm also alerted the entire I. *Gruppe* of Sch.G 1. No sooner had the Hs 129 *Staffeln* scrambled, than the Fw 190s, guided by red and green flares, were taxiing from their dispersal areas to take off.

This co-operation between the two units was a relatively rare occurrence. Although neither was subordinate to the other, a strong bond of comradeship existed between the two commanders which had proved its worth since the days of the French campaign. The absolute trust that the one placed in the report of the other immediately made the *Schlachtgeschwader Kommodore* realise the seriousness of the situation and Meyer's emergency call for close air support with 500 kg SD2 bomb containers was translated into action without delay.

In addition, it was typical of the trust that *General* Seidemann, the commander of VIII. *Fliegerkorps*, had in the ground-support pilots that he did not intervene in such situations but left the units a free hand in every respect. Although this generosity was due to the *General* having known his unit commanders since the Polish campaign, his attitude nevertheless always earned praise.

The Hs 129 and Fw 190 *Staffeln* arrived at Meyer's position at almost the same time and flew in formation with him while he personally directed them to their area of operations. Druschel also flew up close to Meyer's machine to have his

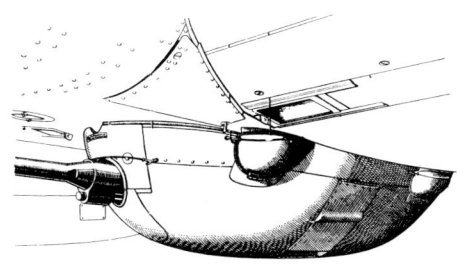

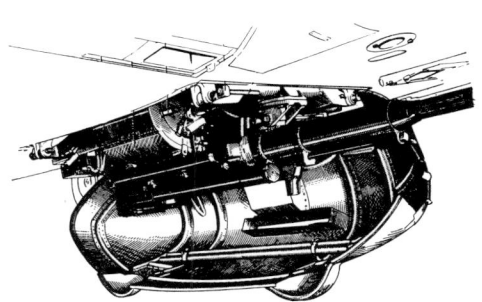

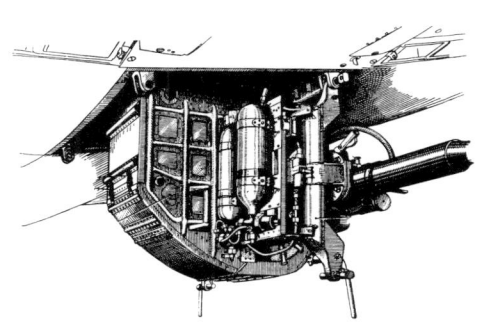

Above top: Left hand view of MK 103 Rüstsatz.
Above centre: MK 103 with fairing hinged open.
Above lower: Lowered MK 103 showing ammunition box fitted and carrier frame.

The MK 103 was introduced into service with the Hs 129 Staffeln in July 1943 - just in time for the major German offensive at Kursk.

An Hs 129 with stained blast troughs and the personal name "Mulle" applied to the nose. Such personal markings were rarely seen on the Hs 129.

targets shown to him. Meyer then took over the command of his anti-tank *Staffeln*: "I had only ever seen such a mass of enemy soldiers once before, and that was at the beginning of the Russian campaign in 1941. Wave after wave emerged from the woods tugging gun mountings, mortars, anti-tank and anti-aircraft guns by hand along behind them. It was a weird sight to see these masses marching straight to the west as obstinately as mules, without taking any fighting action or any defence against our aircraft, as if the Soviet brigadier commanding them was intent on turning the wheel of military history back to pre-First World War times. Man behind man, block beside block, they came over a frontal area some 8 to 10 kilometres (5 to 6 miles) wide."

"Then followed the tanks. Totally obsolete light tanks rolled out of the woods behind the infantry. Medium and heavy tanks followed, using the roads from the villages situated between the woods. After our *Schlachtgruppe Kommandeur* had personally satisfied himself of the enemy's incredible behaviour, the Fw 190s hurtled down from above to drop their SD2 bomb containers into the masses, each direct hit knocking down a whole block of infantry.[1] After the first attack, we viewed what happened next with amazement. Despite the havoc wrought by the Fw 190s' bombs, those men who were not killed or wounded struggled to their feet and hurried to join those blocks which were still intact, only to become the unhappy victims of the next bomb hit. Again more killed and seriously wounded men, but the remainder recovered and tried to join other blocks which spewed out of the woods as if there was no end to them. Such a sight was enough to give even the most hardened soldier the creeps. On they marched, without ever quickening or slowing their pace. It was like watching a sinister steam-roller moving forwards. Even when the first ground-attack aircraft went home and the next *Staffel* dropped its bombs into the masses, they still did not stop their march but moved on without taking defensive action or seeking any cover. Only when the Fw 190s started mowing down their first ranks with cannon and machine-gun fire and bombs began to fall on the outskirts of the woods to the west did this steam-roller slowly grind to a halt. Utter confusion now reigned on the battlefield as the ground-attack

Three Hs 129s set out from Mikoyanovka on a sortie somewhere over the Belgorod sector. In the foreground is the Kursk-Orel railway line.

aircraft continued to strafe the enemy without respite."

"Then, hardly discernibly, the enemy began to retreat. At first it was only a slight hesitation, but gradually there was a marked increase in the speed of withdrawal until, suddenly, the withdrawal turned into an avalanche. One block carried another along with it until all the soldiers ran back and the whole mass of frightened men stampeded into the woods."

Now Meyer's anti-tank aircraft systematically started their slaughter, as *Oblt.* Georg Dornemann recalled: "When we arrived in the area we saw marching infantry well concealed in the woods. Behind them we discovered tanks rolling forward, but it was impossible for us to establish the exact number. As they came out of the woods we counted ten, twenty, thirty and then gave up as more and more appeared - certainly in the strength of an armoured brigade. We were fully aware that the tanks presented a deadly menace to the rear flank of our *Panzerkorps*; we had to go in without delay and stop them."

"My *Staffel*, together with other *Staffeln*, attacked in relays and the enemy suffered heavy losses. Our pilots could see the panic-stricken response of the Russian tank crews and the retreating armour presented splendid targets for us. Each pilot made his run-in at low level and fired his armour-piercing shell at just the right instant, just like on a firing range. When we went in for the kill, a steady approach and a well aimed shot were vital to knock out a tank - I would say that it was a real art."

"When the tanks were knocked out, they belched fire and smoke. Others did not get clear of those which had been knocked out and collided with them. Later, interrogated prisoners confirmed just how successful our attacks had been and that they had been forced to withdraw."

Not a single Russian tank succeeded in attacking the German flank. After three hours of dreadful work the Henschels and Focke-Wulfs flew away, leaving behind them a battlefield littered with the dead and strewn with the gutted remains of knocked-out tanks from which plumes of smoke spiralled high into the air. As dusk fell, the darkening sky was lit with an occasional flash as flames reached a petrol tank or ammunition store.

That evening, after the last of the machines had returned to its airfield, the Staff of the *Panzerkorps* asked for a reconnaissance mission to be carried out early next morning. According to Meyer, the *Panzerkorps* reported that they had heard a great deal of unexplained battle noise during the afternoon and were most surprised when they were told that a Russian attack had already been stopped and beaten back without a single German soldier having to take part. A patrol by a few aircraft was flown over the

Seen here is W.Nr.141859 coded "D". Although a fairing was provided for the MK 101, in favourable conditions, quicker arming turn-round times could be achieved if the aircraft flew without it.

Red "H" of 4.(Pz)/Sch.G 1, believed to be the aircraft of Lt. Lothar Kallerhoff, taxies out.

battlefield next morning, but they reported that the area was completely quiet. Just how successful the Henschel *Staffeln* had been on 8 July is confirmed by *Luftflotte* 4's war diary which states that on that day:

"The Panzerjäger were especially successful. Eighty tanks were completely destroyed and a further number damaged".

Meanwhile, in the Orel sector to the north, Ninth Army had gained a mere 10 km (6 miles) at a cost of 25,000 killed and 200 tanks and 200 aircraft lost. The unimaginably strong and deep Soviet defences proved to be impenetrable and by 10 July the whole of the German strike force in the north, including reserves, had been committed but without any further gains. The German armoured spearheads, blunted by the Russian defences, ground to a halt. Then, on 13 July, the

Soviet infantry rode into battle on the backs of tanks; here the infantry have dismounted to make a combined attack.

Russians launched a counter-attack against Orel from the north and almost at once achieved a deep penetration. This compelled the *Luftwaffe* to weaken its concentration on the southern flank by the transfer of aircraft to the threatened area and 4. and 8./Sch.G 1, 4./Sch.G 2 and Pz.Jä.St./JG 51 were ordered to transfer immediately to Orel West in order to engage the enemy tanks which had broken through. Here the anti-tank *Staffeln* came under the control of the 1. *Fliegerdivision*, part of the newly-established *Luftflotte* 6 which was responsible for operations on the central sector of the front between Smolensk and Orel.

In view of the serious situation, *Luftflotte* 6 "... chased everything that had wings into the air", but anti-tank operations along this sector of the front proved difficult, extremely wasteful and met with little success. Georg Dornemann, the *Staffelkapitän* of 4./Sch.G 1, remembered this as a period of particularly heavy losses and *Luftwaffe* records confirm the loss or serious damage of up to four Hs 129s a day during this period. In total, the Hs 129 anti-tank *Staffeln* lost some 30% of valuable aircraft and pilots to air and ground defences in the 11 days between 14 and 25 July without having the opportunity to carry out the tasks for which they had been intended and specially trained. It seems the battle-tried and tested policies were ignored and, with a complete disregard for the specialised role of the *Panzerjäger Staffeln* which operated best in areas of weak enemy air activity against tanks which had penetrated the front lines and were moving across open ground, the Hs 129s were ordered into the air on fruitless attacks against near-invisible tanks sheltering in forested areas or to carry out virtual suicidal missions of reconnaissance and orientation in an area where enemy aircraft were becoming more and more dangerous.

Normally, targets such as tank assembly areas behind enemy lines were avoided by anti-tank aircraft because of the high losses which would result from the established anti-aircraft defences. Such attacks were better carried out by bomber formations which carried a great number of hollow-charge armour-piercing bombs best dropped from a safer altitude, though when the 4./Sch.G 1 was ordered to attack just such a target, it made a surprise early-morning, low-level, cannon attack which, contrary to expectations, resulted in a marked success. Georg Dornemann, who led this attack flying "Red L+"

recalled that: "Shortly after crossing the front line, we discovered in the first rays of the sun the parked tanks with their crews still asleep near them. After my first armour-piercing rounds struck the tanks and the first of them had been turned into a blazing wreck, the tank crews sprang to life. But I and each of my pilots quickly fired off the rest of our ammunition and were soon heading back to our airfield, flying now in brighter sunlight and already bracketed by some light flak.

"In this attack, our cannon fire proved devastating. Fifty or more Russian tanks littered the ground, burnt out or incapacitated. My own score was three. None of our aircraft was lost in this attack, though my own aircraft was slightly damaged by small arms fire in the port wing immediately outboard of the engine nacelle."

The summer of 1943 marked a turning point as far as the growth of Soviet military power was concerned. On the ground, Soviet armour was changing. The T-34 had been redesigned and, as the T-34/85, was being introduced with an 85 mm gun which could fire shells capable of penetrating German armour at all normal ranges. The SU-152 self-propelled gun also appeared while, in the air, the Soviet Air Force was equipped with Yak-1, Yak-9, LaGG-3 and MiG-3 fighters as well as the excellent Ilyushin Il-2 close support aircraft. Russian aggressiveness in the air also increased; hitherto, Russian fighters had presented no great threat to German anti-tank aircraft. Interceptions had been rare and enemy fighter pilots had shown neither great skill nor determination, but now the situation was to change as enemy fighters became both more numerous and their pilots more combative. Using lone-wolf tactics the Russians now seemed to concentrate on making surprise attacks on vulnerable anti-tank aircraft, focusing their efforts almost exclusively on the wingmen and picking them out of the formation. Henschel pilots who saw Russian fighters in action at this time identified most of them as Yak-9s with conspicuous diamond markings applied to their fuselage sides. Since they had never known Russian pilots to be so aggressive up to this time, the German pilots strongly suspected that the fighters were from the French-manned "Normandie" squadron.

Naturally, the Russians were, by this time, aware of the strengths and weaknesses of the Hs 129, having had ample opportunity to examine a number of them, most of which had crash-landed in their territory. In addition, several examples had been captured intact after being abandoned by the retreating Germans. Additional information had been obtained from prisoner-of-war interrogations and captured German documents, so that all known variants and armament combinations had been accurately identified. Eventually, this information was published in a guide for Russian fighter-pilots which contained notes on the Hs 129's sensitive places. In particular, attention was drawn to such weak spots as the pilot's head and the fuel and oil tanks which were protected, but not entirely, by armour plate, and the engines which were vulnerable to attack from above, from below and from the front. It was noted that the engine nacelles also housed the starter fuel tanks and, as the Germans themselves knew, hits in the engine nacelles and wings usually caused fire which resulted in the loss of the whole aircraft.

Oblt. Georg Dornemann returns from a sortie during the Kursk fighting, July 1943.

A curious problem arose at around this time which, for a while, had the Germans baffled. A large number of Russian tanks had succeeded in penetrating the front line at a relatively weakly defended point and, operating singly or in pairs deep in the German rear area, repeatedly interrupted rail traffic on the Bryansk-Karachev-Orel railway. Having penetrated the front, the Russians had clearly succeeded in establishing a hidden base from which they made their raids, but its exact location remained a mystery for some time. A number of Hs 129s were detached from the front and besides attacking the tanks wherever they were reported also tried to locate their hiding place by following their tracks back to where they originated. Such attempts were frustrated, however, by the fact that all tank tracks vanished within a radius of some 5 km (3 miles) from wherever the tanks were based and their exact location was later only discovered by accident.

An interesting photograph showing a Luftwaffe Hs 129 B-2, coded Red "B", during engine maintenance (note missing cowling) and carrying an MK 101 cannon under the fuselage. Although the aircraft appears to have been painted in a desert scheme, this photograph is believed to have been taken on the Eastern front, a fact perhaps confirmed by the exhausts - clearly visible on either side of the nose - for the windscreen and cockpit heater.

To the east of the railway line were some large woods, where a great number of nocturnal flights by Soviet U2 aircraft suggested that there were numerous partisan groups operating in the area. Indeed, one anti-tank *Staffel* operating from a meadow along the banks of the Desna river to the south of Bryansk had come under such heavy and accurate mortar fire from the partisan-held woods along the river's eastern bank that it was forced to establish another landing field elsewhere. Eventually it was confirmed that these partisans were forcing the local population either to obliterate the tanks' tracks or make heavy wooden frames which the tanks dragged along the ground to eliminate all traces of their movements.

On 19 July, a *Schwarm* of Hs 129s from 4./Sch.G 2 was alerted that five T-34s had again appeared at a point on the railway line where they had stopped a goods train and their crews were busy destroying the tracks with demolition charges. The *Schwarm* immediately engaged the tanks and knocked them out but suffered a major loss in the process. *Major* Matuschek, the *Staffelkapitän*, had expended almost all his ammunition on a tank without causing any apparent damage. In a final and determined assault which he pressed home to point-blank range, he fired off his remaining ammunition but misjudged the moment he should have pulled up and flew full tilt into his intended victim. As his comrades watched in horror, both aircraft and tank disappeared in a single massive explosion.

At the same time as *Major* Matuschek made his attack, *Hptm.* Bruno Meyer was out on a lone reconnaissance flight to the north of Orel. Local attacks and counter-attacks had resulted in a very confused situation and Meyer was under orders to establish and report the exact position of the front. While so pre-occupied, his machine was bounced and set on fire by a Yak-9. Meyer quickly dived his burning aircraft over his own front lines and crash-landed on the edge of a marsh. To his astonishment, Meyer discovered that he had come down in front of a force of some 80 Soviet tanks of all types which had broken through the front line unobserved into German-held territory. They had been so skilfully camouflaged with straw that from the air they were indistinguishable from ordinary haystacks. Fortunately, the tank crews were nowhere to be seen, but purely by accident, Meyer had discovered the hiding place of the tanks which had recently been causing so much damage along the Bryansk-Karachev-Orel railway line!

Throwing off his harness and clambering out of his burning aircraft, Meyer was further surprised to discover

Hptm. Georg Dörffel (centre) was awarded the Knights Cross on 21.8.1941 and the Oak Leaves on 14.4.1942. From early 1943, Dörffel commanded the Fw 190 equipped I./Sch.G 1 which played an important part in "Zitadelle" and shared in the successes of Hptm. Bruno Meyer's Hs 129 Staffeln.

that, as water from the marsh seeped into his machine, the flames were extinguished. Cautiously returning to his aircraft, he was able to radio his adjutant, *Lt.* Weber, and inform him of his discovery. The radio conversation was also picked up by *Major* Georg Dörffel of I./Sch.G 1, who happened to be in the area with a number of Fw 190 fighter-bombers, each loaded with 250 kg high-explosive bombs which had been intended for a different target. Now Dörffel changed course and headed for Meyer's position.

Meanwhile, Meyer made his way to the edge of the marsh where he was picked up by an armoured car and taken to the nearest village. According to Meyer's subsequent report, the sector commander in the village at first refused to believe that an unmanned force of tanks had been discovered on his doorstep and preferred to believe instead that Meyer was still suffering from shock and confusion as a result of his crash-landing. But as they were talking, *Major* Dörffel's Focke-Wulfs appeared in the distance and the explosions and coils of oily black smoke finally convinced the sector commander that what Meyer had seen were no ordinary haystacks after all. Between the Fw 190's attacks, Meyer suggested that the remaining tanks could be captured, but still the commander was reluctant to take any action as control of his rear area was beyond his jurisdiction. As a result, Hs 129 and Fw 190 aircraft had to spend two whole days laboriously destroying the tanks from the air.

By 20 July, the Germans were in full retreat and by the 23rd had been pushed back beyond the start lines they had held prior to the launching of *"Zitadelle"*. But the Russians, now determined to fully exploit their initiative, kept up the pressure and to the end of the year launched a series of blows along the whole length of the front from Smolensk to Rostov. The Battle of Kursk had been a devastating defeat for the Germans. Not only had their reserves of men and armour been squandered, but they were now off balance and open to Russian counter-attack. By mid August, combat losses and wear and tear had reduced the 68 Hs 129 B-2s which had been available before *"Zitadelle"* to 36, of which a mere 27 remained operational.

In gathering its forces at Orel and in the Kharkov-Belgorod area for *"Zitadelle"*, the *Luftwaffe* had seriously weakened its forces on the Lower Donets front and it was here that the Russians, after their joint counter-attacks at Orel and Belgorod, mounted a secondary offensive. The available *Luftwaffe* units were now forced to disperse over the three main areas of Orel, Belgorod and Stalino, and with the strategic initiative now in the hands of the Russians, the *Luftwaffe* was compelled to adopt a makeshift policy of switching its units and its main effort from one sector of the front to another as Russian pressure demanded.

By late August, the Russian advance in I.

A Schwarm of Hs 129s crosses the perimeter of an airfield in Russia.

Fliegerkorps' area of operations had moved into the heavily wooded areas in the northern region of *Luftflotte* 6's sector. Here, the enemy was able to find excellent cover in the forests and the only possibility was to halt the movement of armoured forces on the few roads and paths which cut through the area, but this was not the best of hunting grounds and tank-busting with cannon aircraft proved so difficult that the Hs 129 *Staffeln* in the Bryansk area were transferred to Konotop. No sooner had the Henschels arrived than the airfield was bombed by a tight formation of 30 Russian-flown Bostons. In the summer of 1943, the Soviet Air Force had made great strides in improving its reconnaissance capabilities. *Luftwaffe* bases were kept under constant surveillance and intermittent intruder raids were mounted against forward *Luftwaffe* airfields. Although it is by no means certain, there is every likelihood that transfer of the Hs 129 *Staffeln* to

Konotop had been observed by Russian aerial reconnaissance and that this was an attempt by the Soviet Air Force to destroy the German anti-tank aircraft on the ground. In the event, this particular attack was unsuccessful; casualties and damage to buildings were insignificant and none of the anti-tank or close-support aircraft on the airfield damaged, let alone destroyed. As the runway had also escaped damage, the Henschels were able to operate successfully against a Russian tank offensive launched from Orel. Despite their low numbers and the fact that the German troops were without friendly armoured support, the Hs 129s succeeded in bringing the Russian advance in the Konotop area to a temporary halt.

After moving on to Poltava, where they returned to the control of VIII. *Fliegerkorps*, Meyer's existing four *Staffeln* were strengthened by the arrival of *Oblt.* Oswald's 8./Sch.G 2. After leaving the Mediterranean, 8./Sch.G 2 had been based at Deblin-Irena for re-equipment before being transferred to join all other Hs 129 *Staffeln* on the Eastern Front. The deployment of the anti-tank *Staffeln* to heavily contested sectors of the front was retained temporarily as army units were making increasingly heavy demands on the services of the *Luftwaffe's Panzerjäger* and the ever-increasing number of Soviet tanks presented a threat on all front sectors. All five units under Meyer's command were heavily committed in the bitter defensive fighting which now took place.

As already mentioned, the Russians maintained the momentum of their advance by launching a general offensive on the whole central and southern front. Red Army groups continued to drive westward and despite stubborn resistance, pushed the Germans out of the key towns they had held for more than a year and a half. During August and September, Orel, Belgorod, Taganrog, Stalino, Mariupol, Bryansk and Poltava were all recaptured. Scorching the earth in their wake, the Germans fell back to a line on the great bend of the Dnieper from Gomel down to the Sea of Azov. These Russian advances forced the *Führer der Panzerjäger* to withdraw the Hs 129 support airfield from Zaporozhe (where 8.(Pz)/Sch.G 1, 8.(Pz)/Sch.G 2 and Pz.Jä./JG 51 were then based), to Kirovograd and his supply base from Kirovograd to Uman.

Characteristically, this redeployment as illustrated in the accompanying table, was only temporary, for the fluid situation on the southern front demanded the constant transfer of various *Staffeln* from one sector to another. Aptly regarded as the *Luftwaffe's* "Fire Brigade", the *Panzerjäger Staffeln* were rushed from one "hot-spot" to another and it was inevitable that a short time later, Meyer was required to move his Staff and 8.(Pz)/Sch.G 2 to join 4.(Pz)/Sch.G 2 at Krivoi-Rog. There they were to cover the withdrawal of the German Sixth Army which was then engaged in bitter defensive

The copious and highly mobile Soviet flak units were both feared and highly respected by the German Panzerjäger. This particular battery operated on the southern sector of the Eastern front in mid-1943 and had accounted for five German aircraft shot down at the time of being photographed.

On 28 July 1943, Fw. Hinz of 4.(Pz)/Sch.G 1 was shot down by Russian flak and killed. Here, the remains of his Hs 129 B-2, W.Nr.140519, lies at the top of a Russian scrap heap.

battles against strong armoured forces as it retreated from the Dnepropetrovsk area. Sorties were flown to ward off the enemy's tank attacks at the northern exits of Krivoi-Rog and on the roads to the north, north-east and north-west and within two weeks the FüPZ *Stab* and the two *Staffeln* had claimed over 130 Soviet tanks knocked out, of which Sixth Army was able to confirm more than 100.

Nevertheless, by the end of September the Russians had elsewhere captured the strategic rail and communications centre of Smolensk, keystone of German defences on the central front, and further south had pushed to the Dnieper River on a broad 130 kilometre (80 mile) front from Kremenchug to Dnepropetrovsk. Still further south, the Red Army had pushed Kleist's 14 divisions out of the last German bridgehead in the Kuban and had occupied parts of the Crimea.

Despite their success in slowing down the Russian advance, Hs 129 losses were severe. The 4.(Pz)/Sch.G 1 lost an Hs 129 B-2 when it was destroyed on the ground at Zaporozhe-East during a Russian air attack on 5 September and five more were lost to flak and ground fire over the following month as the *Staffel* pulled back through the Central Ukraine. The 8.(Pz)/Sch.G 1 also lost five aircraft during August and September, of which four are known to have been shot down by flak. In the same period 4.(Pz)/Sch.G 2 lost eight aircraft, of which two were deliberately destroyed when the Germans evacuated Varvarovka airfield, two were lost due to technical trouble and four were shot down. Pilot losses amounted to three killed in action and one injured. In 8.(Pz)/Sch.G 2, flak shot down five Hs 129s, two pilots being killed in action and two posted missing. So far as is known, the only Hs 129 B-2 lost by Pz.Jä.St./JG 51 occurred on 17 September when a machine was shot down by an enemy fighter north-west of Pologi.

To assist in the defence of the front line between Kharkov and Rostov, Bruno Meyer had moved his *Staffeln* to various airfields along the southern sector of the front, particularly to Dnepropetrovsk, Stalino and Zaporozhe East, but the Russians were winning one victory after

DEPLOYMENT OF HS 129 STAFFELN, RUSSIA, SEPTEMBER 1943

4.(Pz)/Sch.G 1	Askania-Nova
4.(Pz)/Sch.G 2	Krivoi-Rog
8.(Pz)/Sch.G 2 & Pz.Jä./JG 51	Kirovograd
8.(Pz)/Sch.G 1	Kiev
Führer der Panzerjäger	Kirovograd

Total: 53 aircraft (35 operational)

another, and day after day the Germans were forced to retreat further westwards as the mass of Soviet armour erupted from the east. On the morning of 10 October, the Russians mounted their final attack against Zaporozhe in the area controlled by *Luftflotte* 4, opening their offensive with a massive artillery barrage, the intensity of which had never before been equalled. This was followed by an attack against German positions by an entire Russian Army Group and although the Germans counter-attacked and pushed the Russians back to their jumping-off positions, on 13 October the Soviets succeeded in making a huge penetration of the German defences. The following day they accomplished another deep tank penetration and during the night of 14-15 October, Soviet advance detachments probed their way into the blazing town. But although Zaporozhe was no spectacular victory for the Russians and there were no huge German losses to be announced, it was one of the most important Soviet victories on the Dnieper in 1943, for it brought about a fundamental change in the situation in the South Ukraine. Now the Russians could reach out for the lower Dnieper, its estuary and the approach to the Crimea. The Soviet High Command did not hesitate to open its attack.

On 6 October, four days before the Russian attack on the airfield at Zaporozhe, 4.(Pz)/Sch.G 1 and Pz.Jä.St./JG 51 were transferred to Orsha for operations in support of Army Group Centre under *Luftflotte* 6.

1 THE CARNAGE MUST HAVE BEEN APPALLING. WHEN RELEASED, THE CONTENTS OF THE AB CONTAINERS COVERED AN AREA 20-30 METRES WIDE (21-32 YDS) X 30-60 METRES LONG (21-65 YDS).

Soviet air power increased significantly during and after "Zitadelle". Airfields often came under attack, especially by Il-2s which were "... an ever present plague". Losses of aircraft and men were usually only slight however, though German morale was impaired. Occasionally, more material damage was caused. Here, bomb blast has flattened a Bf 109 and damaged an Hs 129 though significantly, the Henschel's armoured cockpit has remained intact.

Fighting Retreat

The Withdrawal through the Ukraine   October 1943 – January 1944

12

The autumn of 1943 once more brought low cloud and fog to the battlefields. If the sun appeared at all, it shone only palely and fitfully between heavy rainstorms which fell from a dismal sky and turned the ground into thick mud. At night, the mud froze over and made movement easier, but in this unpredictable weather, the Russian advance was largely confined to colder periods when light snow and frost permitted cross-country movement.

Following the appointment of *Oberstleutnant Dr.jur.* Ernst Kupfer as *General der Schlachtflieger*, the Hs 129 *Staffeln* were amalgamated and reorganised to form the IV.(Pz) *Gruppe* of a new *Schlachtgeschwader*, SG 9. But on 20 October, 11.(Pz)/SG 9, previously 8.(Pz)/Sch.G 1, was withdrawn from front-line service and transferred to Udetfeld in Germany where, as the trials unit *Erprobungskommando* 26, it carried out tests with a variety of anti-tank weapons experimentally installed in Hs 129, Fw 190 and other aircraft. The remaining *Staffeln* did their utmost to try and resist the Soviet tide in the East but their successes were on too small a scale to affect the overall situation.

Aircraft losses arising from the autumn battles in the Ukraine were almost as high as at Kursk three months earlier. The 14.(Pz)/SG 9 experienced a run of particularly bad luck towards the end of October. On 26th of that month, this unit lost its *Staffelführer*, *Lt.* Hans Jentsch, when his aircraft, W.Nr. 141299, received a direct flak hit and he was seen to crash in flames on the north-west exit of Wesseloye. On 30 October, *Uffz.* Rudolf Petzold was shot down in flames by Russian flak 5 km (3 miles) north of Askania-Nova, and on 1 November, *Lt.* Jentsch's replacement was lost when *Staffelführer Oblt.* Friedrich Wilhelm Quilitsch's Hs 129B-2, W.Nr. 141226, was seen to dive into the ground in flames during an attack against tanks 5 km (3 miles) east of Malaya-Mayachka. *Lt.* Wilhelm Abt took his place as the *Staffel*'s third *Staffelführer* in just nine days, but was himself shot down on 15 November in the Alexandria-Melitopol area. He was replaced by *Lt.* Ruffer who acted as *Staffelführer* until *Oblt.* Hans-Hermann Steinkamp arrived as *Staffelkapitän*.

With the struggle for the Dnieper Line already well advanced, the Red Army increased its pressure and its armoured forces continued to drive to the north and south of Nikopol. In the

Engine start on the Hs 129 of Lt. Lothar Kallerhoff of 10.(Pz)/SG 9. The large intake on the side of the nose and the exhaust trail created by the petrol burning cockpit and windscreen heater may be clearly seen.

Heavy rainfall in the autumn of 1943 turned the ground into thick mud. W.Nr.141278 is seen here on a rain soaked airfield.

A rare photograph of W.Nr.141278 and a Rumanian Hs 129 on the same airfield.

north, the Soviet objectives were Kirovograd and Krivoi-Rog, while in the south the Russians pushed from Melitopol towards Kherson. Nearly 30 Hs 129s were lost or damaged during operations in October 1943, the majority due to enemy ground defences, although Soviet fighter pilots also made some claims. On 23 October, the radio command station of Major-General Savistkiy's 3rd IAK informed a flight of four Yak-9Ts patrolling the battlefield in the Melitopol area, that a formation of Hs 129s had been observed over Danilo-Ivanovka. The Russian flight - part of the 812 IAP, was under the command of I.V. Fiodorov, a Soviet ace who would finish the war with 36 confirmed air-to-air kills plus 9 destroyed on the ground - immediately set course to intercept the German aircraft.

Fiodorov had not encountered the Hs 129 before, and although he knew the type had no rear gunner, he resolved to approach cautiously as the German machine was also known to be well-armoured and manouevrable. When Fiodorov first saw the Henschels, there were three of them flying without fighter cover at 100-150 m (328-492 ft). As the four Yaks dived down to attack, Fiodorov took aim at one of the Henschels, opened fire and shot it down. Pulling out, Fiodorov noticed another eight Hs 129s about to attack some Russian trenches. Attacking head-on, the Yaks forced the Henschel pilots to break formation and jettison their bombs. Lt. Shiskin and Lt. Maksimov each claimed a Henschel shot down, but Fiodorov was unlucky; he had already exhausted all his cannon ammunition and was low on fuel, so in his third attack with machine-guns only, he merely succeeded in damaging his prey. In another action by the 812 IAP in the same area on 25 October, a group of Yak-9Ts met two Hs 129s 3 km (1.8 miles) west of Akimovka. In the dogfight which followed, Lt. Maksimienko claimed one of the Henschels shot down.

At this time, the command post of the *Führer der Panzerjäger* - ostensibly the same command as *Kommandeur* of IV.(Pz)/SG 9 - moved to Askania Nova airfield. Since Bruno Meyer was absent, the command was now in the hands of *Hptm.* Franz Oswald. During the morning of 28 October, and as a result of the airfield being threatened by progressively stronger Russian forces, Oswald radioed I. *Fliegerkorps* that

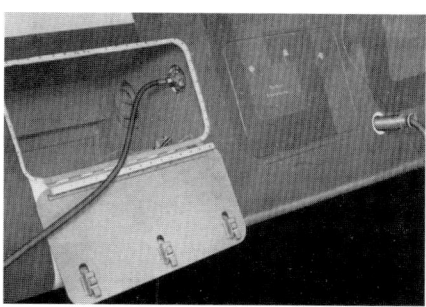
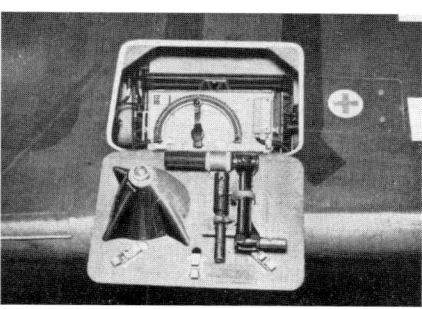

Top: A detail showing the storage and access compartment to the compressed air supply on the starboard side of the Hs 129 fuselage. Note also the external cable for electrical supply.
Above: Hatch showing access to the radio compartment. Note the starting handle with extension together with the fuselage end-cone attached to the door panel. The cone was stored here when the Hs 129 was converted for air-towing the DFS 230. The mechanic in the bottom photograph has just opened the hatch.

Celebration for Ofw. Holtermann, safely returned following a sortie in W.Nr. 140834. From right to left: Fw. Axel, Uffz. Michel, Hauptfeldwebel Scholl, Ogfr. Ströhlhein, Lt. Kallerhoff and Ofw. Holtermann.

A formation of Yak-9 Ds of the Red Air Force.

potential dive-bomber targets comprising enemy infantry, artillery, cavalry and horse-drawn vehicles, had been observed only some 10-20 km (6-12 miles) from the airfield. Some time later, a patrolling *Schwarm* of Hs 129s spotted ammunition tractors and dug-in infantry. By 11:30, 26 Hs 129 sorties had been flown against these forces and as the day progressed, more Soviet infantry, cavalry, anti-tank capability and artillery were reported near Shevtchenko where an armoured spearhead was attacked by two *Schwärme* of Hs 129s. At 14:50, some of Oswald's aircraft, ignoring the presence of strong formations of Soviet fighters and ground-attack aircraft, attacked eleven enemy tanks advancing north-east of Nishnye Sserogosy, despite being fired on at one point by light flak.

The next morning, lacking firm orders from the *Fliegerkorps* and without any information regarding the front line, Oswald decided to mount sorties at his own discretion. An early-morning Hs 129 reconnaissance flight reported Soviet infantry, cavalry and flak concentrations in Malaya Blagovetshenka but aircraft sent out to attack them were forced to return on account of "technical reasons". Nevertheless, the enemy was kept under continual observation and by early afternoon further reports by Hs 129s and Fw 190s revealed an alarming build-up of Soviet forces moving westwards - tanks with mounted infantry, anti-tank guns, horse-drawn artillery and no fewer than 150 lorries.

As the Russians drove ever closer to the airfield, so the flight durations of the attacking German aircraft diminished and with the situation worsening by the hour, it became clear that the airfield would have to be evacuated. In the late afternoon of 29 October, Oswald signalled I. *Fliegerkorps* requesting the services of 13 Ju 52 transports to assist in the transfer out of the Fw 190 ground-attack *Gruppe* based at Askania Nova. Meanwhile, with little information to hand on the local Army situation, the *Luftwaffe* set about organising its own defence of the area.

The evacuation of the airfield started as soon as the first Junkers transports touched down. Equipment was bundled aboard, the ground personnel piled in after it and the first transports took off again, heading for the safer airstrip at Chaplinka. An Me 108 which was supposed to fly out refused to start. Its wings were taken off and strapped to the fuselage so that the machine could be hooked up to a car. It was towed across the steppe to Chaplinka without damage. As the last of the Hs 129s took off, they were protected by others which had flown up from Kherson to cover their withdrawal. Apart from the loss of a little unimportant equipment, not a single man, aircraft or vehicle was left behind and although Askania-Nova airfield was evacuated in perfect order its loss was yet another important setback.

A snow camouflaged Hs 129 B-2 showing that sometimes the spinners and propeller blades were also daubed with white paint.

13

"What should a Tank Destroyer look like?"

A Diversion of Doctrine

On 19 August 1943, *Generaloberst* Hans Jeschonneck, the Chief of the *Luftwaffe* General Staff was found dead. Much criticised by Göring and Hitler, especially after the failure of the Kursk offensive and as a result of the apparent inability of the *Luftwaffe* to mount an effective resistance against the Allied strategic air offensive which was pounding the Reich's cities and production centres, Jeschonneck felt that he was being held solely responsible for the *Luftwaffe's* shortcomings. He subsequently committed suicide. He was succeeded by *Generaloberst* Günther Korten, one of whose first reforms was, in October 1943, to combine the two sub-inspectorates for Stukas and ground-attack units into the single post of an independent *Waffengeneral der Nahkampfflieger*, or General of Close Support Forces, whose task was to co-ordinate all ground-attack units, including the *Stukas*, and to establish the prerequisites for maximum efficiency and readiness for action. This was to be achieved through the supervision, planning and control of progressive technical development in aircraft, weapons and equipment and the collection and analysis of all front-line experience gathered by the ground-attack pilots, upon which the issue and implementation of future operational guidelines and training was to be based.

The first *General der Nahkampfflieger* - the title was soon changed to *General der Schlachtflieger* - was *Oberstleutnant Dr.jur.* Ernst Kupfer, a former Heidelberg law graduate and a greatly respected and experienced Stuka pilot who, from February to September 1943 had successfully led the famous *"Immelmann"* dive-bomber unit, *Stukageschwader* 2. Although once an ardent supporter of the Ju 87, Kupfer was a pragmatist and recognised that by September 1943 it had become obsolete. On 10 September, Kupfer was called from his large headquarters in the former Olympic games restaurant on Rangsdorf Lake to the RLM and, at a conference chaired by Milch, gave an address on the subject of his new command in which he covered in detail the various requirements of the units for which he was now responsible.

Kupfer first explained that the units under his command were the *Stuka* (dive bomber) units, the *Schlachtflieger* (ground-attack units), the *Jabos* (fighter-bombers - with the exception of the long-range fighter-bombers operating as *Schnellkampfverbände*), the *Störkampfstaffeln* (night harassing units) and all *Panzerjäger* (anti-tank units). In a lengthy and detailed account of the *Stuka* and its tactics, Kupfer first called for the immediate conversion of the Ju 87 units to the Fw 190, after which he addressed the subject of anti-tank operations which he recognised as being quite distinct from other types of ground-attack aviation.

It was Kupfer's belief that due to the vast length of the front, it was quite impossible to expect the Army always to have its anti-tank artillery in just the right place to ward off a tank attack. Where sections of the front could only be lightly defended, the enemy would always attempt a breakthrough and once that happened, it was unrealistic to expect ground troops lacking anti-tank weapons to possess the combat spirit and morale necessary to

Obstlt. Dr. Ernst Kupfer, the Luftwaffe's first General der Schlachtflieger.

The Ju 87 G-2 armed with two 37 mm Flak 18 cannon and special ammunition achieved great success against enemy tanks and armoured vehicles but due to the weight and unfavourable aerodynamic effect of these weapons, the aircraft was very slow and could only be operated together with strong fighter escort.

let the tanks roll over them and then jump up and fight the enemy infantry. Facing a tank without the slightest chance of destroying it was a terrifying proposition and since a tank attack could not be stopped by ground troops, enemy armour would always succeed in penetrating the area behind the lines where their mere presence would cause a state of panic. To fully exploit this panic, Russian tank crews appear to have been ordered to break through with a full load of fuel and drive as far as possible. Sometimes, since there was an area immediately behind the front where there were no German troops, they could travel great distances until they reached a small town or village far behind the lines. Here would be the German second-line support troops; baker's columns, supply units, transport detachments and clerical staff, all of whom would be extremely alarmed if enemy armour was reported to be roaming about the area.

Even a small number of enemy tanks could have a devastating effect on the morale of second-line troops and frequently these breakthroughs consisted not of a hundred or so tanks but perhaps five or ten, followed by a few lorries and an anti-tank gun. These would drive as far as they could and then, when their fuel ran out, the tank detachment would conceal itself inside local buildings. Although sometimes scattered over a wide area, the tanks could cause panic completely disproportionate to the numbers involved. Sometimes, also, far larger penetrations could be experienced where there was a very real danger of sections of the front collapsing, but in either case the tanks could be quickly destroyed provided suitable aircraft were available. It was therefore crucial that anti-tank work from the air was seen as an absolute necessity and that the existing capacity should be expanded and improved. Kupfer explained that:

"Today, all the enemy's attacks are tank or tank-supported attacks, and since the Army's anti-tank forces will never be on the spot when they are needed, it falls to the Air Force to ward them off. What we require for the next winter is anything in aircraft that we can muster, whatever the type, and a determined effort should be made to provide the anti-tank aircraft with all the necessary equipment."

"What should a tank-destroyer look like? First of all it must be able to operate against tanks which have already broken through. I mention this event in order to stress the importance of our being able to fight from the air any tanks prowling around behind our lines."

"Anti-tank aircraft must operate at very low level. The types we have now must fly so low that they actually skim the tanks. An anti-tank aircraft must attack from a height of 500 metres (1,640 ft). It has to head straight for the tank without being allowed to take any evasive action and shoot at the target from a distance of 200 down to 100 metres (650 - 330 ft). As a result, after pulling up after his run-in the pilot must fly directly over the tank. This results in another requirement: we must have an anti-tank aircraft which can open fire further away from the target. To a limited extent, this need was filled by fitting the Ju 87 with 3.7 cm cannon but we must also have an anti-tank aircraft

which is provided with adequate armour. Although this may make it slow, it must fly in on the deck with ground-attack aircraft flying with it in order to suppress the enemy's anti-aircraft fire and ward off preying fighters so that the anti-tank pilot can fully concentrate on the target during his run-up."

"We must make a supreme effort in the way of aircraft and equipment for the coming winter. This will be decisive in holding the Eastern Front. Let me insist on the urgency of my demands. We must be able to destroy these tanks and strafe the fuel lorries to set them on fire."

"Of the aircraft fitted with anti-tank weapons, the Ju 88 fitted with a 75 mm cannon seems to be the best solution. The only thing which would make this type unsuitable would be the waste of flying personnel. An anti-tank aircraft does not require three men, one is perfectly adequate. However, a three-man crew would be no great disadvantage since there are sufficient bomber crews at present."

"Our anti-tank aircraft for the future must be twin-engined; a single engined one just will not do. It has happened time and again that an aircraft was able to return on one engine only because when one engine had been hit and failed, the other one brought it back. An anti-tank aircraft must expect to be hit many times. All the Russians blaze away at a low-flying aircraft with all the weapons they have, so a twin-engined machine is essential in order that it may have a chance of survival and still limp back."

"The calibre of the gun carried must be 75 mm. Tanks' armour plating will be growing in thickness and small calibres are quite useless as they don't penetrate. Another requirement is an air-cooled engine so that there is no risk of damage to radiators due to ground fire, in which event ground-attack aircraft are compelled to turn back immediately. Shooting must be possible from a great distance, and the aircraft must be manoeuvrable so that it doesn't have to fly far round towards the rear after a firing pass and also so that we need not attack the enemy's tanks from the rear and hence from his side of the lines where he can concentrate his anti-aircraft guns. Strictly speaking, our existing types are not suitable for frontal attacks against tanks which have either broken through or are ahead of the main front line. Of equal importance, as I have already mentioned, is effective armour protection."

Here it is necessary to stress that Kupfer was himself a dive-bomber pilot and, perhaps because of this, his conclusions concerning anti-tank operations appear flawed in a number of respects. Certainly, his appreciation of anti-tank work does not reflect the views of the Hs 129 *Panzerjäger*, who seem not to have been consulted, nor of the handful of pilots who had flown the Junkers Ju 87s which, experimentally fitted with cannon, had been attached to his *Geschwader* and deployed against armour. After much trial and error, these Ju 87 pilots had evolved tactics which called for attacks on the rear of the tank where the armour was thinnest and so that in the event of damage sustained from enemy anti-aircraft fire, the aircraft was already flying towards its own lines. For Kupfer to suggest frontal attacks was therefore completely contrary to the Ju 87 pilots' battle-tested experience.

However, Kupfer's considerable front-line expertise enabled him clearly to recognise that the course of the war had brought about a change in the duties of the dive-bomber units and that a pure ground-attack aircraft was now needed to replace the Ju 87. Although the meeting with Milch was extremely cordial, neither could subsequently agree on exactly what was needed as a future anti-tank aircraft. Moreover, no practical new or different

Early trials with a Ju 88 fitted with a Pak 40 revealed the need for a redesigned filter muzzle brake and some reinforcement of the nose.

ideas were put forward. Anti-tank rockets were not mentioned, the call being instead for ever larger guns and, as a replacement for the Hs 129, Kupfer's request for a heavily armoured aircraft powered by two air-cooled engines only tended to confirm that, if long development times were to be avoided, the aircraft best suited to the anti-tank role was the existing Hs 129. However, of this aircraft, Kupfer commented:

"*Let me make some comments on the Hs 129 which is now in operational service. This type can definitely only be operated in combination with the ground-attack units to protect it. The existing model is too slow, extremely unwieldy, difficult to get off the ground and it must get too close to its target. Even then its 30 mm cannon is not capable of penetrating the Soviet tanks' frontal armour. I have been told, though, that some experimental Hs 129s fitted with a 75 mm gun have achieved good results.*"

Although the Hs 129 had proved adequate up to mid-1943, it thereafter suffered losses which would only increase as the enemy's defences on the Eastern front continued to improve in quantity and quality, a trend which had been observed since the early days of the campaign and especially since the Kursk offensive. Similarly, the number of enemy tanks appearing at the front was growing at an alarming rate and it was anticipated that they would be protected by increasing thicknesses of armour plating. Clearly there was a growing need for weapons with a greater armour-piercing capability, and in view of the shortage of tungsten (*Wolfram*) which was bound only to become more acute, it was logical - given that armour-piercing rockets had not yet reached front-line service - that consideration should be given to larger calibre weapons. However, to consider the Ju 88 equipped with 75 mm cannon as superior to the Hs 129 was, in the opinion of one highly experienced and successful *Panzerjäger* consulted by the author "... ridiculous". Indeed, Meyer's trials with this type should already have convinced Kupfer that the Ju 88 was too slow and too unmanoeuvrable, a point confirmed exactly three months later when *Obst.* Viktor von Lossberg, an innovative former bomber pilot now serving as departmental chief in the RLM's Technical Office, reported to the *General der Schlachtflieger* that the results of intensive trials carried out with the Ju 88P showed it to be "... unsuitable for employment at the front". By comparison, however, similar trials with an Hs 129 fitted with the 7.5 cm BK showed that this combination was to be preferred. Especially favourable comments were received from front-line officers and *E-Stelle* personnel who were unanimous in their view that an Hs 129 equipped with a 75 mm cannon showed no marked deterioration in either flying quality or performance.

Milch, however, was opposed to the idea of a twin-engined aircraft on the grounds that too much armour would be required to protect the engines, crew, fuel lines and fuel tanks. He felt instead that the anti-tank arm should re-equip with

Trials with various Fw 190s fitted with an MK 103 under each wing were disappointing. Accuracy was insufficient to ensure hits in a tank's weak areas and trials were abandoned in favour of anti-tank rockets.

a single-engined aircraft powered with an air-cooled engine and possessing the speed and manoeuvrability of a fighter. Since no time could be allowed to develop an entirely new anti-tank aircraft, the only existing type which came close to meeting Milch's requirement was the Fw 190.

However, neither the opinions of Kupfer nor Milch are given much credence by former Hs 129 pilots today. As Franz Oswald comments: "Dr Kupfer had obviously not the slightest idea of the excellent features of the Hs 129. Who on earth makes an attack against a tank from the front? And as far as weapons are concerned, the Hs 129 did not require a larger calibre weapon since the MK 103 was first-rate in its effectiveness. The Ju 88 in the anti-tank role on the other hand, was a crazy idea. How could Kupfer say that the Hs 129 was too slow and not manouevrable enough if, obviously, he had never flown the type let alone flown an anti-tank mission? *Generalfeldmarschall* Milch seems to have been equally dumb because with a twin-engine aircraft you could at least return on one engine if the other was out of action. Why didn't Milch and Kupfer talk to experienced and successful Hs 129 pilots?"

It is interesting too, to note that following Kupfer's address, Henschel's records state that

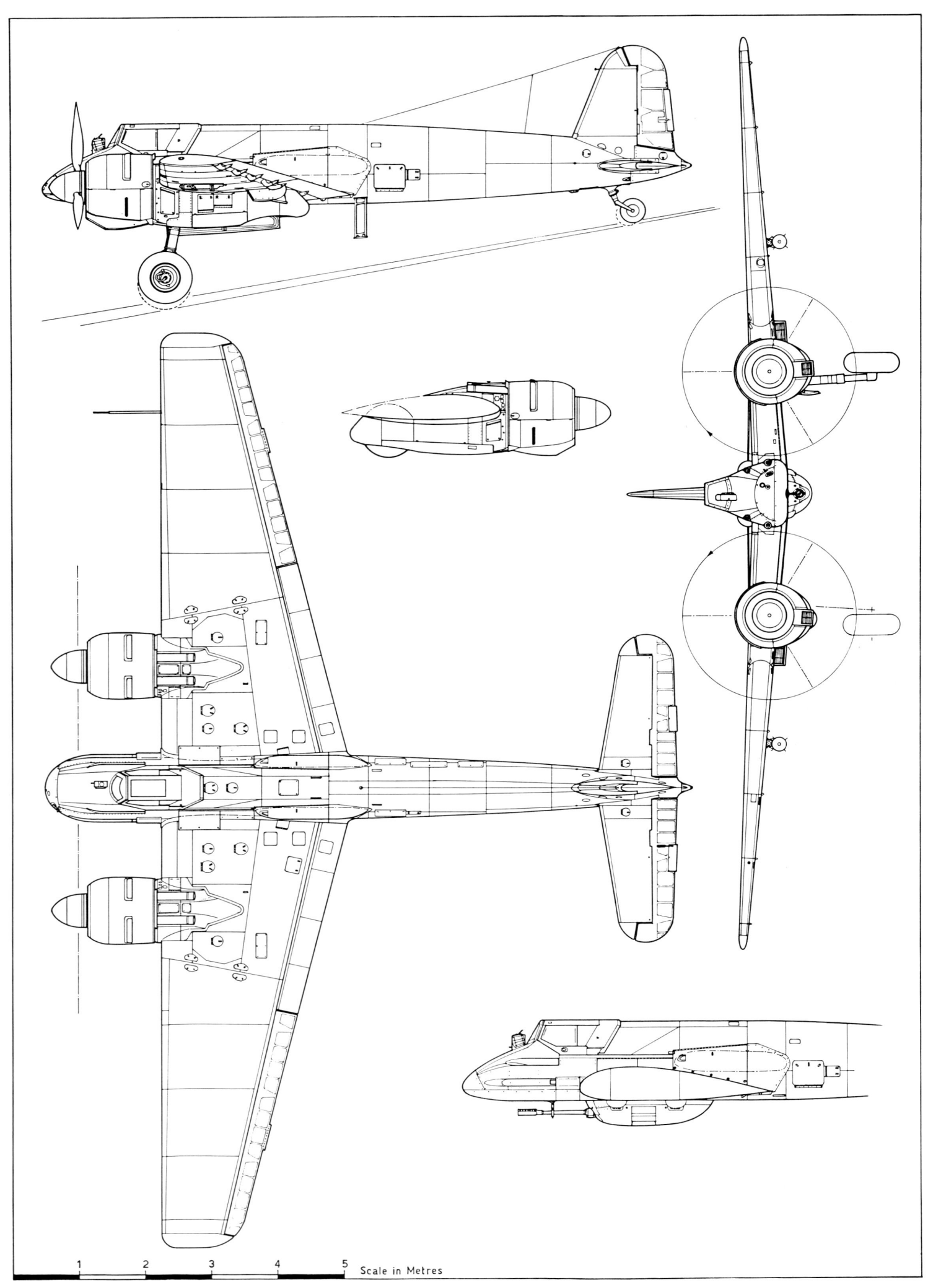

Scale in Metres

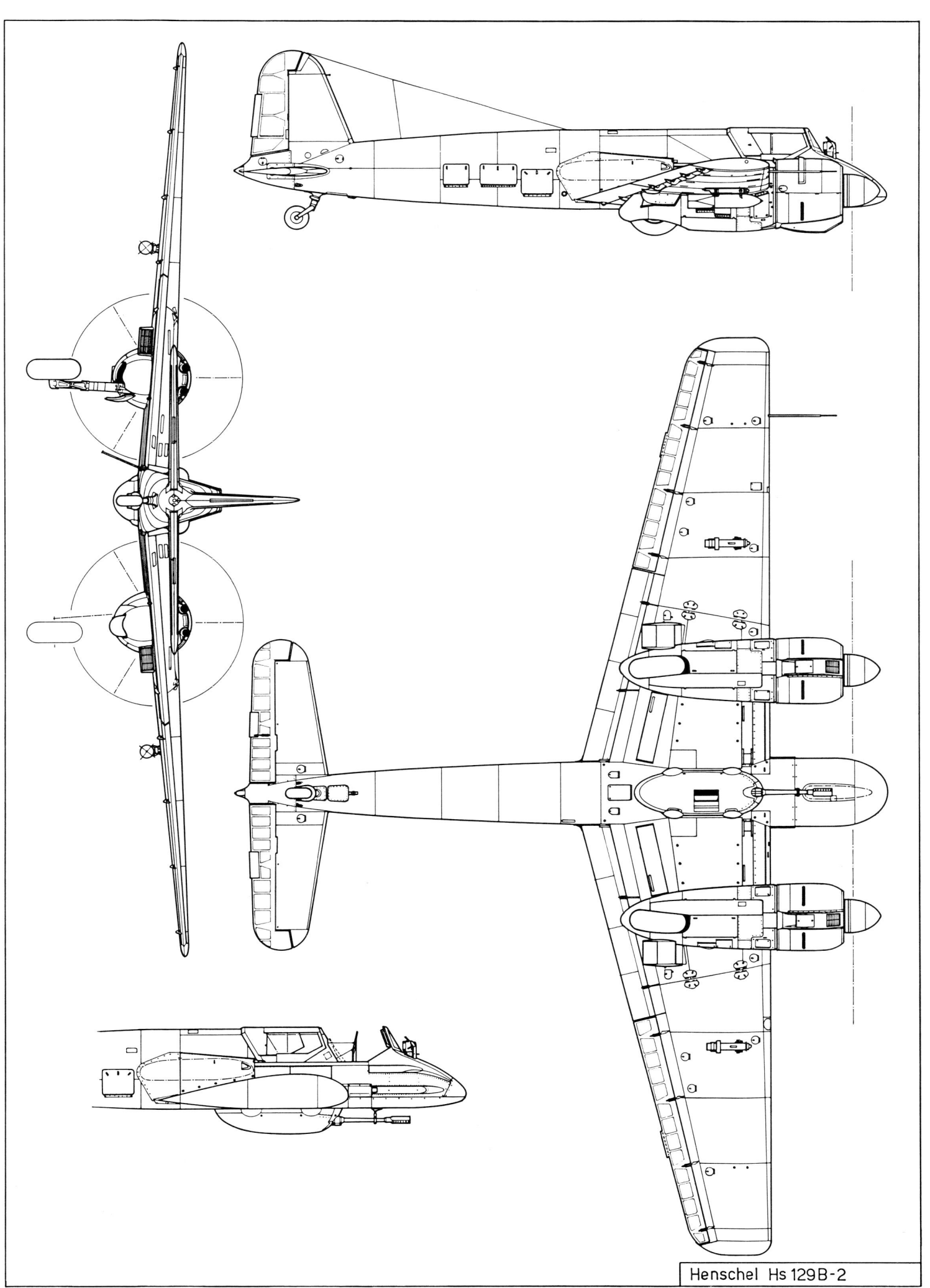

Henschel Hs 129B-2

An interesting sequence of stills taken from a 16 mm cine film showing a pilot boarding his Hs 129, White "L", assisted by a member of the ground crew. In the background is "White "K", both aircraft bearing traces of snow camouflage. Note the position of the hand- and foot-holds. The small pierced lug visible on the upper wing surface behind the engine is for tying on the engine covers.

"... *the situation regarding ground attack aircraft is not quite clear...*". Clearly, Kupfer's remarks tended to confuse rather clarify the situation.

The suitability of the Fw 190 for anti-tank and ground-attack work was at that time largely academic, however, as this aircraft was then desperately needed for home defence and although Göring himself had ordered that fighter and defence-orientated aircraft production had to be stepped up as strongly as possible, even at the expense of other types of aircraft, *General* Galland, as commander of the fighter arm, jealously guarded against any attempt to siphon off his Fw 190s into the ground-attack arm. In any case, although the Fw 190 was undoubtedly an admirable aircraft with which to re-equip the *Stuka* units, it was, like the Ju 88, not entirely suitable as a replacement for the Hs 129. While it was essential that any anti-tank aircraft should be able to take off from wet, muddy, or otherwise un-favourable airfields, experience had earlier shown that those ground-attack units already equipped with the Fw 190 sometimes had great difficulty in taxiing their heavily-laden aircraft on sodden forward airstrips. Instances were reported of Focke-Wulfs becoming bogged down in the mud and, as the pilot applied more power to pull his aircraft free, it simply pivoted helplessly about one wheel. Conversely, dry, sandy conditions also gave rise to difficulties and during fighter-bomber operations in Africa, several Fw 190s of III./SKG 10 had undercarriages so clogged with sand that they failed to retract, forcing the aircraft to return to their airfield as soon as they had taken off.

To be effective in the anti-tank role, the Fw 190 would require armour-piercing weapons and trials were conducted with an Fw 190 fitted with two 30 mm MK 103s, one under each wing, but results were disappointing. It proved impossible to ensure hits were sufficiently closely grouped and tests showed that at a distance of 100 m (110 yds), twelve shots were spread over an area of 568 square cm (88 sq.in.) and, even after the introduction of a special muzzle, spread of shot was still extended over an area of 542 square cm (84 sq.in.). This was simply too great to ensure accurate hits on a tank's weakest points unless the tank was attacked relatively slowly and carefully from extremely close range. But at low speed the weight of the two cannon and their housings affected the Fw 190's performance to such an extent that any advantage to be gained from using it was lost. The alternative, if the type was to avoid rendering itself too slow and vulnerable, was to attack at higher speed but this prevented the pilot from firing more than one or two rounds during each pass. A further disadvantage was that if one cannon jammed or otherwise failed to fire it was not possible to use the other. Despite these setbacks and disadvantages, the Fw 190 trials continued until late 1944, but by this time the development of cannon had at last been over-taken by the introduction of anti-tank rockets.

As a temporary means of raising the quantity of anti-tank aircraft available, the number of Ju 87 *Panzerstaffeln* was increased and a 10.*(Panzer) Staffel* was added to each of the *Stukageschwader*, each *Staffel* consisting of twelve Ju 87s with 37 mm

cannon and four with bombs, the latter being used to attack flak batteries. Although these units were to prove remarkably successful, experiments continued with Ju 88s fitted with a variety of anti-tank weapons, but these trials were eventually discontinued when it became clear that they would lead only to disappointing results. Nothing was done to increase Hs 129 production but, in view of favourable reports, trials continued with an Hs 129 fitted with 75 mm cannon and these eventually produced far more satisfactory results than the similarly equipped Ju 88.

Shortly after Kupfer's address at the RLM, all Luftwaffe ground-attack and anti-tank units were redesignated. The original *Schlachtgeschwader* 1 and 2 were disbanded and their various *Staffeln* used to create new *Schlachtgruppen*. The Hs 129 *Staffeln*, which had in any case already been

Starting the port-side engine of White "L".

operating as a single unit for some time under the overall command of the *Führer der Panzerjäger*, were now officially formed into a single *Gruppe*, the IV.*(Pz)/Schlachtgeschwader* 9. The *Gruppenstab* was formed from personnel drawn from the previous *Stab*/Sch.G 1 and the *Staffeln* redesignated as follows:

    4.(Pz)/Sch.G 1   became   10.(Pz)/SG 9
    8.(Pz)/Sch.G 1   became   11.(Pz)/SG 9
    4.(Pz)/Sch.G 2   became   12.(Pz)/SG 9
    8.(Pz)/Sch.G 2   became   13.(Pz)/SG 9
    Pz.Jä.Sta/JG 51   became   14.(Pz)/SG 9

However, these changes were barely under way when Kupfer was killed in a flying accident in the Balkans on 6 November, 1943. He was succeeded a short time later by *Oberstleutnant* Hubertus Hitschhold who, from the Summer of 1942 until mid-1943, had been *Kommodore* of *Schlachtgeschwader* 1. At last the *Schlachtverbände* possessed a commanding officer with direct personal experience of ground-attack and anti-tank operations; Hitschhold was very well acquainted with the particular problems facing his command and it was he who was really responsible for the subsequent reformation and modernisation of the *Schlachtverbände*.

"*Obstlt.* Hitschhold was more competent," recalls Franz Oswald. "In May or June 1942, as a Technical Officer, I instructed him on flying the Hs 129 and after a couple of minutes he flew the type himself."

The first result in the new command was a burst of reforming energy to make up for lost time. Although the fighter arm still had priority over the *Schlachtflieger* in all areas of equipment and material, large-scale re-equipment of the Ju 87 units with the Fw 190 eventually became possible as the *General der Jagdflieger's* anxiety to obtain the long-nosed Fw 190 D-9 fighter led to his diminished interest in the earlier BMW 801-powered versions of this aircraft and he allowed some of them to be released to the *Schlachtflieger*. Conversion to the Fw 190 was therefore pushed forward with a view to completion by the Summer of 1944, but the critical position on the Eastern Front at that time demanded the use of every available aircraft and crew, so preventing the withdrawal of the Ju 87 units for conversion training. As soon as the Eastern Front had been stabilised, a new problem arose; supplies of C3 fuel used by the Fw 190 became very limited, whereas B4 for Ju 87s and Hs 129s was available in substantially greater quantities. As a result of these problems, full conversion was never achieved and one ground-attack *Gruppe*, III./SG 2, was still flying daylight operations with the Ju 87 when the war ended.

While displaying a keen personal interest in the development and modernisation of the ordinary ground-attack units, Hitschhold also played particular attention to anti-tank operations. He recognised that although the Ju 87 and Hs 129 formations had played a most successful role in the past, their heavy, large-calibre weapons were aerodynamically undesirable and rendered the aircraft slow and unwieldy in the face of ever more effective opposition. Hitschhold therefore enthusiastically explored the previously neglected area of anti-tank rockets and was a frequent visitor to the trials airfields in order to personally push forward as rapidly as possible the development of the new *Panzerschreck* and *Panzerblitz* rockets and the replacement of Ju 87s and Hs 129s with rocket-firing Fw 190s. The daylight ground-attack units would then have been uniformly armed and equipped, but the reorganisation of the *Schlachtflieger* along such up-to-date lines had already come too late. Earlier technical planning had not been sufficiently far-sighted and the office of the *General der Schlachtflieger* was not created until conditions at the front had deteriorated beyond the point where any new policy could change the final outcome of the war.

Major Hubertus Hitschhold.

"Three Cheers for the Henschel Locomotive Works!"

Tank-Buster Training & Tactics

14

Training

Elementary flying training in the *Luftwaffe* began with a first phase at an *A/B Schule* in light aircraft such as Focke-Wulf, Klemm or Bücker bi-planes. During the second flying training phase, the candidate pilot was closely watched and depending on the wishes and temperament of each candidate pilot concerned, his instructors decided if he would be most suitable as a fighter, bomber or ground-attack pilot, etc.

After completion of the basic course and the award of the pilot's badge, further flying training depended on the nature of the specialisation. At first, pilots who wanted to serve with the ground-attack arm and who seemed suitably qualified were posted to various training units, those destined to fly the Hs 129 being transferred to the *Zerstörerschule* 2 at München/Neubiberg or the *Ergänzungs Zerstörergruppe* where they gained the necessary experience of flying twin-engined aircraft. In June 1943 parts of *Zerstörerschule* 2 were redesignated to form parts of the II. *Gruppe* of SG 101 and moved to the French airfield at Paris-Orly where its function was to train crews for ground-attack operations.

The II./SG 101 consisted of three *Staffeln* with a normal strength in aircraft equivalent to that of an operational *Staffel*. The *Gruppe's* aircraft originally consisted of Bf 110s only, but in January, 1944, about half of these aircraft were replaced by Hs 129 A-0s, B-1s and B-2s. Later, some Arado 96s were received to replace losses suffered in an Allied bombing raid on 30 April, when ten of the *Gruppe's* Hs 129s were destroyed on the ground while on detachment at Clermont-Ferrand. In August 1944, SG 101's *Geschwaderkommodore* was *Major* Helmuth Krebs, who had earlier been awarded the *Deutsches Kreuz* in Gold for his work with a *Schnellkampfgeschwader*. *Major* Langemann was the *Kommandeur* of the II. *Gruppe*, and *Oblte*. Richter, Krauspe and Hessel were the *Staffelkapitäne* of the 4., 5. and 6. *Staffeln* respectively.

After February 1943, pilots passing out of SG 101 were transferred to the *Luftwaffe's Ergänzungs-Schlachtgruppe*, or Reserve and Operational Training Unit, which had been formed in February 1943 with four *Staffeln*. This unit was based some 97 km (60 miles) south-east of Warsaw at Deblin-Irena in Poland and pilots posted here received final additional training and instruction on the aircraft they were to fly and its tactical employment for ground-attack missions. By this stage of his career, the ground-attack pilot had practised formation flying, bomb-aiming, firing at ground targets, air-to-air combat and orientation. A pilot also received thorough instruction in Army tactics and material as well as

Right and Far Right: Although under-powered and possessing poor cockpit visibility, a number of Hs 129 A-0s served on well into 1943. The particular machine seen above was not so lucky. With Fw. Otto Braun at the controls it crashed at Deblin-Irena on 19 June 1942 while serving with the Erg.Zerst. Gruppe.

co-operation with the Army and Navy. Armourers were also trained at Deblin-Irena where they studied the armament of the Hs 129.

While serving with the *Ergänzungs-Schlachtgruppe*, pilots were required to attain squadron standards by flying tactical missions under simulated conditions with live bombs and ammunition. Any pilot who did not fully meet the established standards was dismissed as unfit and assigned other duties. On the other hand, pilots showing great skill were additionally trained in the firing of armour-piercing anti-tank cannon and at a later period of the war received training in the use of *Panzerblitz* or *Panzerschreck* hollow-charge rockets. However, because of a lack of fuel which began to be felt in the latter half of the war, the training of new ground-attack pilots was too short and no great level of flying experience could be attained. This often lead to great losses in the first operations and to small successes, especially on operations in difficult situations where enemy defence was strong.

The majority of the instructors at the *Ergänzungs-Schlachtgruppe* were themselves experienced and competent ground-attack pilots, but, due to the demands of the front-line units, the schools could never be staffed with enough suitably qualified officer instructors. There was no reserve of officers who were not fully required at the front, nor was there a system to regularly exchange personnel between front and home to bring the schools and operational units up to sufficient strength.

In October 1943, the *Ergänzungs-Schlachtgruppe* was redesignated I./SG 152, the *Gruppe* consisting of four *Staffeln*.

I./SG 152
1. Staffel	Fw 190
2. Staffel	Fw 190
3. (Pz) Staffel	Hs 129
4. (Pz) Staffel	Ju 87

By 20 February 1944, another training *Geschwader*, *Ritterkreuzträger Obst.* Christ's SG 151 was also operating a number of Hs 129 and Ju 87D aircraft at Pardubitz in its III. *Gruppe* (previously the Erg. Stab/St.G 3 and III./St.G 151) under the command of *Hptm.* Hanschke, but beyond this, the history of the Hs 129 training *Staffeln* becomes difficult to follow due to the constant redesignations, disbandments and reformations which subsequently took place. Certainly by 30 March 1944, 4.(Pz)/SG 152 had a number of Hs 129s on hand and on 31 July 1944, 3.(Pz)/SG 152 was operating Hs 129 aircraft together with a number of Ju 87Gs. On that date the *Staffel* was redesignated 14.(Pz)/SG 151; it was disbanded on 10 October 1944.

As the general war situation deteriorated, the need at the front for every available combat

Top and Centre: An Argus-engined Hs 129 A-0 and Gnôme-Rhône-engined Hs 129s at Paris-Orly
Bottom: A belly-landed Hs 129 A-0 belonging to SG 101 based at Paris-Orly. The Infanteriesturmabzeichen was also used by the training units.

aircraft became so acute that on 11 February 1945, the OKL offered *Luftflotte* 6 the services of all schools and replacement units. The remaining *Staffeln* of SG 151, now equipped with both bomb-carrying and *Panzerblitz* armed Fw 190s and a number of Ju 87s, were frequently successful at the front until the worsening situation finally forced them to the point where operations could no longer be continued. At the end of April 1945, SG 152 began disbanding at Amberg and this was followed by the dissolution of a number of other ground-attack training units which had seen operations on the Eastern Front. Personnel from these units were eventually sent into action as infantry in the defence of Berlin, often under the command of experienced and highly decorated pilots. One such ground fighting unit was led by *Major* Bruno Meyer.

But even before the training units were transferred to the front, life could at times be just as dangerous as with any operational unit. A former member of III./SG 151 recalled that at Pardubitz, during retraining of pilots to the Fw 190, accidents amounted at times to as many as three aircraft per day.

Training units based in occupied countries, where local airfield labour was employed, had to cope also with the additional risk of sabotage, as experienced by *Lt.* Walter Krause: "I was with the *Ergänzungs-Gruppe* in Deblin-Irena from May to November, 1943. The reason for my somewhat prolonged summer stay on the Vistula was a flying accident I had late in May. At this time, *Oblt.* König was getting us into trim on the '129. All that was still necessary was live firing practice on the range at Pulawy to test our shooting abilities. Two days previously, we had been loaded onto lorries in company strength to fight partisans, but after the first stop I jumped from the lorry and sprained my right foot. The result was that I was forbidden to fly for a week, during which time live firing was to take place followed by immediate transfer to the front. I had to get to the front at all costs, so although the doctors had forbidden it, I flew my practice attacks over the Pulawy forest with a bandaged foot.

"I was making my last approach on the range when, as if controlled by a magic hand, both engines suddenly spluttered into complete silence. My first reaction was to switch the fuel supply from the fuselage tank behind me to the wing tanks, but still nothing happened. Are the fuel cocks open? Yes! I was amazed at what had happened but otherwise I was absolutely calm. Height? About fifty metres (165 ft). Below me, there was nothing but woods. Lower flaps. Tighten seat belt. A tiny clearing opened up amid the trees. I pushed the aircraft to the ground and immediately lost consciousness. When I came to, some people were placing me on a stretcher. My eyes were covered with blood and dirt and I felt terrible pains in my head and back. Before I fainted again and fell into a pleasant state of unconsciousness, I heard someone say, *"I'm sure I certified this man unfit to fly."*

"Later, I learned that the mysterious engine failure had been caused by Polish workers employed in the repair depot at Deblin-Irena. An examination of my aircraft showed that the magnetos had been tampered with and similar inexplicable accidents had occurred in the Fw 190 *Staffel*, but always with fatal results. The armoured Hs 129 had saved my life. *Three cheers for the Henschel locomotive works!"*

Despite the training given to pilots in the schools and replacement units, a pilot's first operational sortie was frequently a confusing if not frightening and unnerving experience. No amount of simulated battle experience could prepare new pilots for the shock of the real thing. *Hptm.* Rudolf-Heinz Ruffer, speaking in July 1944 when he was the *Staffelkapitän* of 10.(Pz)/SG 9, recalled his first encounter with a T-34: "I wanted to join an arm of the services which, even in peacetime, would be risky and exciting. That's why I applied to become a member of the *Luftwaffe's* flying personnel. My passion was for hunting and I was obviously very excited when I was sent for fighter-pilot training. Later, though, I was trained as a ground-attack pilot, so now I hunt enemy tanks."

"On my first successful sortie I could hardly believe that one could fight such a steel colossus as a tank, let alone destroy it. On this first mission I spotted a tank, but unfortunately a bit too late. It was just crouching there, big and heavy and wide, as if it was defiantly pressing itself into the ground."

"I completely forgot to squeeze the triggers of my weapons. It simply didn't enter my head that I was supposed to shoot at the tank and I had to wait until I could make another approach. Even then, in my excitement, I merely fired my machine-guns, with the result that only pieces of its camouflage foliage fell away. On my next pass I managed to score a direct hit and inflict fatal damage, though I didn't realise this until my *Rottenführer* told me. At first, the tank began to smoke heavily. Then flames broke out and, slowly, it started to burn with bright flames. It reminded me of a spirit stove, all lit up and giving off a shower of sparks."

"I realised then just what a powerful weapon I possessed and became more confident. After my next sortie, during which I fired short bursts to set these monsters on fire or to blow them up, I gained complete confidence in my aircraft and its armament. Gradually, I gained more experience, which I am now able to pass on to my pilots."

Like any good commanding officer, *Oblt.* Franz Oswald, the *Staffelkapitän* of 8.(Pz)/Sch.G 2 and later, when *Hauptmann*, *Staffelkapitän* of 13.(Pz)/SG 9, was greatly concerned for his men and today takes great pride in the fact that during the entire war he lost only three wingmen: "Our greatest losses were always amongst newcomers, and this became worse as the war progressed. I always told my new pilots that during their first four or five missions they were to concentrate just on their flying and make sure they got back safely. Before anything else, they had to learn to recognise the front, keep formation and recognise

This aircraft, W.Nr.140492, was found on Caen-Carpiquet airfield in France in July 1944. It had been damaged by bomb splinters, wrecked by a demolition charge and looted by both sides. The code "DO+XE" was painted in black on the fuselage sides and under the wings and a 375 mm (15 inch) figure "5" was painted on the outside of each engine cowling. One ETC 50/VII d bomb rack was fitted under each wing and a rack for 4 x 50 kg bombs was fitted under the fuselage. Armament consisted of 2 x MG 151/ 15 mm guns and 2 x MG 17 of 7.92 mm calibre. In addition to the usual comprehensive armour plate, two new pieces were found protecting the engines; one shaped piece around the underside of the engine nacelle protected the air intake and another piece 325 mm x 375 mm (13 in x 15 in) on the side of the engine covered the oil pump.

Hs 129 B-2 Red 'L' W.Nr. 140830
10.(Pz)/SG 9, July 1943.

Underside view of Georg Dornemann's Hs 129 B-2 showing the exposed details of the MK 103 cannon. The aircraft flew operations with the cannon cover removed. The W.Nr. 140830 has been omitted in this view as no proof has been found that it was applied on this side.

Malaya-Viska and I felt it even more from being so keyed up. Only two hours with the *Staffel* and already I was on my first operational mission!"

"The cold start and assembling in the air as Number 2 behind "Drops" was not difficult as I had amassed a large number of flying hours during training at Paris-Orly and Deblin-Irena, but how completely different this was! Endless, misty, snow-covered countryside, with no horizon for navigating and orientation, and to make things worse the aircraft were painted with white camouflage so that I could hardly see the machine in front of me."

""Drops" led the *Schwarm* along the railway line around Kirovograd. The front could be recognised by plumes of smoke and a smell of burning. This smell was typical of the area close to the front. I shall never forget it. We flew at a height of 100 metres (330 ft). Below me I saw some retreating German soldiers in white camouflage smocks and two burning German tanks, but where were the Ivans? "Drops" took us around and made for the edge of a wood. Then he ordered us to release our bombs and make firing passes. His voice was calm over the headphones and, as he waved his hand to me reassuringly, I could see that he had already released his cluster bombs from the ETCs. But where? I couldn't see anything on the edge of the forest, but I dropped the 50 kg cluster bombs in level flight just the same."

"Bank over, but watch out for collision! Where is "Drops"? This snow and the white-painted aircraft make things very difficult! "Drops" makes a strafing pass on the edge of the wood and at last I think I can recognise some Russian anti-tank guns, the notorious "Crash-Boom". There are many gun flashes from the edge of the wood and these weapons are deadly against our Mark IVs. After three firing passes we reassemble for the return flight and make an uneventful return to our airfield. The 10 December is a memorable day for me as the day I joined the 10. *Staffel* and flew my first mission."

"One thing was already quite clear; my flying abilities would enable me to accomplish my missions and, although I had been highly strung at the beginning of the sortie, I discovered then, as I did time after time before take-off, that once I had strapped myself into my seat, I became completely calm."

In general, the quality of new pilots posted to

Above Left: Hs 129 B-1, White "7", of a training unit.
Left: The only Hs 129s to carry a four-character unit code (as opposed to factory markings) was the Ergänzungs-Schlachtgruppe (Reserve and Replacement Ground Attack Group), established in April 1943 at Deblin-Irena, Poland and redesignated I./SG 152 in October 1943. This aircraft, "4M+RD", appears to be an early Hs 129 B-1.

the *Schlachtverbände* was very high. Pilots not suitable for ground-attack operations were relieved in the Schools and Operational Training Units by the skilled instructors. The good pilots were instilled with a love of ground-attack work so that they volunteered for that branch and the palming off of poor pilots to the *Schlachtverbände* was therefore avoided. This careful selection ensured that only well-trained, good quality pilots, found their way into the anti-tank units and it is not altogether surprising, therefore, that some of these pilots were to particularly distinguish themselves as tank-hunters or unit leaders. Just as the fighter, destroyer and bomber units had their *"Experten"*, so too did the *Panzerjäger*, and although their individual exploits and achievements are far less well known, they won the respect and admiration of the ground troops and their *Staffel* comrades for their sheer tenacity in pressing home attacks through walls of flak and small arms fire.

Some pilots had themselves served earlier as flying instructors. Georg Dornemann, for example, was an instructor from 1936 until late 1942 when he was recruited at Paris-Orly by the *Eichenlaubträger* and *Inspizient für Schlacht- und Zerstörerflieger, Obslt.* Otto Weiss. After a six to eight week conversion course at Deblin-Irena, Georg Dornemann joined the Staff of the *Panzerjagdkommando Weiss* in January 1943 as Weiss's adjutant. During his first familiarisation flights in the early Hs 129 A at Deblin-Irena, Dornemann was not overly impressed with this particular version's flying characteristics, but once he had joined a front-line unit and flew the Hs 129 B-2, he changed his views and this operational sub-type made a "very favourable impression" on him.

Tactics

In January 1943, Dornemann was appointed *Staffelkapitän* of 4.(Pz)/Sch.G 1 based at Stalino, but between February and May, 1943, he was unable to obtain a single confirmed tank kill, despite his repeated and determined cannon attacks. He knew he was hitting the target and the tanks often clattered to a standstill, but without any visible sign of damage a confirmed kill could not be awarded.[1] It was while flying in the Kuban in May that he finally succeeded in scoring his first five confirmed kills, and it was on one of these missions that he was shot down for the first time. Making a wheels-up landing in no-man's-land, he managed to clamber clear of the smouldering aircraft only seconds before it exploded and burst into flames.

Georg Dornemann's technique for destroying tanks was to attack them from the side so that if his shells failed to penetrate the interior, he at least stood a good chance of immobilising the vehicle by damaging its tracks or wheels. Occasionally, he would approach his intended victims from behind and endeavour to destroy the fuel tanks. If successful, such attacks frequently started a "... brilliant firework display". Almost all the Soviet tanks Dornemann encountered were of the T-34 type, but other targets such as infantry, vehicles and field guns also received attention. During the run-up to a tank target, Dornemann frequently used his 20 mm guns loaded with tracer and high-explosive shells to aim, but on some occasions he was so certain of a hit he fired only his tungsten-cored ammunition. If struck in the right place, a tank could be destroyed or disabled with just two or three of the armour-piercing rounds. If his aircraft was hit, Dornemann always tried to get back to the safety of the German lines, and although this was sometimes managed under the most heavy anti-aircraft fire, he survived being shot down no fewer than six times before a heavy crash-landing finally finished his career as an Hs 129 pilot. With a total of more than 50 tanks destroyed, plus an Il-2 which he shot down in air-to-air combat, Georg Dornemann was mentioned in numerous citations but otherwise his achievements received little recognition. For the *Panzer-Schlachtflieger* it was not at all easy to be awarded a high decoration and it is no exaggeration to say that a unit's best pilot often wore no more than the Iron Cross First Class! Georg Dornemann remembered the Hs 129 as an "...excellent aircraft, with no particular airframe or engine faults except being underpowered".

It was not until 1944 that a training manual for attacking tanks was completed and until this time no standard method existed. Instead, it would seem that each individual *Staffelkapitän* operated more or less as he saw fit, and two different methods of attack were evolved, each of which had its favourable points. Franz Oswald and Bruno Meyer preferred to approach from behind, where the tank's armour was thinnest, a method which had the added advantage that, if the German aircraft was hit during its approach to the target it was already flying in the direction of its own lines where it could make a forced-landing. The disadvantage of such attacks was that the T-34 was a very small vehicle. With a length of 7.544 m (24ft 9in) and an overall width of only 2.997 m (9ft 10in), (hull width 1.854 m (6ft 1in)) the T-34 presented an even smaller target when viewed from behind, so that attacks against the rear of a tank called for a particularly high standard of marksmanship. A further disadvantage in making attacks from the rear was that, in order to ensure that hits were scored at 90 degrees to the tank's sloping rear armour, the pilot had to open fire while in a dive and, in order to avoid making contact with the ground, had to pull out at a range greater than if he were attacking horizontally. Walter Krause, who flew with 10.(Pz)/SG 9, first under Georg Dornemann and later Gebhard Weber, confirmed that it was for this reason that horizontal strikes were standard in his *Staffel*. After using the fuselage-mounted weapons to correct his aim, the pilot would open fire at close range with his MK 101 or MK 103 cannon, usually from around 250 m (820 ft) down to 50 m (164 ft), banking away immediately after firing to avoid any explosion should his target detonate immediately it was hit.

In order that each pilot could attack a different target without disturbing the concentration of the others, the *Panzerjäger* always flew in a *Schwarm* formation consisting of two pairs, or *Rotten*.

The leader, Number One, was the *Schwarmführer* and, like Number Three, was also a *Rottenführer*. The wingmen (Numbers Two and Four) were known as *"Kettenhunde"*, or "Chained Dogs".

The problem of accurately identifying the location of friendly troops had first arisen as early as the Polish and French campaigns when, on a number of occasions, German aircraft had bombed their own men in error. Experiments with bomb-lines, beyond which German aircraft could not release their bombs, met with little success as the speed of the German advances often meant that friendly units frequently drove forward beyond those lines. The result of this was that air support failed to arrive at the critical strongpoint obstructing further advances.

The problem was finally solved by the use of coloured smoke and ground panels, the latter laid out in such a way that very precise information could be conveyed to friendly aircraft.

On some occasions the Hs 129 *Staffeln* were required to fly armed reconnaissance missions. In view of the standing instruction that these units could only mount operations on their own initiative against tanks which had broken through the front lines, reconnaissance sorties had to be assigned by some higher authority. Such missions were mainly ordered when, as a result of recent ground fighting, the exact position of the lines or location of the enemy was not known and the objective was to discover where friendly and enemy troops were. Sometimes, the only way to

Panzerjäger Schwarm formation

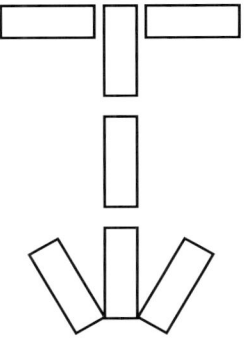

German ground to air signal: Enemy tank has broken through (in direction of arrow)

Each vertical marker represents 1000 metres

Russian anti-aircraft fire was viewed as a constant hazard to Hs 129 pilots. Here, Soviet troops man a quadruple AA machine-gun.

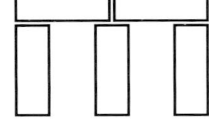

German ground to air signals:
Top: Drop point for message.
Below: Strong opposition 3000 metres ahead.

determine who was occupying a particularly ragged section of the front was to fly low over the area and look down into the soldiers' foxholes to discover if the occupants wore German or Russian uniforms. Any targets of opportunity discovered during such flights could be engaged, though on account of their heavy flak protection, static troop and tank concentrations would not normally be attacked as any success would not compensate for the expected losses. Such targets were left to horizontal bombers, dive-bombers and fighter-bombers.

Unlike Bruno Meyer, who clearly had a healthy respect for Russian small-arms fire, Franz Oswald developed his own tactics for eliminating such a threat. Before attacking the tank with his 30 mm armament, Oswald would first silence the dismounted crews or accompanying infantry with bursts from his fuselage-mounted weapons, but as he points out: "While the pilots themselves were at little risk from infantry fire due to the excellent protection afforded by the armoured cockpit and *Panzerglass* windscreen, there was too little armour protection around the engines and aircraft were therefore most likely to be lost due to engine damage from a lucky shot. Since our engines were easily shot on fire, the only thing to do in such an event was to crash land and get out as soon as possible. I saw this happen many times, but I can't recall a single case of anyone parachuting from an Hs 129 as our operating altitude was so low."

"We would normally open fire at a distance from the target of between 45 and 60 metres, and from such a close range the 30 to 40 degree firing angle brought the aircraft dangerously close to its target. There was always the risk that if the pilot failed to pull up over the tank in time he would crash into it or, if the tank exploded when it was hit the attacking aircraft could be damaged or even destroyed by blast and flying debris."

However, such instantaneous explosions were relatively rare and would only occur if a shell struck the tank's magazine. More often, as we have seen, there was no immediate outward sign of damage; pilots would see only the flash of shell hits and perhaps a cloud of debris as dust and camouflage material was dislodged by the impact of the aircraft's shells striking the tank's hull or upper decking. Only later would smoke be visible, eventually turning to flames as the tank caught fire and perhaps exploded.

Franz Oswald was awarded the German Cross in Gold on 4 June 1943, and, after destroying more than fifty tanks as well as numerous lorries, anti-aircraft positions, artillery emplacements and horse-drawn transport, received a well-deserved Knight's Cross on 24 October 1944. He made seven wheels-up or crash-landings with the Hs 129 - some with burning engines - and his aircraft twice cartwheeled while landing. He is one of only four pilots actually awarded the *Ritterkreuz* while flying the Hs 129, an aircraft which he remembers as perfect for low-level flying and anti-tank operations on the Eastern Front. The aircraft's speed left ample time to take aim at the small T-34, even from behind, and also allowed the pilot to follow the contours of the landscape which were used for surprise and escape. Although sometimes engaged by Russian fighters during the later stages of his operational career, Franz Oswald maintains they were rarely any real menace. If fighters were seen, the best course of action was to rely on the Henschel's excellent ground-hugging ability and fly as low as possible.

Such low-level flying saved Oswald's life on more than one occasion. Once, after attacking enemy tanks during the fighting in East Prussia late in 1944, Oswald's *Schwarm* was itself set upon by Russian fighters. The *Schwarm* immediately broke up, each pilot heading home alone. Franz

With the necessary gunnery skills, an Hs 129 pilot could often destroy or disable a T-34 (*far left*), or even heavier tanks such as the KV-2 (*left*), with just two or three well-aimed armour-piercing rounds.

Oswald's flight path took him over an airfield occupied by JG 52 where, looking up at the sound of aircraft engines low overhead, the fighter commander and ace, Hermann Graf saw a solitary Hs 129 pass over the airfield but with a Russian fighter in hot pursuit. Two Bf 109s were immediately scrambled and, once they had caught up, forced the fighter off the Henschel's tail. Blissfully unaware that he was being stalked, it was only Oswald's low-level flight which prevented the Russian fighter from bringing its guns to bear and he only learned of the threat from Graf.

By employing sound judgement throughout his period as *Staffelkapitän* and occasionally ignoring senseless orders, Oswald was sometimes able to prevent his pilots being sent out on missions which held no hope of success and which would have resulted only in unnecessary losses. At the end of the war, Franz Oswald was in the unique position of being able to examine his own service records. He found that his superiors had a very high opinion of him, though some thought him too critical. Today, he is proud of his war record and considers his method of attacking tanks from the rear was best, pointing out that the most highly decorated Ju 87 pilot, *Obst*. Hans-Ulrich Rudel, destroyed over 500 tanks using precisely the same tactics. Regardless of the approach adopted, however, what was of prime importance when attacking tanks was that the pilot should have complete control of his aircraft and possess good marksmanship.

Gebhard Weber saw two years of operational flying, solely on the Hs 129. After completing his training as a *Schlachtflieger*, Weber was posted to *Panzerjagdkommando Weiss*. Arriving on the morning of Easter Day, 1943, he found this organisation located near Kharkov with a *Stabsschwarm* and two *Staffeln*. No sooner had he got there and reported to *Obstlt*. Weiss, than Weber was ordered to take command of the entire ground personnel and march them along the highway to Kharkov. It was probably because he carried out this, his first assignment in Russia, in good order that he became Weiss's adjutant. Later, when the unit was renamed *Führer der Panzerjäger* and placed under the command of *Major* Meyer, Weber became Meyer's adjutant.

At the end of 1943 Weber was transferred to 13.(Pz)/SG 9 and sometimes acted as Oswald's deputy. In March, 1944, Weber was given his own command and became *Staffelkapitän* of 10.(Pz)/SG 9, leading it until the end of the war. He remembers the Hs 129 as a perfectly satisfactory tank-busting aircraft: "In the cockpit of the operational Hs 129 B-2 we had much more room than in the earlier Hs 129 A-0 which we used only for training. In the B-2, the view to the front, the sides and above was excellent. To look behind was simply a question of getting in the habit of using the rear-view mirror."

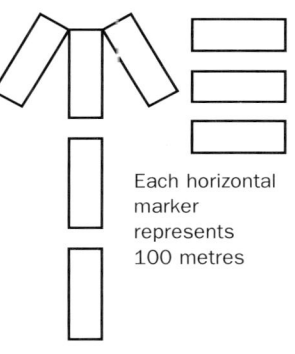

Each horizontal marker represents 100 metres

German ground to air signals: *Top*: Danger from this direction at 300 metres. *Below*: Danger from this direction at 2000 metres.

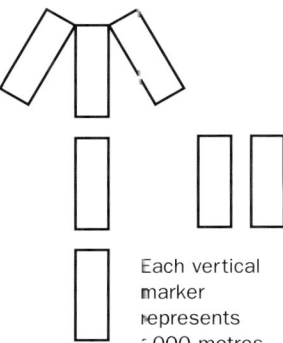

Each vertical marker represents 1000 metres

Oblt. Gebhard Weber, (shown here as a Leutnant), led 10.(Pz)/SG 9 from March 1944 to the end of the war. He remembers the Hs 129 as an extremely satisfactory tank-busting aircraft.

"As the engines had a tendency to catch fire quite easily on the ground during start-up, we had to have fire extinguishers close to hand, though I personally never experienced an engine fire while in the air."

"Naturally, we had some problems with the cannon in winter. The airfields in Russia were mostly meadows or uncultivated fields and depending on the weather conditions they could be wet, half-frozen, slushy or covered in snow. During our take-off runs the aircraft often resembled snow-ploughs, and the propellers threw water, snow or dirt - sometimes all three - against the cannon under the fuselage. There was a fairing which was designed to cover and protect the cannon, but these extreme conditions were just too much. Some days after we had taken off we found the cannon had accumulated a very heavy deposit of ice which sometimes prevented the gun from functioning properly. Otherwise, there was the occasional malfunction and jamming, just like any weapon, but I had to break off an attack only once because the cannon went on strike, and this was not the rule."

"Russian fighters were no problem to us if we saw them in time. On the contrary, they respected the range of our weapons and would turn away if we manoeuvred to engage them. I agree with Major Meyer though, when he says that they later became more aggressive with air superiority. Their advantage then was their greater height and they would attack us from out of the sun, either while we were engaged in attacking tanks, when we had no fighter escort with us, or when the escort itself had gone off to attack some other ground target."

"The Hs 129 *Staffeln* fought mainly against tanks which had broken through and were still on the move. Parked tanks were the target for Fw 190 fighter-bombers, or bombers like the Ju 87, Ju 88 or He 111. Flying towards the front of the tanks was highly dangerous and ineffective due to the thickness of the frontal armour, so we flew in so that we could attack them from the rear where the engine was located. Later, we attacked from the side and aimed at their hull and tracks. We were very successful in these methods of attack and in the case of attacks against the rear of a tank, I found that my aircraft was so stable that I could actually aim to shoot through the mesh grills on the tank's top decking. Hits scored in this way with incendiary shells could be most spectacular, especially if the tank crew didn't realise they had been hit and continued to drive around with flames and smoke belching from their engine compartment. Eventually, though, the tank crews got wise to us and would rotate the turret gun to fire backwards at us as we made our run-in."

"Then the Russians tried fixing moveable shutters in place of the grill. These were open when the tanks were on the move but, when attacked, the shutters were closed to protect the engine. This was not an effective method of protection, however."

"Later on in the war we made low-level attacks from the side of the tanks and tried to penetrate the hull between the tracks and the wheels. One or two shells were sufficient to put a tank out of action and sometimes, when a tank exploded, the whole force of the blast went through the bottom of the hull and the earth was scorched in a large circular area all around the tank. However, as one could never tell in which direction the blast from an exploding tank would go, I would bank away after firing in order to avoid possible blast damage to my aircraft."

By the time Gebhard Weber was given command of his own *Staffel*, the Henschel Flugzeugwerke had increased the amount of armour plate around the aircraft's engines. Although this further affected the aircraft's speed and manoeuvrability, the added protection gave the pilots even more confidence in their machines and, as Weber recalls: "Apart from the odd lucky shot, we considered infantry fire of little importance. First we would fire at any mounted infantry with our 20 mm guns, then attack the tanks with our cannon. We had such confidence in our invulnerability that, if we saw tracers coming up from the sides, we would protect ourselves by banking over to present our armoured undersurfaces to the hostile fire."

"Our escort fighters hardly ever attacked targets already under attack by Hs 129s. Sometimes, though, in the course of an operation, and provided there was no enemy fighter opposition, I would release the fighters from escort duty so that they could, for example, attack lorries, horse-drawn carts, etc. I often practised this after August 1944 and the fighters were frequently successful. On the southern sector of the Eastern Front we were mainly escorted by JG 52."

In his two years of operational flying, Gebhard Weber was shot down four times and, on 28 February 1945, was awarded the German Cross in Gold. Shortly before the collapse, he was nominated for the *Ritterkreuz*, but final confirmation was delayed in the chaos of the last months of the war and this prized decoration was never actually awarded.

Because of their individual temperament which made them suitable as ground-attack and anti-tank pilots in the first place, Hs 129 pilots were not inclined to become involved in air-to-air combat. Indeed, occasions arose when formations of German and Russian ground-attack aircraft would fly past one another, each intent on completing his mission rather than be distracted by air combat. Nevertheless, while it was not the business of the *Schlachtflieger* to seek or engage in aerial combat, a small number of pilots found themselves in a favourable position during an engagement and were able to shoot down faster, more manoeuvrable fighters. On 13 March 1944, for example, Hs 129 aircraft not only destroyed seven heavy tanks, 13 assault guns and over 80 vehicles of the advancing Soviet Army, they also succeeded in shooting down an Il-2 and a Yak-5. One Hs 129 pilot with confirmed air-to-air kills was *Fw* Otto Ritz who wrote:

An Fw 190 taxying through the mud and slush on a Russian airfield. Of Hs 129 operations in these conditions, Gebhard Weber wrote "... during our take-off runs, the aircraft often resembled snow-ploughs."

Spring rains turned the Russian airfields into quagmires. Here an He 111 ploughs through slush and rain water. One Hs 129 pilot wrote: "... the mud is indescribable".

"When I shot down an R-5[2], my cannon shells and bullets streamed at him but I didn't know whether I actually succeeded in downing him. Later, my comrades confirmed the kill and said they saw the 'plane go down in a steep plunging dive and crash. I also shot down a Pe-2 over the Korsun pocket. Here, however, I saw my bursts pour into the victim and strike home. At first the Pe-2 tried to avoid me by ducking into some clouds but I waited until it emerged again. Then I let loose burst after burst, my shells and bullets thudding into both engines. The aircraft was already fiercely belching fire and smoke when the rear gunner opened up at me, but he had hardly done so when the machine suddenly burst apart in the air leaving nothing but lots of aluminium debris sailing downwards."

For Franz Oswald, the expected exhilaration of aerial combat proved to be something of an anti-climax. Flying from Tazinskaya on 23 July 1942 in company with *Oblt.* Kent, the pair of Hs 129s were flying at 1,200 m (3,936 ft) with the sun behind them when they saw, 200 m (656 ft) below, two Russian fighters flying in the opposite direction. As the Henschel pilots swung round and dived behind the fighters, two more Russians appeared and in no time ten to twelve Russian fighters were milling about the sky. When one of them flew across the nose of Oswald's aircraft and passed exactly through the reflector sight, he opened fire, but although the Henschel was "spitting flame at him", the Russian fighter flew on unscathed. As he manouevred to attack another fighter, Oswald noticed a third Russian on his tail but with the premise that discretion was the better part of valour, he recalls: "That was enough for me! With throttles wide open, I got down on the deck and flew in the direction of our own forward lines."

---

1 As well as tank "kills", pilots could claim tanks "hit with measureable effect"; in other words, damaged to an extent which would temporarily put them out of action.

2 The Polikarpov R-5 was a late twenties reconnaissance/bomber/general purpose design still in widespread first-line use long after the German Invasion of Russia.

"So low, I could have shaken hands with Ivan"

Non-Stop Ground-Support
January 1944

For the German Army on the Eastern Front, 1943 ended with gloomy military prospects. The Crimea was isolated, the northern half of the Dnieper bend was in Soviet hands and only a part of the Western Ukraine still remained under German control. In the five months since "*Zitadelle*", 104,000 men had been lost and resistance was on the verge of collapse. By the beginning of December 1943, von Manstein's Army Group South still held a fragile line which leant towards the east, but compared to six months earlier, this had reduced considerably in size and strength and had fallen back westwards some 400 km (250 miles). On the 24th, the Russians opened their winter offensive on either side of the Kiev-Zhitomir road and within a few weeks the whole of Army Group South was committed. General Vatutin's First Ukrainian Front and General Rokossovski's Belorussian Front threatened to separate von Kluge's Army Group Centre from Army Group South. Through winter snow and biting cold the Red Army's onslaught continued unabated, giving the hard-pressed German forces no respite. During the first days of January 1944, the Russians were observed assembling strong artillery and armoured forces in the rear and at 06:00 on 5 January, they launched another attack towards Kirovograd. Massed infantry poured through gaps torn in the German front by artillery and air strikes. The infantry, supported by armour, achieved deep penetrations and all German attempts to block the Russian advance failed. The enemy's forces crossed the Ingul and assembled on the west bank before they again thrust westward in a major breakthrough. Apart from the adverse weather conditions - which reduced the *Luftwaffe's* scale of effort proportional to the forces available - the poor state of airfields and general dislocation due to frequent moves all combined to reduce operational readiness and to limit the number of sorties which could be mounted. Yet despite these difficulties it is conceded that the *Luftwaffe* played an important part in closing the gaps between the retreating German formations and whenever conditions permitted, gave valuable support to the army's counter-attacks which succeeded in delaying the Russian advance.

Substantial accommodation was essential in the cruel Russian winter and wherever possible German personnel were billeted with the local population and lived together with them in their primitive, peasant huts. Upon joining 10.(Pz)/SG 9, *Lt.* Walter Krause shared a hut with "Drops" Dornemann, not far from Malaya-Viska airfield, together with some Russian peasants who slept on a large brick-built oven. As *Lt.* Krause found: "The huts were quite warm and snug if one ignored the other occupants - the bugs and lice - but the treeless, unpaved village street was downright bleak and desolate. Nevertheless, these quarters were a welcome place in which to seek refuge from the harsh, icy Russian winter nights."

On 11 December, *Lt.* Krause flew his second mission when again the target was in the Kirovograd area. The following day, 10. and 12.(Pz)/SG 9 were once more ordered to attack

Oblt. Georg Dornemann came to 4.(Pz)/Sch.G 1 in January 1943. Although Staffelkapitän of this unit and 10.(Pz)/SG 9 for a brief period until 13.12.1943 when he was shot down and seriously injured, Dornemann was greatly loved and respected by all members of his Staffel. This photograph was taken after his long recovery; the Wound Badge in Gold is visible on his left breast pocket.

Russian columns, as a result of which Dornemann's *Staffel* was credited with the destruction of eleven tanks, Dornemann himself destroying a number of ammunition lorries and supporting infantry, plus one T-34. But life with an anti-tank *Staffel* was not all flying and fighting, as *Lt.* Krause was about to discover.

On the morning of the 13th, Dornemann ordered Krause 50 kilometres (31 miles) to the rear to an Army rations depot to draw two weeks' provisions for the *Staffel's* 120 men. Krause's Opel Blitz truck struggled over the rutted, frozen highway and it was late in the afternoon before he returned, tired almost to the point of exhaustion, to Malaya-Viska. At first he was bewildered to be met only with embarrassed looks until, eventually, he was told that "Drops" Dornemann had not returned from a sortie.

That day, the 11. Panzer Division had mounted a counter-attack, in support of which 10. and 12.(Pz)/SG 9 had been heavily committed and had made a major contribution to the successes achieved. Although *General der Infanterie* Wehler signalled Eighth Army's "heartfelt thanks" to the units involved, it was no compensation for the loss of 10.(Pz)/SG 9's *Staffelkapitän*.

Dornemann had already destroyed three tanks in the day's operations and had been leading a *Schwarm* in another attack against a Russian armoured column. But as he banked W.Nr. 141531 over while leaving the target area he failed to notice that the column also included light flak vehicles which opened fire on his aircraft. A high-explosive shell hit the cockpit and exploded, sending steel splinters into Dornemann's face. Soon his eyes were full of blood, yet he somehow managed to feather both propellers, lower his flaps and swing round so that his aircraft was flying back towards German lines. However, the crippled machine was already losing airspeed and was too badly damaged to make the safety of friendly positions. As Dornemann later explained: "My aircraft fell like a stone from 50 metres (164 ft) and I made a heavy crash-landing in no-man's-land. The impact of the crash was so severe that my back was badly injured, the canopy was jammed in the closed position and I was rendered unconscious".

Fortunately, Dornemann's crash had been observed by soldiers of the *Waffen*-SS who sent out an assault gun to the downed aircraft. At the crash site the SS men found the pilot paralysed, bleeding and trapped in the wreckage. Unable to open the jammed canopy, the SS troops smashed a hole in the glazing and pulled the still unconscious airman out through the opening, but in their haste to extract him and to vacate no-man's land, they unwittingly added to Dornemann's back injuries. This was his seventh and last crash-landing. Eventually, after a long and painful recovery, Dornemann was given command of a rocket-firing Fw 190 *Staffel* which operated as part of the I./SG 9, but in the last days of the war the situation was so confused that receipt of the unit's first operational orders virtually coincided with orders to surrender.

Now, as a result of Dornemann's hospitalisation, 10.(Pz)/SG 9 came under the temporary command of the inexperienced, twenty-year old *Lt.* Walter Krause, the *Staffel's* only other officer present at that time and its youngest member. Landed with the daunting responsibility of leading the *Staffel*, even if only temporarily, Krause admits that for the next 24 hours he was at panic stations. During his training he had attended courses at the air warfare academy which, he felt, had taught him everything; everything except, of course, the everyday practicalities and routine required for leading an independent anti-tank *Staffel*! It was a hectic and worrying responsibility. Apart from attending to the unit's administrative and technical personnel's problems, the Staff of VIII. *Fliegerkorps* constantly rang up to give information on the latest position of the front lines and at the same time requested details of the *Staffel's* fuel and ammunition consumption, sorties flown, aircraft losses and so on.

Despite this responsibility, Krause was still keen to fly more combat missions and while he took charge of the *Staffel* on the ground, *Fw.* Dietrich and *Fw.* Otto Ritz were assigned command of flying activities. The more experienced Otto Ritz personally took *Lt.* Krause under his wing and it was with Ritz that Krause flew his next few missions. During his third mission, an attack on a target east of Kirovograd, the *Schwarm* ran into heavy anti-aircraft fire put up by Soviet ground troops. As Krause recalls: "My aircraft was hit several times but I didn't notice it in all the excitement. I still had to become accustomed to all the confusion and chaos of a mission with aerobatics on the deck, dropping bombs, firing the cannon and staying in formation. Otto Ritz had seen I had been hit, though. He suddenly ended our firing passes and pulled up on my starboard wing. Once in position

During the night of 8/9 January 1944, Russian forces broke through German lines and drove onto the German-held airfield at Malaya-Viska. To meet the threat, resident Hs 129 Staffeln raised the tails of their aircraft in order to use them as conventional anti-tank guns. In the event, this action was not necessary but these photographs of 10.(Pz)/SG 9's Gebhard Weber (*right*) and Jupp Oehl (*far right*) taken the following morning, show the aircraft still jacked up and ready for action.

alongside my aircraft he pointed to my starboard engine and there was the tell-tale plume of black smoke. But my brave '129 made it back to our airfield where, as I couldn't lower the undercarriage, I had to put the Henschel gently down on its belly into the snow of Malaya-Viska."

On 4 January, 1944, *Lt.* Krause and part of 10.(Pz)/SG 9 transferred to Starokonstantinov, where the unit's new *Staffelführer* arrived, the young Berliner, *Lt.* Hans-Werner Wenzel. For the next few days, non-stop missions were flown from first light until dusk in order to stop a Russian breakthrough near Berdichev. On 5 January, the *Staffel* knocked out twelve tanks and twelve lorries, Krause himself making a modest contribution to the German war effort by setting ablaze a lorry which was towing a "Goulash Cannon" - a field kitchen!

On 7 January, a strong Soviet armoured force - the entire 67th Tank Brigade - advanced deep into German-held territory as far as Malaya-Viska and encircled the airfield where *Hptm.* Franz Oswald, as the *Führer der Panzerjäger*, was in overall control of the anti-tank *Staffeln*. At 02:00 on the night of 8-9 January, the Russians attacked Malaya-Viska, their tanks with mounted infantry moving through the village, firing at anything they saw. Vehicles were set ablaze, houses shelled and the village - where XLVII *Panzer Korps* command post was overrun - reduced to ruins. They then swung towards the airfield.

During an anxious night in which *Hptm.* Oswald and his pilots stayed close to their aircraft, they were joined by the famous fighter ace Erich Hartmann and other members of JG 52. In the darkness, some T-34s had smashed into some airfield huts and blundered into a number of JG 52's Bf 109s, crushing the tail units beneath their tracks. One Bf 109 pilot, believed to have been Hartmann, taxied over to the "safer" side of the airfield, but the enemy tanks withdrew before causing any further damage, either to report their findings or because they had run short of fuel.

The respite was to be short-lived. At around 05:00, tanks, accompanied by armoured cars, reappeared close to the airfield. Because XLVII *Panzer Korps* possessed no armour-piercing weapons, the Hs 129 personnel began to position their aircraft around the airfield in a defensive "hedgehog". The tails of their aircraft were lifted and rested on empty petrol drums so that the 30 mm cannon were horizontal and, with the pilots sitting in the cockpits, the aircraft were made ready for action as if they were conventional anti-tank guns. With the ground personnel organised to swing the aircraft in whichever direction the Russians might appear, the waiting became almost intolerable; the night was still pitch black and everyone was keyed up for the expected Russian attack.

With the dawn came a dense fog and though it gradually lifted, it proved impossible for the Henschels to take-off since in the bitter cold temperatures of - 25 degrees, the engines could not be started without first being warmed. The situation was even more frustrating since the airfield's flight servicing company had already departed taking their heating equipment with them. Consequently, it was not until 10:00 that the Hs 129s were finally airborne, but by that time the situation had largely been brought under control by the Ju 87s of SG 2 which, operating from a neighbouring airfield, hunted down tank after tank on the snow swept plain between Malaya-Viska and Gruzkoye.

On 10 January the *Stab* of IV.(Pz)/SG 9 and all four of its subordinate *Staffeln* was ordered to transfer to Kalinovka, 23 km (14 miles) north of Vinnitsa, in order to stop Russian armour which had broken through the German lines north-east of that city. But just as a *Schwarm* from 10.(Pz) *Staffel* was about to take off on its transfer flight, fully armed and packed with luggage, 25 Il-2s and their fighter escort swept over Starokonstantinov airstrip to make a low-level attack.

As Walter Krause recalls: "We had no choice but to take off with engines at full power into the chaos of manoeuvring enemy aircraft, exploding bombs and tracers from our own flak. Then, on a signal from the *Schwarmführer*, the four *Schlachtflieger* turned into the enemy formation in an attempt to break up or at least disrupt the attack and so protect a number of Ju 52 transports which were still standing on the airfield being loaded. In the air, quite a dog-fight took place. The German machines formed a kind of flying hedgehog, firing in all directions, while the airfield's quadruple flak fired into the midst of it all. The firepower of the Hs 129s soon gained the Il-2s' respect and they dropped their remaining bombs at random and made off in all directions. Those ground personnel not involved in the airfield defence peered warily from their trenches until the attackers were turned away, pursued by the Hs 129s".

"I chased one Il-2 over the ground at very low level until I realised that I had inadvertently followed him across the front line and that I was now in enemy territory. But when I decided to turn back, four Yak-3s pounced on me. Only by flying at extra low level was I able to evade their repeated attacks and I reached Kalinovka airstrip drenched in sweat and with my hair practically standing on end. Safely back on the ground I was met by Otto Ritz who had evidently already heard about my escapade. *"You won't grow old at the front if you carry on like that!"* was his dry comment."

Later, the Hs 129s were able to carry out their original mission and used their guns and cannon to shoot up a Soviet-occupied village where lorries and various other vehicles were set on fire. But Ritz's prediction concerning Krause's life-expectancy came alarmingly close to reality the very next day. All airmen are superstitious, and as Krause's next mission would be his thirteenth, Ritz was heard to mutter one of his less than encouraging remarks, commenting wryly that Krause's mission was "bound to go wrong!" As Krause remembered: "At first, all was quite normal. Otto led us to an area south of Progrebitchi where we were at first unable to find any tank targets but attacked columns of lorries instead. Then, immediately after leaving the target area to make our way home, we discovered a large column of tanks just north of the nearest village. Otto banked over at once and led us round in a turn. I was flying as his Number 4 in the *Schwarm* and approached the tanks in a gentle turn to his starboard at 100 metres (330 ft), directly over the village. I could see that the place was full of Ivans and a stream of red tracers from 3.7 cm flak flashed vertically up past my "Mill"[1]. I must have presented a splendid target, but perhaps a bit too low and a bit too fast. Despite the already almost unbearable tension, I was frightened out of my mind when there was a sudden big bang. Direct hit in the port wing! My aircraft went into a kind of sideways skid and

Hs 129 B-2 with MK 103 and canvas cockpit cover.

started to lose height rapidly."

"Then, beyond the village, I saw to my horror that I was flying straight towards a Russian flak position! I was now down to around 50 metres (165 ft) and when I saw the flak position right where I wanted to make an emergency landing, my blood froze. An instant before the Russians could open fire on me, however, a '129 shot past me from above, firing at the enemy gun position from all four barrels. It was Otto Ritz!"

"Once over the flak position - I was now so low that I could have shaken hands with any Ivan who might have survived - Otto headed west. Miraculously, my "Mill" stayed in the air and, waggling his wings as a signal for me to follow him, Otto led me back to base where we both made normal landings. Today, I have the tip of the 3.7 cm shell which hit my aircraft on my desk as a souvenir."

Other anti-tank pilots in action at this time were not so fortunate. On 8 January, 12.(Pz)/SG 9's *Staffelführer*, *Lt.* Erhard Fuchs, collided in mid-air with *Uffz.* Werner Vosseler, both pilots being killed, and during a sortie on the 12th, 10.(Pz)/SG 9's *Ofhr.* Egon Pfaff was killed when his aircraft, W.Nr. 141395 broke up in the air and crashed near Losovataya. On 16 January, *Uffz.* Gerd Logemann was injured when he crashed while trying to land his damaged W.Nr.141392 at Kalinovka. After turning his machine back to the airfield on its left engine only, he attempted an emergency landing. In the Hs 129, the pilot's heavy head and back armour plate was retained only by a relatively flimsy aluminium alloy fixture. As Logemann banked his aircraft on final approach, it stalled and plunged 10 m (30 ft) to the ground, the impact causing the armour plate behind him to break free and thrust his head forward into the windscreen. Although he was knocked unconscious when his skull hit the armoured glass, Logemann survived.

On the 24 and 26 January, following their fierce attacks during the middle of the month in the Kirovograd area, which the Germans had succeeded in holding for a while, the Russians launched a pincer attack against a German salient west of Cherkassy. On the 30th another salient east of Krivoi-Rog was also attacked. Russian superiority in strength was considerable and both these Soviet operations were successful. On 25 January, 10.(Pz)/SG 9 prevented a Russian tank breakthrough on the left flank of a German counter-attack and subsequently made a considerable contribution to the successful defence of Progrebitchi, for which the *Staffel* received a letter of appreciation from *General der Flieger* Seidemann. At this time the *Staffel's* score of tanks destroyed in the three months since its redesignation in October 1943 stood at 219 and despite the Russian's numerical superiority, morale in the *Staffel* was high. The pilots were young, aggressive, and confident that if anybody could stop the enemy then it was the two *Panzerjägerstaffeln* at Kirovograd, 10. and 12.(Pz)/SG 9. But this abundance of youthful confidence was severely shaken in early February when 10.(Pz)/SG 9 was transferred to Uman close to the Rumanian border to help open what the German High Command referred to in their communiqués as the "Cherkassy Pocket". More accurately known as the "Korsun Pocket", six and a half German divisions had been encircled and trapped by the Red Army on 28 February. Surrounded and cut off far behind enemy lines, the entire pocket was then trying to migrate westwards and rejoin the main German front. It was here at Uman airfield, overcrowded with VIII. *Fliegerkorps*' aircraft, including He 111 and

General der Flieger Hans Seidemann, commander VIII. Fliegerkorps

Ju 52 units which had flown supplies into the pocket and brought out wounded on their return trips, that the younger anti-tank pilots of the *Staffel* saw for the first time emaciated, exhausted and dispirited German soldiers in ragged, filthy uniforms. They found it a deeply shocking experience. To make matters worse, the Russians had brought up large numbers of anti-aircraft guns and for the first time the flak defences were so strong that the Henschel pilots were forced to abandon their attacks.

Georg Dornemann and Gebhard Weber were not the only successful Hs 129 pilots shot down that winter for also in January, Hans-Hermann Steinkamp, at that time the *Staffelführer* of 14.(Pz)/SG 9, was forced to make an emergency landing behind enemy lines. Steinkamp was renowned for his excellent marksmanship, exceptional eyesight and his ability to sense an enemy flak trap from many miles. While flying low over a column of retreating German vehicles which had congregated in front of a collapsed river bridge, Steinkamp saw two tanks swing onto the road behind them. At first he assumed they were friendly tanks moving up to provide cover for the rear of the column, but then he pulled up out of formation and banked round. "Follow me!" Steinkamp shouted over the radio. "There's something wrong down there!"

The other pilots of the *Schwarm* watched as Steinkamp closed in on one of the two tanks, took careful aim and squeezed the triggers on his control column. A short but concentrated burst of cannon shells set the machine alight and it started to burn fiercely. When the other three pilots flew over the column, they saw that the drivers of the German vehicles had thrown themselves in the roadside ditch for cover. Only then did they finally realise why Steinkamp had attacked - the second tank's turret was marked with the stars of the Red Army and supporting Soviet infantry could be seen nearby. After the second vehicle had been knocked out, its sole survivor was captured by the German soldiers, who were now able to leave the ditch.

But Steinkamp's aircraft had been hit by light flak during his attack and he was forced to make an emergency landing close to the T-34 he had just destroyed. Safely on the ground, he jumped out of the burning Henschel and ran towards his own positions, only to find that three lines of Soviet infantry stood between him and safety. While running through the third line of Russians he was spotted by one of their officers but, before the man could unshoulder his machine-gun, Steinkamp shot him with his pistol. Alerted by the shot, the other Russian soldiers now opened fire on the fleeing German pilot, wounding him in the shoulder and smashing his forearm. Despite these wounds, Steinkamp somehow managed to get away and even succeeded in swimming the river in a desperate attempt to reach his own lines. Only after he had met up with a German patrol did he collapse, completely exhausted. After making a remarkably speedy recovery, Steinkamp returned to operations where his great successes earned him the *Deutsches Kreuz* in Gold on 29 March 1944 and the *Ritterkreuz* on 24 October of that year.

Oblt. Hans-Hermann Steinkamp came to the Panzerjäger on 4.3.1942 via Gr.Kampf.Sch. 1 at Tutow. He is reported to have possessed exceptional eyesight and an ability to detect flak traps. In January 1944, whilst Staffelführer of 14.(Pz)/SG 9, he was shot down behind enemy lines and although wounded as he tried to avoid a Russian patrol, he managed to reach the safety of his own lines.

An unknown pilot seated in his aircraft. Interesting details include the dive angles engraved on the canopy side panel, mirror, manufacturer's data plates and the generally worn appearance of canopy frame.

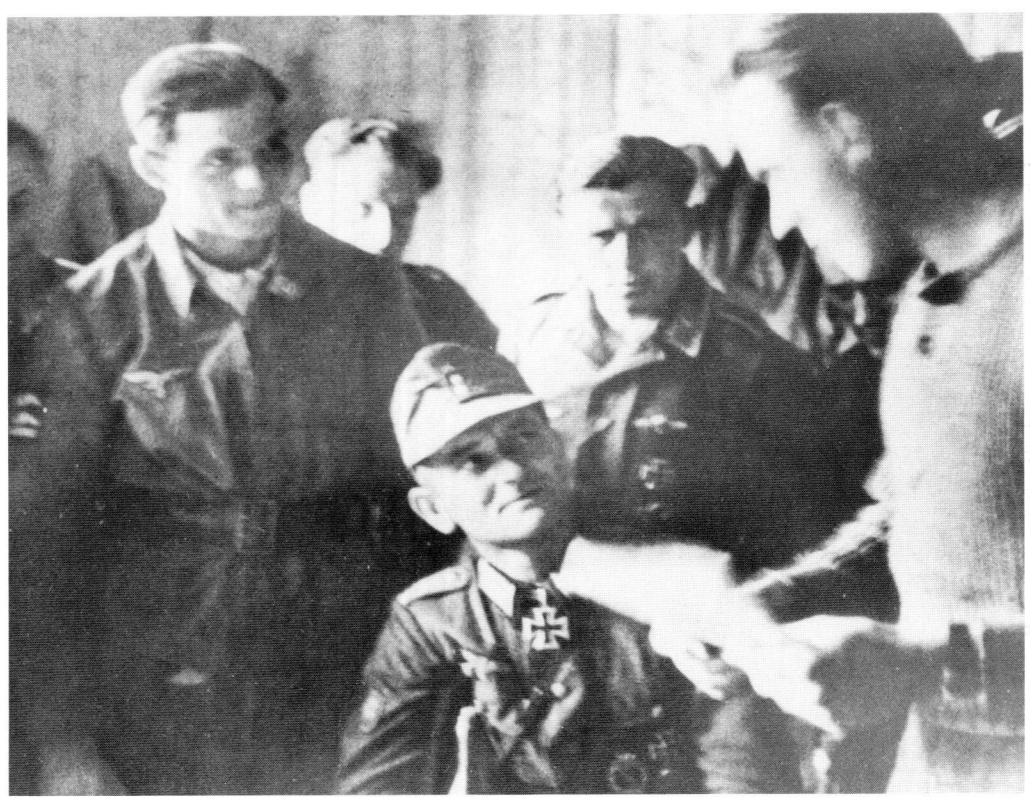

Though this photograph was taken earlier in the war, it demonstrates the close co-operation between the Panzerjäger and German ground troops - in this case, the Gerbirgsjäger, or Mountain Troops. Here, Oblt. Ruffer together with pilots of 8.(Pz)/Sch.G 1 discuss operations with a Ritterkreuzträger from the Gebirgsjäger, believed to be General Georg Ritter von Hengl, commander of 59th Corps.

On 27 January, 10.(Pz)/SG 9 lost *Lt.* Horst Michel. He was leading a *Schwarm* in an operation against tanks south-west of Ocherenya, but after making his sixth attack his aircraft, W.Nr.141589, developed engine trouble. Michel nevertheless decided to make another pass. According to his *Rottenflieger, Uffz.* Scholz, *Lt.* Michel's aircraft was last seen to the north-east of Ocherenya, where it was presumed to have crashed in enemy territory.

Although the main objective of the Hs 129 *Staffeln* was to attack and destroy enemy troops and vehicles, particularly armour, there were occasions when an opportunity arose to employ the aircraft's heavy weapons against other targets. During the battles for the lower Dnieper, for example, some German soldiers of a mountain division found that their positions were in full view of a Russian observation post set up in a church tower on the opposite bank. As a result, enemy artillery fire was landing in the German positions and making life particularly uncomfortable for the soldiers there. No friendly artillery was available to knock out the observation post and although an attack had been made by German aircraft, it was without effect.

VIII. *Fliegerkorps* had just learned of the failure of this attack when a report was received from *Lt.* Weber of 10.(Pz)/SG 9 stating that he had a *Schwarm* of Hs 129s available for operations. Although the weather was not favourable - the cloud base was down to 300 m (1,000 ft) - *Fliegerkorps* asked if this formation would make an attempt on the same target, to which Weber eagerly replied it would.

Since armour-piercing shot would not be required for such a mission, the aircraft were loaded with bombs and armed with high-explosive shells. The four Hs 129s took off and climbed into the low clouds. Crossing into enemy territory, they flew past the target and then turned back to attack it from behind. Their first run-in was with bombs, during which they scored some good hits. The pilots then strafed with their cannon, pouring their high-explosive shells into the tower until they were sure that the observation post would do no more harm to the German front. Even before the formation had landed, news of its success had already reached the *Fliegerkorps* via the *Flivo*[2] at IV.(Pz)/SG 9's command post who reported, "Mission accomplished without any trouble. The church tower is still burning." A few days later the *Gruppe* received thanks from the *Gebirgsjäger* division.

---

1 Rather than being a specific reference to the Hs 129, "Mill", or "Mühle" was a term used by German airmen in the same way as British and American pilots would refer to their "kite", "crate" or "ship".

2 Flivo: abbreviation for Flieger Verbindungs Offizier (Air Liaison Officer, i.e. Forward Air Controller).

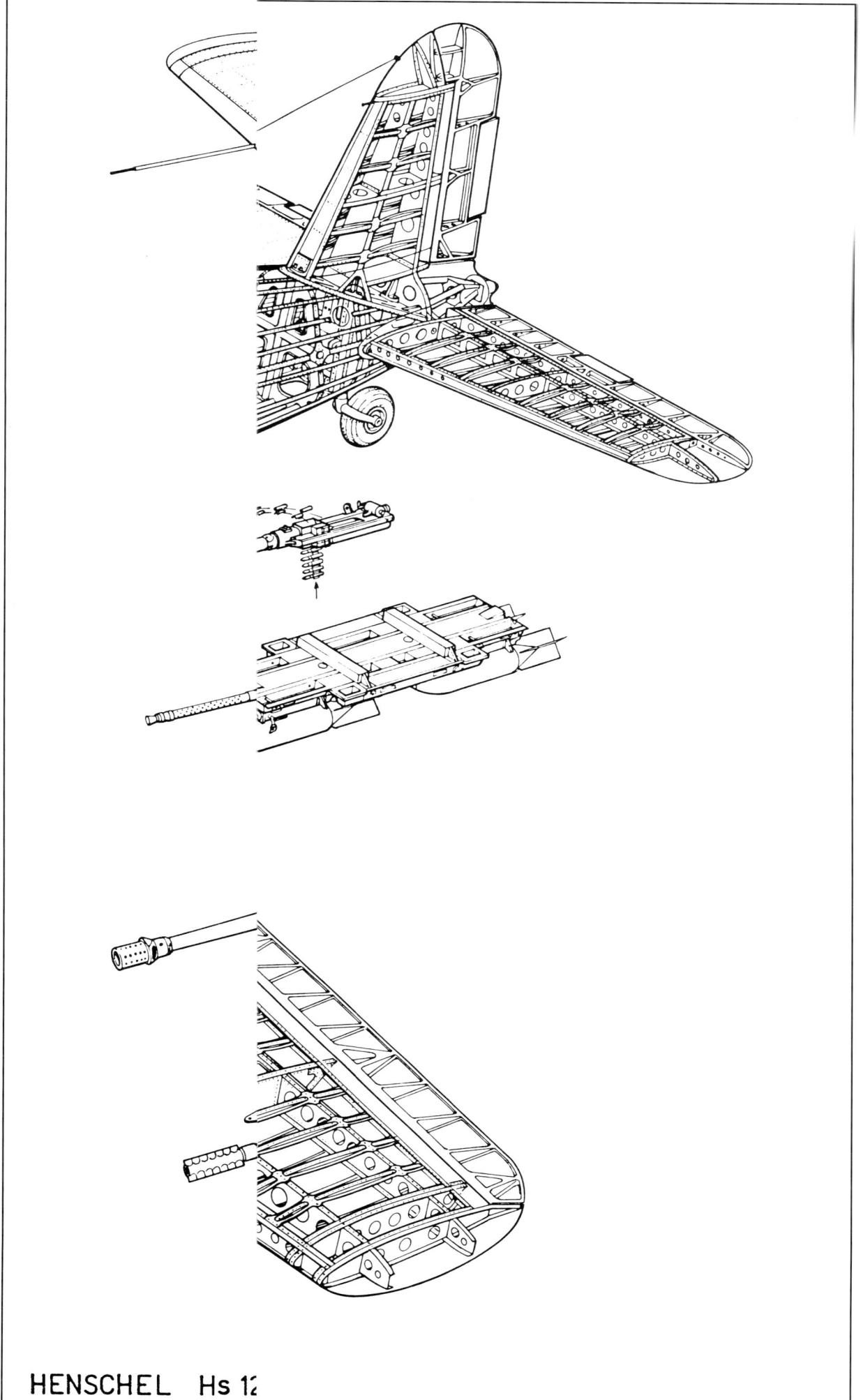

HENSCHEL Hs 12

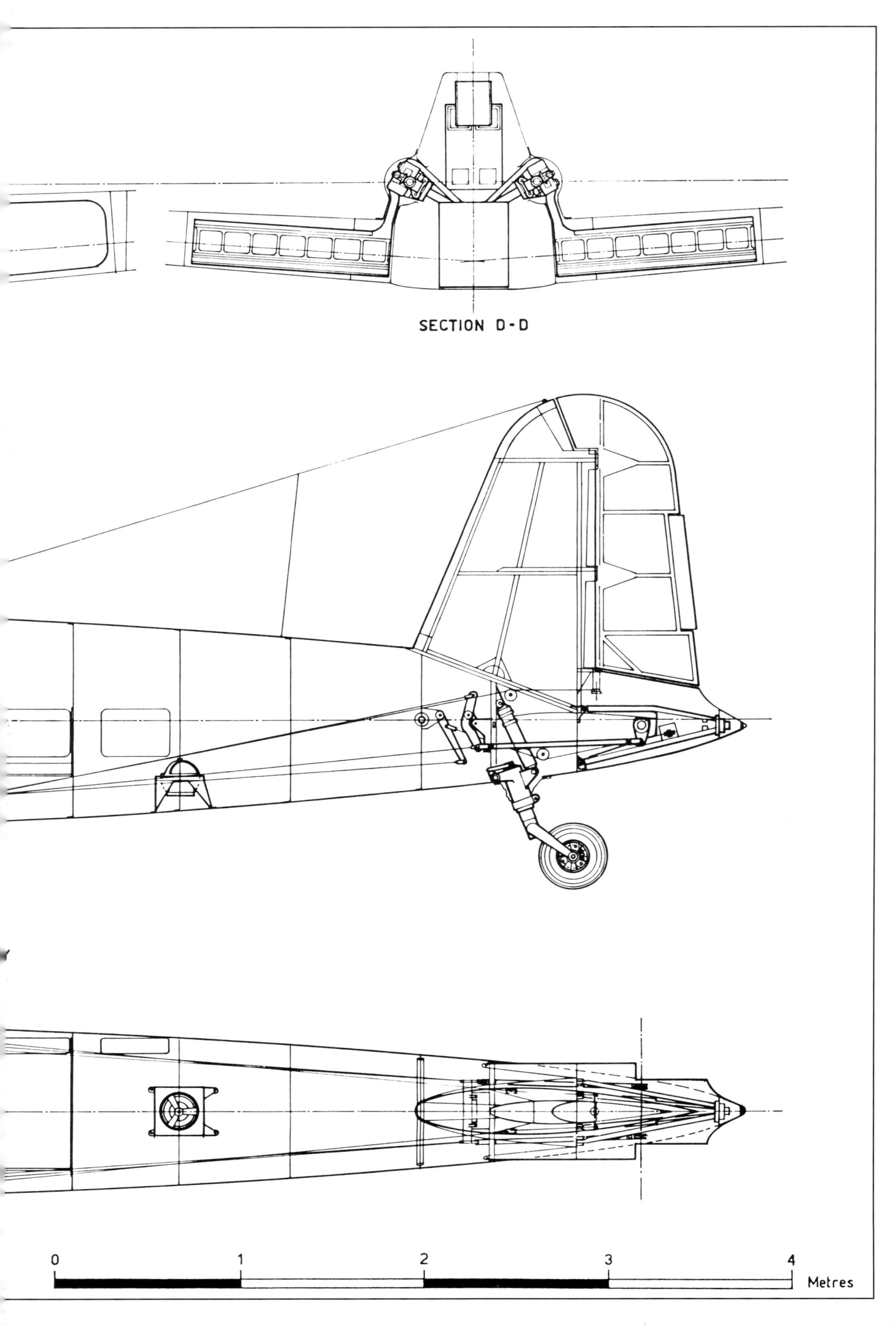

SECTION D-D

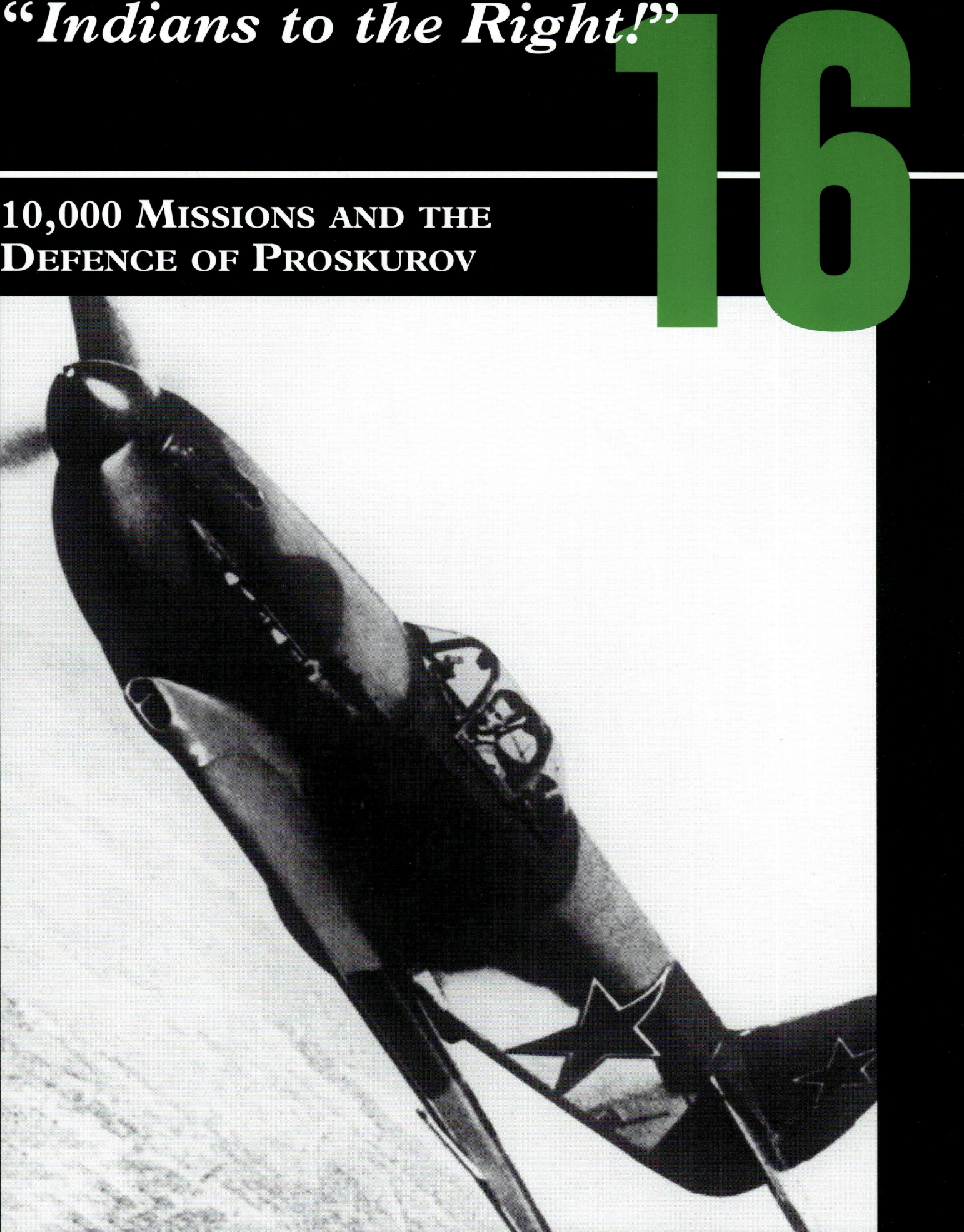

"*Indians to the Right!*"

10,000 Missions and the Defence of Proskurov

16

In February, 1944, the key positions on the Dnieper bend, Nikopol and Krivoi-Rog, finally fell to the continuing Soviet advance. The Russian winter was at its height with bad weather and extreme cold grounding virtually all *Luftwaffe* flying units. The pilots of 10.(Pz)/SG 9 at Uman spent most of their time at readiness in their operations room, an abandoned road-worker's wagon still bearing the former owner's original red and white paint scheme and the lettering: *"Bauunternehmer Aloys Tscherny, Vienna XVII"*. The Russian Air Force, apparently less restrained by the poor flying weather, mounted frequent attacks on Uman airfield where the brightly painted wagon presented a fine target.

For their own self-protection, the pilots had dug a slit trench and although only about 300 mm (12 inches) deep it was to prove its worth. One day in February, four of the *Staffel's* pilots were sitting in their cockpits at immediate readiness when a number of Il-2s made a head-on attack against their parked aircraft. Leaping out of their machines, the pilots made a dash for cover, each throwing himself into the trench with his head between the legs of the man in front. There was a fearful whistle and bombs exploded about 20 m (60 ft) from where they lay, but the gallantly conspicuous *"Gefechtsstand Aloys Tscherny"* escaped completely undamaged and, still defiantly uncamouflaged, remained in use for many more months.

When the weather permitted, the *Staffel* was able to fly a number of missions in aid of troops surrounded in the Cherkassy/Korsun pocket. The soldiers were attempting to make contact with the outside force trying to relieve them and finally succeeded in breaking through the Russian ring during the night of 16-17 February. When the temperature rose slightly, a thaw set in bringing mud and rain. On 1 March, due mainly to the state of Uman airfield, which was in any case captured by the Russians on the 10th, 10.(Pz)/SG 9 transferred to Vinnitsa where flying operations were conducted from a concrete runway.

On 11 March *Lt.* Wenzel was ordered to fly a sortie with six aircraft, all that were serviceable. As usual at Vinnitsa, refuelling was carried out after the aircraft had been towed by caterpillar tractor onto a small concrete pad near flying control and it was shortly after they had been drawn up on the refuelling pad close to an Me 323 "Gigant" transport aircraft, and the pilots had strapped themselves in, that JG 52's Technical Officer, *Hptm.* Schinkel, came over to the parked Henschels. "You should not park your mills so close together", he called out. "*General* Seidemann (VIII. *Fliegerkorps'* commanding officer) is on the airfield and he has issued orders that all aircraft must be parked at least 15 metres apart."

"So how are we supposed to fuel up?" retorted the Henschel pilots, but the brief argument was

In June 1942, Henschel established a Front Repair Station at Zaporozhe to service aircraft close to the front. As the front moved further east, so too did the Front Repair Station, transferring first to Kharkov and later to Tagowrog. This Hs 129 B-2, still in its factory codes, is being tested before being sent to a Luftwaffe unit.

Spring thaws in March 1944 brought mud and rain. At Vinnitsa, 10.(Pz)/SG 9 refuelled after the aircraft had been towed by caterpillar tractor onto a small concrete pad near flying control.

ended abruptly when a red flare shot up into the sky and in the same instant some 20 Il-2s swept over the field at tree-top height looking for targets. The flying control building, the huge Me 323 with its 55 m (108 ft) wingspan, and the six parked Henschels were sitting ducks. Walter Krause: "We jumped out of our aircraft and made for the nearest slit trenches. The Russians' 2 kg bombs burst all around us, aircraft exploded, and the wounded could be heard crying out. *Lt. Wenzel* was carried off with injuries caused by bomb splinters and our last six Hs 129s presented a very sorry sight. As we surveyed the scene, a loud voice behind me demanded, *"Where is the Staffelkapitän of the Panzerjäger?"* Spinning round, I saw to my horror that standing in front of me was *General* Seidemann himself. I brushed the dirt from my flying overalls. *"Herr General, Lt. Wenzel has been taken away wounded."* He gave me a glacial stare. *"If the Panzerjäger disobey my orders regarding the parking of aircraft they'll have to make up for it in other ways or they'll be court-martialled"*. I felt crushed. The 10.(Pz) didn't have a single airworthy aircraft left. After the *General* had stormed off, Otto Ritz took me to one side. *"Never mind, Herr Leutnant"*, he said kindly. *"We'll make up for it!"*

"The next day we transferred to Proskurov, not in our Henschels but in a lumbering Ju 52. Here in Proskurov we were to jump out of the frying pan and into the fire. We took delivery of new Henschels but the situation at the front and within the *Staffel* was pretty grim. We had received a severe mauling; the *Staffelführer* was wounded; part of the *Staffel* was still in Vinnitsa and another part with *Lt.* Jech and *Fw.* Heinrich Michalczak had left for the Brody area. But there was one bright spot. In Proskurov a new era began for the 10.(Pz) when *Hptm.* Ruffer took over the *Staffel*."

At this time, the Russians had surrounded Proskurov on three sides and were occupying the heights around the city. Apart from the Staff of *General* Hans Hube's 54th *Panzerkorps*, the city had been evacuated. Although airfield conditions at Proskurov were primitive they were reasonably comfortable and while *Lt.* Krause, *Hptm.* Ruffer and *Lt.* von Chamiev sat in their hut reminiscing about old times, from the window they could watch the *Staffel's* Henschels making their cannon attacks against Russian armour only some 8 km (5 miles) away. With the enemy so close, the pilots felt certain that yet another withdrawal was imminent and were therefore surprised when the situation at the front died down. Becoming suspicious, "Pan" Ruffer decided to investigate.

The two aircraft climbed into brilliant sunshine and were soon over the front. Everything looked quiet, though from time to time black smoke signals were fired into the air. The pilots presumed these were to indicate that German aircraft had crossed the lines.

"Then Ruffer called me over the radio," Krause recalls, ""*Lets fly to the rear for a while and find out what's going on there*". But again there was nothing to be seen and the countryside remained

Refuelling one of the 205 litre wing tanks of White "I", W.Nr. 141584 of 10.(Pz)/SG 9. Traces of the factory code may still be seen on the fuselage.

Lt. Walter Krause's White "K" of 10.(Pz)/SG 9 and a Ju 87 D. The role of the Hs 129 was to attack tanks which had broken through the front line and were operating in areas where anti-aircraft defences were weak. Armour concentrations or tanks parked behind the front were attacked by bomb carrying Ju 87s and Fw 190s which also provided close-support.
Below: Ground crew working on White "K".

Technical and flying personnel of 10.(Pz)/SG 9 at Proskurov, March 1944. At the head of the column with map tucked into his flying boot is Lt. Walter Krause with, bareheaded, Fw. Heinrich Michalczak

Hs 129 B-2 White 'K'
as flown by Lt. Walter Krause, 10.(Pz)/SG 9, early 1944.

This aircraft carried the standard 70/71/65 splinter camouflage pattern and **yellow** theatre markings with random temporary **white** winter scheme overpainted. The **white** paint although appearing to be haphazardly applied was clearly brushed on with care so as not to obliterate the aircraft code letter or national insignia. The National insignia were: B2 crosses on the wing undersides, B6 crosses on wing upper-surfaces, B5 crosses on fuselage sides and H2a *Hakenkreuze*. This aircraft was fitted with an MK 103 cannon.

Ofw. Hermann Holtermann, (centre, with map), was one of 10.(Pz)/SG 9's most experienced pilots. He was awarded a posthumous German Cross in Gold on 1 January 1945.

peaceful in the spring sunshine. We flew on until a formation of what at first looked like dancing birds appeared in the distance. Recognising them as enemy fighters, I called Ruffer: *"Herr Hauptmann, Indians to the right!" "I've seen them"*, he replied. *"Let's stay down low"*. But the Russians had already seen us and in no time at all eight Yak-3s had closed in on us and, dividing up into two flights, proceeded to attack us from each side. *"Make for home!"* Ruffer cried, *"But stay down low! Keep weaving and keep firing!"*

"At a height of only 9 metres (30 ft) we flew at once towards Proskurov, criss-crossing each other for mutual protection as we went. We both fired at the attacking fighters from all barrels and were so busy that we hardly had any time to be afraid of the Ivans. After about twenty minutes of this we reached our airfield with the Russians still in hot pursuit, but when our light flak opened up on them they turned away and we were able to land safely. Neither of our machines had been hit once and, although Ruffer said with his inimitable grin, *"Didn't we do a grand job?"*, we were both dripping with sweat."

However, the overall situation was anything but grand. This was still the period of the Russian mud season and both men and machines were taxed to the limit when the Red Army re-opened its attack with massed armour and drove on with its advance. In the next few days the Henschels of 10.(Pz)/SG 9 flew without pause against enemy tanks which had broken through the German front line and it again became clear that the Hs 129, flown by a competent pilot, could knock out any type of enemy tank. *Hptm.* Ruffer, acting as deputy for *Major* Meyer, led some aircraft from the Staff and two flights from 10.(Pz)/SG 9 and actually managed to stop the Russian onslaught near Vinnitsa and Tarnopol.

In this way, ground-attack and anti-tank aircraft operating in the area were frequently able to prevent a disaster only at the last minute and in some cases, as a result of their considerable operational experience, the pilots themselves were able accurately to assess a dangerous situation on the ground and a crisis was often averted without friendly ground troops even being aware of the threat. Such an occasion arose on 12 March, when a strong spearhead of Russian tanks approached the by now greatly advanced airfield from which the 10.(Pz) was operating. *Hptm.* Ruffer, realised at once that strong enemy armoured forces were renewing their push towards Proskurov and that the airfield was threatened. On his own initiative, Ruffer led wave-by-wave attacks against the T-34s while the groundcrews were kept very busy reloading and refuelling the aircraft for the next mission; from their airfield they could clearly see how the Henschels banked and dived to attack and, in between rearming and refuelling they themselves made arrangements to defend the airstrip.

To no avail the Russians camouflaged their tanks using every trick of the trade. Some also set off smoke canisters to imitate being set on fire, while others drove through the walls of houses and hid inside, but by the time dusk fell, the *Staffel* had destroyed 19 tanks and immobilised 5 others. Ruffer himself achieved his 50th victory, *Fw.* Ritz claimed 5 tanks bringing his score to 27 destroyed in 90 missions and *Lt.* Krause claimed 2 tanks destroyed. *Ofw.* Erhardt Dittrich, who up until this time had 100 missions, 37 tanks, 13 assault guns, 80 to 100 vehicles, an Il-2 and an La-5 to his credit, increased his score by a further 7 tanks. Furthermore, while flying an armed reconnaissance mission in the Proskurov area, Dittrich encountered an enemy armoured spearhead close to his own tank forces. Through radio contact with the German Panzer commander and by making mock attacks against the Russian armour after his own ammunition was exhausted, he was able to direct 12 Hs 129s to the target area where they destroyed 46 T-34s.

The Henschels' repeated low-level wave-by-wave attacks also routed the enemy's accompanying infantry and although a number of T-34s were only destroyed after they had penetrated to the immediate vicinity of 54th *Panzerkorps'* command post, the Russians' intentions had been defeated and Proskurov saved from immediate capture. For this action the 10.(Pz)/SG 9 received a mention in the *Wehrmacht* communiqué of 13 March, though it stated only tersely that *"A Schlachtstaffel under the command of Hptm. Ruffer has particularly distinguished itself"*.

Some time later, when another attack was made on Proskurov with significantly stronger forces, the Fw 190s of *Major* Karl Henze's I./SG 77 stopped the enemy's drive so effectively that First Panzer Army was able to escape encirclement and German troops gained the necessary time to evacuate the fully occupied field hospitals and supply dumps in good order and to build up a new defensive line.

During these operations the *Staffel's* ground staff worked ceaselessly to keep the Henschels fuelled, armed and airworthy. On the evening of 15 March, *General* Seidemann arrived to personally express his appreciation and, no doubt to everyone's relief, said that the Vinnitsa incident would now be forgotten. General Hube, the one-armed, former World War One infantryman and now commander of the First Panzer Army, also came to the airfield and presented the *Staffel* with a letter of his personal recognition. With this success and a score of 50 tanks destroyed to his credit, Ruffer's *Staffel* comrades felt sure that his achievements would be recognised by the award of the *Ritterkreuz*, but several months were yet to pass before this speculation became a reality.

At this time most of Ruffer's kills had been achieved using the MK 101 cannon. Use of the improved MK 103 had increased since its service introduction in July 1943, but it was not without its teething troubles and Ruffer's score would

The commander of a T-34 peers cautiously around his turret hatch.

German vehicles fight their way through the mud of the Russian spring thaw. As wheeled vehicles easily became bogged down in such adverse conditions, a tracked type, such as the one shown was necessary to pull them free.

White "A" of 10.(Pz)/SG 9. The snow camouflage on this aircraft has extended to the propeller blades and the weapons technician working under the aircraft has the steel bar required for levering the loaded MK 103 back into position.

Two pictures showing 10.(Pz)/SG 9 armourers reloading the MK 103 cannon of White "A". By early 1944, when these photographs were taken, the MK 103's earlier teething troubles had been eliminated and the Panzerjäger possessed a very reliable and effective weapon. Points of interest are the variously coloured tips to the 30 mm rounds, the quick release pins which enabled the weapon to be easily swung down for reloading and the steel bar required to lever the loaded gun back into position.

have been higher had the MK 103 proved more reliable. He once took off eight times with an aircraft equipped with the MK 103, and on all eight occasions the cannon failed. Nevertheless, by the end of March, Ruffer was still the leading Hs 129 *Experte* and had increased his score to 63 tank kills. As for the MK 103, the cannon later became a very reliable weapon when used under normal conditions. Interestingly, the 10.(Pz) *Staffel's* Heinrich Michalczak was able to make some proposals to improve its performance via his father who worked as a weapons engineer at the Rheinmetall-Borsig armaments factory in Berlin.

Soon only a small part of Proskurov and the airfield itself remained in German hands. As the Russians drove still closer, thick fog at first prevented the *Staffel* from flying either offensive operations or evacuating the airfield. German tanks standing near the airstrip fired at the attacking Russians and also had to be used to pull the aircraft from the deep mud. By 24 March, the situation was so desperate that the Henschels simply had to take off despite the weather and after a "dreadful flight" arrived in Kamenets-Podolski. But this was only a temporary move, for no sooner had they arrived than they had to flee again, this time to the beautiful little Rumanian town of Chernovtsy. Two days later the *Staffel* transferred to Lemberg (now Lvov) inside the Polish border. Here almost the entire VIII. *Fliegerkorps* had assembled and operations by all types of aircraft were mounted from the airfield's single overcrowded concrete runway. By the end of March the 10. *Staffel* alone had accounted for the destruction of 100 T-34s, six Russian aircraft, approximately 30 assault guns and hundreds of vehicles of all types, all for the loss of two 10. *Staffel* pilots killed when their aircraft crashed and caught fire.

While the 10. *Staffel's* recent attacks had been directed principally against tank targets, the 13. and 14. *Staffeln* efforts had been directed mainly against columns of vehicles and infantry. In the sector covered by 13.(Pz)/SG 9, flying had been impossible because of the weather conditions which lasted for most of February, as recorded by Franz Oswald:

***3 February**. No missions flown. Now we are in the midst of the muddy season and the roads and most of the airfield look awful although our landing strip is still good. This muddy season will last for some four to six weeks, during which no vehicle will be able to get through.*

***5 February**. Fog today. The situation here is driving me mad; almost the whole of the Eastern Front is afire and only our sector is quiet. Nothing happens which requires our intervention. And this terrible weather. All the roads are now so muddy that no Staffel vehicle can be driven and in these conditions our airfield is an hour's march from where we are billeted.*

***6 February**. The Staffel is off duty today for the first time in many months. The airfield is now closed down because of the muddy ground.*

Breakfast! In the vast open spaces of southern Russia, troops were encouraged wherever possible to live off the land. Here, personnel from 10.(Pz)/SG 9 round up some vital and much-cherished items from the Staffel's inventory!

On 13 March, *Lt.* Gebhard Weber was transferred from 13.(Pz)/SG 9 to replace the 10.(Pz) *Staffel's* injured *Lt.* Wenzel. On the same day, 13.(Pz)/SG 9 was posted to another operational area and although the weather was still poor with a great deal of rain, many missions were flown so that the *Staffel* was in action almost continuously until the end of the month. Losses

White "O" of 10.(Pz)/SG 9 arrives on a muddy Eastern front airfield, believed to be Proskurov, in March 1944. The aircraft appears well-used and weathered and has heavy carbon deposits around its gun troughs.

were slight and no pilots were lost, although Franz Oswald was shot down on 20 March and made a forced landing in no-man's-land, during which his only injury was a slightly sprained hand. He ran to his own lines where, after 45 minutes he was picked up by a *"Storch"*. In the two weeks leading up to the end of March that Oswald's 13.(Pz) *Staffel* was in action, it claimed 41 tanks destroyed with another 21 attacked with noticeable effect. During the afternoon of 5 April, Franz Oswald led two pilots in "a fine and successful mission". Although the take-off was "awful" - it was raining and the airfield was wet and muddy - the weather in the target area was much better. No tanks were seen, but the three Henschels strafed some enemy vehicles, setting eight lorries on fire. The pilots then flew to some eight to ten gun emplacements, strafing these too before making a safe return to their airfield.

A report prepared by one of Henschel's fitters who visited the units at this time confirmed that, irrespective of the mission types undertaken, all Hs 129 pilots had been very successful with the type and had great confidence in the aircraft. Despite formidable Russian defences, attacks were always pressed home regardless and the pilots were pleased to state that the Hs 129 was insensitive to hits. Despite shot-up control surfaces or bullet and flak damage to its fuselage and wing surfaces, the aircraft could always be relied upon to take the pilot safely home. As well as anti-tank work and strafing attacks against enemy infantry and vehicles, the machine was also ideal for the low-flying reconnaissance role where the excellent view from the cockpit enabled even well-camouflaged and hidden targets to be identified.

Meanwhile, the German Seventeenth Army had been forced to evacuate the Kuban bridgehead and had crossed over the Strait of Kerch to the Crimea. This had been accomplished without appreciable loss, but when the Russian Army broke through the front north of Melitopol and thrust past the Perekop Isthmus, Seventeenth Army was completely cut off from the mainland. By 30 October 1943, the Russians had entered the Crimea, trapping the German forces who had been ordered to hold fast by Hitler. After the Russian offensives in the Ukraine during the first four months of 1944, the Germans had been pushed back to the Carpathians and almost to the borders of Poland. It was not, therefore, until 8 April 1944 that the Russian assault in the Crimea began.

Luftwaffe anti-tank support for the trapped army units began to arrive on 10 April, when five He 111s landed at Karankut, southwest of Dzhankoi, loaded with key anti-tank personnel from 10.(Pz)/SG 9 and the Ju 87-equipped anti-tank *Staffel* 10.(Pz)/SG 3. The Henschel *Staffel* went into action immediately and so distinguished itself, particularly in operations on the Feodosia strip, that only three days after its arrival, it had already assisted in the destruction of 82 Soviet tanks and was mentioned in the OKW's daily bulletin of 13 April. Nevertheless, Seventeenth Army was forced to retreat until it held only a defensive position in the fortified belt around Sevastopol. Although the *Luftwaffe* still held runways and airstrips there, they were the subject of concentrated bombing and strafing attacks by the Soviet Air Force. During one such strafing attack carried out by Il-2s against Chersones airfield on 15 April, three of 10.(Pz)/SG 9's pilots were involved in an unusual incident. While making a low-level pass, one of the Russian aircraft was hit by anti-aircraft fire and was forced to make an emergency landing on the airfield. *Ofw.* Dittrich, *Fw.* Anton Becker and *Fw.* Heinrich Michalczak jumped into one of the *Staffel's* cars and raced out to capture the pilot, but as the three Germans climbed out of their vehicle and advanced towards the downed aircraft, the Russian drew his pistol and fired at all three Germans before shooting himself. Michalczak escaped with light wounds, but Dittrich and Becker were killed.

By 17 April, Russian air attacks on the German-held airfields in the Crimea were being supported by artillery fire and by 27 April, the "fortress" was under assault by 29 Soviet divisions, a tank corps, three artillery divisions and a dozen independent brigades. The final full-scale Russian attack against Sevastopol's northern front began on 5 May and was followed by attacks on the southern and eastern fronts. Eventually as their defences were pushed in, only the German held airstrip on the Chersones peninsula remained. This became subjected to accurate shelling from the Sapun hills where the Russians had a clear field of view of the tip of the peninsula. The 10.(Pz)/SG 9 was ordered to relocate to Kishinev, but the *Staffel's* technical personnel only managed to escape when, on 8 May, and with T-34s already on the airfield, a Ju 52 made the last

Hptm. Franz Oswald, (right), Staffelkapitän of 13.(Pz)/SG 9, describing a successful mission to an unidentified Leutnant, Eastern front, Spring 1944.

Ofw. Corell, with map, and Lt. Lothar Kallerhof (left) with other members of 10.(Pz)/SG 9. On 28 April 1944, Kallerhof was injured when his aircraft crashed on the airfield at Bacau due to the failure of one engine at low altitude. Ofw. Corell was killed during the Soviet summer offensive in July.

A column of Russian horse drawn transport, a mode that was used throughout the war.

flight out. Although various items of equipment had to be abandoned, great care was taken to ensure that as much as possible of the valuable tungsten-cored anti-tank ammunition was saved. German resistance in the Crimea finally collapsed on 17 May.

The IV.(Pz) *Gruppe* of SG 9 reached a milestone in its history when, on 1 May 1944, it flew its 10,000th operational sortie. The *Gruppe* had now destroyed a total of 1,500 Russian tanks and its numerous decisive actions had been repeatedly stressed in *Wehrmacht* communiqués. Apart from the direct tank losses it had inflicted upon the Russians it had also knocked out tank spearheads, helped seal off enemy advances and generally frustrated his intentions on many occasions. In recognition of the *Gruppe's* achievements, *Generaloberst* Dessloch, officer commanding *Luftflotte* 4, sent a letter of appreciation to all officers, NCOs and men in which he expressed his "heartfelt recognition" of the *Gruppe's* 10,000th sortie.

Another operation mounted soon afterwards by IV.(Pz)/SG 9 met with considerable success. This started one afternoon when a *Rotte* (pair) of Hs 129s took off to pin-point the location of some lorries which had earlier been reported behind the Russian lines. However, before they could find the enemy transport, the German aircraft were intercepted by a formation of nine Russian Lavochkin La-5 fighters and forced to turn back. While re-crossing the front line the German pilots noticed that, sheltering in a gorge where they could not be seen from the German positions, was a Russian strongpoint consisting of a large number of soldiers with gun limbers, flak, horse-drawn carts and more than 100 horses.

The enemy was obviously preparing to camp overnight, for they had already started to set up tents and were lighting fires and digging in and certainly didn't expect to be seen by the two German aircraft. When the Henschel pilots landed and reported their findings it was already late in the afternoon but, despite the hour, the *Staffelkapitän* had all his men made ready and, shortly before dusk, the *Staffel* took off to locate the enemy strongpoint.

They flew up close to the gorge were the enemy had made camp and split into two sections. The aircraft then dived with all guns firing onto the assembly of men, horses and material. Utter confusion reigned; the animals galloped away; the men scrambled to find cover; an anti-aircraft machine-gun crew was killed even before it could open fire. Each aircraft made more than ten passes and fired off all its ammunition before the Russian strongpoint was annihilated. In the last light the *Staffel* flew home, satisfied, as it reported, that it had "... *struck a large number of Russians off the ration list*". The destruction caused during this attack was confirmed the next morning when a reconnaissance flight was flown by a *Rotte* of Hs 129s. In the gorge, there was not a single living soul to be seen.

"Now the Hs 129 Wears the Knight's Cross"

Operations in Rumania
1944

17

Above: A carriage ride for the newly decorated Hptm. Ruffer in Bacau, 9 June 1944. Seated next to Ruffer is Oblt. Wenzel and, behind the young Rumanian driver, Lt. Krause.

Right: Fellow pilots of 10.(Pz)/SG 9 congratulate Hptm. Ruffer on the award of the Ritterkreuz. In the foreground, from left to right: Lt. Krause, Hptm. Ruffer, Ofw. Holtermann, Uffz. Wille and Ofw. Corell.

The bitterest fighting in this sector centred around the ruins of the castle of Stanca on the so-called Castle Hill which for a long time had changed hands repeatedly as a result of attack and counter-attack. On 1 June, a *Schwarm* of Hs 129s was attacked by Russian fighters near the castle. When the Henschels landed, one of their number was missing and one of I. *Fliegerkorps* forward command posts later reported having seen a lone Hs 129 fall out of the sky and crash in flames south-west of Stanca. This could only have been the aircraft flown by the 10.(Pz)'s *Fhj. Uffz.* Ernst Berg. *Uffz.* Moninger was also lost in the bitterly contested Stanca area on 16 June.

Most Hs 129 losses were due to enemy ground fire and occasions when aircraft were lost as a result of air combat with Russian fighters are relatively rare; details of air battles where the names of the victorious Soviet pilots are known are even more so. However, one such incident occurred on 29 April when the famous Soviet pilot Ivan Kozedub was leading a formation of six La-5s from the 240th Fighter Regiment on a patrol over Jassy. The Lavochkin pilots observed a formation of no fewer than ten Hs 129s, escorted by four Bf 109s. Making two attacks, Kozedub shot down two of the Henschels, both of which were seen to crash near the front line. Towards the end of the war, Kozedub shot down a third Hs 129 and with a total of 62 kills was the Soviet Air Force's leading fighter ace at war's end.

A similar incident is known to have occurred several months later in Hungary on 21 December 1944, when a pair of Yak-9s flown by Lt. V.A. Mierienkov and Leading Pilot M.S. Dvornikov from the Seventeenth Air Army's 288 IAP was escorting a formation of Il-2s in the Székesfehérvár area when they were attacked by six Bf 109s. In the air battle which followed Mierenkov claimed three of the German fighters shot down and, shortly afterwards, the Russian fighter pilots sighted another group of German aircraft consisting of Hs 129s with a Bf 109 escort. This time, Dvornikov is said to have shot down three Bf 109s and one Hs 129.

Another loss to occur in Rumania was that of 12.(Pz)/SG 9's *Staffelkapitän*, *Hptm.* Marufka.

Ruffer's Staffel comrades hoist their hero onto their shoulders.

As a result of an emergency landing during a ferry flight on 12 March 1944, Marufka was in the underground hospital at Focsani-South when, on 11 June, American bombers operating against Eastern Front targets from their bases in Italy attacked the airfield there. Unfortunately, some of the American bombs fell on the hospital; among the fatalities was Marufka.

Hans-Günther Marufka (seen here as an Oblt.) came to 12.(Pz)/SG 9 on 26.5.1943 after earlier service with ZG 26, NJG 3 and 10.(Nachtjagd.)/ZG 1. As a Hauptmann, he became Staffelkapitän of 12.(Pz)/SG 9 which he lead on the southern sector of the Eastern front until his death on 11.6.1944.

PART FIVE

Friend and Foe
The Rumanian Role

Trials and Tribulations
Special Weapons

Although most of Germany's Allies showed interest in the Hs 129, only the Rumanian Air Force was to receive the type in any quantity and from July to end September 1943, it took delivery of 42 Hs 129 B-2s. This photograph shows the Michael's Cross and yellow fuselage band carried by all Rumanian Henschels while operating as an Axis partner.

Pilots of the 42nd Escadrila on the major airbase at Nikolayev, southern Russia, December 1943.

A bombed-up aircraft of the Rumanian 41st Asalt Escadrila is prepared for a mission on Chaplinka advanced airfield in southern Russia, November 1943.

In Rumanian Service

OPERATIONS BY THE 8. RUMANIAN *SCHLACHTGRUPPE*

18

Preparing a Rumanian Hs 129 B-2 for a mission in Transylvania, October 1944. This machine appears to have the lower parts of its engine cowlings painted white. All Hs 129s operated by the Rumanian Air Force were equipped with bomb racks, this machine apparently being fitted with a rack for a 250 kg bomb. Unusually, the spiral spinners have been retained.

The Hs 129 Fights the Wehrmacht

RUMANIAN OPERATIONS TO MAY 1945

19

The final Russian drive into Rumania opened on 20 August 1944, and at 22:00 on the 22nd, Radio Bucharest broadcast a cease-fire order to all Rumanian forces. Embittered by German air attacks on the Rumanian Royal Palace, Rumania then declared war on the Third Reich on the 25th. This was to bring the 32 Hs 129 B-2s of the Rumanian 8. *Schlachtgruppe's* three *Escadrile* into action against German forces. On the same date, a total of 22 operational *Luftwaffe* Hs 129s were stationed in Rumania under *Luftflotte 4*. However, the following day the only German-operated Henschels remaining in Rumania were from a detachment of 14.(Pz)/SG 9, and although most of these were evacuated to rejoin the parent *Staffel* which, together with other *Luftwaffe* units had been forced to retreat to Hungary, a further 22 machines were left behind. A *Luftwaffe* report listing German aircraft in the Rumanian Air Force shows that by making use of the former *Luftwaffe* Hs 129s abandoned in Rumania, a total of 54 machines were on the strength of their former ally on 1 September 1944. When originally captured some of these aircraft were equipped with 30 mm cannon, but the Rumanians had neither the experience nor the ammunition to enable them to use these weapons and in Rumanian service they were replaced with bomb racks.

All the captured Henschels were now incorporated into a mixed air unit which flew sorties in support of Rumanian troops fighting against German forces in Western Transylvania. However, losses were heavy and due not only to German opposition but also to Russian anti-aircraft defences which failed to recognise the Henschels as friendly. When Rumanian troops reached the Hungarian border, at which time the pace of operations was slowed by the weather, the surviving Henschels were reorganised into the 8th Dive-Bombing and Attack Group with a total of 31 aircraft divided between the 74th Dive-Bombing Squadron with Ju 87Ds and the 41st Attack Squadron with Hs 129s.

By the second half of December, when a period of cold weather had frozen the airfields and improved operating conditions so that sorties could be flown over Slovakia, the Group's strength had been reduced to 25 aircraft including 16 Hs 129s. Owing to a shortage of spares and frequent breakdowns, operational readiness was reduced to 30-40% and although a maximum of six aircraft could be put into the air at any one time, operations were normally mounted with only four flying as a *Schwarm* in the German way. Nevertheless, the Soviets appreciated the support these aircraft provided and acknowledged the effectiveness of the Rumanian pilots' attacks in much the same way as the German Army was acknowledging the assistance provided by the *Luftwaffe's* Hs 129 *Staffeln*. Similarly, the Rumanian pilots appreciated the sturdy construction of the cockpit area which enabled a number of them to survive crash-landings.

In the four weeks from 25 March to 24 April 1945, the Hs 129s of the *Escadrila 41 Asalt* flew 160 sorties, against enemy columns, railway stations and tracks, road traffic and various other military targets. Claims during this period included 122 motor vehicles and 91 other vehicles destroyed as well as 4 railway trains, 3 artillery positions, 1 tank and a bridge. Losses amounted to two aircraft shot down by anti-aircraft fire.

When the war in Europe came to an end, the Rumanians still possessed 14 airworthy Hs 129s, twelve of which were then based at Zvolen (Tri Duby) airfield. Their final sorties were flown on 11 May, 1945, and were mounted against troops belonging to General Vlassov's "Russian Liberation Army" of defectors and disaffected prisoners-of-war located in a wood near Uherské Brod. After the war, the Rumanian Henschels stayed in Czechoslovakia until 27 July 1945, when they flew to Ghimbav airfield near Brasov in Central Rumania. There, the aircraft remained in service until the late 1940s, long after the last of the *Luftwaffe's* Hs 129s had been abandoned, destroyed or scrapped. Only then were the last three Rumanian machines broken up for scrap.

Just like their German counterparts, Rumanian pilots who flew the Hs 129 remain convinced that this aircraft was ideal for the tasks it was called upon to perform. All Rumanian airmen who had any connection with the Hs 129 praised its efficiency; it could accurately deliver its bombs onto the target, it possessed good flying characteristics and protected its pilot in all circumstances.

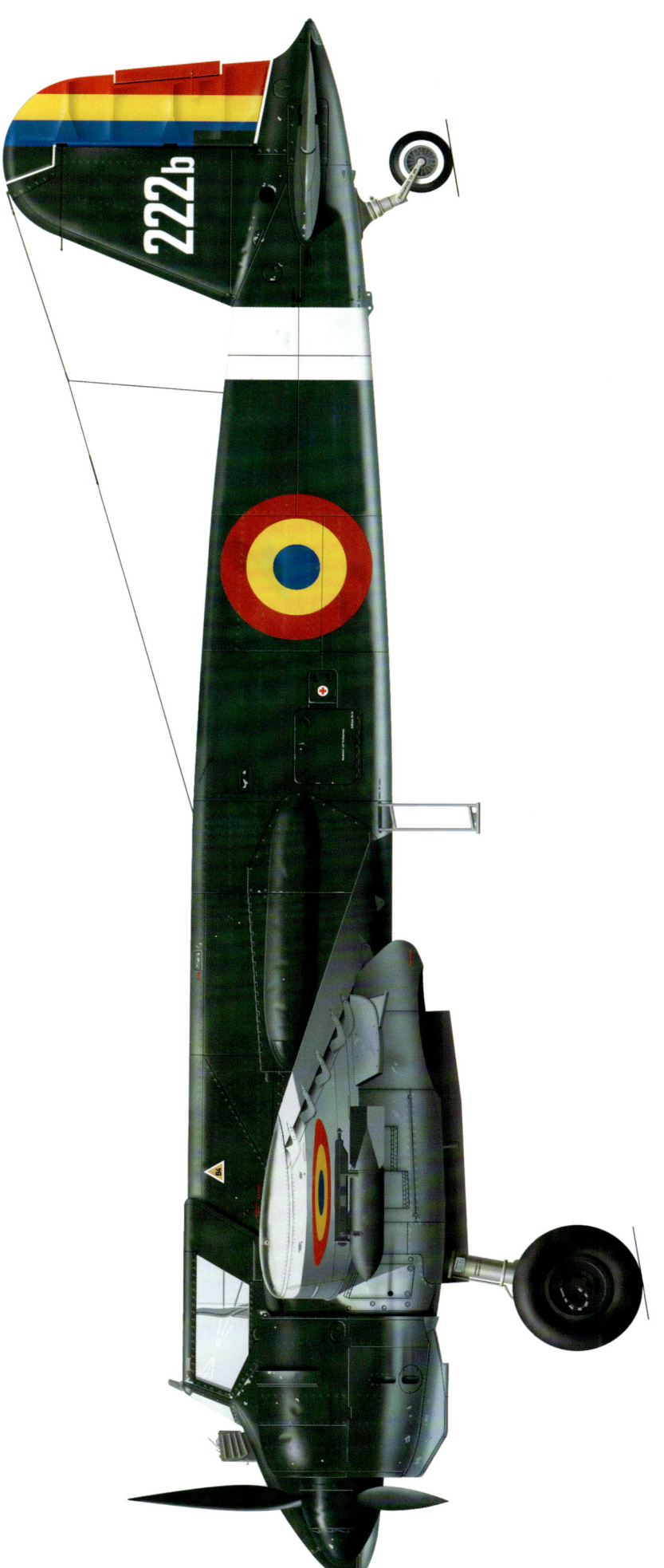

Hs 129 B-2 Number 222b

Escadrila 42, Rumanian Air Force, Transylvania, 1944.

Freshly repainted in an overall **green** believed to be of Russian origin, this aircraft is depicted after the Rumanians changed sides to fight against their former German allies. The earlier Michael's crosses have been replaced by roundels and the fin flash now extends down the whole length of the rudder. The Rumanian system of individual aircraft markings allowed for aircraft lost to be replaced by aircraft carrying a small suffix letter to the **white** code number; this Aircraft 222 would have been replaced by 222a and this in turn by 222b. The **white** fuselage band, wing tip undersides and nose were recognition markings intended to indicate to Soviet forces that the German aircraft was friendly. Bomb racks only were fitted.

A formation of Hs 129 B-2s of 42 "Asalt" Escadrila pass low over their Slovakian airfield, Spring 1945.

Winter camouflage for a Rumanian Hs 129 B-2.

Adj. av. Anghel Vasile poses for a propaganda shot with a female Russian soldier at Miskolc in North East Hungary, October 1944.

The 42 "Asalt" Escadrila in Transylvania, September 1944, showing the blue, yellow and red tail stripes and roundels applied after August 1944.

Trials and Tribulations

EXPERIMENTS WITH SPECIAL WEAPONS

20

For almost the entire period that the Hs 129 was in production, various trials took place to test possible improvements to both the aircraft's design and its offensive capability. In October 1942, for example, the flat canopy side panels of W.Nr. 0266 were replaced with new ones incorporating a tear-drop shaped bulge, but further development was discontinued when it was found that these bulges caused an unacceptable degree of distortion. The same aircraft was used to test a Robot camera. In November 1942, W.Nr. 0267 was tested with right-handed propellers on both sides, after which left-handed propellers were fitted to both sides and, in each case, flights were conducted with one engine shut down. Other trials involved numerous test flights with different types of ailerons and a wheel fairing was also evaluated, presumably intended to protect the otherwise exposed tyres from ground fire. In June 1943, flight-tests were carried out with W.Nr. 0267 to compare the normal series-production engine cowling with armoured cowlings and two types developed by Potez, the standard and long models, were also flight tested.

Further trials centred on the power plants. In August 1943, W.Nr. 0267 flew for the first time with a pair of 820 horsepower Gnôme-Rhône 14M38 engines for tests in connection with the proposed new production variant, the Hs 129 C-1. At that time, the RLM had placed orders for some 600-700 Hs 129 C-1s, series production of which was scheduled to commence in April 1944. This variant was intended to carry two MK 103s beneath the fuselage, placed side-by-side, on special mountings. The mountings possessed limited traverse, thus permitting the pilot to align the weapons on targets either side of the aircraft's line of flight. In addition to the standard MG 151s and MG 17s of the Hs 129 B-2, the HS 129 C-1 was to feature two fixed rearward-firing MG 17s in the aft fuselage, to provide some measure of rear defence. W.Nr. 0267 subsequently made two further speed and temperature measurement flights but on 26 September it collided with a Ju 88 while landing. Although damage was slight, a ground run of the engines after repairs revealed that the starboard carburettor had to be changed and, as no replacement was to hand, the machine was grounded. In the meantime, W.Nr. 0266 which had earlier suffered an engine fire and had also been grounded to await a new carburettor, rejoined the test programme and conducted performance trials with the 14M38 engines. Unfortunately, it was found that Gnôme-Rhône had not kept their promise to reduce the high cylinder temperatures which characterised the 14M series, with the result that cooling problems still existed. Anticipating this, Henschel had already explored the possibility of fitting the Hs 129 C with 840 hp Isotta-Fraschini Delta 12-

The proposed armament of the Hs 129 C was to include two rearward-firing machine-guns. The aiming of these weapons was to have been achieved by the use of a rearward-facing periscopic Revi 5 gunsight and although development of the Hs 129 C was abandoned, the rearward sight was also employed in connection with the development of a flame-thrower. The test bed for this rearward-firing device was Hs 129 B-2 coded "DE+ZR", the aircraft seen here at Tarnewitz.

Hs 129 B-1 coded 'KG+GI' was fitted with the Rüstsatz II comprising four 7.9 mm MG 17 machine guns. The gun pack is shown here swung down.

cylinder inverted-vee air-cooled engines. However, further development was discontinued in October 1943 when *Obst*. Georg Pasewaldt, the *Entwicklungs-Chef* in the *Technisches Amt*, reported that it was unlikely that these alternative powerplants could be obtained from Italy.

Meanwhile, trials with wing racks carrying bombs weighing up to 500 kg had been carried out and in January 1944, the RLM placed an order calling for six prototype B-2s and C-1s to operate as heavy tank-destroyer aircraft fitted with the BK 7.5 cm cannon. The four MG 17s and the option of two MK 103s were deleted and the standard built-in armament changed to one (jettisonable) BK 7.5 with 12 rounds and two fuselage-mounted 13 mm MG 131s each with 250 rounds. Further development and production planning relating to the Hs 129 C-1 was finally abandoned when a letter dated 7 March arrived from the RLM advising Henschel that the C-1 series had been deleted from the Ministry's procurement programme. With the exception of the near completed Hs 129 V 4 W.Nr. 220001 - the first prototype of the C-1 - construction of further prototypes was ordered to be discontinued and all parts which could not be used for the B-3 series were to be scrapped.

Thereafter, although series production of the C-1 had been abandoned and there was little official interest in the C-1/V 4 prototype, work continued to complete the machine and it made a number of flights before being grounded on 13 July 1944 at the request of the RLM and as a result of the prevailing fuel shortage in the Third Reich. As the Allied bombing offensive against the German oil industry intensified during the summer of 1944 and fuel output declined, strict measures were called for in order to conserve existing stocks. Since the RLM now considered fuel consumption of the Hs 129 series generally to be excessive, it was planned that the type would be completely withdrawn from operational service in April 1945.

However, throughout the greater part of the Hs 129's service with the *Luftwaffe*, key Henschel design and technical personnel maintained a close working relationship with the operational units assigned to fly the aircraft. *Hptm*. Eggers and *Lt*. Scholz of Pz.Jä.St./JG 51 in particular made a number of visits to the Henschel factories in Berlin during which current operational experiences and future requirements were discussed. Meetings were also held with the *General der Jagdflieger's* inspector for ground-attack units and later, officers representing the *General der Schlachtflieger*.

Spearheading this deliberate drive towards co-

COMPARISON Hs 129 C-1 / B-2		
	C-1	B-2
Engines	Gnôme-Rhône R14M38	Gnôme-Rhône R14M4/5
Flying Weight	5300 kg	5100 kg
Maximum Loaded	5700 kg (est)	5250 kg
Maximum Speed	400 km/h	350 km/h
Standard Armament	2 MG 151	2 MG 151
	2 MG 17	2 MG 17
	2 MG 17 (firing backwards)	
Additional Armament	2 MK 103 (2 x 60 rounds)	1 MK 101 (1 x 30 rounds)
Bomb Load	3 x 250 kg or	1 x 250 kg and
	1 x 1000 kg	2 x 50 kg
Armour	Improved for engines	
Fuel Tanks	2 in fuselage	1 in fuselage
		2 in wings

operation was Henschel's chief designer, *Dipl.Ing.* Friedrich Nicolaus who, in conjunction with the *Kommandeur der Erprobungsstellen*, is known to have held discussions as early as June 1942 - immediately following the type's service debut - with such *Panzerjagdflieger* as *Oblt.* Franz Oswald and *Lt.* Wörl of II./Sch.G 1, concerning their operational experiences with the MK 101 cannon and the feasibility of using heavier calibre weapons in the Hs 129. The following month, and at the request of the RLM's *Technisches Amt*, investigations began into the possibility of installing such weapons as the 3 cm MK 103, 3.7cm *Flak* 18 with 12 rounds, the 5cm *Pak* 38 complete with a reloading unit and 40 to 50 rounds and the 5cm *Flak* C/41. Of these, the C/41 was deemed to be too heavy for consideration but the other options were thought feasible.

For their part, the pilots welcomed and appreciated such effort on the part of the aircraft manufacturer and strived to keep Henschel informed of their observations and any grievances that arose. In January 1943 for example, Nicolaus met *Major* Hitschhold, *Kommodore* of Sch.G 1, to discuss operational experience and further development possibilities and later that same month, *Leutnant* Orth from 4.(Pz)/Sch.G 2 spent two days at Schönefeld reporting to Nicolaus on the Hs 129's poor performance in Libya. There were similar meetings with *Generalmajor* Galland and *Hptm.* Meinardus, Galland's aide on Hs 129 affairs, to discuss operations in Tunisia.

Practical investigation with the *Flak* 18 began in November 1942 and was test-flown in December in W.Nr. 0280. Later that month, the aircraft was transferred to Rechlin - which called for an improved mounting - but the weapon installation had an adverse effect on the aircraft's flying characteristics, especially when landing, and trials were eventually discontinued in October 1943.

Meanwhile, on 2 October, the Hs 129 B-2 W.Nr. 141291 was transferred from *Werk* II to Schönefeld, followed two days later by W.Nr. 141292, where they were both to be fitted with a 50 cm BK 5 cannon installation. Simultaneously, however, tests at Tarnewitz with W.Nr. 140494 had shown that the far larger BK 7.5 could be mounted with more favourable results and on 1 October this aircraft was transferred to Schönefeld where its BK 7.5 equipment was modified. In December, the aircraft was fitted with ballast and a mock-up of the cannon and made a number of flights including some with one engine shut down. By March 1943, three aircraft, W.Nr. 140494, 141291 and 141292 had been fully converted to accept the BK 7.5 and the first firing tests were carried out in May with W.Nr. 141292. Test flights at Rechlin and the RLM followed and both aircraft were later moved to the weapons research facility at Tarnewitz.

On 4 August 1943, *Hptm.* Eggers and *Lt.* Scholz arrived at Henschel's

Installation and detail of Rüstsatz II comprising four 7.9 mm MG 17 machine guns mounted beneath an Hs 129 B-1.

The 3.7 cm Flak 18 (also known as the BK 3.7) shown installed beneath the Hs 129 B-2. The aircraft left is almost certainly W.Nr.0280, photographed at Rechlin in December 1942.

Investigations regarding the installation of the Flak 18 began in March 1942 and an aircraft fitted with the weapon was flown in December. Trials were discontinued in October 1943 due to the adverse effect on the aircraft's flying and landing characteristics. In the accompanying sequence of photographs, the Flak 18 is seen (*right*) less its barrel and fairing, with the 12-round magazine visible top left. The photo (*above*) shows the light alloy fairing swung down, whilst the photo (*above right*) shows it in position over the gun. Photo (*right*) shows the complete installation.

Hs 129 B-2, W.Nr.140494 was used during the development of the Pak 40 75 mm cannon. Here the aircraft is shown at Rechlin in September 1943. Note the cannon fairing bulge visible under the fuselage. Captured Allied machines can be seen in the background.

Schönefeld plant. The Battle of Kursk had only recently been fought and lost and *Dipl.Ing.* Nicolaus and *Fl.Stabs.Ing.* Helmut Czolbe were anxious to learn how the Hs 129 B-2 had performed in the anti-tank role, especially with the newly introduced MK 103. Talks continued over the next two months with Eggers, Scholz, Nicolaus and Czolbe holding a number of meetings to discuss further potential armament developments, in particular the installation of 2.5 cm and 7.5 cm cannon, the *Nebelwerfer* mortar, a flame thrower and the electrostatically operated SG 113A *"Förstersonde"*.

One of the problems inherent in attacks with a fixed cannon was that the aircraft was forced to approach along a straight line which made it vulnerable to ground fire. It was for this reason that consideration had been given to mounting a WK 28/35 *Nebelwerfer* mortar with limited traverse under the fuselage of the Hs 129. Two Hs 129 B-2s, W.Nr. 141253 and 141256, were fitted with the weapon at Schönefeld and handed over to Rechlin on 4 October. At the same time, and in accordance with a suggestion put forward by *Hptm.* Eggers, attempts were made to equip the Hs 129 with 21 cm rocket projectile launchers. Initial trials seemed promising and it was thought that it might have been possible to mount two of these launchers under each wing. In both cases, however, the accuracy of these weapons was found to be insufficient for anti-tank work and although W.Nr. 141689 was converted to accept a fin stabilised WK 28 mortar for improved accuracy, both these weapons were eventually rejected in favour of heavy calibre cannon armament.

On 27 December 1943, the Hs 129 equipped 11.(Pz.)/SG 9 was withdrawn from front-line operations and on 20 January, 1944, the *Staffel* was redesignated *Erprobungskommando* 26, an experimental and test unit which, although directly subordinate to the *General der Schlachtflieger's* headquarters at Rangsdorf, worked in close co-operation with the *Kommandeur der Erprobungsstellen*. The K.d.E., *Oberst* Edgar Petersen, was at the head of the directorate which controlled eight research establishments located at Rechlin, Travemünde, Tarnewitz, Karlshagen, Münster Nord, Werneuchen, Udetfeld and Gotenhafen. Each one of these *Erprobungsstelle* specialised in one particular area of aeronautical testing, with the exception of Rechlin, which covered a much wider field of research. *Erpobungskommando* 26 evaluated new types and combinations of weapons intended for ground-attack, especially anti-tank weapons. The unit was based at Udetfeld, near Gleiwitz and comprised 5 officers, 16 aircrew, of whom, 6 were radio operators/gunners and 82 technical personnel to attend to engines, bombs, armament, radio, hydraulics or electrics depending on their trade speciality. The *Kommando* was completely self-supporting in that it also had its own transport and (civilian) clerical personnel. The aircraft establishment was 18, typically consisting of 4 Ju 87s, 4 Fw 190s and, from June 1944, 4 Hs 129s. There were also four night ground-attack aircraft and, for communications purposes, a Bf 108 and Fi 156.

During the time it was in existence - it was disbanded at Greifswald in late April 1945 - *Ekdo.* 26 tested a wide variety of bombs, rockets and special ammunition and only those projects which seemed promising were recommended for further development. Especially successful were the trials undertaken with the Army's 5.5 cm and 8.8 cm *Panzerschreck* and *Panzerblitz* armour-piercing rockets. After the necessary installation and adjustment of the special equipment required to mount and fire these rockets, it was also *Ekdo.* 26's responsibility to carry out the instruction and training of the groundcrews and pilots of the operational units destined to use such weapons.

Perhaps two of the most radical armament proposals associated with the Hs 129 were put forward during the first half of 1943, when Nicolaus was invited to the RLM to discuss both the feasibility of installing a flame thrower in the aircraft as well as an electrically activated, perpendicularly firing anti-tank mortar.

The first of these proposals - the *Flammenwerfereinbau* or flame-thrower installation - was to use a petroleum and benzene based substance known as "Aeroflame". Initially, a few experiments using this highly volatile weapon were carried out at the Army's gas and chemical warfare training ground at Raubkammer. A Do 217E was selected as the carrier and a special tank was built into the aircraft, a motor pumping the oil towards the tail of the aircraft where it emerged under pressure for igniting. It is not clear whether any air-trials were performed before this aircraft was destroyed after catching fire.

The next step was to use the Hs 129. As with the earlier attempt on the Do 217, a special carrying tank was fitted into a Henschel in August 1943, though this time a four metre long emission pipe was also attached which could be hydraulically raised and lowered. The substance for emission consisted of a petrol/benzene compound thickened with 4% to 8% of Oppanol. This was pressurised with nitrogen and ignited with a thermite cartridge which burned during the whole emission period.

At the end of August and in very early September 1943, meetings to discuss the possible operational use of the *Flammenwerfereinbau*, were held at the Henschel works at Schönefeld between Nicolaus and members of his team and *Hptm.* Eggers and *Lt.* Scholz of Pz.Jä.St./JG 51. Though the outcome of these meetings is not known, the notion of the Hs 129 carrying a rearward-firing flame-thrower has always been viewed as an experiment and to date, little firm evidence has been found to suggest that it progressed much beyond that stage. However, it is known that modifications to the elevator, tail wheel and electrical system of W.Nr. 142001 were carried out in August 1944 and, after making a test flight, the aircraft was handed over to the Münster-Nord test centre near Fassberg on 26 August where the flame-thrower itself was installed. This aircraft was still in existence at the end of the war.

The second curious form of offensive armament to be associated with the Hs 129 was the *Sondergerät* - or "Special Device" - SG 113A, known alternatively as the *Forstersönde*. Shortly after the war, Dr P. Hackemann, a ballistics specialist previously employed by the *Institut für Waffenforschung* - Institute for Weapons Research - at the *Luftfahrtforschungsanstalt* (Aeronautical Research Establishment) (LFA) *Hermann Göring* at Volkenrode, Braunschweig wrote:

> "... The idea has often been expressed of having the firing mechanism of a weapon controlled by the target itself. If we think of the alignment process which takes place, i.e. in aligning a rifle by hand, the gunner sees the line of sight fluctuating around and across the target and endeavours to fire at the right moment. So as not to let this moment slip, he should be provided with a technical aid which fires automatically. We have to eliminate the human time lag in the gunner, that is the time which elapses from recognising when the line of sight passes through the target until the moment the gunner activates the firing mechanism."

A considerable amount of both theoretical and practical trials work relative to this idea was performed at Volkenrode between 1942 and 1945, which ultimately led to the involvement of the Hs 129. Volkenrode was one of two major research institutes established in Germany during the late thirties and run jointly by the military, a number of eminent government-funded scientific research bodies and a selection of industrialists. The primary areas of research at Volkenrode included aerodynamics, gas dynamics, engines, air armament, rockets, flak and associated equipment. There was also a unique 400 metre long (1,300 ft) high altitude firing tunnel for ballistics experiments.

Hackemann extended his theory to aircraft armament, believing that a human air gunner (or gunners) on board an aeroplane could be replaced by highly sensitive instruments and automatic, electrically fired weapons. Hackemann's theory was first applied to anti-tank work on the basis that the attacking aircraft would fly over the tank at an altitude of between 5 and 20 m (16.5ft-65.6ft) and then fire vertically downwards, the pilot having made his approach either in a shallow dive or in low-level horizontal flight. Should the pilot not succeed in flying horizontally over the target, it was assumed that he could put the vertical axis through the target by banking his aircraft. By using such methods, the required accuracy of alignment would be low

Hs 129 B-0, W.Nr.0016, was one of three Hs 129s fitted with the SG 113 A mortar in July 1943 and it made three test flights the following month. This interesting sequence of photographs, taken at the LFA Volkenrode shows the installation of the mortar in the forward fuselage of 0016. Of note in the photograph (*top*) is the antenna fitted to the aircraft's nose and the Fw 189 parked in the background, which was probably the machine used for the earlier MG 131 automatic firing tests. Photo (*left*) shows the top view of the SG 113 A casing enclosing its six barrels designed for the ejection of the counter-weight. The 7.5 cm J-Gr. 38 HL/A armour-piercing shell with which early firing trials were conducted (*opposite page*), was later abandoned in favour of a special 1.5 kg shell encased in an aluminium sabot. The Opta-Radio control apparatus for the weapon was installed in a metal box behind the pilot's seat (*opposite top left*). The pilot activated the weapon by use of a special selector switch installed on his instrument panel to the right of the control column. The pilot could also regulate the sensitivity of the photo-electric cell by means of a device located to the far left of the instrument panel, while the arming button was mounted on the control column.

EXPERIMENTS WITH SPECIAL WEAPONS

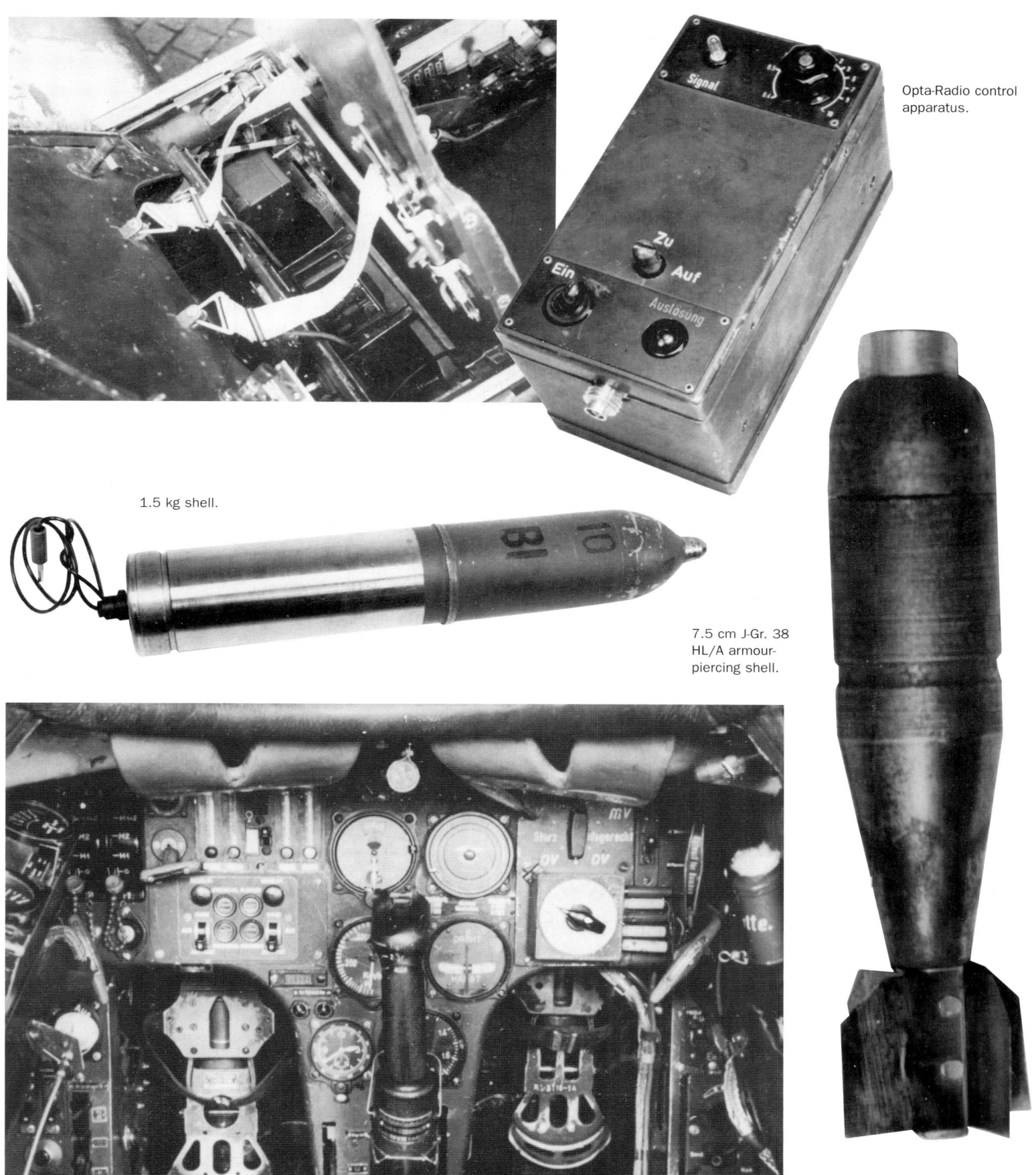

Opta-Radio control apparatus.

1.5 kg shell.

7.5 cm J-Gr. 38 HL/A armour-piercing shell.

Instrument panel of W.Nr.00_6 showing the special selector switch installed to the right of the control column.

Another of the three Hs 129s fitted with the SG 113 A Förstersonde was W.Nr.140499, photographed here abandoned at the LFA Hermann Göring, Volkenrode. This sequence also offers another clear view of the upper casing of the mortar with its set of six ejection barrels.

Hs 129 W.Nr. 0249 was the third aircraft used to test the SG 113 A at Volkenrode. This sequence shows to advantage the nose mounted target detection antenna as well as offering a clear view of the mortar's underside casing from where the shells were electrically fired.

113A as a practical and efficient operational weapon arose when, during the only other flight to register a hit, the projectile was fired from a height of 2 m (6.5 ft) and is thought to have completely disintegrated upon impact. The scores of resulting splinters embedded themselves in the firmly enclosed front compartment of the tank. One such splinter, found within the turret interior was noted to have part of a thread on it, suggesting that it came from the end of the projectile. Although the cover plate was torn from its mounting it was only bent.

Trials limped on at Volkenrode, Rechlin and Tarnewitz into the final months of the war, before lack of fuel, specialist ammunition and gun components ended the programme. Photographs taken by Allied troops at the LFA *Hermann Göring* Volkenrode, shortly after the cessation of hostilities, provide evidence that at least two Hs 129s remained equipped with the SG 113A, including W.Nr.0016, which had previously been used to test cold starts, tropical filters, non-standard propellers, FuG 16 radio equipment, cameras and the MK 113 cannon.

Referring to trials conducted with the SG 113A, *Oberstabsingenieur* Ossenbühn, head of *Abteilung* Fl-E6 at Tarnewitz and responsible for the development and testing of aircraft guns and rocket projectiles, stated that "... results on the whole were unsatisfactory owing to the insufficient possibility of hits."

Walter Raufelder held a similar opinion: "The *Forstersönde* would not have been suitable for operations. The system worked, but it had one major drawback: the target tank would explode immediately after the aircraft had passed over it so that the target and the Hs 129 would be blown to pieces by the tank's explosion."

Elsewhere, having handed over the 13.(Pz)/SG 9 to his successor in East Prussia, *Hptm.* Franz Oswald transferred somewhat reluctantly to *Ekdo.* 26 at Udetfeld in south-east Silesia on 17 January 1945. At this time, the airfield lay close to the path of the Soviet advance and when Oswald arrived, the unit was already preparing to transfer to Greifswald. The aircraft were quickly flown out and after the unit's equipment, weapons and vehicles

Uffz. Walter Raufelder of 10.(Pz)/SG 9, pictured second from right at Radom, Poland, July 1944. Later he would flight-test the Hs 129 fitted with the SG 113 A Förstersonde mortar at Volkenrode.

Viewing from right to left, a sequence of stills from a cine film showing Uffz. Walter Raufelder in W.Nr. 0249 during firing trials with the SG 113 A at Volkenrode in January 1945.

had left by road, Oswald took command of those elements which were to transfer by rail.

It was a hazardous journey and at one point, east of Oppeln, with Russian tanks only 18 kms (11 miles) away from the train, all personnel aboard were ordered to report with their weapons to the local commander so that they could be committed to the ground fighting. However, in the event, the unit was eventually allowed to continue its journey. After three days, the train reached Frankfurt/Oder, Franz Oswald now driving ahead in a car to announce the arrival of the train at each station. On 21 January, Oswald drove from Frankfurt/Oder to Berlin in order to report personally to the *General der Schlachtflieger*, *Generalmajor* Hubertus Hitschhold, before continuing to Greifswald that evening by rail.

Serving with *Ekdo.* 26 was not to Oswald's liking. On 25 January 1945, he wrote that he very much regretted he had to remain at home when times were so critical and "... *the hour of the Panzerjäger had arrived.*" Now, more than at any other time, the need was to defend Germany from the mass of approaching Russian armour, but Oswald also recognised that *"Befehl ist Befehl"* - orders are orders. Most of the unit's other pilots felt the same way, some of them having been with *Ekdo.* 26 for more than a year. Having learned that his old *Staffel* was preparing to convert to the Fw 190, Oswald hated sitting around in the knowledge that he could achieve so much elsewhere. Nevertheless, he applied himself to his work as diligently and as expertly as he could, the hope never far from his mind that perhaps in the late summer or autumn of 1945, he would be given command of a *Gruppe* and allowed to return to the front.

Hptm. Franz Oswald, Kommandoführer, Erprobungskommando 26.

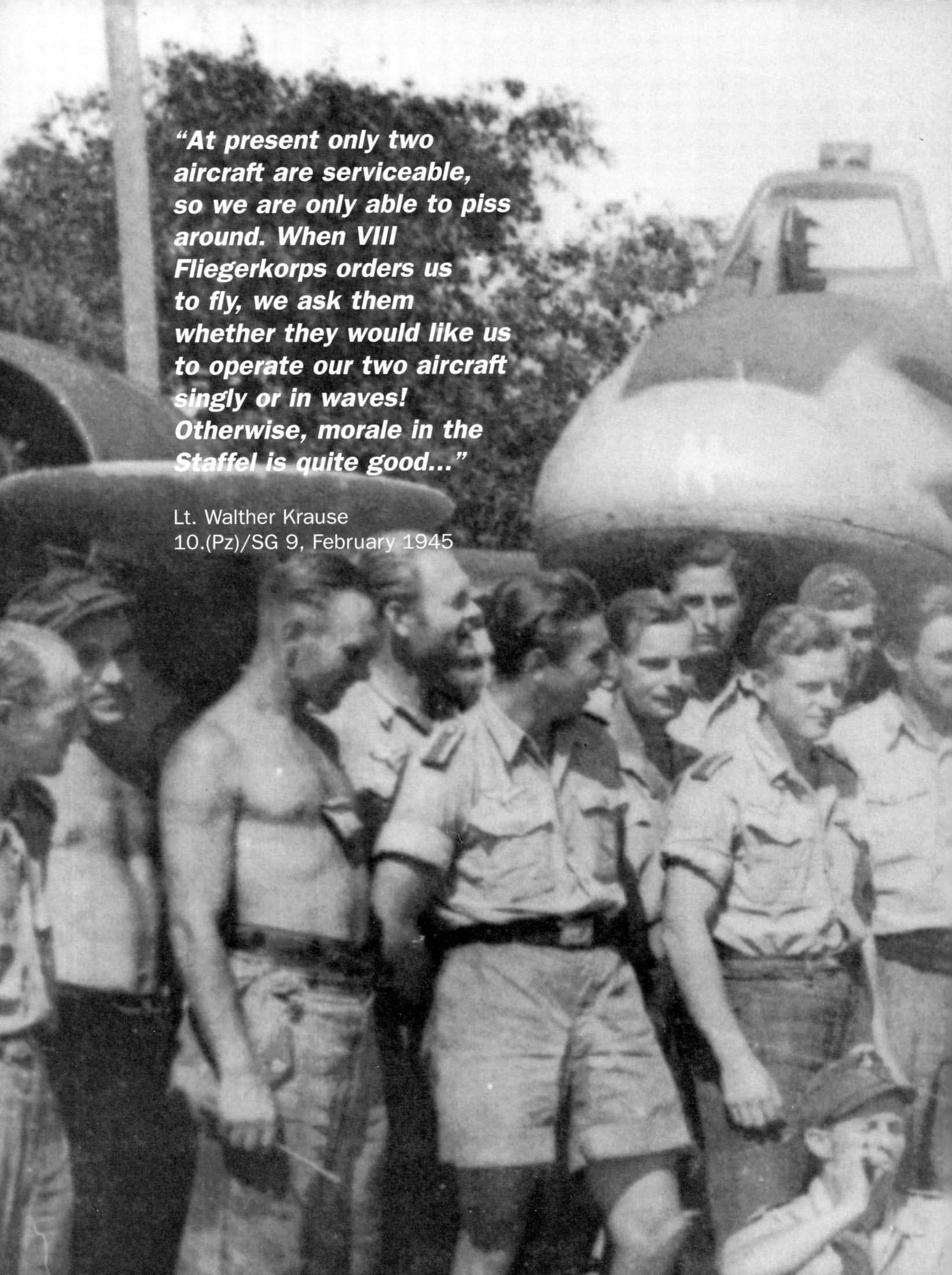

"At present only two aircraft are serviceable, so we are only able to piss around. When VIII Fliegerkorps orders us to fly, we ask them whether they would like us to operate our two aircraft singly or in waves! Otherwise, morale in the Staffel is quite good..."

Lt. Walther Krause
10.(Pz)/SG 9, February 1945

PART SIX
BLOOD RED HORIZON

The distinctive outline and straight leading edge wings of the Hs 129 are clearly shown in this view of two aircraft in the landing circuit. The nearest aircraft already has its wheels and flaps down.

Although the strong shadows suggest this photograph was taken during the summer months, this aircraft appears to be still wearing traces of a winter scheme. The aircraft is equipped with an MK 101 and although the improved MK 103 had been introduced to service some twelve months earlier, production problems created a shortage which caused the older MK 101 to be retained.

Belly-landed W.Nr.141868, Red "F" (or "E"), victim of Russian flak showing direct hits in the starboard wing and tail assembly, as well as numerous shrapnel holes in the port wing, fuselage, engines and propeller blades. Unfortunately, neither the date nor the unit to which this machine belonged are known, though spiral spinners place this photograph after the end of July 1944. The canopy was evidently jettisoned before the pilot set the aircraft down, a recommended precaution in case the aircraft should overturn.

"Keep Your Eyes Skinned at All Times"

The Russian Summer Offensives of 1944

21

If German forces on the Eastern Front had been allowed to use the spring of 1944 to fall back to a shorter front and reorganise in strong defensive positions, there might have been some hope of blunting the Russian offensives that summer. However, OKW's obsession with holding territory at all costs left German forces dangerously stretched over a vast 2,250 km (1,400 mile) front with few reserves. Especially vulnerable was the German central front where earlier fighting had left Army Group Centre holding a salient. If the enemy attacked here in any strength, the dangerously over-extended Army Group's position was such that it could not expect to hold out.

To make the Germans' position worse, Army Group Centre was further weakened when nearly all the armoured forces in Russia were switched to the area of Army Group North Ukraine, where OKW was convinced that as soon as the ground was sufficiently hard again the Russians would mount an enveloping operation from Galicia via Lvov to Königsberg in East Prussia. Despite reports from the front from early June onwards, all of which seemed to indicate the progressive build-up of a powerful assault force against Army Group Centre, the belief that an attack would be launched further south was so firmly held at Supreme *Wehrmacht* Headquarters that German forces, including 300 ground-attack aircraft of all types, were still being held in the area of Army Group North Ukraine when the Russian offensive against Army Group Centre opened.

The attack opened on 10 June with, contrary to all expectations, a major assault in the north against the Finns. Then, on 22 June, the Russians attacked either side of Vitebsk, to the north of Army Group Centre and followed up on the 23rd with an offensive to the south. The success of these two attacks either side of the German central front allowed the Russians to employ their armoured formations in a giant pincer movement which converged on Minsk and surrounded 100,000 Germans. By 3 July, Vitebsk, Mogilev and Minsk had already fallen to the Red Army and on the 17th the Russian First Guards Tank Army crossed the Bug and entered Poland. On the 23rd, Russian troops reached Lublin and four days later took Bialystok and Lvov.

As the scale of the catastrophe began to dawn on OKW, *Luftflotte 4's* ground-attack aircraft were progressively moved northwards to the area controlled by *Luftflotte 6* in order to ease the strain on the rapidly disintegrating front, but the Germans were unable to balance their forces to match the Russian advance along so wide a front and such was the rate of collapse that, finally, all possible forces had to be thrown in, even at the risk of laying open the Carpathian and Balkan fronts in Rumania. By the end of July, by which time the Russians had captured Brest-Litovsk, so clearing the whole of Belorussia, *Luftflotte* 4 had

Hptm. Hans-Günther Marufka, Staffelkapitän of 12.(Pz)/SG 9 briefing his pilots before a mission. Ground-attack pilots generally needed 1:500,000 and 1:300,000 maps for approaching and leaving targets, but for target location 1:100,000 - scale maps were used.

been stripped of its forces and almost all bomber, fighter and ground-attack aircraft had been transferred to *Luftflotte* 6 until, finally, there was nothing else left which could be committed to the battle. These widespread transfers, however, resulted in dislocation and a serious decline in serviceability. Thus the strengthening of the central front was still wholly inadequate to relieve the hard-pressed and harassed ground forces. By 1 August, the Russians had crossed the Vistula and reached Praga; elsewhere they were only 24 km (15 miles) from the East Prussian border.

The Russian successes against Army Group Centre had also created highly favourable conditions for other Red Army groups to come into action. All along the line from the Baltic to the Black Sea, the Russians constantly shifted the weight of their attacks so that as operations on one front were slowed, powerful offensives began on another. In this way the Germans were kept continually off balance, never able to find enough breathing space to rebuild their lines.

From mid-May, 13.(Pz)/SG 9 had been held in reserve and in this *Staffel's* sector all remained quiet, though the mood was tense: in the West, the Allied invasion was expected at any time and it was felt that the Russians would certainly take advantage of this and attack in the East. Transfers to the *Reichsverteidigung* - Defence of the Reich - had been allowed for some time and by the end of June this *Staffel* found itself short of pilots and temporarily without officers apart from *Hptm.* Oswald. On 8 July, *Oblt.* Bartel joined the *Staffel* but in the same week no fewer than five pilots left, four of them experienced *Schlachtflieger* with the Iron Cross First Class. Although replacements were received, they would require breaking-in before the unit returned to action.

The blow fell on 14 July when two Soviet armies struck at the First Panzer Army's left flank due east of Lvov. For the next week 13.(Pz)/SG 9 flew non stop, Franz Oswald flying his first mission on the 14th after exactly two months. Over the next two weeks the *Staffel* knocked out 38 tanks, Oswald claiming 10 in 13 missions and on 24 July, 13(Pz.)/SG 9 flew its 3,000th sortie and celebrated its 50th tank kill in ten days.

From mid-July and throughout August most of the Hs 129 *Staffeln*, although woefully inadequate in numbers, were constantly in the thick of the action. The 12.(Pz)/SG 9, now led by *Oblt.* Lehmann, lost two pilots on 15 July; *Uffz.* Walter Hetzel, a former reconnaissance pilot, was killed when his aircraft, coded "F+", W.Nr. 141720, was

Oblt. Arnold Plümer (with telephone) in IV.(Pz)/SG 9's battle headquarters. Plümer was shot down and seriously injured on 17.8.1942 but although his flying days were over, he returned to service in June 1944 and became Gruppe adjutant.

hit by flak and crashed in the German lines near Loyki, and *Ofw.* Hans Kaschel made an emergency landing north of Krasny when both engines were damaged by ground fire. Although he was seen to clamber apparently unhurt from his aircraft, W.Nr. 141556 coded "B+", Kaschel had the misfortune to have crash-landed in an area held by partisans and he was never seen again. On 20 July, *Uffz.* Karl Böttcher of 14.(Pz)/SG 9 was wounded and had to make an emergency landing at Stry in south-eastern Poland when his W.Nr. 141878 was hit by flak and on 25 July, 13.(Pz)/SG 9's *Uffz.* Rolf Ruthmann was taking off from Triciana airfield near Reichshof when Russian fighters attacked the airfield. Ruthmann's Red "C" W.Nr. 141837, was badly shot up, caught fire and crashed in flames. The pilot died from burns later the same day. Two days later, 14.(Pz)/SG 9's *Lt.* Oskar Bressler was wounded while making an emergency landing at Przemysl in W.Nr. 141858, and on 31 July, *Fw.* Walter Lippstreu of 12.(Pz)/SG 9 was killed north-east of Kowno when his aircraft, coded "O+" W.Nr. 141713, was hit by flak, crashed and burst into flames.

Among the Soviet units taking part in this action was the 9th Fighter Aviation Division equipped with the American Bell P-39 Airacobra, an aircraft which the Russians nicknamed *britchik*,

Russian fighters engaged the escort, the others attacked the main formation, first shooting down one Ju 87 and one Hs 129 and forcing the German aircraft to scatter. In the ensuing chase, four Soviet pilots each shot down a Ju 87 but the remaining Henschels appear to have escaped without casualties.

Typically, however, the most severe Henschel losses were due to flak and ground fire, and the heaviest casualties were inflicted upon 10.(Pz)/SG 9. On 16 July, the *Staffel* lost two aircraft north-east of Volkasusanka near Lublin; *Uffz*. Karl Bayrle was killed in aircraft "F+" W.Nr. 141973, when it received a direct AA hit and plunged into Russian lines. The other machine, "G+" W.Nr. 141966, was flown by the much-loved and respected *Staffelkapitän* and Knight's Cross holder *Hptm*. Ruffer. Witnesses who observed the crash said that Ruffer's aircraft was hit by flak and came down in enemy territory in such a way that there was no possibility the pilot could have survived.

Ofw. Helmut Corell was lost on 17 July in W.Nr. 141749 "J+", when he too fell victim to the ferocious AA fire and his aircraft crashed into a pond in enemy territory about 60 km (37 miles) south of Sokal. The *Staffelführer*, *Oblt*. Hans-Werner Wenzel, was posted missing on 22 July; he was last seen attacking tanks in W.Nr. 141880, coded "K+". On 27 July, *Ofw*. Hermann Holtermann was lost in W.Nr. 141872, "W+" and although other pilots of his *Schwarm* were themselves too busy taking evasive action to notice exactly what happened to him, he was presumed to have been shot down when his *Schwarm* ran into heavy flak at Jaroslau, near Deblin-Irena. Holtermann was posthumously awarded the *Deutsches Kreuz* in Gold on 1 January 1945.

On 20 July 1944, a bomb exploded at Adolf Hitler's mosquito-infested *Wolfsschanze* forest headquarters in East Prussia, arranged and planted there by officers acting in opposition to the Nazi leadership. In a lucky escape from assassination, Hitler was shaken, but relatively unharmed. That same day 13.(Pz)/SG 9's *Staffelkapitän*, *Hptm*. Franz Oswald, experienced what he described as his "luckiest moment of the

Britchik Aces: Considered obsolete by the Allied air forces, the P-39 found its place on the Eastern Front during 1943 where it outpaced both the Spitfire and the P-40. Seen here in front of one of the machines are Soviet aces (*left to right*) L.I. Goreglyad, A.F. Klubov, not known, V.A. Berezkin, A.I. Pokryshkin and N.L. Trofimov.

or "Little Shaver". This unit was commanded by Aleksandre Pokryshkin, a Siberian pilot finally credited as the second highest-scoring Soviet fighter ace with 59 victories. The destruction of most German records for this period makes any comparison between Russian claims and German losses impossible, but Pokryshkin claimed one Hs 129 shot down at the beginning of the Lvov-Sandomiertz operation. During this action Pokryshkin's own machine was damaged when another Hs 129 opened fire on him.

On 16 July, in the Carpathians area, three groups of Red Air Force fighters from the 16th Guards IAP were providing cover for their own ground troops when they spotted a mixed formation of some 30 Ju 87s and Hs 129s escorted by eight Bf 109s. While one group of

Among the Panzerjäger lost during July 1944 was the recently decorated Knight's Cross holder and Staffelkapitän of 10.(Pz.)/SG 9, Hptm. Rudolf-Heinz Ruffer. His aircraft W.Nr.141966, coded "G+", received a direct flak hit, crashed and burned. Here, he is seen in front of Hs 129 W.Nr.141749, White "J".

war". For some days the *Staffel* had been operating from the airfield at Lysiatycze in Southern Poland, since June also the base of *Stab* IV./SG 9. The aircraft were loaded with AB-50 anti-personnel containers, one of which was mounted under each wing. Each container held fifty 1 kg bombs and was designed to open over the target and scatter the deadly bomblets over a wide area. Once released, the bomblets armed themselves almost immediately and, despite their small size, exploded with a carpet effect of considerable destructive power. On this occasion, the *Abwurfbehälter* on the right wing only half released over the target and hung up on the wing rack. In Oswald's words: "I came within an ace of being killed. I was unable to drop the container under the right wing. Jettisoning it did not work and although I tried everything to shake the container free, it wouldn't go. I feared it would come off when my aircraft landed and these containers explode on contact even though the fuse is not armed."

Although Oswald's first thought was to bale out, this was out of the question; his map showed large zones marked with a letter "P" and encircled by a red ring indicating that the surrounding area of forest was infested with partisans. There was only one alternative; Oswald planned to land in a 200 kph (120 mph) high-speed approach, touch down hard to jolt the container free and hope that his high landing speed would enable him to outrun the bomblets before they exploded. First, he circled Lysiatycze airfield with flaps and undercarriage lowered to show that there was something wrong. Then he made his high speed run-in and bounced his wheels down hard on the ground. This succeeded in shaking free the container which then opened up and released the bomblets. Carried along by the aircraft's forward speed, the bomblets - each comparable to a direct hit by an anti-aircraft shell - bounced and tumbled about the machine: "My touchdown still gives me nightmares! When the wheels touched the ground the container sprung open and its contents exploded, tearing some 400 to 600 holes in my aircraft. Three splinters actually penetrated the cockpit and it was a miracle that I wasn't injured or killed."

Since stemming the Russian advance proved impossible with the resources available, German forces could do little but save what they could from complete catastrophe and withdraw as quickly as possible to safer airfields, destroying all airfield installations, equipment and stocks before leaving. The only supplies which were not evacuated or destroyed were bombs, but these were put to practical use in the demolition of airfields. Some demolition, however, was to prove a little premature. At the end of July, 10.(Pz)/SG 9 was stationed at Radom in Poland. *Lt.* Walter Krause remembers his stay there as a positive nightmare: "The airfield had been prepared for evacuation and armourers had placed 250 kg bombs everywhere, including in our huts, and then connected them to a special electrical circuit. One such beast was even placed under my bed. I hated to sleep there."

"On 31 July, at around noon, while we were having our lunch in a remote hut a short distance from the airfield, there was a gigantic explosion. Window frames were blown in and we were almost thrown from our chairs. There were clouds of dust everywhere and as we staggered

A formation of Hs 129s set out on a "free-hunt".

outside we could see a pall of thick yellow smoke over our barracks. *Luftwaffe* soldiers were laying in the streets and the cries from the wounded could be heard everywhere. It was a terrible sight. We learned later that this inferno had been caused by a telephone party which was trying to locate a fault. They had connected up the wrong line by mistake and detonated all the bombs! In addition to this, the Russians bombed our airfield every night. This was completely new to us and our new *Staffelkapitän*, *Lt.* Gebhard Weber, pressed VIII. *Fliegerkorps* to allow us to be transferred. We were glad to show Radom a clean pair of heels!"

This was a time of heavy fighting against an enemy who was greatly superior in both manpower and material. Although their numbers were too small to affect the overall situation, the *Panzerjäger* continued to fly without respite and their successes were often sufficient

The Diary of Feldwebel Otto Ritz, 10.(Pz)/SG 9

July - August 1944

Day 1, July.

The Soviets are trying to cross the River Bug in order to encircle our rear guards. I lead a Schwarm of Hs 129s to attack the Russian tanks and infantry as they try to take our last bridge over the Bug in grid square 'Q'. Their anti-aircraft guns open up from a great range and their anti-aircraft machine guns are also in action. I am still trying to manoeuvre the Schwarm into the best tactical position when Russian fighters appear. We take evasive action, mutually covering each others' tails and at last manage to make a steady approach to the tank targets. A T-34 moves along the bank of the river and tries to engage our guards from the side. Near the bridge is a German anti-aircraft gun but it has jammed and although the gunners work desperately on the breech, they are unable to fire. I close in on the tank and fire my guns, but at the same time I feel that my aircraft has been hit. The Russian anti-aircraft shells have set my Henschel on fire and I am forced to make an emergency landing. When I thump it down on the opposite bank of the river, I see that another Hs 129 has knocked out the first T-34 and black smoke is already rising from another one.

I clamber out of my machine and, seeking cover, climb into a friendly 88-mm anti-aircraft gun emplacement. Here I can watch my comrades' attack. It is over an hour before they leave the area. During this time I notice how, although all kinds of ironmongery is hurled up by the anti-aircraft defences, very little of it can be seen from the Henschel's cockpit. The last few German soldiers cross the bridge and even the wounded can be brought over before the bridge is blown up. Soviet ground-attack aircraft make an appearance, but they are too late. They drop their fragmentation bombs between our foxholes and then make a low-level strafing attack in tight formation, during which they are surrounded by our light flak. Two are hit. Pieces come from them and they crash. I would like to go to the crash sites but the area is under heavy Russian machine-gun fire. Late in the evening I am back with my Staffel.

Day 2, July.

The Bolsheviks must have suffered heavy losses, for now all their men and equipment are perfectly camouflaged and hardly any movement is to be seen. The cloud height is 75 metres (250 ft) when we are suddenly ordered to mount a close-support operation against Russians which have assaulted our positions north of Lublin. A small group of Waffen-SS men are

defending themselves in a quarry against hordes of Russians and there is bitter hand-to-hand combat everywhere. As we fly over them, we are so low that we can see their faces and as we turn to approach flanking Soviet troops we can see machine-guns open up. Dead and wounded Russians are laying between the bomb craters in the fields and gardens below. This must be the results of earlier attacks carried out by our Focke-Wulf and Stuka Staffeln.

We finally find the tanks we have been briefed to attack. They are standing in a plantation with Soviet infantry waiting between them. We start by dropping our bombs and then make low-level attacks with our cannon. An anti-aircraft machine-gun mounted on a Sherman opens fire on me and scores a number of hits in my ammunition box. I am trying to bank round and fly back over Lublin when, suddenly, one round after another explodes. Various parts and panelling of my aircraft fly off and I have to crash-land between two lines of Soviet soldiers about three kilometres from the outskirts of the town. Before I hit the ground, I have to slide back the cockpit canopy because of the intense heat, and when my aircraft crashes I am flung out of the cockpit.

Blood is running over my eyes and although I can hardly see, I start running to where I presume our lines are. This long-distance running has taken me back several kilometres when I come across an armoured train. But no one aboard has seen me, and just when I have almost reached it, it moves off along the open track.

I hear explosions behind me and see that a small railway station which I have just left has been blown up. Thinking that it has been destroyed by German engineers I go back, only to discover to my bewilderment that the station was not blown up by our engineers but by partisans. The devil knows why they should do this, for their action can only be to the detriment of the advancing Russians. I resume my walk back until I reach a deserted German command post. There is a telephone and I make a call which is answered by our commanding general himself! Now I am saved. Shortly afterwards I am picked up by a motor-bike and driven back behind our lines. There I am given some food and the General sees to it that my injuries are properly attended to. The next morning, his Fi 156 Storch brings me back to my Staffel. Here I learn that my boys have knocked out three T-34s and I console myself with their success.

Day 3, July.

I can't stand this inactivity any more. When you have been knocked down, the best thing to do is climb into the cockpit again without delay and fly a mission, then your self-confidence remains and you have no time to ponder over your mishap.

I am keen for action and so resume flying operations at once. On the outward flight, and while still over our own territory, a formation of Russian fighters flies towards us head-on and I am attacked by an La-5. I fire at him a little before he can shoot at me, but I don't know whether I have scored any hits. Then, by flying into a layer of mist we are lucky and get rid of our opponents. A downward glance shows that four Russian tanks, camouflaged with green shrubbery, are standing between our positions. I make low-level attacks and immobilise all four of them. Only the crew from the last one are able to bale out, though one of them seems to be wounded for he can't get away and lays beside the turret where he is burned by the flames of his burning tank. The other members of the crew have run away and are trying to reach their own men, but when they realise they have been encircled by our soldiers they stop, raise their hands, and are taken prisoner. As I bank round I can see our men waving to me.

I fly on. I find four trucks and a radio vehicle driving along a dirt road; they are new American types and probably belong to a tank unit. I open fire and cut them to pieces. When we are far behind our own lines we are attacked by six Yak-9s. Two of them streak down and although they fire bursts from too great a range they manage to hit Number 2 in the Schwarm.

Day 4, July.

*Y*esterday, we were briefed to attack some tanks but although the target was accurately marked on our maps, we couldn't find them. We managed to find some trucks, though, most probably loaded with tank ammunition, for when they blew up, the force of the explosion almost tore my engines from the wings. I was able to destroy four of the trucks and while we continued to look for the tanks a number of Russian fighters found us! We were lucky however; our Messerschmitts came to help us and while the fighters were all milling about above us I discovered a scout car between some fir trees. My bursts set it alight at once. Then we strafe some Russian infantry positions on the western side of a slight rise and we are making a slow turn for another run in when we see a column of Russians marching straight towards us. The Russians throw themselves to the ground and lay there, perfectly staggered, just as if they were on a barracks square. We open up with all we have and our guns sweep the column. Parts of bodies are thrown into the air and a huge cloud of dust is generated from our bullets striking the ground. It must be terrible down there.

Day 5, July.

*O*ne morning, in the bridgehead at B., we see heavy attacks by Soviet infantry although there is no sign of their tanks. At first we think they must be holding them in reserve, but then we see the unmistakable marks in the ground left by tank tracks. They end under some sheaves of corn. Light anti-aircraft guns located in a nearby village fire madly at us but our bursts set the camouflaged tanks alight and they burn splendidly. Russian P-39 Airacobras hurtle down from above into our formation, spitting flame from all their guns. At first, we are surprised that instead of pulling around to make another pass at us they make a getaway. Then we see a second formation of fighters. Me 109s! Now we know why they made off so quickly without making another attack.

Day 6, July.

*O*ur anti-tank guns and machine-guns have caused a Russian attack designed to expand their bridgehead to fail. The harvested cornfields are covered with hundreds of Russian dead who, with the bodies of their dead horses, have been left behind in the parching heat. When we fly low over the countryside, rooks and magpies soar up from the inflated horse bodies. The hordes of Russian soldiers have moved on and are crossing open country. We attack them where they march the closest. By the evening, although our Tiger tanks and infantry have advanced again and have overtaken some of the surviving Russian tanks, the crews do not give away the places where they have parked up.

The next morning an enemy counter-attack is thwarted. While we make our low-level strafing attacks the Russian artillery pounds away at a wood, but our own artillery has left its emplacements there during the night and transferred to other positions. Becker continually sneers at the enemy's futile attempts over the R/T, but he has to stop laughing when seven La-5s attack out of the sun. We dive down to the ground in desperate curves before turning slowly towards our own lines and our first anti-aircraft positions. Here we are saved again by our own Bf 109 fighters. One of the Russians was shot down and dives vertically into a pond. When we land, we are soaking wet and admit that we have never perspired so profusely.

Day 7, August.

*T*oday I have achieved a Staffel record with seven kills. I was able to knock out the last tank and set it on fire with my very last armour-piercing shell. The rest of the Staffel could account for a further four T-34s. In some places the T-34s have overrun our grenadiers' positions before they were knocked out and now we see our grenadiers approach the burning tanks from all sides. We hunt down the Russians before they can find cover and also strafe five horse-drawn wagons.

Day 8, August.

*O*n the Vistula, four T-34s are knocked out and set alight by my cannon bursts. Anti-aircraft guns attached to the tanks with steel cables are unable to fire a single shot and are devoured by the burning fuel which leaks out of the armoured vehicles' fuel tanks. The effect of our cannon fire must be terrific, for during one of my attacks I saw the body of one of the mounted infantrymen sail over some trees.

Day 9, August.

*D*uring an early morning attack across the Vistula we head right into a force of Soviet ground-attack aircraft complete with fighter escort. While an air battle develops, we break away. We see three T-34s without accompanying infantry drive out of a small wood and move directly into the river. While I am attacking them, the other pilots discover five more tanks in the wood. The colossi roar around like mad, tearing down trees so that clearings are made. Russian soldiers rush to and fro in the undergrowth and we can see that some of them are manning machine-guns, but the effect of our strafing attacks cannot be determined as Russian fighters approach from the east and we head back to our airfield.

When we land, our groundcrews find that all of our aircraft have been hit by machine-gun fire. They set to work immediately to repair the damage, though this is their sixth night without an hour's sleep. How they manage to mend and restore our damaged machines to working order is often unbelievable. Last night, one of the fitters was working on an aircraft when he fell fast asleep and remained laying on the wing with his screwdriver still in his hand.

The personnel of 10.(Pz)/SG 9 line up for a photograph at Radom in July 1944 to commemorate Otto Ritz's 50th tank "kill"; front row (sitting) *Left to Right*: Fw. Franz Preiner, Uffz. H. Wille, Uffz. Walter Raufelder, Uffz. Eberhard Scholz (all pilots). Known to be back row from right: Uffz. Jüpp Spix (technical specialist), Uffz. Werner Benter (pilot), Fw. Artur Neumann (pilot), Uffz. Willi Tholen (engine specialist), Fw. G. Beker (pilot), Otto Ritz, Uffz. Heini Kelber (engine specialist).

to influence the result of a local ground engagement.

On 6 August 1944, for example, the Russians succeeded in penetrating the left flank of Fourth Panzer Army on the Vistula. Since there were no ground reserves which could go into action to seal up the penetration, the whole Army was in danger of being rolled up. For three days *Fw.* Otto Ritz led his anti-tank *Schwarm* against the Russian forces which had broken through and in fierce attacks succeeded in destroying 25 tanks and other equipment.

Ritz had been a medical student before joining the *Luftwaffe* and after pilot training at Memmingen and Schroda-Ost near Posen, he was posted to 10.(Pz)/SG 9 in October 1943. He soon became one of the most successful anti-tank fighters and by April 1944 had destroyed 30 tanks. Extracts from his diary for the period July-August (see pages 254-255) provide an excellent personal account of the operations he flew at this time and, overall, his attacks were so successful that they enabled the Army to regroup and redeploy, so preventing Fourth Panzer Army from suffering a disastrous defeat.

The Fourth Panzer Army also reported that Ritz's attacks had been so decisive that they wished to recommend him for the award of the Knight's Cross. Seidemann asked the *Staffel* to forward all the necessary documentation, but Ritz was confused. A necessary requirement before the *Ritterkreuz* could be awarded was that the nominee should first possess the *Deutsches Kreuz* in Gold, yet Ritz did not have this decoration. In one of the rare instances where the rules appear to have been waived, Ritz received his *Ritterkreuz* some three months before the official award of the *Deutsches Kreuz* in Gold on 1 January 1945, though, inexplicably, photographs taken on the day Ritz received his *Ritterkreuz* clearly show a German Cross on his uniform.

At the end of July 1944, forward units of the Russian First Ukranian Front had elsewhere succeeded in crossing the Vistula and established what later became known as the Baranov bridgehead with Sandomierz on the west bank. This came as some surprise to the Germans, not least to the personnel of 10.(Pz)/SG 9 whose airfield lay directly in the path of the Russian advance. Having sufficiently recovered from the wounds he received in the Crimea in March and after completing an Fw 190 conversion course, *Fw.* Michalczak had now returned to the *Staffel*. Michalczak and *Fw.* Otto Ritz were the closest of friends and the two had previously flown many missions together. Once, the two men, having already surprised and destroyed a group of five T-34s in a ravine, were flying past a nearby hilltop when they found a second group of seven tanks parked as if for a drive-past. The crews were standing in a semi-circle around an officer with a map. Before the Russians could even turn their heads, the Henschel pilots had opened fire and gunned them down.

On another occasion Ritz and Michalczak were flying together as part of a *Schwarm* when the Henschels flew past a Russian anti-aircraft battery on the Dnieper. The guns opened fire and hit one of the aircraft, which spun into the ground. Then they hit a second aircraft, forcing the pilot to make a crash-landing.

"I had never before been so furious as on this mission", wrote Ritz later: *"During my low-level attacks I looked straight into the muzzle flashes of the AA guns but we kept our firing buttons depressed until there was complete silence in the gun positions. While I was streaking in, my own aircraft was hit and a fine spider's web of cracks appeared in the thick armoured windscreen. It must have been a direct hit from a 37 mm shell, but the gunners could not celebrate. They received a severe mauling and their distorted bodies lay between the guns which our fire had torn from their mountings."*

In early August 1944, although he had then flown only 78 missions, Michalczak had already set on fire or immobilised 61 Russian tanks, destroyed 78 lorries and shot down two Russian aircraft. After one particular entry in his log book for that period, he entered ten exclamation marks to show that during an unexpected Russian attack he had during the course of one day flown no fewer than ten missions.

The story behind those ten missions began early one morning, when a guard's alarm call had summoned the *Staffel* personnel from their huts into the dawn. Outside, a convoy of Army supply vehicles was rumbling past loaded with

grenadiers and wounded, the remnants of a retreating advance detachment. Other soldiers were trying to put together some hasty defence, calling for mines and helping to push a 20 mm anti-aircraft gun from a muddy lane into the main road. Then the 20 mm flak batteries and anti-aircraft machine-guns on the nearby airfield started firing. As there were no enemy aircraft to be seen they must have been shooting at ground targets and this indicated that enemy tanks were in the area.

For a moment the pilots were confused; the previous evening the front line had been on the other side of the Vistula and a *Schwarm* of Hs 129s flying home from a close support mission had reported that the countryside was calm and peaceful in the dusk.

Michalczak was the first to rouse himself from the shock and dismay and urged some pilots and ground staff onto a lorry which made off for the airfield at top speed. As they

Pilots of 10.(Pz)/SG 9 congratulate Otto Ritz upon achieving his 50th tank "kill". From left to right: Fw. Georg Eicher, Fw. Franz Preiner, Fw. Otto Ritz and the ill-fated Fw. Artur Neumann who was killed on 11 August 1944 while attempting to make a single-engined landing at Warzyn.

In July 1944, Soviet aircraft made fierce attacks against German held airfields in Poland. A right raid at Radom on 31 July caused many casualties and Obgfr. Friedrich Vollmer - Otto Ritz's faithful first mechanic - died as a result of his injuries.

A Schwarm of Hs 129s from 13.(Pz)/SG 9 return after a sortie.

passed some machine-gun emplacements, they saw the gunners waving wildly, warning them of immediate danger. Only then did it become clear exactly what had happened. By advancing through woods and swamps the Russians had managed to cross the Vistula and by first light had successfully penetrated the German lines. Suddenly, tracer bullets started to fly, criss-crossing the runway and ricocheting off the paving. One of the men in the truck tried to jump off, but it was still moving at full speed and Michalczak shouted to him to stay. When the lorry finally drove up to the airfield's entrance they found it blocked by a burning vehicle, but Michalczak jumped down and ran as fast as he could towards the *Staffel's* parked Henschels. Only one man managed to follow him; his fitter, *Obgfr.* Classen, who had instinctively leapt off the truck behind him. Classen ran for some 20 paces and then paused to see who else had followed. As shells howled from the Russian tanks, he noticed that his comrades, the lorry and the burning vehicle were all hidden from view behind a wall of dust which the shells threw up into the morning mist.

A nearby shell-burst threw Classen to the ground. Although he shouted out three times for his comrades to follow him, he received no reply. The shriek of more incoming shells tore at the air as he picked himself up and ran after Michalczak who had meanwhile reached one of the parked aircraft and had climbed up into its cockpit. As Classen came running up, Michalczak threw the aircraft starting handle down to him and pointed towards the runway. Two T-34s had stopped at the airfield briefing hut. One rolled on for a couple of yards and then both began firing down the runway. Behind the tanks were Russian soldiers, alternately running and throwing themselves down for cover.

Obgfr. Classen could clearly see the approaching tanks and infantry but, as yet, the enemy had not seen him. If just one of the soldiers had observed the two men on the aircraft, all would have been lost, so he started to turn the starting handle, pushing with his whole body against the resistance of the inertia starter because Michalczak was his only hope, the only man who could fly the machine and perhaps stop the tanks.

But starting an engine was just too much for one man on his own and Michalczak had to leap off the wing and help. Once the engine had fired, Michalczak climbed back into the cockpit and pulled back the throttle lever. To his utter dismay, the revolution counter needle fell and the propeller ground to a stop. They tried to start the engines for a second and then a third time, jointly operating the starting crank. Finally, one engine and then the other roared into life, drowning out the nearby noise of battle. After climbing back into the cockpit again, Michalczak started to slowly taxi away, shouting, "*Classen! You stay here.*

Regardless of what happens, crank up the engines. If we can't stop the Russians I'll land and stow you away in the baggage compartment!"

Shells were bursting all around the Henschel as it gathered speed and rolled over the grass. Gradually, the tail rose and the mainwheels left the ground, only to bounce back again. Michalczak pulled the stick back into his stomach and the aircraft barely lurched into the air, but its speed was still insufficient and it started to lose height as it passed low over the pair of T-34s. From his cockpit, Michalczak could see a frightened face as one of the tank's crew hastily withdrew into the turret and closed the hatch.

Despite his dangerously low speed, Michalczak banked round to attack. He had to prevent the Russians from reaching the aircraft parking area and from destroying the machines. He made his run up to his target and had almost closed to firing range when the front of the nearest T-34 erupted in flames. At once, Michalczak realised that the crew of the airfield AA gun had at last managed to move it up from the road and had brought it, partially concealed by its camouflage of bushes and branches into position. Behind the gun's protective shield the crew could be seen waving a piece of yellow cloth and the pilot realised that they were trying to tell him that they were unable to aim at the second tank because it was shielded by the one they had already knocked out. But this tank too was doomed.

As the Henschel swept down for the kill, Michalczak's cannon shells hammered into the T-34's steel hull. The crew baled out, but were hit by the next burst of fire. A third tank moved over the open field towards the runway, but this, too, was hit by the Hs 129's cannon. Flames burst out of the visor slits and hatches. Michalczak just had time to note that none of the crew had baled out before he saw something which almost caused him to lose his courage. Large groups of yet more Russians were advancing from a hollow, pulling pack horses and light guns behind them. He doubted whether he could stop such a formidable avalanche but he attacked just the same, scattering it and forcing them to cower on the ground for protection. Despite his vision being impaired by clouds of dust from the impact of bullets hitting the ground, he managed to shoot up three horse-drawn carts, a mortar troop and the line of soldiers near the runway. A few Russians, their nerves shattered, hurried back towards the woods from which they had emerged, but the majority of them remained laying on the ground, either hit or rooted to the spot from fear.

Meanwhile, about 30 Russian soldiers had almost managed to reach the *Staffel's* parked aircraft and Michalczak could see the small black shape of *Obgfr.* Classen close by. Michalczak shot the 30 soldiers down, firing off all his ammunition until nothing stirred. He landed his aircraft and jumped from the cockpit. Another aircraft was started up and Michalczak took off for the second time. Even with the undercarriage still extended he fired burst after burst from all his guns into more Russians who had approached. Horse-drawn carts carrying tank ammunition blew up; horses and men cartwheeled through the air. An anti-tank gun and its crew were put out of action. The gunners of two machine-guns were hit. Each time the Henschel made a firing pass, panic-stricken Russians threw themselves into the ditches beside a dirt road, ran behind the trees lining the runway or tried to crawl into the earth. Michalczak made one run after another and fired at everything that moved. When he had again expended all his ammunition, he landed, cranked up the next Henschel, took off yet again, fired, landed... And so it went on...

When he landed for the fifth time, the rest of the *Staffel's* pilots and ground crews ran up to him, breathless. Although he hadn't realised it at the time, the two machine-guns Michalczak had destroyed were the ones which had held down his comrades from the lorry. They had sought shelter in a ditch and had been unable to move until Michalczak had killed the enemy gunners.

Four of the *Staffel's* pilots took off immediately while the others helped with the rearming, pulling the empty belts from the ammunition boxes and refilling them. Meanwhile, the Russians had renewed their efforts and brought artillery into position on the edge of the wood. Shells whistled

Luftwaffe ground crew with an Hs 129 3-2 on the Eastern front. Their existence was largely one of hard work and privation. In summer, temperatures could reach 40-50° C and in winter, temperatures down to -40° C often had to be endured, sometimes without adequate clothing.

Below and Far Right: Ground crews of 10.(Pz)/SG 9 wait for a Ju 52 transport aircraft which will transfer them to an airfield near Lublin, eastern Poland during the summer of 1944. Temporary distraction is caused by the flames and smoke from a shot down Soviet Il-2 close to the airfield.

onto the airfield, one round bursting in the middle of the four Henschels which were taking off. By some miracle, none of them was damaged and, once in the air, Michalczak directed the pilots by radio onto individual targets he had already identified. The additional firepower arrived at a critical moment, for Russian cavalry now began to emerge from a copse and charge towards the runway. The aircraft's 20 guns caused havoc among the men and horses and the *Schwarm* encountered only spasmodic defensive fire from the woods and the copse. When the aircraft took off for the last time that morning there were very few signs of life. Dead and wounded Russians lay on the field and on the edges of the wood, while elsewhere there were dead horses and abandoned weapons.

During this action, Michalczak himself had made no fewer than ten flights. When his machine landed for the last time and rolled to a standstill, he remained sitting quietly in the cockpit for some minutes, eyes closed, completely exhausted. When he eventually managed to haul himself out of his aircraft and lower himself to the ground, he merely slapped his fitter on his back. Although no words were spoken, Classen understood. It was Michalczak's way of saying thanks for holding out. Between them the two men had forced the enemy to withdraw and had saved the *Staffel's* aircraft.

But other strong Russian forces were already nearby and the risk of remaining in place was too great. Before dusk fell the *Staffel* was transferred to another advanced landing strip and here Heinrich Michalczak was awarded the *Deutsches Kreuz* in Gold. In a simple ceremony, the *Staffel's* personnel were lined up in a village street and between the peasant huts, the *Staffelkapitän*, Gebhard Weber, pinned the medal on Michalczak's tunic. In March, 1945, Michalczak was nominated for the Knight's Cross but, as with Weber, the war ended before it could be awarded.

Shortly after this award ceremony, 10.(Pz)/SG 9 moved to Warzyn, a remote forward field half way between Kielce and Krakow. Warzyn, like Bacau, became another milestone in the history of 10.(Pz)/SG 9, for the unit was to spend longer there - from August 1944 to 13 January, 1945 - than at any other place. At first the airfield was the scene of the usual hectic activity as it was

prepared for operations, and the pilots were soon flying missions continuously in the Opatov-Staszov sector on the edge of the Lysa-Gora mountain range. In the course of these operations the *Staffel* claimed no less than 40 tanks and on 13 August was visited again by *General* Seidemann. He proved to be most enthusiastic about the *Staffel's* success and confirmed that the Hs 129 units were mainly responsible for the Russian attacks west of Sandomierz being repulsed. More ominously, the *Staffel* also learned that the Russians had transferred no fewer than 2,000 aircraft to the area of the front in which the unit was operating.

On 11 August, the pilots of four Henschel 129s were briefed for an operation in which they were to prevent scattered remnants of German Army units from being surrounded by Russian armour attacking them from both sides of the Sandomierz-Opatov road. *Oblt.* Weber led the *Schwarm*, and *Lt.* Krause led the second *Rotte* with *Fw.* Artur Neumann as his wingman. While the *Schwarm* was climbing out after take-off, Krause saw that Neumann's starboard engine was streaming a trail of blue smoke. As the aircraft were still over friendly territory, enemy action could be ruled out and the cause was probably due to a seized piston.

Krause had no sooner pointed out the smoke trail to Neumann than a vibration seemed to pass through Neumann's aircraft and the large three-bladed propeller of the port engine came off and cartwheeled close over Krause's machine. "Naturally, I was frightened out of my wits", Krause recalled. "It could easily have hit me!"

Krause watched as Neumann's aircraft turned back towards the airfield. Then joining up on the formation as its Number Three, Krause and the other two pilots settled down to enjoy the rest of the flight to the front in the beautiful August weather. The sky was a brilliant blue and the pilots' spirits were further raised by the fact that compared to usual conditions they were accompanied by a "huge" escort of eight Messerschmitt 109s under the command of *Oblt.* Friedrich Obleser, the *Staffelkapitän* of 8./JG 52. The two formations flew on, the Henschel pilots happy that this unaccustomed number of fighters had been assigned to escort them and safe in the belief that they were promised absolute security.

As *Lt.* Krause recalled: "In the Sandomierz-Opatov area we started a *"Hund-Such-Kurve"*, a low-level weaving search manoeuvre named after the zig-zag way in which a dog will run about,

sniffing the ground. From our height of 400 metres (1,312 ft) we could see that the retreating German soldiers on the road were being threatened from both sides by Russian tanks and lorries. We attacked at once. After three or four low-level strikes, Obleser's voice came over the radio. Above us, all seemed quiet and the fighter leader was anxious to join in the action. *"Man Alive, Weber! It's bloody boring up here. No Indians for miles around. Haven't you got anything for us to attack down there, lorries for instance?"* *"Of course"*, replied Weber. *"Provided everything is quiet, there are plenty of lorry targets for you."*

"Weber had hardly released his R/T button when the eight Me 109s came down in a steep plunging dive and streaked past us towards the lorries. But they were not alone! Behind them, almost as if they were part of the '109 formation, more aircraft dived steeply out of the sun. Russian P-39 Airacobras with the red noses of the famous Stalin Squadron! Since I was Number Three, I was at the end of the line of *Panzerjäger* and, as the saying goes, *"The devil takes the hindmost"*. Cannon shells flashed past me from the P-39s' 37 mm nose cannon. I just had time to call out over the R/T: *"Achtung! Indians behind us!"* when cannon shells thudded into my aircraft and an Airacobra overtook me. It was only about ten metres (30 ft) away and I could clearly see its olive camouflage paint and the huge Soviet star markings. My height was now around 100 metres (328 ft) and my machine was diving towards the ground. I pulled back on the stick... but nothing happened! In desperation, I pressed the electrical elevator trim with my left hand and the aircraft's nose came up so sharply that it felt as if the aircraft had been grasped by a giant's fist. I had only narrowly missed hitting the ground, but now the aircraft was climbing too steeply. I pushed the trimming control forward again to flatten out since there was still no response from the joystick. Unable to maintain control by use of the stick, I had to keep trimming the aircraft, but each time I did so I could not help over-correcting. It was like a roller-coaster - up and down, up and down - until I reached the airfield. I made a careful approach, then trimmed out as best I could. Throttle off - *Bang*! - and I am down on the airstrip in a formidable belly-landing! Dust and quiet. The first person to approach my aircraft was *Oblt*. Lehmann, the *Staffelkapitän* of the 12.(Pz)/SG 9, who asked me if I had been hurt. Apart from a twisted back I was unharmed, but my aircraft had been well and truly shot up by the Airacobras and, of the horizontal tail surfaces, only the starboard stabiliser remained."

The Russian fighters had also attacked and hit Weber's aircraft. Oil leaked back over the wings and petrol gushed from the perforated wing tanks. Although the fuel did not ignite, it was clear to Weber that the machine would not fly far before it ran dry. Both engines stopped completely when the aircraft was flying over a forested area, but as Weber still maintained complete control over his aircraft, he was able to bring it down in a gentle landing on top of the trees. As the treetops took the weight of the Henschel, they had a braking, cushioning effect and the machine gradually descended until it came to rest in a clearing. Fortunately, the engines and tail were resting on two small mounds of sand so that later, the valuable cannon could be easily dismantled and salvaged before the aircraft was burned.

The unfortunate Neumann, who had not long been with the *Staffel*, had been able to return to the airfield on one engine but crashed fatally on landing. The fourth machine also made it back but had been so badly damaged in the fighter attack that when it came to rest in one piece in a clearing and the pilot put his foot in the footstep it was just too much. As the weakened structure took the pilot's weight it gave way and the fuselage simply folded in half and collapsed to the ground.

Throughout the summer battles on the Vistula and the forelands of the Carpathian Mountains, the German anti-tank units were in action constantly. The enemy's tank brigades had suffered heavy losses, and each mission flown by the *Panzerjäger* meant fighting from take-off to touchdown, until the pilots' eyes ached from the constant searching of the ground and surrounding airspace. Scores of Soviet fighters patrolled the area providing cover for their armoured spearheads and even though *Luftwaffe* fighter units engaged the Russians, some of the enemy always managed to penetrate the fighter screen and attack the anti-tank aircraft. At the approach of hostile aircraft, the Russian AA gun crews accompanying the tanks could unlimber their guns and be in action in a matter of seconds, firing magazine after magazine skywards to form an almost impenetrable wall. Consequently, the enemy fighters had to be outwitted and the AA guns destroyed before the T-34s could be caught and attacked.

In the summer of 1944, *Oblt*. Hans Hermann Steinkamp was the *Staffelkapitän* of 14.(Pz)/SG 9, and it was upon his shoulders that the main responsibility fell to ensure that everyone in the *Staffel* maintained a high degree of efficiency, both in the air and on the ground. When he returned to his unit after recovering from the wounds sustained in the incident described in an earlier chapter, the 23 year old pilot had lost none of his fighting spirit. Almost every operation resulted in a tank kill, four T-34s being knocked out on one day alone, then three, then two and several with one well-aimed burst, one even with

The grave of Fw. Artur Neumann who crashed and was killed on 11 August 1944 while attempting a single-engined landing at Warzyn.

a single cannon shell. By 9 August, Steinkamp had personally knocked out 65 tanks, put another 62 out of action and destroyed 83 lorries.

Steinkamp's 65th tank kill was obtained when a *Schwarm* he was leading attacked a number of tanks in a village. During this action another pilot, *Fw.* Helmut Herrnberger, had attacked from the wrong direction and the fierce Russian anti-aircraft fire had forced him to break off his firing pass. Turning away and making another run in, Herrnberger was disappointed to discover that what should have been his twenty-second kill was already burning so fiercely it had also set on fire the thatched roof of the house behind which it had tried to find protection; Steinkamp had meanwhile selected the same tank and, attacking out of the sun, set it on fire with a single short burst. As he left the target through the anti-aircraft fire, Steinkamp clearly saw two of the tank's crew stumble over the village street and throw themselves into a garden. Apart from being Steinkamp's 65th kill, which at that time made him the *Gruppe's* most successful pilot, it was also the *Staffel's* 330th.

All the aircraft returned safely and, back on the ground, the tall, sun-tanned Steinkamp, still dripping with sweat, stood among his pilots and ground crews. The sleeves of his summer shirt were rolled up, he wore the *Deutsches Kreuz* in Gold on his right breast pocket, and there was still a red stripe over his face where the tight flying helmet had left an imprint. "Man alive, Herrnberger", he said with a laugh, "*you were lucky! You should have attacked from the sun so that it would have been impossible for the flak to shoot at you and you would also have been in a much more favourable firing position. I'm telling you, keep your eyes skinned at all times!*" For a moment the tall *Feldwebel* looked shamefaced, but then he waved his hand towards his aircraft; he had indeed been lucky for this time his aircraft had returned without so much as a scratch.[1]

According to a contemporary report, the *Staffel's* pilots always preferred to fly sorties when Steinkamp led the *Schwarm*. "Once you had been out with the Old Man two or three times", said a *Feldwebel* from Berlin who, although newly assigned to the *Staffel*, achieved his third tank kill on the same day as Steinkamp got his 65th, "you soon learned what it was all about." "If only I could have shot as calmly as he did", said an *Unteroffizier* who, with almost 20 kills to his credit, still found that the *Oberleutnant's* shooting abilities were unrivalled.

STRENGTH OF VIII. FLIEGERKORPS, NOVEMBER, 1944.

Stab/VIII. Fliegerkorps - Luftflotte 6

Krakow

1.and 2./NAG 2	Bf 109	25	(13)
NSGr 4	Ju 87 and Si 204	27	(16)
Stab and I./JG 52	Bf 109	49	(38)
Stab and I./SG 77	Fw 190	47	(35)
10.(Pz)/SG 77	Ju 87	25	(15)
Warzyn			
III./JG 52	Bf 109	41	(33)
10.(Pz)/SG 9	**Hs 129**	**14**	**(14)**
Naglowice			
II./SG 77	Fw 190	42	(32)
NAG 15	Bf 109 and Fw 189	23	(14)
Rudniki			
III./SG 77	Fw 190	42	(28)
Total:		**335**	**(238)**
			(71% Serviceable)

Still in their flying suits, these men crawled out of their tents early in the morning and crawled back into them late at night. Between take-offs and landings, the *Staffelkapitän* was called to the telephone to check the situation map. New messages arrived by teleprinter. Ground crews waited impatiently for his decision whether a damaged or bullet-riddled aircraft should be flown back to the repair depot or whether repairs should be done in the field. A pilot going to fetch spare parts asked for more orders; the chief engine fitter who, with his spectacles and conscientiousness resembled a school teacher, made suggestions concerning an engine change on "*Cäsar*", asked permission to make an airframe test on "*Dora*" and to remove the radio equipment from the unserviceable "*Kurfürst*". Orders, judgements and advice had to be given promptly and called for total dedication and utmost responsibility. It was the *Staffelkapitän* himself who looked for his men's quarters, who directed the alignment of the anti-tank cannon in the firing butts and listened to every engine which was test flown. Even the cook who reported that the vehicle with the meat and vegetable supply had broken down 10 km (6 miles) away turned to the *Staffelkapitän* for assistance in his desperate situation. He knew that all the men on the airfield would be looking forward to their meal and that

Above: General der Flieger Seidemann awarding Fw. Otto Ritz the Ritterkreuz on Warzyn airfield, Poland, 30 September 1944.
Centre: Fw. Ritz receives the congratulations of his Staffel. To the right of Ritz is Fw. Heinrich Michalczak.
Right: Twenty-four year old Fw. Otto Ritz was one of the most successful Hs 129 pilots, joining 10.(Pz)/SG 9 in October 1943 and being awarded the Ritterkreuz less than a year later after flying more than 100 operations and destroying 60 tanks. Note the Deutsches Kreuz in Gold on Ritz's uniform.

the *Oberleutnant* always ate together with his men. No matter what the problem, the 23-year old *Staffelkapitän* always had to find an answer.

The Russian victories in Belorussia were amongst the greatest of the war but from about 25 July to the end of August their progress was much slower due to long lines of communication, fatigue among the troops and the commitment of heavy German reserves in counter attacks against Russian attempts to advance into East Prussia and Central Poland. By the end of August, when the front ran from half way across Latvia and down to Central Poland, Russian operations were called off on orders from the Soviet High Command and their offensive came to a standstill. Nevertheless, although the situation had stabilised, the Soviets had gained 650 km (400 miles) since 22 June and Red Army troops were on the very borders of the Reich itself, only 570 km (350 miles) from Berlin.

It was fortunate for the Germans that the main thrust of the Russian advance in Poland had for a brief spell spent itself, for in September 1944 a fuel shortage made itself felt and *Luftwaffe* operations had to be ruthlessly cut down. For the remainder of the year, therefore, a period of relative inactivity set in and there was little change in the position of the front which now ran from East Prussia down to the Carpathians.

For 10.(Pz)/SG 9 at Warzyn, all flying activity came to a standstill until mid January, 1945. The unit's personnel set to, building hardened shelters for the aircraft, there were field training exercises, aircraft maintenance and a great deal of boredom in what was considered to have been a "... godforsaken Polish place". Although the situation was as quiet as in peacetime, there was no electric lighting and most of the personnel were in bed by 19:15 where they listened to a battery-powered radio. For some, rifle shooting parties were organised to hunt hares, and while the NCO pilots started secretly brewing schnapps, the officers preferred to pass the time playing cards.

The boredom was relieved on 30 September 1944, when Otto Ritz became the second *Panzerjäger* to be awarded the *Ritterkreuz*. The award came more unexpectedly than it had to Ruffer; the *Staffel* was lined up on parade and Ritz was ordered to march to the front where *General* Seidemann hung the Knight's Cross around his neck. Ritz had now flown more than 100 missions and destroyed over 66 tanks, but the award was also made in recognition of the part he had played in stopping the Soviet advance on the Vistula.

At this time, too, 10.(Pz)/SG 9's aircraft were refitted with FuG 7a radio equipment and as a result of the quiet situation, were able to receive the mechanics' constant attention and serviceability reached 100%, a record throughout the entire VIII. *Fliegerkorps*.

Further south, the Russians had overextended themselves in their advance into Hungary. Here the Germans were to prove that they could still turn and fight, preventing the Russians from reaching Budapest until the end of December and remaining in control of the city until the middle of February, 1945. On 23 September 1944, 14.(Pz)/SG 9 had been transferred to Gyoma in south-eastern Hungary where it operated under the command of *Einsatzstab Banat*. The *Staffel* was still at Gyoma on 3 October with 14 of its 16 aircraft operational

The 10.(Pz)/SG 9 on parade following the award of the Ritterkreuz to Fw. Otto Ritz. The NCO standing next to Ritz is Fw. Heinrich Michalczak while the officers are, from left to right, Obit. Schlachte, Lt. Jech and Lt. Krause. Note that Krause wears the Rumanian pilot's badge in addition to his Luftwaffe pilot's badge and that both Ritz and Michalczak are wearing the Deutsches Kreuz in Gold on their right breast.

The NCO pilots of 10.(Pz)/SG 9; from l. to r.: Uffz. Eberhard Scholz, Uffz. Kureck (KIA), Uffz. Schaber, Fw. Michalczak, Fw. Otto Ritz (KIA), Fw. Georg Schönthoner, Uffz. Hannes Gehlhaus, Uffz. Heirowsk (KIA), Uffz. Wille, Uffz. Benter.

The NCO pilots of 10.(Pz)/SG 9 are joined for this photograph by Lt. Jech and the Staffel's ground personnel.

under I. *Fliegerkorps*. By 29 November, the *Staffel* was at Magyarmecske where, with 13 of its 19 aircraft operational, it came under the command of *Stab*/SG 10. The 14.(Pz)/SG 9 under *Oblt.* Steinkamp remained in Hungary until December.

Meanwhile, in East Prussia, the Russian advance continued and Soviet forces encountered particularly stiff German opposition at Stalluponen, a town which they captured and lost several times in succession. Also operating in East Prussia in support of the Soviet Third Belorussian Front was the First Air Army, part of which consisted of the French volunteer pilots of

With the arrival of a cold autumn in Poland in 1944, Fw. Jüpp Weber, Uffz. Karl Bretschneider, Fw. Willi Tholen, Uffz. Hans Gehlhaus and other ground personnel from 10.(Pz)/SG 9 formed a forestry party to cut wood in the local forests around Warzyn for winter warmth.

the Normandie-Niemen Fighter Regiment, a unit which was particularly active around Pilluponen and Stalluponen. On 18 October the Regiment flew 88 sorties in this area, during the course of which it claimed 12 victories. The first of these losses occurred at 11:25 when *Asp.* Joseph Risso and *Asp.* Alexandre Laurent pounced upon a number of unescorted Hs 129s. In the short engagement which followed, Risso succeeded in shooting down one of them, almost certainly the aircraft flown by *Ofw.* Bey of 13.(Pz)/SG 9 who is known to have been killed that day. Then, at 12:45, nine of the Yaks located another formation of Hs 129s probably from 12.(Pz)/SG 9, and shot down four of them near the front line, the "kills" being shared by *Cne.* Pierre Matras, *Asp.* Francois de Geoffre, *Lt.* Leon Cuffant, *Lt.* Maurice Amarger, *Asp.* Marcel Albert, *Asp.* Roland de la Poype and *Asp.* Robert Marchi.

For 13.(Pz)/SG 9 in East Prussia, October was a depressing month, especially for Franz Oswald. The transfer of pilots to the Defence of the Reich had changed the atmosphere which had previously existed and the old *Staffel* spirit was a thing of the past. Most depressing of all, Oswald found, was that for most of the month there was little activity and only a few sorties were flown. None were flown at all during the last week of the month, at which time it became very cold and the first winter snow fell.

On 3 November, Franz Oswald was awarded the *Ritterkreuz*, the presentation being made by *Generalmajor* Franz Reuss, commander of the 4. *Fliegerdivision*, but even this event was tinged with sadness. Apart from the war situation which was certainly not in Germany's favour, Oswald's association with the *Staffel* and his operational flying career were to come to an end in December and, in January 1945 he was ordered to *Erprobungskommando* 26 at Udetfeld.

For 10.(Pz)/SG 9, too, the weeks leading up to the last wartime Christmas dragged by. Snow fell in November and was followed by a thaw which brought with it the customary mud and slush. Then came a great, dry cold, as is common in central Poland at this time of year. With the front at the Baranov bridgehead static, 10.(Pz)/SG 9 flew no more missions for the remainder of 1944 and for a while there was insufficient fuel even for training flights. An extract from one of *Lt.* Krause's letters home illustrates the dismal situation. On 24 November he wrote: *"I hadn't seen any aircraft in the sky for two months, but yesterday a fighter Staffel transferred to our airfield. When the '109s flew over our heads we cheered and waved like little children. German aircraft have become such a rarity, not only over the Reich but also here, that we were as pleased as Punch"*.

Some days later, however, after a break of three months, VIII. *Fliegerkorps* allocated its units some fuel for training flights. For two days 10.(Pz)/SG 9 slaved away, overhauling the aircraft and making them airworthy after the long period of enforced idleness. *"The mud is indescribable"*, wrote Walter Krause, *"but although the aircraft were bogged down over their axles we managed to get four Henschels into the air. The Staffel was transformed. Thank God we're flying again"*.

---

1 Fw. Herrnberger's luck finally ran out when he was killed in Hungary in March 1945.

"They nailed us to the ground"

FROM THE VISTULA TO THE ODER
JANUARY – MARCH 1945

22

The second half of 1944 was a period of unparalleled disaster for German arms both in the East and West. In the East, the gains so easily won in 1941 had been lost and on all sides German forces had been overwhelmed by sheer weight of manpower and material. Although many local victories were achieved, they were but pinpricks to the vast might of the Soviet Army and whereas the enemy had a seemingly endless supply of replacement armour and material, German losses were irreplaceable. By now the situation was past saving and, although the Germans were to throw

An Hs 129 B-2 at an Aircraft Forwarding Station.

all possible resources into the final struggle in the East in 1945, they were powerless to avert the impending catastrophe. On the airfield at Warzyn in Poland, 10.(Pz)/SG 9's personnel reflected on the gloomy outlook, *Lt* Walter Krause recalling: "I can well remember the turn of the year 1944/45. It was a starry night on New Year's Eve. We'd had some drinks, but not as many as the year before. Exactly at midnight, the light flak on the airfield gaily blasted away to greet the New Year, but we pilots stood around in the village street with serious faces. What would 1945 bring for us? Certainly not anything good for there was every indication of an imminent large-scale Russian attack from the Baranow, Pulawy and Magnuzev bridgeheads. The *Staffel* was ordered to stand by at immediate readiness."

"For the first time, VIII. *Fliegerkorps* had issued its units with a volume of aerial reconnaissance photographs showing the bridgeheads. The front lines could be easily recognised and there was a great number of Russian tank concentrations and artillery positions to be seen. The Russians' superiority in guns, tanks and aircraft was obvious, yet there still remained a certain level of confidence and this was not only felt in the *Luftwaffe*. For example, a young tank *Leutnant* came to the *Staffel* one day to agree on co-ordinated operational practices and radio frequencies, etc. He, too, was optimistic and said that his regiment was in position near Staszov with sixty Panther tanks. He felt his regiment was not only stronger than ever before but he believed it was impossible for the Russians to break through".

Shortly before midnight on the night of 11/12 January, the Russians opened their offensive to break out of the Baranow bridgehead and the inferno was let loose. Walter Krause remembers being woken by an increasingly stronger rumble and went outside to investigate. "I was terrified to see that although the front was some 60 kilometres (37 miles) away, the entire horizon in the east was blood red."

Deploying as many as 420 heavy- and medium-calibre guns for every two kilometres of front, the Russians opened their attack with a sustained artillery bombardment which blasted away everything in its path. This artillery fire was so devastating that, some days later, when 10.(Pz)/SG 9 tried to find the young *Panzer Leutnant's* regiment at Staszov, they discovered that not one of the its Panthers had survived. They had all been blown to pieces in their assembly positions.

In the early hours of 12 January the temperature stood a few degrees above freezing. Towards 01:00, VIII. *Fliegerkorps* telephoned orders that its units were to come to urgent readiness, but the men of 10.(Pz)/SG 9 had already left their beds. Despite the biting cold, the ground crews were already working on the machines and the pilots were dressed in their flying overalls and sitting in the command post awaiting orders. Soon the first messages came in telling of breaches torn in the front lines through which the Russians had launched their armoured formations. At the same time, at the Pulavy and Magnusev bridgeheads to the north, a great convergence of offensive force was observed. Thousands of enemy vehicles were counted. Here, too, the enemy was obviously about to launch an offensive on a massive scale.

But while the battle raged on the ground, air activity was slight. The first day of the Russian Sandomierz-Baranow attack was marked by bad weather which grounded both Russian and German air forces. In a situation of stable high pressure, low-hanging clouds and thick fog covered the front lines and it was late afternoon before it had cleared sufficiently to enable the *Panzerjäger* to fly. By this time the Russian Third Guards and Fourth Tank Armies had made an appearance and the total Soviet force committed in this sector amounted to 32 rifle divisions and 8 tank corps. This was the greatest mass of force in one area since the beginning of the war and whole concentrations of up to 200 T-34s had been reported pushing through gaps in the front opened by artillery and infantry. Despite the extremely poor visibility, the 10.(Pz)/SG 9's *Lt.* Rolf Aigner took off with a *Rotte* on an armed reconnaissance sortie and although he saw columns of burning German vehicles on the Staszov-Chmielnik road, he was unable to establish the position of the front line.

On the morning of 13 January the weather was at last clear enough to carry out low-level attacks. The Russians had now broken through on a wide front and their tank spearheads had advanced to the Nida river east of Jedreszow, just 30 km (19 miles) from Warzyn airfield. Across the Nida a broad 65 kilometre (40 mile) path to Upper Silesia and the Oder lay wide open. With two *Schwärme* 10.(Pz)/SG 9 made rolling wave-by-wave attacks. As *Lt.* Krause recalled: "The situation was appalling. Everywhere burning German vehicles. Not a trace of any coherent units. During one of these missions we flew past the edge of a sizeable forest from which the Russians were about to attack with a large number of T-34s - at a glance I estimated about 50 or 60. Without delay we swung round, manoeuvred into position, and with our remaining ammunition destroyed three T-34s. At a farmstead near the forest was a single German tank which had just been set alight. A member of the crew, dressed in his black Panzer uniform, clambered out of the turret and walked away from this burning coffin, dejectedly dragging his feet. The nearest Russian tanks were about 200 metres (656 ft) away, but I swung round past the burning German tank at a height of around 10 metres (33 ft) and rocked my wings to encourage the lone figure. He looked up at me and made a despairing gesture with his hand. I shall never forget that look. He was a young *Leutnant* about the same age as myself."

During the *Staffel's* second mission that day they attacked armour concentrations in the area near Chmielnik. Low clouds had forced the aircraft to fly at low level over the target area and, without any warning, the pilots ran head-on into a formation of Il-2 *Shturmoviks*. A wild melee began, German and Russian aircraft wheeling around in the sky, during which an Il-2 banked round and began to fly in the same direction as the Hs 129 flown by Heinrich Michalczak.

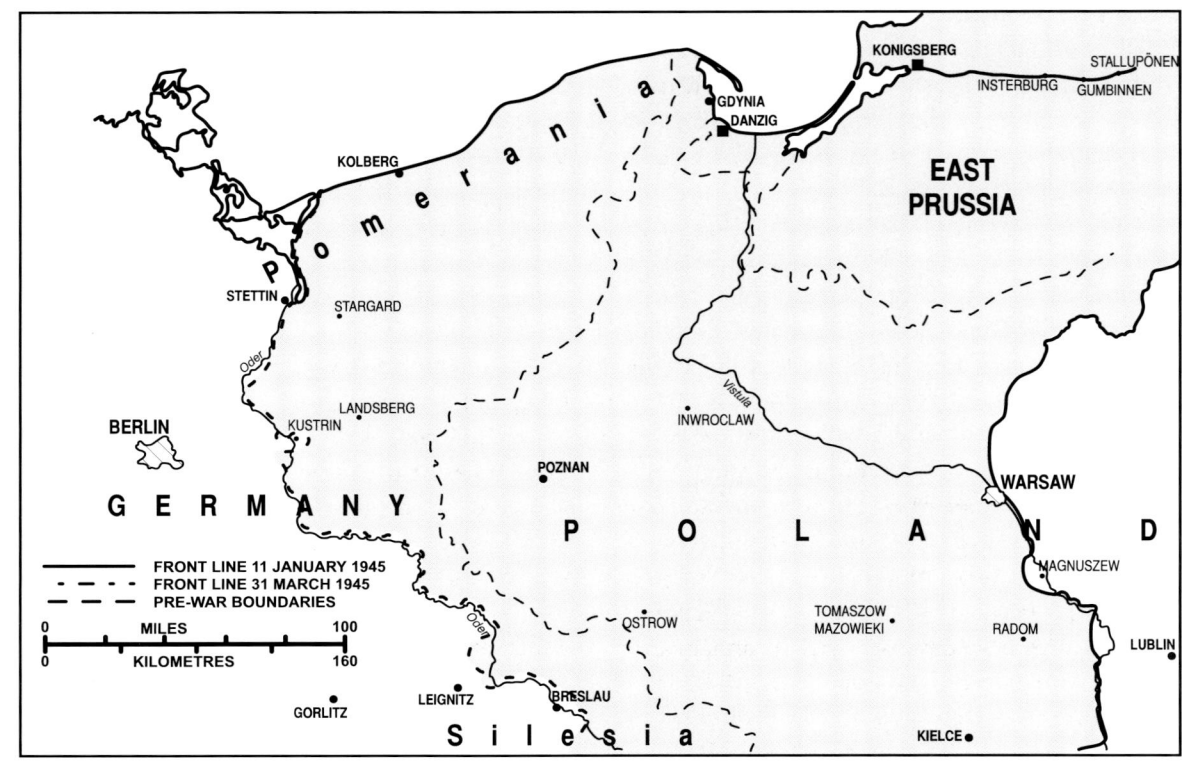

Michalczak reacted at once. Manoeuvring into position behind the Il-2, he opened fire with all his weapons. The *Shturmovik* burst apart in a huge fireball and all that remained was a mass of tattered fragments falling to the ground.

Captions to this previously published photograph claim the aircraft was coded Blue "F" and was flown by Georg Dornemann. Latest research shows this to be incorrect; the spiral spinners date the picture as post-July 1944 at which time Dornemann was not flying as a result of injuries sustained in a crash-landing in December 1943. Furthermore, blue codes were extremely rare at this time and the machine is therefore believed to be Red "F" of 14.(Pz)/SG 9. The yellow "V" marking, just visible on the left wing, was a recognition marking seen on aircraft from 29.9.1944 to 7.3.1945 after which date, Luftflotte 4 ordered it to be replaced by yellow nose bands and rudders.

On 14 January, the Russians launched their expected offensive from the Pulavy and Magnusev bridgeheads near Warsaw. Although the German Ninth Army had expected these attacks it lost half its strength in the first day alone. Four Hs 129 B-2 aircraft from 10.(Pz)/SG 9 were lost or had to be destroyed as a result of the day's operations, *Ofw.* Hans Fleddermann crashing in flames to his death 2 km (1¼ miles) north-west of Motkewice when his W.Nr.141738 White "4", received a direct hit from flak; *Uffz.* Franz Matzen being posted missing in the same area in W.Nr. 140405 White "1"; at Warzyn, W.Nr. 141759 White "7", belly-landed onto the airfield with flak damage and was later blown up to prevent it falling intact into Russian hands. Similarly, W.Nr. 141970 White "2", had to be destroyed after it broke its tailwheel while taxiing to take off on an operation.

With the German Vistula defence line torn apart and with no natural barrier in their way, the Russians raced across the Polish plains towards Germany. Outflanking and encircling Warsaw, they drove straight for the Oder River while to the south the Red Army rolled into Silesia. In these circumstances, 10.(Pz)/SG 9 fully expected to be transferred at any moment. An airfield was prepared near Czestochowa but it was overrun by Russian armour before it could be used. Instead, the *Staffel* moved to a new airstrip concealed in a wooded area near Kreuzberg on the Polish-German border, but this, too, had to be evacuated after a few days and by 19 January the *Staffel* was operating from Oppeln-Stubendorf in Germany. From here, missions were mounted continuously and with some success, only one Hs 129 being lost. However, the airfield was protected only by a weak ring of light flak and on 20 January, when the Russians reached the Oder to the south of Oppeln and threatened the landing-ground, preparations were made to transfer to a more secure airfield.

After an anxious night spent beside their aircraft, the *Staffel's* pilots found that yet again thick early morning fog prevented an immediate transfer. Other aircraft sharing the field tried to take off before the fog had lifted and came to grief, two Fw 190s and an Si 204 crashing and catching fire. Despite this dismal start to the day, the *Panzerjäger* remained calm and waited for the fog to disperse. Eventually they were able to take off into a clear January sky bound for Weidengut, a small airfield situated some 20 km (12 miles) west of the Oder and close to the troop training ground at Lamsdorf.

Meanwhile, in the north, the Russians had continued their advance into East Prussia. Here German ground forces launched fierce counter-attacks against Russian assault troops, tank columns and lorried infantry attempting to batter their way through the well-prepared German defences. Although flying operations on both sides were frequently hampered by bad weather, there were the occasional clear spells when the Russian and German aircraft were able to take to the air. Operating in East Prussia at this time were the Hs 129 units 12.(Pz) and 13.(Pz)/SG 9, these units later being joined for a short time by 10.(Pz)/SG 9. The Russian advance into East Prussia was marked by speed and savagery, the 10.(Pz)/SG 9's *Staffelkapitän* recalling that attacks were made to prevent Russian tanks from running down German refugees on the roads. Similarly, the *Staffelkapitän* of 13.(Pz)/SG 9 remembers reports that the Russians had tied civilians to their tanks to protect them from attack.

On 19 January both sides mounted numerous missions and despite poor visibility the day was a particularly successful one for the French-manned Normandie-Niemen Regiment. The Regiment's Yaks shot down three Fw 190s over Schillen and had just regrouped when *Asp.* Jacques André spotted three Hs 129s from 13.(Pz)/SG 9 flying at low altitude between Gumbinnen and Insterburg. With two other pilots, André attacked the German machines and shot down two Hs 129 B-2s in flames 20 km (12 miles) east of Insterburg. One of these was flown by *Ofw.* Heinz Heger who wrote the following account of his ordeal:

"Early in the morning of 19 January 1945, I was given instructions to fly an exceptionally dangerous mission. Besides myself, my flight should have comprised Oblt. Bartels as No.2, Kraus as No.3 and Piper as No.4, but Oblt. Bartels' aircraft apparently became defective on take-off. We then failed to meet our escort fighters over Insterburg but, in view of Germany's desperate situation, we felt we had no choice but to press on with our attack to the best of our abilities. On our approach to the target I saw a formation of Ju 87s in the distance whose crews were making a lot of noise over the radio and, immediately afterwards, I saw a big swarm of Russian fighters. In accordance with our well-tried and proven practice, I swung round to make a feint withdrawal and after five minutes returned to the front at low level. The coast seemed to be clear. Then we met a flock of 190s heading back to their base at full speed. When another gaggle of 190s came towards us, dashing past in the same manner, I thought that something was very wrong and, better to be safe than sorry, I withdrew again."

"My dark feeling had not deceived me, but it was too late. Russian fighters appeared from nowhere and we were suddenly in the thick of an air battle. I slid out of the formation and changed places with Kraus who then became the leader, while I hung on at the rear of our three-aircraft section. This gave me the chance of covering the withdrawal of the other two and in this I was successful, but now I had to fight my way out to save my own skin. The Russians hunted me like a hare. The sky was full of frantically twisting aircraft and I was able to count 17 Yak-3s. I tried all the tricks of the trade to escape them and although cannon shells from five of the fighters sometimes streamed at me at the same time, I could not resist the temptation of firing an occasional burst if I was in a particularly favourable shooting position. While I was pulling up into a steep climbing curve to the left, I was able to put a full burst into the belly of victim number one and the fighter spun into the ground. Almost at the same time, my aircraft was hit by a short burst from the right rear, some of the shells thudding into the instrument panel and one actually shattering the retaining lock of my armoured back plate causing it to fall backwards. At first this was just a nuisance, but it was to have dangerous consequences later."

"Making further evasive manoeuvres, I tried to shake off my pursuers who had by this time chased me about 25 kilometres (16 miles) behind our lines, a slightly unusual practice for the Russians (Heger was not, of course, aware that the pilots of the Yaks were French). I continued to take every opportunity to attack and get some breathing space and when I got another fighter in front of my cannon I sent a burst into it causing it to hurtle over its right wing and hit the ground. At the same time there was a loud bang in my machine, the fuselage tank started burning and

Hptm. Oswald, Hptm. Hanschke, Fw. Kotter and Ofw. Heger shortly after Hanschke took over IV.(Pz)/SG 9 from Bruno Meyer. Oswald, Kotter and Heger were all experienced Hs 129 pilots.

Hs 129 B-2 Red 'F'

14.(Pz)/SG 9, Hungary 1945.

This aircraft was finished in the RLM standard 70/71/65 splinter pattern and carried a late-war variation of the **yellow** theatre markings. In lieu of the standard **yellow** wing undersides and nose, this machine retained the **yellow** fuselage band but the starboard wing underside carried a large **yellow** 'V' marking. This marking was applied to many aircraft operating in Hungary between 29 September 1944 to 7 March 1945. The open end of the 'V' was wrapped around the leading edge of the wing and terminated in a position approximately level with the leading edge of the upper wing cross. A six-figure *Werk Nummer* appeared at the base of the fin in **white** and in accordance with an order dated 20 July 1944, 'handed' **white** spirals were applied to the spinners over the 70 **Black-Green**. The aircraft carried an MK 103 cannon. The National insignia were: B2 crosses on wing undersides, B6 crosses on wing upper-surfaces, B5 crosses on fuselage and H2a *Hakenkreuze*.

things became very hot for me. Bailing out was impossible as I was too low so, close the throttle, ignition off, flaps down, undercarriage down. The cockpit canopy was of no use either, so off with that too and head for the ground."

"Shortly before hitting the ground, I tucked up the undercarriage again and side-slipped. When the aircraft belly-landed, the sudden deceleration caused the burning fuel from the fuselage tank to spurt forwards and I had to protect my face from the flames with my arms. I slid over the snow-covered ground for what seemed like ages, during which time, in order to escape the flames and be able to get out of the cockpit as quickly as possible, I released my harness and, using the windscreen framing, pulled myself up from my seat. Thus when the machine finally ran into a ditch or a slope and came to a sudden stop, I was half leaning over the windscreen and the loose armour plate behind me was thrown forwards and hit my back with such a force that I was knocked unconscious for a while. When I came to, I used my last ounce of strength and managed to crawl onto the wing and then collapsed next to the nose section of the forward fuselage."

"As luck would have it, my wrecked 129 had come to rest just 150 metres (490 ft) from an advanced field dressing station! But it was not possible for anyone to come to my aid as the 129's ammunition was exploding in the flames. At first I thought it was the clatter of small-arms fire somewhere in the distance, but I soon realised that the noise originated from my own ammunition and that I was in a highly dangerous situation. In this case too my guardian angel was there; about one and a half metres (5 ft) away was a foxhole."

"When soldiers later helped me out of the foxhole to take me to the field dressing station, my entire scalp was no longer there, the lower part of my forehead bone, my two cheekbones and my chin lay bare, my nose and upper lip were very battered and my eyebrows and eyelashes had disappeared completely."

Within two hours of his crash, Heinz Heger lay aboard a hospital train in Insterburg where his wounds were dressed. After many unpleasant experiences, including narrowly avoiding capture by the Russians at Preussisch-Holland, Heger discharged himself from hospital some five weeks after his crash-landing and despite various attempts by the authorities to assign him to a *Luftwaffe* sanatorium, the railway flak or to a reserve battalion as platoon leader, Heger managed to arrange a transfer to his former unit. The *Staffel* had, in the meantime, lost all its aircraft and was converting to the Fw 190 at Perleberg where his arrival caused quite a surprise, as Heger explained:

"I arrived at Perleberg on Easter Saturday, 1945, late at 23:00 hours. Some of my old comrades were already in bed, others were playing Skat. Otto Kiefer was the first one I met - on the lavatory, the first place I had to go very urgently. When Otto saw me he turned deathly pale, for I had been placed on the official list of those killed in action. Much the same happened to Egon Kotter whom I shook out of his sleep, his first thought being that God had shown him a vision. This was soon followed by an enthusiastic welcome by Kotter and the other pilots. As we were off the next day, Easter Sunday, we had a boozy celebration."

The pilot of the second Henschel shot down by the three French pilots in the engagement of 19 January was *Ofw*. Wilhelm Piper who was wounded and forced to belly-land his Hs 129 B-2 W.Nr. 141855 close to the front lines 15 km (9 miles) south-east of Insterburg. On 20 January, W.Nr. 141744 from the *Gruppenstab* crash-landed due to engine damage on Kreysing airfield near Posen and exploded and in similar circumstances, 13.(Pz)/SG 9's Pak 40-armed Hs 129 B-3 W.Nr. 162044 crash-landed on the airfield at Inovroclav in north-west Poland and was completely destroyed.

As already seen, on occasions, the *Luftwaffe's* Hs 129 encountered its near-equivalent in the Soviet Air Force, the superior Ilyushin Il-2 *Shturmovik*. On 20 January 1945, a group of Il-2s belonging to the 90 Guards ShAP[1] under Captain T.S. Liadskiy was returning from a mission over German lines in the Budapest area when they observed a formation of Hs 129s about to attack Soviet troops. Since the Russian pilots had already completed their mission and lacked a fighter escort, the Il-2 pilots attacked and shot down three of the Henschels themselves.

The 13.(Pz)/SG 9's association with the Hs 129 came to an end on 22 January 1945, when almost all the *Staffel's* remaining aircraft were concentrated on the airfield at Wagrowiec (Tonndorf). Grounded by fog and mist when the Russians made a surprise breakthrough, no fewer than 13 of the *Staffel's* Hs 129s, including three Hs 129 B-3s, had to be deliberately destroyed to prevent them falling intact into enemy hands. In this way the aircraft of 13.(Pz)/SG 9 came to an ignominious end, the *Staffel's* flying personnel, as already related, being subsequently withdrawn to Perleberg for retraining on the Fw 190.

By 28 January, the Russians had crossed the

The most outstanding all-purpose ground-attack aircraft of WWII was the Il-2 Shturmovik. Although almost equivalent to the Hs 129 in its role, the Il-2 was superior in performance and earned the complete trust and confidence of its crews, many of which survived the severest combat damage to their aircraft, thanks to the armour plate protecting the engine and cockpit. Large, rugged and with tremendous destructive capacity, the Il-2 was capable of delivering a large volume of bombs, rockets and shells. To its pilots, it was known as Ilyusha, and to Soviet soldiers below it was the "Flying Tank" and "Flying Infantryman". The Germans called it "Schwartz Tod" - "Black Death".

Oder on either side of Oppeln, yet despite this change in the situation, which several times threatened Weidengut, the airfield remained the home of 10.(Pz)/SG 9 for the next eight weeks. In late January, too, by which time the *Staffel* had received a few replacement aircraft, continuous missions were being flown to hunt down Russian tanks which employed every trick at their disposal to try and mislead the German tank-hunters. Always the masters of camouflage and deception, the Russians had earlier set off smoke canisters attached to their vehicles in order to simulate combat damage, but the experienced anti-tank pilots were not easily misled and knew that a genuinely disabled vehicle burned with bright flames and sparks. So it was that the Russian tank drivers hit upon a new idea, something which, curiously, the German anti-tank pilots only encountered in Silesia. When attacked, the tank drivers drove at full throttle, in reverse if possible, straight through the brick walls of houses. In this way they attempted to hide and protect themselves. Only the barrels of their guns were then visible, rising and falling amid clouds of dust and rubble.

After a few weeks of flying constant combat sorties, the men and machines were worn out. In early February, Lt. Walter Krause wrote:

"At present only two aircraft are serviceable, so we are only able to piss around. When VIII. Fliegerkorps orders us to fly, we ask them whether they would like us to operate our two aircraft singly or in waves! Otherwise, morale in the Staffel is quite good."

Although there were signs that the Russians were obviously preparing further attacks across the Oder, for the time being the German front held though it was very thin and contained large gaps. When flying on operations, the pilots not only had to find and attack the Russians but also had to establish the position of their own troops as well. During one such mission flown in an area south of Oppeln, about 20 km (12 miles) east of the Oder, pilots from 10.(Pz)/SG 9 observed that "everything on the ground looked dead". There were no German soldiers or civilians to be seen, and in the Blechhammer area the countryside resembled a lunar landscape, the ground bearing the marks of crater upon crater where the Americans had carpet-bombed the local hydrogenation plants. At low level, the Henschel pilots approached a small railway bridge on the Oder. The bridge itself had been destroyed and columns of black smoke rose upwards from various fires in the nearby area.

"What a picture!" wrote Krause: *"On the Eastern bank there was a shallow dugout and in it were two German soldiers with a large number of Panzerfäusten laying around. In front of them were five burning T-34s. We couldn't believe our eyes. Far and wide there were no other German troops; just these two men. They even waved to us. What thoughts were in their heads? Heroism? Despair? I don't know, perhaps both."*

"One day I drove my Kubelwagen to a village about 30 kilometres (19 miles) west of Weidengut where we had knocked out three T-34s. The village had since been re-occupied and we wanted to evaluate the effects of our 30 mm cannon. Some of the things I witnessed during this journey are still lodged vividly in my memory. First there was the countryside, devoid of almost all human life. Obviously the civilian population had been evacuated in time, but we saw hardly any German soldiers either. Eventually we found just a single 105 mm artillery piece behind a barn with a Hauptmann and his gun crew standing next to it. Using his map, the Hauptmann explained the situation to us and said that he only had a few rounds left and could only fire in an emergency. Then, in the village with the three destroyed T-34s we had come to find, we met a single German soldier, the Quartermaster from the assault-gun battalion which had retaken the village. He helped us find the knocked-out T-34s and they showed to advantage the remarkable effects of our 30 mm armour-piercing shells, the tungsten cores of which had punched through the tank's armoured plating

Grounded by fog and mist at Wagrowizc (Tonndorf) when the Russians made a surprise break-through, 13 Hs 129s from IV/SG 9 and Oblt. Bartel's 13.(Pz)/SG 9 had to be destroyed by retreating Luftwaffe personnel. Here, Soviet soldiers have pulled out one of the ammunition belts during an examination of the burnt-out remains of W.Nr.141537.

Oblt. Bartel (2nd from left) joined 13.(Pz)/SG 9 as Hptm. Oswald's deputy on 8.7.1944 and took over the Staffel in January 1945. A few weeks later, 13.(Pz)/SG 9 was withdrawn from operations to convert to the Fw 190. On the right is Jupp Oehl who had flown at Zaporozhe, Apostalovo, Kherson, Bacau, Lysatycze - all the "hot spots" on the Eastern front - and made several flights in the Hs 129 B-3 at Jürgenfelde. Note the "victory sticks".

Although this Hs 129 is almost over the camera, the sloping nose still permits an excellent view forwards and downwards. Spiral spinner markings were introduced as a recognition aid on 20 July 1944.

and, bursting into thousands of pieces, had caused terrible damage to the occupants and the interior. The Quartermaster also led us to a knocked out German assault-gun and then to two more which were defending the edge of the village. The Russians were visible in the next village only about 3 kilometres (2 miles) away. We returned to our airfield in silence. If this was the kind of land war which was to follow, we were bound to lose. I was deeply depressed".

Gebhard Weber, too, recalls that this was the time he also lost faith in any hope of a German victory. Leading a *Schwarm* on an operation in the Breslau area on 25 February, he was appalled to see huge numbers of Russian tanks, mainly T-34s, driving nose-to-tail down all four lanes and the central reservation of the Breslau *Autobahn*. Anti-aircraft guns of all calibres had been set up to protect the column which also contained a number of special anti-aircraft tanks dispersed at intervals. To attack would have been suicidal and the operation had to be abandoned. It was at that moment, when he saw this mass of unbeatable armour, that Weber realised that he may as well give up - the war was already lost.

The futility of Weber's low-level attacks was again brought home to him during another mission in the Breslau area when 10.(Pz)/SG 9 was ordered to seal a breach in the front line where Russian cavalry and infantry were pouring through into the German rear area. Weber's aircraft was hit by Russian flak, the shells splintering his canopy side panels and blowing a metre (3 ft) off his left wing. The Henschel came down in the snow, but the crash-landing had been witnessed by Russian troops. Although concussed and suffering from a sprained back, Weber made off on foot with the Russians in hot pursuit.

Due to the gravity of the situation, the normally grounded Bruno Meyer had also taken part in this operation and, after making his attacks, saw the empty cockpit of Weber's crashed aircraft. Returning to his headquarters, Meyer immediately informed the Army that one of his pilots was down and was evidently trying to make his way back to the German lines. A tank was sent out and returned Weber to the safety of his own lines, but his aircraft had been lost and no significant damage had been caused to the enemy.

On 12 February, the *Staffel* was dealt a cruel blow when Otto Ritz was posted missing in action. *Oblt.* Weber had taken half the *Staffel* to Schweidnitz and it had been arranged that of the pilots left at Weidengut, Otto Ritz and his wingman, Max Benter, would fly an armed reconnaissance mission to cover the area from Schweidnitz to the north of the River Neisse. But just before take-off, Benter's aircraft became unserviceable and Otto Ritz took off alone in W.Nr. 141722. He did not return. The exact circumstances surrounding Ritz's disappearance are not clear, but fighter-pilots from JG 52 reported that they had last seen his aircraft attacking tanks south of Spalte, while a vague report received from an Army unit said that they had seen a single German aircraft, presumed to be Ritz's, drop from the sky after making several low-level attacks over enemy lines. With Ritz gone, the *Staffel* lost one of its most prominent and successful pilots. At the time of his disappearance, Ritz had destroyed over 70 tanks, damaged another 34 and shot down two Russian aircraft.

By this time Russian tank spearheads had advanced as far as Lamsdorf, only some ten kilometres (six miles) away from the airfield. From here, Rolf Aigner's *Rotte* could be seen one day making low-level attacks behind the Lamsdorf forest. Suddenly, his aircraft disappeared and it was presumed that he had been shot down. Some hours later, a T-34 appeared on the road on the far side of the airfield and everyone was starting to dash for cover when it was seen that the tank carried German markings. A large *Balkenkreuz* had been painted on the turret and Rolf Aigner was waving from the turret hatch. As was learned later, Aigner had indeed been brought down but had been rescued by Estonian *Waffen*-SS men who used the captured Russian tank to return him safe and sound to his unit.

The modest combat activity of February and early March is reflected in the serviceability figures submitted by 10.(Pz)/SG 9 at this time. On 1 March, when the only sorties flown were by two Hs 129s which carried out a battle reconnaissance in the area from the south of Breslau to Zobten, the unit possessed seventeen aircraft, all of which were serviceable. On 6 March, however, four of the *Staffel's* Hs 129s (and one of JG 52's Bf 109s) were destroyed on the ground at Weidengut during a Russian air attack. By 8 March, 10.(Pz)/SG 9's headquarters reported that it had ten of its remaining 13 aircraft serviceable, of which a separate detachment was operating at Schweidnitz where all aircraft were concentrated a short time later due to the continued Russian advance.

There was still snow on the ground in mid-March, but the skies were now beautifully clear and sunny and in the fine Spring weather the Russian and German air forces became more active: Soviet Pe-2 bombers and P-39 fighters frequently attacked the German airfields while the Henschels flew many missions, acting as the Army's "fire-brigade" in support of the extremely fragile front. On 17 and 18 March, 10.(Pz)/SG 9 knocked out 37 tanks and assault guns and damaged another 17 so severely that the majority of these, too, could be considered destroyed. However, the *Staffel* met with no success at all on 22 March when 11 sorties were flown against tanks and lorry columns in the Leobschütz - Neustadt area. These sorties had to be abandoned due to the strong enemy flak and fighter defences, but not before one of the Henschels was shot down. Nevertheless, with a total of almost 600 "kills" to its credit 10.(Pz)/SG 9 is believed to have been the top-scoring *Panzerjägerstaffel* at this time and some of its pilots were decorated accordingly. *Oblt.* Weber had been awarded the German Cross in Gold on 28 February, *Fw.* Michalczak had been nominated for the *Ritterkreuz* and *Lt.* Krause the Iron Cross First Class. In addition, the *Staffel* had received a fine letter of commendation from

When the Russians launched their offensive from the Baranow bridgehead, the preliminary artillery bombardment was so intense that Walter Krause of 10.(Pz)/SG 9 wrote, "…the entire horizon in the east was blood red." By 24 February 1945, in one of the most massive, costly and fastest advances of the war, the Russian Army reached the Oder, less than 64 km (40 miles) from Berlin.

Lt. Walter Krause of 10.(Pz)/SG 9 in the cockpit of his Hs 129. When Oblt. Dornemann was injured in December 1943, the newly arrived Lt. Krause assumed temporary command of the Staffel on the ground; flying operations were led by the more experienced Fw. Otto Ritz. In the Luftwaffe, leadership in the air was assigned to the most experienced pilots rather than being a privilege of rank.

Generaloberst Schörner, the commander of Army Group Centre, and had also earned praise from the commanding general of VIII. *Fliegerkorps*.

On 23 March, 10.(Pz)/SG 9 mounted 17 sorties in the Leobschütz - Neustadt area and although eight of these again had to be broken off due to strong flak and fighter defences, eight tanks were destroyed and another three damaged. On the same day the *Staffel* was again mentioned in the OKW communiqué for its successes on 17/18 March. Although the unit had also taken part in many retreats, the improved spring weather and the *Staffel's* achievements, as well as the various awards and commendations, caused spirits to rise and the pilots regained their conviction that although the war was already lost they could still give "Ivan" a blow he would not forget.

Although 10. and 14.(Pz)/SG 9 were now the only two *Staffeln* still operating the Hs 129, overall successes were high and in March alone 10.(Pz)/SG 9 destroyed 100 tanks, 30 assault guns, several hundred vehicles and six aircraft for the loss of only two Hs 129s shot down by the enemy. But by now the aircraft was long overdue for replacement and latest operational experience was beginning to show that, although good results could still be achieved by Hs 129s operating under ideal conditions, the increased use of the anti-tank Fw 190 now coming into service equipped with *Panzerblitz* rockets produced especially successful results. Indeed, the development of anti-tank rockets had been accelerated not only to overcome the shortage of tungsten - which limited the quantities of hard-core ammunition which could be expended - but was also intended to eliminate the vulnerability of existing anti-tank aircraft which were handicapped by the large reduction in their speed due to their heavy armour and armament. In marked comparison with the Ju87 G and Hs 129, the Focke-Wulf possessed greater speed, was less

vulnerable and had a greater ability to absorb battle damage. Despite the spread of the rockets, which were usually fired in salvoes of six, the accuracy was considered sufficient and during the fighting in Upper Silesia especially, where the terrain restricted the tank packs' freedom of movement, the Fw 190s so excelled that the Russians were forced to pull back from their attacking positions and seek shelter until more anti-aircraft guns could be brought up to protect them.

Operations with the Fw 190 in Kurland and Upper Silesia confirmed also that the most effective way of holding back Soviet armoured packs protected by anti-aircraft weapons was to escort each Focke-Wulf anti-tank *Schwarm* with two *Schwärme* carrying bombs. In this way the fighter-bombers could hold down the flak while the rocket-firing machines made their attacks and, in areas where friendly fighter protection was weak, could also act as fighter escort for the anti-tank aircraft. However, although this method of escorting Focke-Wulf anti-tank aircraft with Focke-Wulf fighter-bombers was clearly effective, no attempt was made to provide similar counter-measures for the Hs 129 and its pilots found that enemy flak defences made it increasingly dangerous if not impossible to press home their attacks.

As for enemy fighters, although they operated freely and in great numbers over the battle areas, *Luftflotte* 6 decreed that their mere presence was not considered a good enough reason for the Henschel pilots to call off their attacks as due to their extra-low level flying, the Henschels may not have been seen by the fighters. Consequently, a report submitted at this time to the *General der Schlachtflieger* proposed that the Henschels should only abandon their mission if actually attacked by fighters. There was, in fact, some logic to this belief and as one former Hs 129 pilot put it - "... low and extra-low level flying was our life insurance". Because of these abilities, the Hs 129 was still considered a useful aircraft with which to counter armoured breakthroughs in bad weather or when there was a low cloudbase which grounded more modern types such as the Fw 190. Although the engine mechanics had discovered a way to fine tune the Gnôme-Rhône engines to give 1,000 hp, banking and manoeuvring a fully fuelled and armed cannon-equipped aircraft still caused the speed to drop off

The lack of a yellow nose and spinner colours suggests this is a late-war photograph but the use of a bomb-rack in lieu of cannon in this period is unusual for a Luftwaffe aircraft.

very rapidly and it was necessary to have a safe height before making any turns. For this reason, attacks were made with as little deviation from a straight line of flight as possible.

On 1 April 1945, the flying personnel of 10.(Pz)/SG 9 at Seyring were ordered to transfer immediately from *Luftflotte* 6 to *Luftflotte* 4's area of control and in particular to Moravska-Ostrava in Czechoslovakia where strong Russian armoured forces had broken through. Ground crews were ordered to follow by road and rail and, until their arrival, the *Staffel's* aircraft were serviced by the ground crews of 14.(Pz)/SG 9 which was already in the area. From Moravska-Ostrava, 10.(Pz)/SG 9 took-off the same day on a late-morning mission in the Schwarzwasser area. Although weather conditions were perfect and the sun was shining beautifully, the mission was unsuccessful due to the ferocious anti-aircraft defences which put up a barrage of such intensity that the Henschel pilots were unable to get anywhere near the new JS-2 tanks.

From Moravska-Ostrava 10.(Pz)/SG 9 moved via Bruno to Fels am Wagram in Austria in order to combat the tank spearheads of a large-scale Soviet attack directed towards Vienna. One of the *Staffel's* pilots, Rolf Aigner, knew the Vienna area well and acted as *Schwarmführer* during attacks against Russian armour in the Augarten. Walter Krause flew two such missions to Vienna and remembers: "We flew along the Danube towards Vienna in splendid sunshine. In the western suburbs things were quite quiet and we could see women in their summer clothes strolling or pushing prams in the sun. One after the other, the four machines of our *Schwarm* flew low along the *Ring* but we could already see Russian flak shells exploding above the rooftops. Then I heard Rolf

Aigner's voice over the R/T. *"On the right, at Karlspalast, the third street on the left leads to the Augarten"*. I'd never imagined that I'd get to know Vienna in such circumstances! In the Augarten there were two flak towers which were still occupied by German troops. Their twin 88-mm anti-aircraft guns could be seen firing at distant targets and although we could see T-34s driving around below us, we had no opportunity to attack them."

The Bf 109s of II./JG 51 were also based at Fels am Wagram at this time and on 9 April the *Gruppe* flew its last mission of the war when it was ordered to escort a number of Hs 129s in an attack to destroy oil storage tanks near Vienna which had fallen into Russian hands. In the target area, a *Schwarm* of II./JG 51's fighters under *Oblt.* Ziehm ran into a formation of Il-2s and their Yak-9 escort. Although Ziehm was seen to go after an Il-2 which he attacked through the dense smoke cloud from a burning oil tank, he was not seen again and remains missing to this day. His wingman, *Fhr.* Hainisch, fell in combat with Russian fighters. Although little is known of the effects of the Hs 129 attack, it may be deduced from the mention of "dense black smoke" in JG 51's post-action report that the Henschels succeeded in setting at least some of the oil storage tanks alight.

During one of 10.(Pz)/SG 9's following missions, it was discovered that Russian armour had pushed through the Vienna forest and was now close to Fels am Wagram. Soon afterwards, on 14 April, the *Staffel* transferred in pairs to Wels, the ground staff following with a number of civilians who, like camp-followers from the middle-ages, had attached themselves to the unit. Although Wels was not directly threatened by the Russians, a new menace arose in the form of American aircraft. The German pilots had not encountered American aircraft before but now long-range Lightning and Mustang fighters flew about over the airfield in broad daylight and, as *Lt.* Walter Krause put it: "... they nailed us Eastern Front *Schlachtflieger* to the ground".

By this time, the only other unit besides 10.(Pz)/SG 9 flying the Hs 129 on operations was *Hptm.* Steinkamp's 14.(Pz)/SG 9. Although in April it possessed its full complement of four *Schwarm* leaders, it had only six aircraft left and plans were already under way to disband the *Staffel* and assign its personnel to ground fighting. The fate of the *Staffel* in the final days of the Third Reich is not known.[2]

---

1 SHAP: SHTURMOVOY AVIATSIONNYY POLK - LIT. RUSSIAN GROUND-ATTACK AIR REGIMENT.
2 STEINKAMP SURVIVED THE WAR BUT WAS KILLED ON 13 APRIL 1952 WHILE FLYING A SEA-PLANE FROM ARGENTINA TO CHILE.

Extraordinary Impact

The Hs 129 B-3 with BK 7.5
Operations in East Prussia 1945

23

Hs 129 B-2, W.Nr.140494 "DO+XG", modified to B-3 standard. In June 1944, after making a number of general test flights, the aircraft was test-flown six times by the RLM and the E-stelle Rechlin. Eighteen further flights were made to assess control vibrations, flying and approach characteristics. After an enlarged rudder was fitted, the machine was transferred to Tarnewitz on 8 July 1944.

When the RLM issued instructions at the beginning of 1942 for the 7.5 cm Pak 40 to be installed in aircraft, it was a rush solution to the problem of ensuring that front-line troops had an effective gun at their disposal for combating the heaviest types of Soviet tanks such as the KV-1 and KV-2. Among the aircraft which could be considered, the Ju 88 took first place because, apart from its strength, there was room in the aircraft for a crew member to manually assist the operation of a semi-automatic loading device. Since this promised fewer difficulties than the development of a fully automatic one, its construction took priority over the installation of a 7.5 cm cannon in the Hs 129 since some time would be needed to design and develop a fully automatic loading apparatus suitable for this single-seat type.

The first bench trials with the Pak 40 and a Ju 88 as the carrier were made in February 1942, but it was found that the recoil and dense gas jets from the muzzle seriously affected the aircraft's propellers, cockpit and engine cowlings. The muzzle brake was redesigned to break the gasses down into smaller jets, all cockpit instruments were seated on anti-vibration mountings and the canopy frame and glazing reinforced, as were the engine cowlings, spinners and undercarriage doors. Further bench tests conducted after these modifications had been carried out showed that the gun's 4 tonne recoil was absorbed without difficulty and the muzzle blast caused no further damage. After approximately 100 rounds had been fired on the ground, air testing commenced at Roggentin, a satellite of the *E-stelle* Rechlin, using captured Russian T-34 tanks as targets.

The first rounds, fired at cruising speed, again caused damage to the engine cowlings, propellers, spinners and cockpit glazing. Further reinforcement failed to satisfactorily prolong the life of these components and after fewer than 100 rounds severe damage was found in the Ju 88's laminated wooden propeller blades. However, in order that the air tests should continue, the explosive charge in the ammunition was reduced from 2.75 to 2.45 kg (6.06 to 5.40 lbs) and 200 of the reduced-charge rounds were fired at flying speeds of up to 600 kph (372 mph) without damage to the airframe. After a further redesign of the muzzle brake, which broke the gas jets down yet smaller, it was again possible to resume the firing of normal charge rounds without damage to the aircraft. Moreover, it was

Hs 129 B-3

The aircraft illustrated is a standard Hs 129 B-2 W.Nr. 140404 which was converted in June 1944 to a B-3, carrying the 7.5cm BK cannon. The machine was tested at Rechlin and Tarnewitz still retaining its original C/12 D gun sight. The standard RLM splinter finish had been applied together with the **yellow** Eastern Front theatre markings. From this evidence it would appear that the theatre markings were applied at the factory as the aircraft still carries its call sign of 'DO + XG' on the fuselage as also on the underside of the wings. The National insignia were: B2 crosses on wing undersides, B6 crosses on wing upper-surfaces, B5 crosses on fuselage and H2a *Hakenkreuze*.

This design of muzzle brake, which broke down the gases of the muzzle blast into small jets to avoid damage to the airframe, is seen here mounted with a Ju 88 but it was later adopted for the more successful Hs 129.

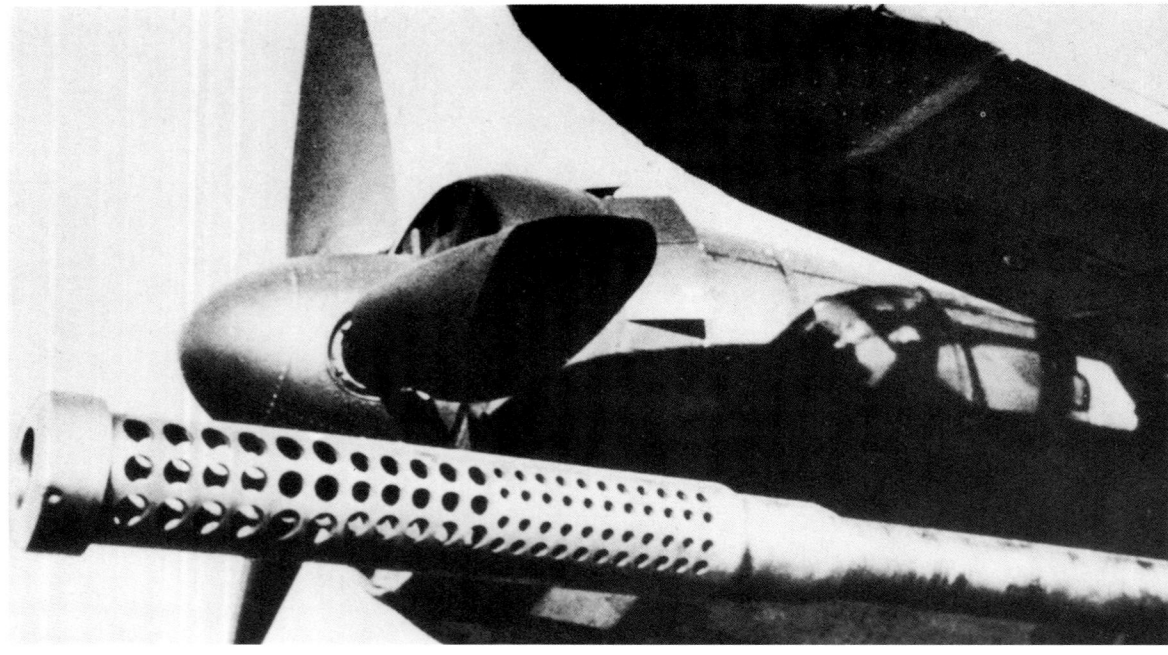

Crash-landed Ju 88 P with Pak 40 showing an early version of the muzzle brake. Trials with heavy cannon were considered necessary to compensate for Germany's shortage of tungsten and continued despite a report stating that the Ju 88 P was "...unsuitable for employment at the front."

discovered that the new muzzle brake not only possessed a more satisfactory weight, better aerodynamic qualities and was both cheaper and easier to manufacture, but it also gave a better shot pattern. Even after 800 rounds the aircraft was still perfectly airworthy, though a modification to the angle of the shell ejector chute was required to protect the fuselage undersurface, the dipole aerial and tail leading edges from damage by the ejection of empty shell cases.

One of the principal objectives of the Ju 88 air trials was to test the loading operation and ensure it was not interrupted by gravitational effects. The semi-automatic loading device held ten rounds arranged one above the other in a box magazine. A crew member, acting as loader, swung the loading tray by hand from the magazine to the axis of the gun in which position a pneumatically operated piston inserted the round. The return of the loading tray was also effected by hand, but the progress of the cartridge out of the magazine was automatic. As a result of the air tests, further extensive changes in design were necessary but, eventually, with an experienced loader, a firing rate of one round every two seconds could be achieved. Armour plate up to 110 mm (4.3 ins) thickness could be penetrated from 1,500 m (4,922 ft) range and practice firing also showed that if the approach was made by a skilled pilot firing two rounds, on average, one would hit a stationary target. The most favourable range for the two shots was between 400 and 300 m (1,312 and 984 ft) for the first and not less than 250 m (820 ft) for the second.

Despite the flying weight of the Ju 88, its manoeuvrability and stability were so satisfactory that very good results were obtained against the practice targets and armoured cars. Once the pilot became accustomed to the violent vibration which resulted from the firing of each shot, the recoil had no effect on aiming or firing and the aircraft did not swerve from the line of flight.

Although 20 examples of the Pak 40-equipped Ju 88 were built, the aircraft failed principally because it presented too large a target and was therefore too vulnerable. In addition, its liquid-cooled engines did not meet the requirements of a ground-attack aircraft and supplementary armour fitted to protect the engines and crew had a serious effect on its speed. The machine also had insufficient power to fly on one engine, so that the gun installation had to be jettisoned if a powerplant failed or was put out of action .

These experiences with the Ju 88 were used to good advantage during the subsequent installation of the Pak 40 in the Hs 129 and this aircraft's comprehensive armouring proved much more resistant to the effects of recoil and blast pressure than the "soft" nose of the Ju 88. The standard Pak 40 was used without any extensive development or modification to the breech, cradle, barrel, barrel brake or barrel recuperator, though the breech block had to be modified for electrical firing, a heater was provided to ensure the barrel brake liquid continued to function at low temperatures and, of course, yet another new muzzle brake had to be developed.

The actual installation of the cannon in the Hs 129 was achieved, perhaps surprisingly, without great difficulty or modification to the fuselage, though problems did arise later with the operation of the weapon. Covered by an aerodynamically shaped fairing, the gun was attached below the fuselage by means of a cradle and cradle support with the magazine and feed mechanism inside the fuselage and the barrel projecting about a metre (3 ft) ahead of the aircraft's nose. Gas jet diversion was so arranged that no parts of the aircraft were in the path of the gasses apart from the armoured nose and undersurfaces, though one disadvantage of this arrangement was that it was at first not possible to conduct bench firing on account of blast deflection from the ground and the aircraft had to be set up over a deep and specially constructed concrete-lined pit.

Once development had been completed, air-to-ground firing trials by Rheinmetall-Borsig began in August 1944, initially with a B-2, W.Nr. 140494, converted to carry a 7.5 cm BK. At this stage the cannon still lacked its magazine installation but single-shot trials were conducted, during which eight rounds were fired. It was found that the engine cowlings and undercarriage were far enough away from the impact of the gases that only slight damage occurred, this being restricted to the cowling of the left engine and adjacent wing leading edge, where some rivets had been loosened and even pulled out, though in one instance the cockpit canopy also became jammed. These weak spots were reinforced by adding strengtheners beneath the aircraft's skin and these slight modifications subsequently proved perfectly satisfactory.

As with the Ju 88, the narrow cannon fairing increased lateral stability and in shallow dive attacks and at speeds of up to 600 kph (372 mph) the ejection of the shell cases caused no damage to the aircraft's undersurfaces or tailplane. One disadvantage, however, was that as in the Ju 88, single-engined flight was only possible without the 750 kg cannon and the mounting cradle had to be designed so the fairing, feed mechanism and gun could all be jettisoned in an emergency.

The special 12-round automatic loading device required for the Hs 129 was constructed in the form of a drum which rotated and fed the shells into the gun electro-pneumatically. Air

Official handbook drawing showing installation of BK 7.5 and the weapon's 12-round rotating drum.

1. TELESCOPIC GUN SIGHT ZFR 3 B
2. SUPPORT BEAM
3. HEIGHT ADJUSTMENT SCREW FOR LOAD ADJUSTING
4. ADJUSTMENT
5. LOADING CYLINDER
6. LOADER
7. TO THE COMPRESSED AIR EXTERIOR CONNECTION
8. THERMO SWITCH
9. LOCKING HANDLE
10. REAR SPRING ASSEMBLY
11. 7.5 CM BK
12. MUZZLE BREAK

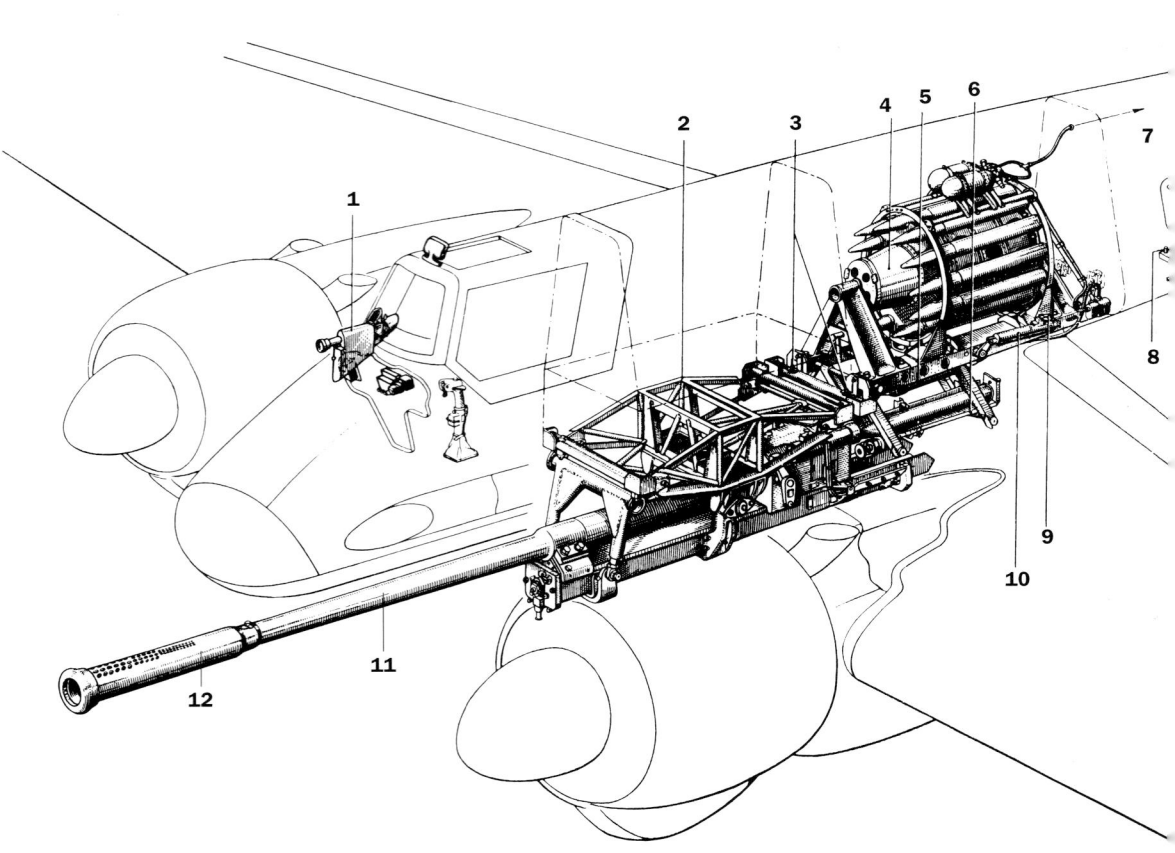

Hs 129 B-2, W.Nr.141258 coded "BH+ZS", was fitted with a wooden mock-up of the Pak 40 installation (cannon and fairing) and during May 1944 was used by the Erprobungsstelle für Seeflug to carry out trials over the Baltic. Note the vertical aerial vane above the cockpit canopy in the photograph of the aircraft in the hangar. The in-flight close-up of the rear fuselage shows wool tufts to measure airflow.

The 75 mm Pak 40 under an Hs 129. Not visible in this view is the magazine and automatic loading mechanism housed inside the fuselage.

In accordance with an order placed by GL/G-E 2/A in January 1944, a number of series production Hs 129 B-2s were modified as prototypes for the proposed B-3 series with 75 mm cannon. This B-2 has had its normal armament removed and some local strengthening of the nose and engine cowlings has been carried out.

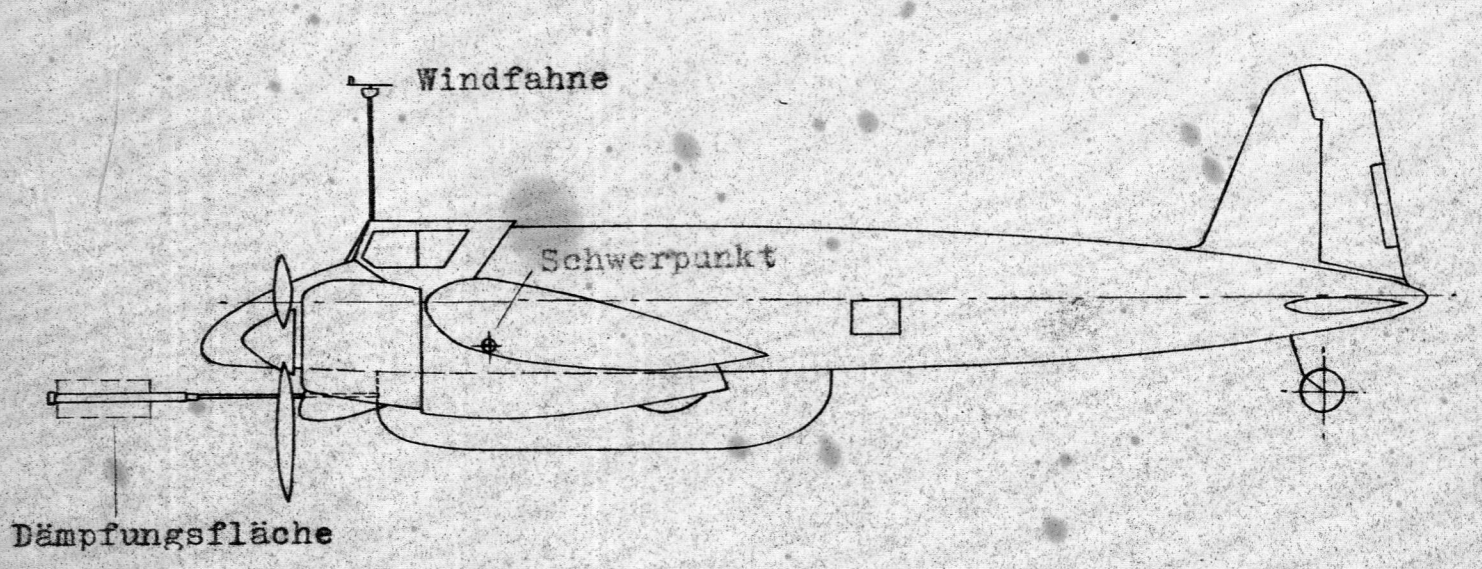

Drawing from original German report on the trials installation of the BK 7.5 in the Hs 129.

trials conducted at Rechlin and Tarnewitz showed the rhythm of the feed mechanism was such that the interval between shots was approximately 1.5 seconds. The shot dispersal pattern was good and, owing to the Hs 129's low approach speed, it was possible to fire approximately four rounds at one target during an approach from 1,000 m (3,281 ft), the last round from 200 m (656 ft).

At the end of August, the *E-Stelle* Tarnewitz handed over the first three Hs 129 B-3s - the designation applied to the aircraft modified to carry the 75 mm Pak 40, or "BK 7.5" cannon as the *Luftwaffe* named the weapon - when W.Nr.162033, 162034 and 162035, were assigned to *Erprobungskommando* 26 for testing. Due to renewed troubles with the shell-case ejection, which Rheinmetall-Borsig had not yet completely cured, the weapon was cleared for limited operational use only. The first deliveries of the Hs 129 B-3 were made to Franz Oswald's 13.(Pz)/SG 9 at the end of October. This unit subsequently conducted firing trials at Jürgenfeld and Shippenbeil which showed that when subjected to the rigours of combat conditions, additional difficulties with the electrical operation of the magazine arose which again prevented the weapon from being cleared for operational use. Unable to rectify the troubles itself, the *Staffel* was sent a number of specialist technicians from Rheinmetall and Tarnewitz. These specialists spent the best part of November servicing the weapons of the seven B-3s which had by then reached the *Staffel*, as well as other machines held in an aircraft park at Blomberg, but they had no sooner completed their task when they were instructed to investigate IV.(Pz)/SG 9's further complaints. It was now reported that airframe damage was being caused during operational air firing which was believed to have been due to a combination of possibly faulty ammunition and structural differences between the test and operational aircraft. These complaints were still being investigated in January when, as already mentioned, 13.(Pz)/SG 9, now under *Oblt.* Bartel, had to destroy all its aircraft at Tonndorf.

Although it was originally intended that production of the Hs 129 B-3 would run on to at least February 1945, and completely replace the B-2 by October 1944, this plan had to be scrapped as the French factories producing Hs 129 components had been overrun by the Allies in July 1944. As a result of this total loss of the production plants and earlier delays caused by Allied bombing which damaged the factories, interrupted electricity supplies and caused transportation bottlenecks, only 25 BK 7.5-equipped Hs 129s could be assembled at Henschel's Berlin-Schönefeld works. In August, production of the Hs 129 B-3 was ordered to be stopped by the *Rüstungsstab* and by the following month, all output of this variant had terminated. Despite its mechanical difficulties, when the fully-automatic cannon operated correctly, these aircraft were particularly successful in the defence of the East during the winter of 1944/45, even against the formidable Josef Stalin tank which had been developed from the earlier KV series. In 14 sorties flown during one period in 1945, nine tanks were destroyed including two of the heaviest types. The weapon was also deployed against other targets such as artillery positions and fortifications. Even if no direct hit was scored, the effect was considerable, the shell making a hole similar to that of a 50 kg bomb.

The Hs 129 B-3 was also delivered to 12.(Pz)/SG 9, but its service with this *Staffel* was somewhat limited as, by 10 November 1944, the unit had been withdrawn from front-line operations to Finsterwalde where it began converting to the Fw 190 under *Luftflotte* 10. On 1 January 1945, 12.(Pz)/SG 9 was redesignated 1.(Pz) *Staffel* of the newly created I.(Pz)/SG 9 and the *Staffel's* Hs 129s were eventually taken over by the remaining two Hs 129 *Staffeln*, 10. and 14.(Pz)/SG 9. During operations as part of 4. *Fliegerdivision* under *Luftflotte* 6, the 12.(Pz)/SG 9 flew 26 Fw 190 sorties, during which it claimed the destruction of four tanks and recorded one aircraft lost and one damaged.

Among the Hs 129s which 12. *Staffel* left behind were five B-3s which were later handed over to 10.(Pz)/SG 9. As Gebhard Weber recalled: "The Hs 129 B-3 was not the official equipment of my *Staffel*, the 10.(Pz)/SG 9. I believe that five of these machines, equipped with the 75 mm BK 7.5 cannon, were flown to me at Schweidnitz in Silesia. They came from *Oblt.* Lehmann's 12.(Pz)/SG 9 in East Prussia after the Red Army had launched its offensive there and that *Staffel* had been forced to abandon its airfield. During one of the following nights however, the Red Air Force attacked our base with bombs and destroyed all but two of the five

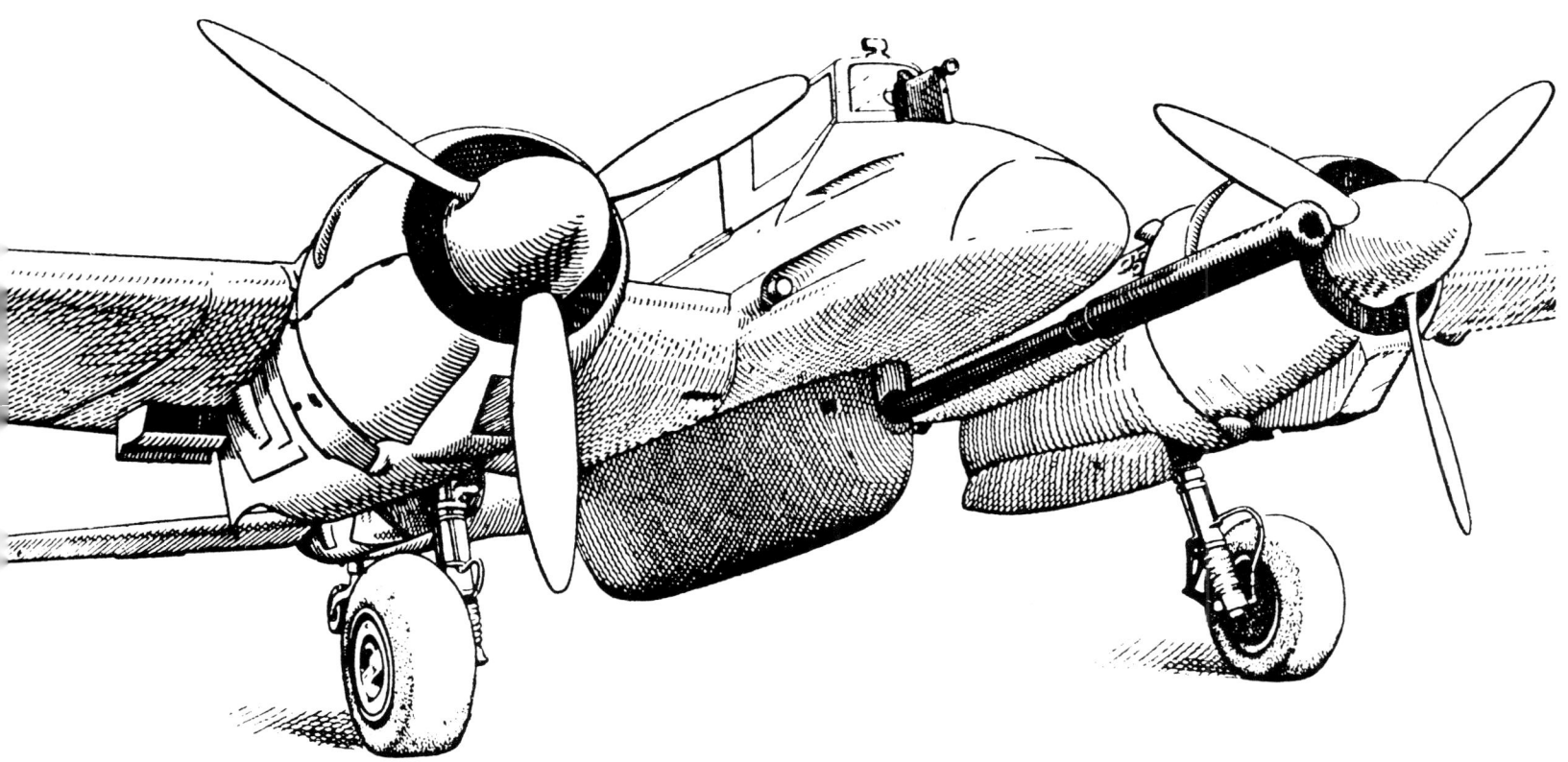

Drawing of Hs 129 B-3 as taken from official handbook.

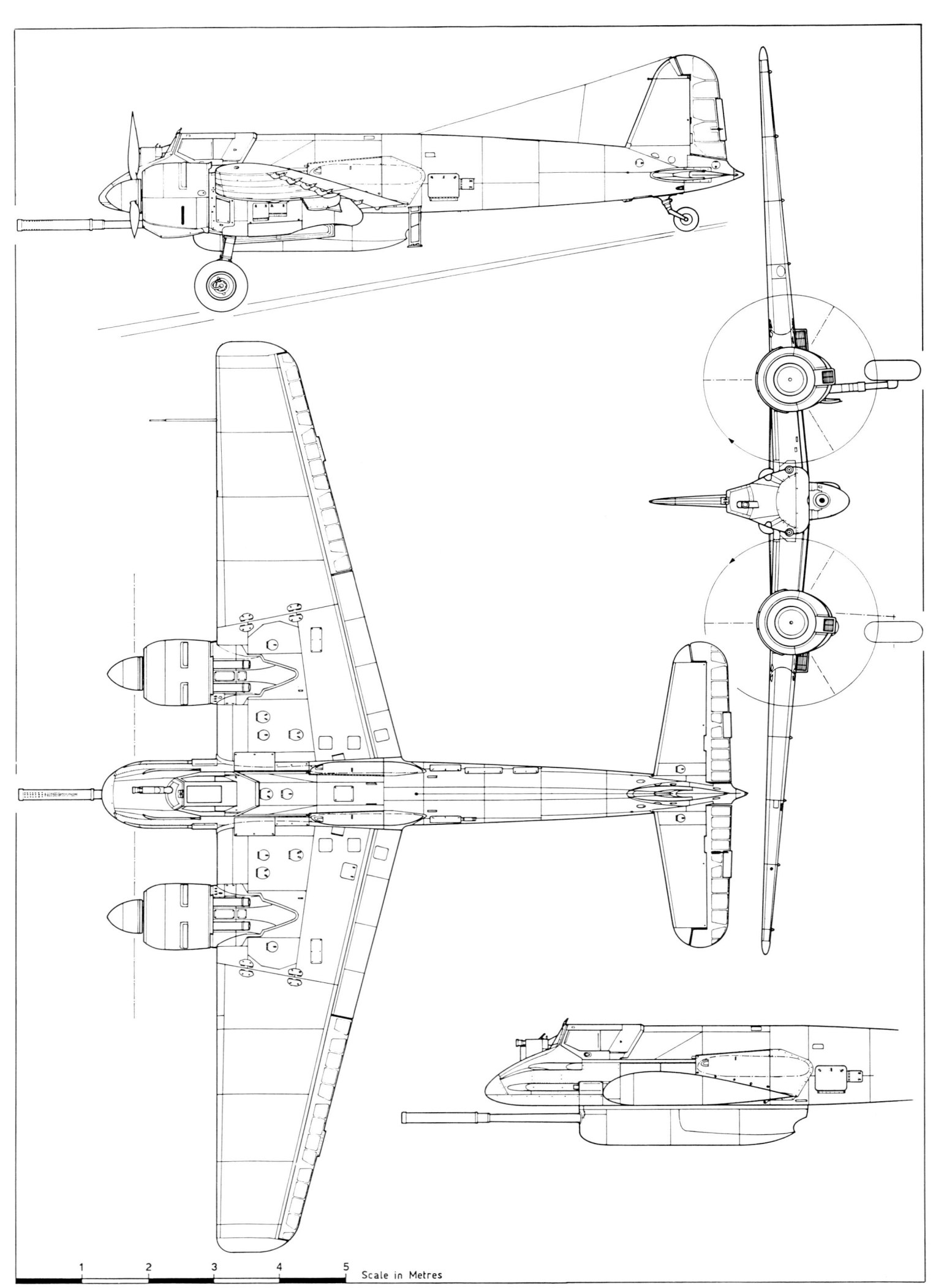

Scale in Metres

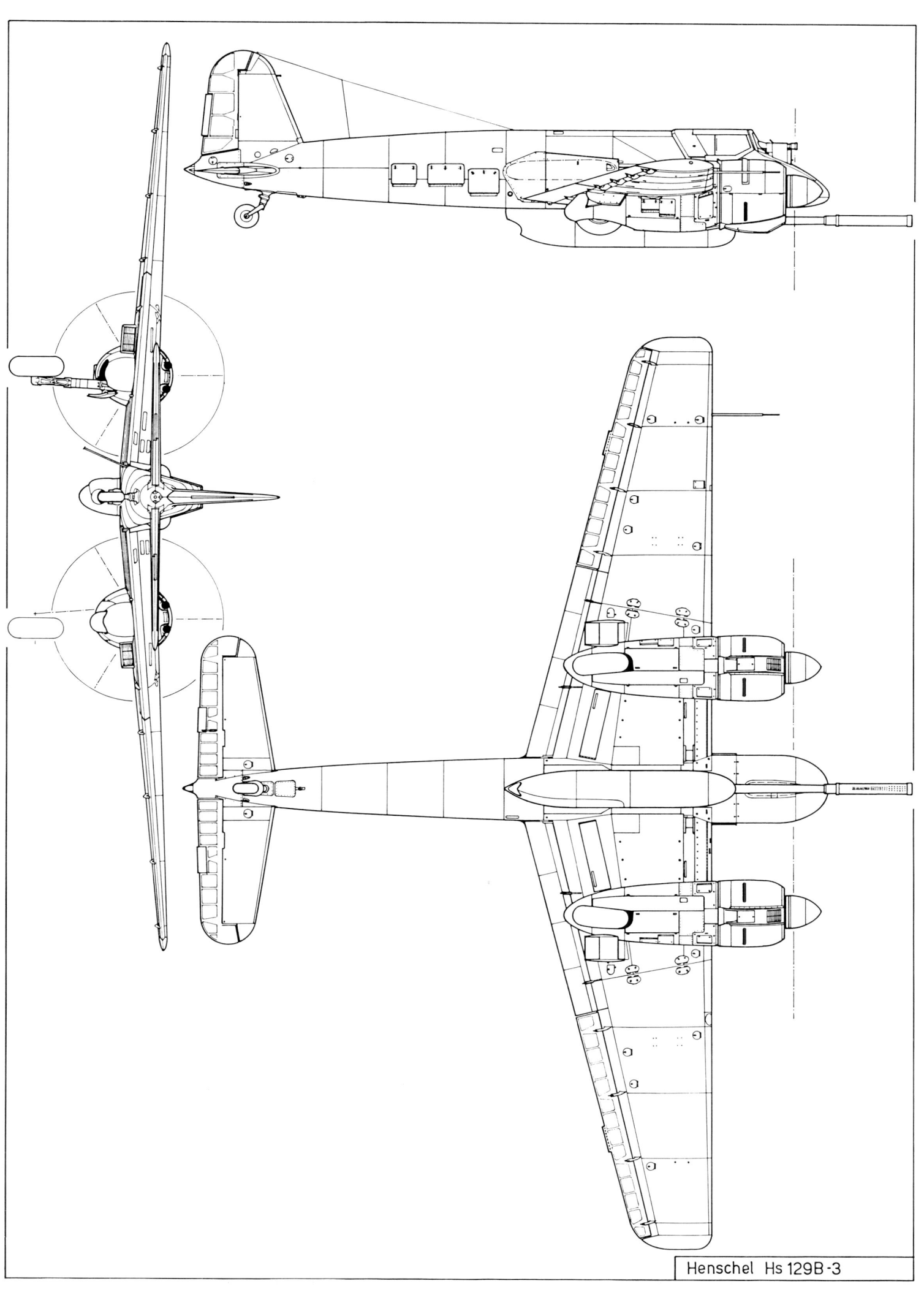

Henschel Hs 129B-3

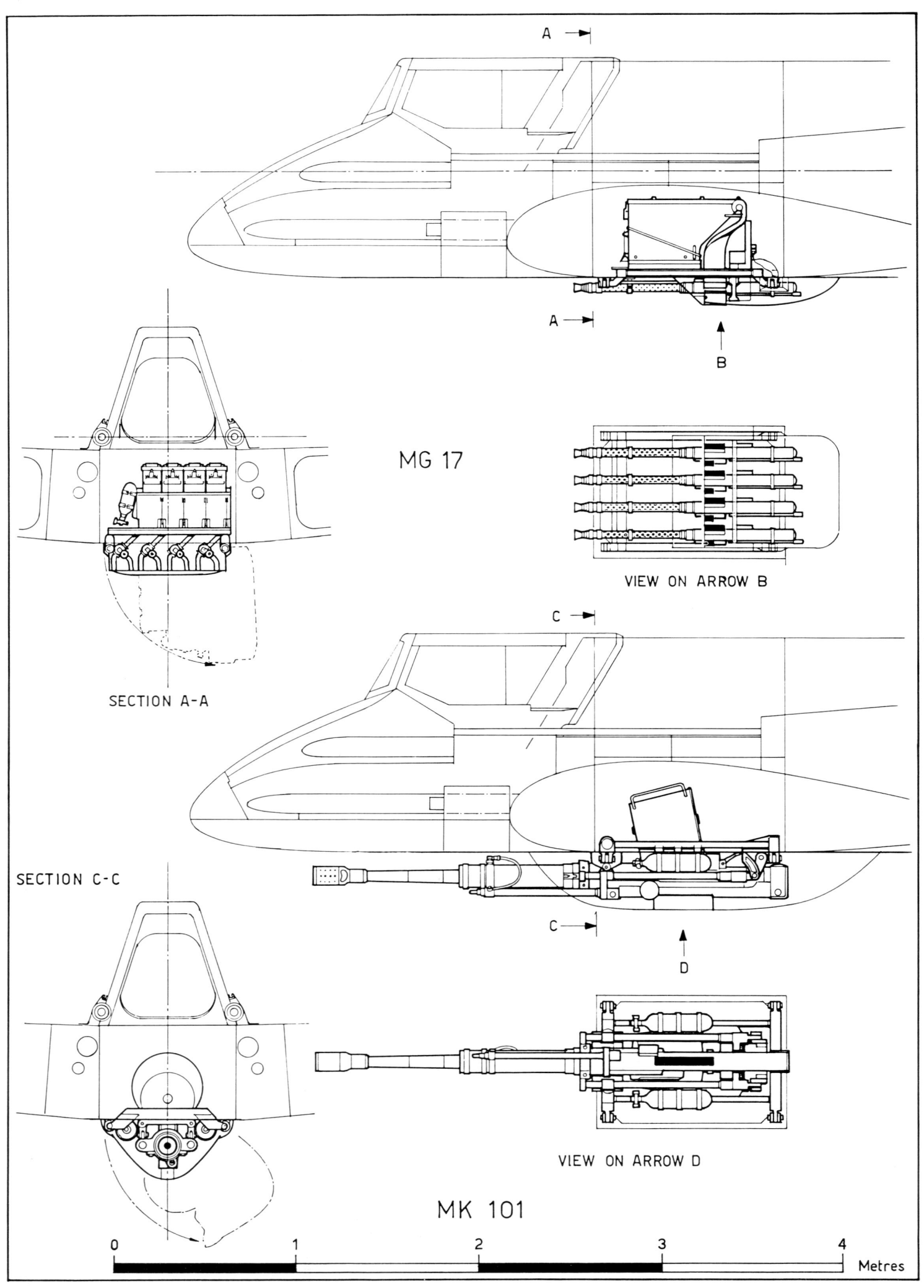

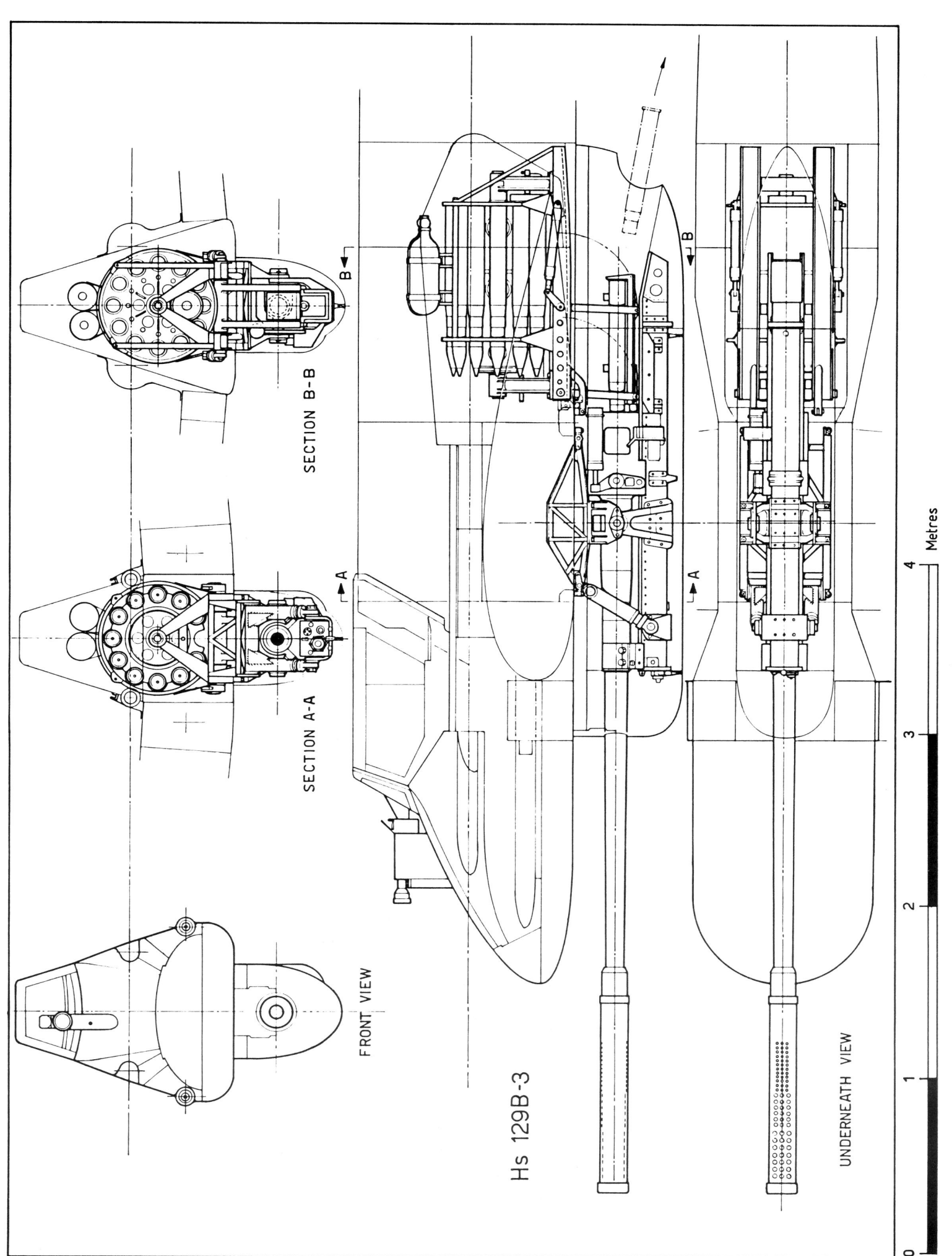

aircraft which had been handed over to us."

While the magazine of the Hs 129 B-3's cannon was constructed to hold twelve of the 75 mm shells, in fact, thirteen rounds could be carried, the additional shell being loaded straight into the breech by the armourers when the aircraft was being armed. When the cannon was fired, the muzzle blast and recoil caused a momentary loss of speed in the order of 10 kph (6 mph), but the few Hs 129 B-3s which were used in combat generally created a very favourable impression with the pilots who flew them. However, one criticism made by Franz Oswald, who flew a machine delivered to 13.(Pz)/SG 9, was that the ZFR 3 B telescopic gunsight made target acquisition difficult.

Gebhard Weber remembers two operations in particular when the B-3 was employed: "We took off from Schweidnitz to attack a Russian tank column which was advancing between Streigau and Jauer. Flying with me in an Hs 129 B-3 as Number 2 in my *Schwarm* was a young pilot with fewer than ten operational missions to his credit. On our third approach against a T-34, his shot hit the side of the tank, just below its turret. The 75 mm round blew a hole about one metre (3 ft) in diameter in the left hand side of the hull and the tank immediately caught fire. During the following operation that day, while we were operating against tanks in the city of Streigau, a tank exploded after the first shot. The impact of the 75 mm cannon was extraordinary."

Despite the appearance of newer types of Russian tanks with even thicker armour, the effects of the 30 mm MK 103 cannon could sometimes be as devastating as the BK 7.5 of the Hs 129 B-3. Gebhard Weber recalled a successful attack he made against a Russian tank in a street in Breslau. As the tank was situated in a built-up area, an attack from the side was not possible and Weber made his approach against its rear. Flying along the street at low level, Weber opened fire. The tank exploded almost immediately, the force of the explosion sending the turret cartwheeling through the air high above the attacking aircraft. It eventually crashed through the roof of a house some distance away.

On another operation, Weber was shot down for the fourth time. He had taken off on a long-range flight to the south of Schweidnitz but discovered en route that his fuselage fuel tank was failing to feed and he was therefore forced to switch over to his wing tanks earlier than he had planned. On the flight out Weber had flown a long dog-leg course to avoid flying over a railway station which was heavily defended by friendly flak, but now, with his wing tanks rapidly running short of fuel, he banked left to cut the corner off the route he had flown earlier. In doing so, he had no choice but to fly directly over the railway station where the 10. Panzer Division was in the process of unloading. When the flak gunners - members of the Hitler Youth under the command of *Luftwaffe* personnel - saw Weber's Henschel, they mistakenly identified it as a Russian Pe-2 and opened fire. Unfortunately for Weber, the *Hitler Jugend* gunners were considerably better at shooting than they were at aircraft recognition and they hit the Hs 129 with their first burst.

Weber belly-landed in open ground near a village where the locals, also convinced that he was a Russian, gave him such a hostile reception that they had to be persuaded at pistol point that he was a member of the *Luftwaffe*. Eventually Weber was picked up by car and returned to his unit, but an interesting sequel to this story occurred in May, 1945, when after the German surrender, Weber was among other POWs being transferred by rail to a POW camp. On the train, he overheard an *Oberleutnant* from a flak unit describing how one day, towards the end of the war, his guns had been set up to protect the 10. Panzer Division while it detrained at a station near Schweidnitz. A lone aircraft had flown over, he said, which his gunners had hit with their first salvo, but he didn't know whether or not the aircraft had been brought down. Weber was pleased to confirm that the battery had indeed scored a kill and introduced himself as the victim!

Zielfernrohr ZFR 3 B telescopic gunsight

This heavily retouched view, apparently of an Hs 129 B-3, first appeared in a 1944 German aircraft recognition booklet. If genuine, it is the only known photograph of an operational B-3, though the style of muzzle brake and the trace of a II.Gruppe bar behind the fuselage cross gives some reason to doubt its authenticity.

"With Panzerfäusten and Machine Pistols"

The Final Ordeal
May 1945

24

The end of the war was rapidly drawing near. On the Austrian airfield at Wels, 10.(Pz)/SG 9 received an order to transfer to Havlíčkův-Brod, between Olmuce and Prague in Czechoslovakia where it was to cover the retreat of Army Group Schörner. The bulk of the *Staffel* transferred first, leaving behind a rear party which was to follow up the next day. This splitting of the *Staffel* into two separate groups resulted in the members of each being led to greatly different fates.

The rear party comprised three Hs 129s, three pilots - Franzl Jech, Georg Schönthoner and Franzl Preiner - and 20 technicians under Willi Tholen. But on the morning they were due to follow the bulk of the *Staffel* to Havlíčkův-Brod, the airfield was smothered in a dense ground fog which delayed their take-off with fateful results. When it cleared, and as the three Hs 129s stood ready for take-off, in came the omnipresent USAAF Mustangs which strafed the airfield. When the Americans flew away, they left all three Henschels burning and destroyed. Unable to move, the three pilots - all of whom were Austrian - and their ground crews decided to remain at Wels and await developments. When the US Third Army reached Linz, the members of the rear party decided that they would surrender to the Americans and, during the night of 8/9 May, they boarded their last remaining roadworthy lorry and drove into US captivity.

On 16 May, the Americans assembled a convoy to transport German POWs to Bremerhaven. On 20 May, just before arriving there and unseen by his US guards, Willi Tholen managed to jump out of the lorry in which he was travelling. Keeping to the minor roads, he evaded recapture and walked to his home in Cloppenburg where he arrived the following day. For him, the war was over, but a very different fate awaited the *Staffel* personnel who had flown to Czechoslovakia. Although he was unaware of it at the time, the transfer flight to Havlíčkův-Brod was to be *Lt.* Walter Krause's last in the Hs 129: "We were very experienced and, as true veterans, felt that we knew everything. Normally we would approach at low level, lower the undercarriage and flaps, pull out and touch down at full throttle. But the airfield at Havlíčkův-Brod was idiotically short and, to make things worse, just on the other side of a hill. We shot over this hill at a speed of about 200 kph (124 mph), only to find that the Bf 109s of JG 52 were all neatly lined up about 100 metres (328 ft) in front of us. I had no time in which to be frightened. Ahead and to my right, probably where two *Staffeln* had lined up, there was a small gap. Using my rudder and brakes, I just about managed to squeeze my '129 through this gap and only came to a standstill at the very edge of the airfield."

For the remaining members of 10.(Pz)/SG 9, as with German units everywhere, Hitler's suicide on 30 April, the surrender of the capital, Berlin, on 2 May and the total collapse of the German Reich came as a great shock. They had lost everything for which they had fought and suffered and for which many of their comrades had been killed. The uncertainty of their own fate as individuals weighed heavily upon them.

Similar uncertainties befell those civilian managers, designers, engineers and technicians who had been employed to work on the Hs 129 at the Henschel factories in Berlin. Though the works at Schönefeld was known to have established its own *Werkschar*[1], the Hs 129's chief designer, *Dipl. Ing.* Friedrich Nicolaus opted instead for service in a Berlin *Volkssturm*[2] company with which he manned part of the hastily prepared anti-tank defences that ringed the capital. Along with other personnel from the factory, Nicolaus took part in the bitter street fighting that raged

This Hs 129, photographed close to the autobahn near Munich, was relatively complete when first found but due to the ravages of time - and souvenir hunters - gradually deteriorated until it was little more than a skeleton.

As the Allies moved into Germany, a number of abandoned Hs 129s were discovered on various airfields. These two photographs, show one example, "PA+UC", found at Wiesbaden.

close to his home near Fehrbelliner Platz during late April and his company suffered heavy losses under the constant Russian shelling, Nicolaus himself being badly wounded in the valiant but futile defence of the capital. On 4 May 1945, Russian units occupied the Henschel factory at Schönefeld.

On 6 May, all action by German forces in the West ceased, but in Czechoslovakia the cessation of hostilities was yet to take effect and German control of occupied areas within Czechoslovakia was deteriorating rapidly. Although the American Third Army had surged into the country, it was obliged to return to a prearranged line thereby leaving all Czechoslovakia to Soviet occupation. In view of this frightening prospect, local *Luftwaffe* personnel and their dependants were hurriedly assembled at various points where they prepared to make a hazardous migration westwards through partisan infested territory where it was hoped they could surrender to American forces.

On 8 May 1945, 10.(Pz)/ SG 9 received the order that only its flying personnel were to fly out to Neubiberg where they were to surrender to American forces on 9 May. The *Geschwaderkommodore* of JG 52, *Brillantenträger Obstlt.* Hermann Graf, had also received the same order but the pilots of both units were reluctant to leave their faithful ground crews behind to an uncertain fate. After a brief discussion between Graf and the pilots the matter was decided. Since they had all gone through the war together they would not be split from their ground crews now. Instead, the aircraft would be blown up and all personnel, air and groundcrews alike, would attempt to drive overland to the Americans.

In the early morning of 9 May, the lorries were

The Eastern Front, Spring 1945: the last photograph taken of pilots of 10.(Pz)/SG 9. Foreground from left: Lt. Krause, Oblt. Weber, Oblt. Aigner, Fw. Ritz. On the fuselage: Uffz. Scholz and Lt. Jech.

loaded and the aircraft destroyed using incendiary ammunition and hand grenades. It was a sight which *Lt.* Krause never forgot: "It was a grandiose but very depressing spectacle when the '109s of JG 52 and our faithful Hs 129s exploded and burned out. In the late morning a column of lorries was formed in which we would travel through Czechoslovakia, where a rebellion against the Germans had broken out, to the Moldau in order to surrender to the Americans. The 9 May was to become a very hard and memorable day. Those of us from the *Staffel* had mounted a three-barrelled 20 mm flak gun on an Opel *Blitz* lorry. This mightily armed vehicle was to drive at the head of the column and I received the order to lead this vanguard. And so, with the sun shining brilliantly, we set off along the road to Tabor and into uncertainty."

"After about 30 kilometres (19 miles), the road made a sharp right-hand curve and our driver braked abruptly. Ahead of us the road led into a village but it was blocked by a tank barricade. I climbed down from the lorry to take a look at the situation. It didn't look too threatening although some Czechs, wearing German helmets and carrying machine-pistols under their arms, were standing by the barrier. I asked one of them what this was all about. He spoke German and said that the Germans had capitulated, that we had to get out of the lorries and surrender our weapons. I told him that under no circumstances would we do this. First, we wanted to go to the Americans and, second, we were strong enough to see ourselves through. At this point our discussion was interrupted by some Czechs under cover who started firing, followed by return fire from our lorry. I dived into a roadside ditch and felt rather helpless despite the large crowd of German soldiers behind me. But the Czechs, about twenty of them, turned and ran back into the village and we were able to quickly clear the barricade. Then it was back into the trucks and our driver accelerated to full speed. We hurtled into the village only to find the place was teeming with armed Czechs! Our driver swerved round the market square and we hardly had time to think, let alone take any action, before we were out the other side of the village. There we discovered to our dismay that the rest of the column had not kept up and was stranded on the other side of the village. We could hear a lot of wild shooting and the situation with our lorry and just ten men gave me reason to be concerned."

"I left seven men on the *flak* lorry while we other four, clutching our machine-pistols, crept cautiously round the village. In the market place, standing in the centre of the square in a leather jacket, his steel helmet sitting lop-sidedly on his head and a machine-pistol under his arm, was *Oberstleutnant* Graf. While I was spending the last day of the war as an infantry soldier, the *Jagdgeschwader Kommodore* was leading his men like an infantry battalion commander. With *Panzerfäusten* and machine-pistols, groups of us stormed the houses from which the Czechs were firing. In a moment the nightmare was over and we had captured about thirty Czechs. From the cellar of the school we released a company of Army prisoners which had earlier been captured by surprise and a large number of German women and children who were also being held captive. After a short discussion it was decided that we would continue our journey, taking with us on each lorry a Czech carrying a white flag."

"We had driven on through several other villages without further disturbance when things again became critical. Ahead of us, the road passed through Tabor, a town of about 20,000 inhabitants. We drove on at walking pace, past houses all flying home-made British, American and Russian flags. With bated breath we drove slowly past thousands of people who were standing silently on the curbside. If a single shot had been fired it would have resulted in a bloodbath for all concerned and I do not think we would have stood a chance of getting out of Tabor alive. Thank goodness everything remained quiet, but it was an uncanny experience".

Late in the afternoon the convoy reached the Moldau near Piesek. Parked on each side of the road, the large white stars of the US Army on its turret plainly visible, was a Sherman tank. After some discussion and argument with the American troops and after the Czech hostages had been released, the convoy was allowed to drive on unhindered to Strakanitz. Here, in a large field surrounded by hills, the Americans had assembled around 10,000 German soldiers, a large number of women, including about 500 female signals auxiliaries, and some children.

The Americans seemed little bothered about their prisoners. They had formed a loose ring of armoured personnel carriers and tanks around the field, but the guards "... were Czechs who liked to play at soldiers". At night, the Czechs' campfires could be seen on the hillsides and around the field, while the Germans slept in tents and relied upon their own supplies of food. During the daytime, every now and then a Mustang would fly low over the field, presumably in an attempt to intimidate the prisoners lest they get out of hand.

As Walter Krause recalls: "At first the mood was one of hope, especially as we were expecting to be released from American captivity soon, but this quickly transformed into a feeling of desperate concern about our uncertain future. On 12 May, a sudden rumour circulated that we were to be handed over to the Russians. As is so often the case with rumours, nobody knew where it started but each of us had the uneasy feeling that there might be some truth in it. On 17 May, our fears were confirmed, when, in the early morning, a regiment of drunken Russian paratroops entered our camp. An unimaginable drama began. The drunken Russians raped, pillaged and fired their weapons at random. All Hell was let loose on the German servicemen and women. All this time, the Americans were still there. They sat on their tanks filming and photographing the barbaric scenes and - I have to say it - they gave the impression that they were greatly amused by this inferno".

Eventually, in a wooded camp at Neubistriz, the Russians separated the German officers from the NCOs and men, loaded them on a lorry and drove them to České Budějovice where they camped at the edge of an airfield. On the runway

---

Dipl.Ing. Nicolaus
Berlin-Wilmersdorf
Zähringer Str.2
26 Sept. 1945

Dear Herr Henschel,

As you probably know, Herr Hormel was arrested a few days after the occupation of the factory on 4 May 1945. Neither the reason for his arrest, nor whether there was any trial, could be ascertained... Following this, Frau Hormel received the sad news that Herr Hormel died on 22 July in Weesow... Herr Hormel often discussed with me the problem of whether he should leave Schönefeld at what was an extremely critical time, or stay on. On every instance, he stated that he would stay, since he felt obliged to do everything possible to ensure the survival of the factory. Since his death was doubtless on account of his arrest, one can safely say that he died for the factory. I would like to add that, after long years of co-operation with Herr Hormel, you too, have lost a true friend of the company...

Frau Hormel has given me details of her present situation... After the occupation, her house in the country was so badly looted, with just a few pieces of furniture being left, that she was forced to beg from her friends for a few pieces of clothing and bed linen... All bank accounts have been frozen, but, in any case, Frau Hormel would not have been granted access to any funds since Herr Hormel was, some time ago, appointed an honorary NSFK-Standartenführer (and later Oberführer) in recognition of Henschel Flugzeugwerke's support of the apprentices' gliding group... The son is still in English captivity... there is no chance of his being released to Schönefeld... the daughter-in-law has been refused permission to move to Schönefeld...

Meanwhile, Frau Hormel lives from what she can raise in her garden. This is very little, since her garden has repeatedly been plundered. Frau Hormel faces an uncertain future, the more so, since - as you may know - her health is not the best and she is not capable of any physical exertion....

As for myself, it will be several weeks before I can show up anywhere, since the fighting here in the West lasted much longer than anticipated and I was wounded and became very ill. I do hope to be able to participate in any new and important ventures. Despite all the problems, unknown to anyone not living in Berlin, I am sufficiently optimistic to believe that the Henschel-Werke, within the foreseeable future, will not only provide bread for a considerable number of people, but also share in the reconstruction of our so terribly punished fatherland.

With best wishes to you and your family,

(signed) Friedrich Nicolaus

By May 1945, only the Luftwaffe's 10.(Pz)/SG 9 was still equipped with the Hs 129 and aircraft operating in the final six months of the war lacked the earlier distinctive yellow nose marking. This particular Hs 129 B-2 with 30 mm cannon was photographed on České Budějovice airfield shortly after the capitulation and is the aircraft which Walter Krause and other POW Henschel pilots wished they could have flown to freedom.

there sat a single but obviously airworthy Hs 129, and more than one of the Henschel pilots must have wished he could fly it away to freedom. But this was an impossible dream. Instead, the *Panzerjäger* officers were split up and Walter Krause found himself aboard a miserable goods train with several pilots from JG 52 and NAG 14. For four weeks the train travelled eastwards, ever deeper into Russia. It finally unloaded its human cargo at Krasno-Uralsk, north of Sverdlovsk in Western Siberia. Here the Germans were put to work in the copper mines and in the forests felling trees. Remarkably, due to their excellent physical condition and the close bond of comradeship which existed between the flying officer prisoners in the Siberian labour camps, they survived the physical and mental rigours of captivity, although the last members of 10.(Pz)/SG 9 were not released by the Russians until the end of 1949.

Four months after the end of the war, in September 1945, *Dipl. Ing.* Friedrich Nicolaus wrote to his erstwhile employer and company chairman, Oskar Henschel, in an attempt to acquaint him with the varying fates of some of the firm's managers and design engineers. This letter contained a telling account of the final days of *Herr* Walter Hormel, a former naval officer and director of the firm and is also indicative of the suffering inflicted upon his wife as a result of the recent conflict. Research conducted by the author indicates that Hormel was tortured to death by the Russians in a prison camp and his body quickly buried in the local cemetery at Weesow.

It is perhaps fitting that the last words in this history of the Hs 129 and some of the men who flew it should come from Walter Krause who flew with the last remaining Hs 129 *Staffel* until the final days of the war: *"The tragic events we lived through in our younger years ensured that such an everlasting bond of comradeship was forged that we cannot forget the 10.(Pz)/SG 9, nor our faithful Henschel Hs 129s."*

End of the road: An Hs 129 lies stripped of its external panelling at Frankfurt-Rebstock. This photograph offers an excellent view of engine and internal construction details.

1 Werkschar - lit. a volunteer "factory platoon" or "works squad" established initially as factory fire fighters and air raid wardens.

2 Volkssturm: Armed or semi-armed civilian home defence force established by the Nazi Party in October 1944 and comprised mainly of elderly men, young boys and reservists declared unfit for front-line service, analogous to the British Home Guard.

Abschrift. Geheime Kommandosache

10.(Pz.)/Schlachtgeschwader 9   O.U., den 3. 43. Fliegerdivision
L - 53 215/Lgp. Dresden
Br.B.Nr. 155/45 g.Kdos.   Nr.: ....

Bezug: D.R.d.L. u. Ob.d.L. Gen.d.Schlachtflg. Gr. I
Nr. 155/43 g.Kdos. v. 1.11.43   2 Ausfertigungen
(über 3. Fliegerdivision)   1.Ausfertigung

Betr.: Fragebogen für den G.d.S.

An
OKL General der Schlachtflieger
— Gruppe I —
(über 3. Fliegerdivision)

Zu o.a. Bezug wird wie folgt gemeldet:

Zu B.) Besatzungen:

1.) Monatl. Durchschnittsbestand an K.-Besatzungen:
(errechnet aus der tägl. E-Meldung)

Einheit:	Baumuster:	Durchschn. Istbestand	Durchschn. einsatzber.
10.(Pz.)/S.G. 9		15 dav. 4Offz.14 dav. 4 O.

4.) Zugänge an FF od. Bf. Dienst- N a m e , Vorname   Dat.d. Eintr.
    Lfd.Nr. FF od. Bf. Dienst-   v. welch.Dienst.
            grad

	FF	Uffz.	Balzer, Hans	1.3.45 von IV (Pz.)/S.G. 9

6.) Verliehene Auszeichnungen:(Deutsches Kreuz 1.Gold usw.)

Lfd. Nr.	FF od.Bf. Dienst- grad	Name Vorname	Auszeich. verl.am
1	FF	Oblt. (Kr.O)	Weber, Gebhard	Deutsch.Kr. in Gold 28.2.1945

Zu C.) Flugzeuge:

1.) Monatlicher Durchschnittsbestand an Flugzeugen:
(errechnet aus den täglichen E-Meldungen).

Einheit:	Baumuster:	Durchschn. Istbestand	Durchschn. einsatzbereit
10.(Pz.)/S.G. 9	Hs 129 B-2	10	8
	B-3	2	2

2.) Totalabgänge an Flugzeugen (K- u. sonstige Flugzeuge) im vergangenen Monat:

Baumuster:	Anzahl:
a) Hs 129	4
Hs 129	3
Fl 156 C	1
b) Hs 129	6 b.w.

— 2 —

3.) Zugänge an Flugzeugen (K- u. sonstige Flugzeuge) in vergangenen Monat:

		Ist	Fehl	Durchschn. z.V.
Hs 129	B - 2		8	
Hs 129	B - 3		1	

Zu D.) Bodenpersonal:

Personalgruppen		Ist	Fehl	Durchschn. z. Verfg.
1.) Allgemeines Personal: (Stamm)		4	—	4
2.) Technisches Personal:		Ist	Fehl	Durchschn. z. Verfg.
Davon a)	Flzg.Ofw.	1	—	1
b)	Fl.Waffenofw. (Abw.)	1	—	1
c)	" (Bordw.)	1	—	1
e)	Flzg.Mechaniker, 1.Warte	16	—	14
f)	Flugmotorenschlosser	9	—	8
g)	Flzg.-Elektriker	2	—	2
h)	Fl.Waffenwarte (Bordw.)	2	—	2
r)	" (Abw.)	15	—	14
s)	"	8	—	7
t)	F.u.S.-Personal	1	—	1
u)	Flzg.-Gerätverw.	1	—	1

Zu E.) Einsatz:

1.) Zahl der eingesetzten Maschinen: 31 bei 13 Einsatztagen.
2.) Verbrauchte Schuß- und Abwurfmunition: (getrennt nach Arten)

```
1015   Schuß   3 cm Pz.H. 103
  20     "     3 cm Pz.Spr. 103
 210     "     2 cm Pz.Spr.Pat. 151
 210     "     2cm  Brdsprgr. Pat. 151
5000     "     7,9 mm S m K l
5000     "     7,9 mm P m K
  47     "     7,9 mm B-Pat.
           "   7,5 cm (Pak 40)
  10   AB/70   (Bomben)
```

5.) Vernichtete und beschädigte Panzer und sonstige Fahrzeuge:
   a) im Berichtsmonat:
      51 Panzer vernichtet, 27 Panzer wirksam beschossen, 1 Lkw. und 1 Flakgeschütz (3,7 cm) vernichtet.
   b) Insgesamt:
      625 Panzer vernichtet, 475 Panzer wirksam besch ossen, 266 Lkw., 13 Pkw., 6 Kräder, 2 Zugmaschinen, 3 Munifahrzeuge, 259 bespannte Fahrzeuge, 11 Pakgeschütze, 2 Plakgeschütze, 2 Granatwerfer vernichtet.
      Sonst "F e h l a n z e i g e".

                    (gez.) W e b e r
                    Oberleutnant und Staffelkptn.

F.d.R.d.A.:

Report dated 3 April 1945 showing a summary of 10.(Pz)/SG 9's strength and operations for March 1945. Note the award of the Deutsches Kreuz in Gold for the Staffelkapitän, Oblt. Gebhard Weber and the mention of the unit's Hs 129 B-3s. Also of interest, under Paragraph E, is a list of ammunition expended during the Staffel's operations which shows, as well as 7.9 mm and 20 mm rounds, 1,015 30 mm hard core (ie, tungsten) and twenty 30 mm high-explosive MK 103 rounds, plus 47 Pak 40 rounds. The Staffel's record of tanks and other vehicles claimed destroyed and damaged to good effect are shown in Paragraphs E.5a and b and are, respectively, the Staffel's claims for the month and total claims up to the end of March.

"As it so happened I was working in the field that day. I heard a plane real low and I looked up and saw it go over. I thought to myself, the war was over and what was a German plane doing flying around here...?"

W.B. Bate, Jr., commenting on sighting an Hs 129 over Mrs W.Y. Allen's farm at Gallatin, Tennessee, USA, 24 July 1946

APPENDICES

ONE:
ENEMY WITHIN THE CAMP

TWO:
CAMOUFLAGE, MARKINGS & MANUFACTURER'S DATA

THREE:
LOSS LISTS

FOUR:
TECHNICAL AND WEAPONS SPECIFICATIONS

FIVE:
LOGBOOKS AND AWARD CITATIONS

Described by "*Flight*" magazine in March 1944 as an "Enemy within the Camp", this sequence shows Hs 129 B-2, W.Nr.0297 formerly Blue "C", of 4.(Pz)/Sch.G 2. The photo below depicts Blue "C" still in her original German desert scheme being examined by RAF fitters probably at Collyweston and variously awaiting panels for the tail, wing undersurfaces and nose.
The aircraft also lacks engine cowling and spinners. The remaining three photos on these pages show the aircraft after repair and repainting in British markings as NF756 of No.1426 Flight, RAF Collyweston. Refurbishing the aircraft to flyable condition took more than a year to complete.

APPENDIX ONE

Enemy Within The Camp
THE CAPTURED HS 129S

A photograph of an early Hs 129 B-1 believed to show an aircraft after capture by Soviet forces. All German markings appear to have been painted out and the port-side propeller blade shows signs of having been straightened and balanced.

THE SOVIET UNION

On 15 August 1942, an Hs 129 B-1 flown by *Uffz*. Karl Wultsch of 5./Sch.G 1 was lost behind Soviet lines near Rshev. At first, the *Luftwaffe* recorded the aircraft as having been lost to flak and posted the pilot "missing", but on 4 November 1942, a Russian prisoner of war interrogated by members of *Stab*./JG 51 revealed that Soviet troops had found the aircraft almost intact. In this way, the Germans first learned that *Uffz*. Wultsch had been captured alive and that his machine, complete with MK 101 cannon, was neither burned nor badly damaged. To have in their hands the aircraft, pilot and cannon was a major coup for the Russians; for the first time they were able to obtain the latest information on what was still a newly introduced type of German aircraft. Unfortunately, little else is known about this or other Hs 129s captured by the Russians although TsAGI - the Soviet Aerodynamic Research Institute - subsequently had ample opportunities to examine and test a number of Hs 129s, other examples being shot down over their lines or abandoned by retreating German units. It is to be presumed that some of these were repaired and flown in the Soviet Union and one machine, apparently in good condition, is reported to have been included in the grand war booty exhibition displayed in the *Park Kultury* - Culture Park - in Moscow at the end of June 1944.

GREAT BRITAIN

Almost three months after the Soviet Union acquired its first Hs 129, the British in North Africa were able to examine W.Nr. 0296 - Blue "A" - which was captured at El Adam on 17 November 1942. A thorough examination was carried out and some useful information obtained relating to the aircraft's construction and armament, but as it had been damaged in a bad landing and then largely destroyed by demolition charges which the Germans had placed in the engines and fuel tanks, it was by no means complete. Other shot down or captured examples were similarly damaged and it was not until W.Nr. 0297 was captured on Melaha aerodrome in February 1943 that the British obtained an example worth restoring to flying condition.

W.Nr. 0297 - Blue "C" - was one of 98 Axis aircraft abandoned at Melaha. When found, the tail unit was almost complete and lacked only what was described in a list of the aircraft found as the "mid unit", which is presumed to refer to a panel on the vertical tail surfaces. No other positive information concerning the salvage or transportation of this aircraft from the Middle East has been discovered though it is thought that the dismantled airframe was delivered to RAF Collyweston on 27 June 1943. Interestingly, however, a further report from the Middle East dated 29 June states that a "fairly complete" Hs 129 together with Gnôme-Rhône engine was being despatched to the United Kingdom from Tunisia. This would suggest that, if this latter report refers to W.Nr. 0297, the machine must have arrived in the UK some time later than previously believed or that, alternatively, a second - and so far unidentified - machine was despatched to the UK, perhaps the aircraft examined at Farnborough. In any event, sources are agreed that by the time the aircraft reached the UK, it was in a bad state of repair when it was recorded as being on the strength of No. 1426 (Enemy Aircraft) Flight.

Formed at Duxford on 21 November 1941, the RAF's No. 1426 (Enemy Aircraft) Flight was created specifically for the task of demonstrating ex-*Luftwaffe* aircraft in the UK in order to familiarise Allied personnel with their recognition features and performance. Many fighter-liaison flights were made, as were visits to RAF and, later, USAAF stations, and the Flight also arranged various demonstrations for the benefit of anti-aircraft units and the civilian Royal Observer Corps. The Flight was transferred to RAF Collyweston on 12

April 1943, the dismantled W.Nr. 0297 arriving there on 27 June 1943.

After the aircraft had been examined by engineers from the RAE Farnborough, a party of airmen from No.65 Maintenance Unit was attached to the Flight to help with reassembly which, due to the poor condition of the component parts and a general unfamiliarity with the type, took more than a year to rebuild. When originally reassembled, the machine retained its German camouflage but was soon repainted in RAF colours with all-yellow undersurfaces. Allocated the RAF serial NF756, the Hs 129 made its first flight after reassembly on 3 September 1944 and, when No. 1426 Flight was disbanded on 21 January 1944 and transferred to RAF Tangmere as the Enemy Aircraft Flight of the Central Fighter Establishment, it took its surviving German aircraft with it. Although allocated to No.47 Maintenance Unit at Sealand on 1 November 1945, NF756/W.Nr. 0297 remained at Tangmere with the rest of the enemy aircraft until examined by the Air Historical Branch in March 1946 who were to decide whether the aircraft was worth preserving. Unfortunately, AHB did not see fit to keep the aircraft and it was sent to No.6 Maintenance Unit at RAF Brize Norton, arriving during week ending 15 August 1946. Together with most other ex-*Luftwaffe* aircraft held there, it was finally struck off charge on 14 August 1947 and scrapped.

USA

For years the identity of the Hs 129 taken to the USA has remained a mystery, but it may, at last, be possible to state exactly which aircraft this was, despite the fact that its *Werk Nummer* is not documented in any US records.

With the capture of the last Germans on Cap Bon, the campaign in North Africa was finally completed. The *Luftwaffe* and *Regia Aeronautica*, which had once threatened to dominate African skies, were thrown out altogether, leaving behind them a trail of abandoned aircraft and stores stretching from El Alamein to Bizerte. The Mediterranean Allied Air Forces (MAAF) Intelligence Section, led exclusively and staffed mainly by RAF personnel but aided by a few USAAF officers, found their task of gathering information from captured enemy equipment in order to gain foreknowledge of new enemy weapons, hard, tedious and often dangerous work, made more difficult by the distances involved and a lack of transport. Nevertheless, in the combined Western Desert and Tunisian campaigns following the battle of El Alamein, over 2,000 aircraft were examined by Technical Intelligence teams and their reports on their findings, ranging from engines, instruments, guns, bombs and radios, to the first specimens of new aircraft, deserve credit given the circumstances in which they were prepared.

Owing to the demands of urgent operational commitments, no special salvage facilities could be made available and at no time during the desert campaigns was any special organisation for the salvage of enemy aircraft, or parts of them, made available to Technical Intelligence. Nevertheless, continual requests were made for whole aircraft, engines, or items of equipment to be shipped back to the UK or USA and, as requests for material poured in, Technical Intelligence units were faced with a difficult problem. They had, of necessity, to make use of whatever facilities were available, and the fact that a large amount of material was, in the end, shipped is a tribute to their efforts.

As already noted earlier in this work, Technical Intelligence recorded ten Hs 129s at El Aouina, but although the US Capture Intelligence Report No.134 dated 7 June 1943 lists some of these, only two, W.Nr. 0326 - Red "K" - and 0408, Red "T", were considered to be good enough condition when found to warrant being "salved for shipment." However, as photographic evidence reproduced in this book shows, W.Nr. 0326 was soon reduced to a severely damaged condition and no report has so far been located which records the fate of W.Nr. 0408.

Nevertheless, the fact remains that from 20 August 1943, an Hs 129 was recorded as being at Wright Field, Ohio, USA. Records show that although it was the Americans' intention to restore it to flying condition in order to test its operational capabilities, it was not until January 1944 that Lt.Col. J.N.Hayward, Chief of the Technical Data Laboratory, at Material Command, Wright Field issued a written enquiry to various aircraft companies in which he stated that the need to put the Hs 129 and an Italian Macchi 202 fighter into flying condition was then "pressing." Enquiries were issued to six companies including the Spartan Aircraft Company of Tulsa, Oklahoma. Interested parties were to respond accordingly.

All the companies approached declined this work, stating that, at that time, they were unable to bid as they either did not have suitable repair facilities or that all their capacity had already been allocated to the war effort. Spartan, however, wrote to advise that although the company's aircraft plant and personnel were taken up with an existing contract, the Overhaul Department at their School of Aeronautics, also based in Tulsa, might be able to take on the work depending on the amount of fabrication, manufacturing of missing items or engineering work required.

It would seem that by early April, the USAAF Material Command (AAFMC) had issued the contract for the repair of the Hs 129 and Macchi 202 airframes and that both aircraft had been delivered to Spartan, though both machines were delivered less their engines. Almost immediately, the Evaluation Branch at Wright Field directed that the propeller control units of the Hs 129, together with all wiring and gauges, should be removed from the cockpit and returned to the Captured Equipment Unit as it was carrying out test runs with the propellers and related equipment on the Gnôme-Rhône engines before the completed engines were reinstalled.

By mid-April Spartan had started work. The entire centre-section with wings and horizontal stabilisers still attached was

All that now remains of FE-4600 is the nose section, currently in Australia.

The Hs 129 taken to the USA is now believed to have been W.Nr.0385. After capture in North Africa, the machine was shipped to the USA and, like the aircraft taken to the UK, more than a year was to elapse before refurbishment was complete. Originally allocated the Foreign Evaluation number FE-105, it later became FE-4600.

put on jacks, cleaned and the necessary repairs marked out. Some of the fuel and oil tanks and lines were flushed and tested; the fabric of the control surfaces was removed in order to straighten and repair them and both wing tips were also repaired. As work progressed, Spartan discovered that certain parts were missing and the first shortage list was submitted for items required. Work proceeded and by 24 April all the original paint had been removed from the centre-section which was then repainted silver. Only faulty or damaged flight and engine instruments were replaced with items of US manufacture, otherwise they were retained in order to simplify repair and assembly and to keep the aircraft in a condition as near as possible to the original. The oxygen and radio equipment were replaced with standard USAAF equipment, but the aircraft's armament was retained as removal would have affected the weight and centre of gravity.

The aircraft had evidently suffered some battle damage during its operational career and while bullet and flak holes in the fuselage and engine nacelles were patched with little trouble, considerably more work was required to repair areas of more serious damage under the centre-section and fuselage. Damage to some electrical wiring was repaired but the original floor under the fuselage fuel tank had been so badly shot up by flak that a new floor had to be built and installed in its place. It was also discovered that the left wing fuel tank had a 75 mm (3 in.) shrapnel hole in it and required complete replacement, while a damaged engine ring and engine cowling had to be straightened, patched and repaired.

A telegram from AAFMC dated 6 June 1944, confirmed that for the purpose of radio call signs the Hs 129 was to be assigned the Evaluation Branch Number EB-105 and, on the same day, Spartan's Weekly Progress Report confirmed that the aircraft was in the process of final examination by their Inspector, though at that time it still lacked some cockpit glazing, engines, engine mounts, propellers and wheels, those received earlier being too corroded to use. On 7 June, W.T. Neal, the Assistant Director of the Spartan School of Aeronautics' Overhaul and Maintenance Department wrote to AAFMC pointing out that both the Hs 129 and the Macchi 202 (EB-300) were then at the stage where very little work could be accomplished towards the completion of the project until engines were received. Neal asked if Wright Field could carry out the fuel tank repairs in order to eliminate difficulties in locating a replacement.

By 15 July, re-inspection of the corroded wheel hubs showed that they were not as bad as first thought and with the delivery of all other parts, the Hs 129 now lacked only its engines. Enquiries for a firm delivery date indicated that they would not be ready until 27 August, AAFMC explaining that the engine repair work had been seriously impaired by a lack of personnel and the pressure of other, high priority engine work. In the event, and as a result of further delays to the completion of both the German and Italian aircraft (for which Spartan was claiming reimbursement by the US Government for the extra expense incurred in storing the aircraft under guard), AAFMC agreed to terminate its contract and arrange for the final assembly to be completed at Wright Field as and when the engines and propellers became available. AAFMC's instructions for the return of both aircraft were telegraphed to Spartan on 2 September 1944.

Whether the same "pressing" requirement to flight test the Hs 129 still existed once Wright Field had installed the engines is not known, but, with the end of the war in sight, the rush to evaluate the ex-*Luftwaffe* aircraft ceased. Besides, American interest was already beginning to concentrate on Axis jet and rocket powered aircraft and it is likely that apart from one or two unusual features, interest in such piston-engined types as the Hs 129 was waning. Confirming a discussion with personnel of the Technical Data Laboratory on 7 May 1945, Capt. W.E. Lamar, Chief of Aircraft and Test Control at the Engineering and Procurement Office at Wright Field, stated that the Hs 129 would be available for laboratory evaluation and, apart from specially authorised flight tests, would be maintained in flying condition for publicity and familiarisation purposes. In future the Hs 129 was to be stationed at Dayton Airfield in Ohio.

At the end of September 1945, EB-105, since renumbered with the "Foreign Equipment" Number FE-4600, was at Freeman Field, Seymour, Indiana, for a public display of ex-*Luftwaffe* aircraft. It was still there in May 1946, subsequently allotted for storage at Davis-Monthan AFB in Arizona. At 12:18 on 24 July 1946, twenty-two year-old 1st Lt. Kenneth P. Almond, an experienced USAAF Flight Test and Maintenence Officer, took-off from Freeman Field in FE-4600 for the 90 minute transfer flight to Berry Field, Nashville, Tennessee en route to Tucson. The Hs 129 was escorted by a C-45 transport carrying a mechanic to help start the engines at each stop and, flying with the escorting C-45, Almond had to use minimum power settings.

The aircraft's tanks were still half-full by the time Almond reached Bowling Green, Kentucky, which was well over half way to the aircraft's ultimate destination. Between Bowling Green and Gallatin, Tennessee, the Hs 129 developed fuel feed problems, probably as a result of a leak. Almond realised that he did not have enough fuel to reach the auxiliary field at Gallatin. At the time, the aircraft was close to a farm belonging to Mrs W.Y. Allen about one mile south-east of Gallatin and, seeing an apparently suitable looking meadow on the farm, Almond decided to make a forced landing. As the aircraft made its final approach, both engines stopped due to fuel exhaustion.

Down in the field, twenty-two year-old W.B. Bate Jr. was cutting the grass and he stopped work to watch the aircraft as it made its final approach. He recalls: "As it so happened, I was working in the field that day. It was a long, narrow field, close to a quarter or half a mile long. I was mowing or clipping the grass in the field with a mowing machine. Best I can remember, I was nearly through with it and it looked nice and smooth. Then I heard a plane real low and I looked up and saw it go over. I thought to myself, the war was over and what was a German plane doing flying around here. He made a low pass over the field and I knew he was going to try to land for I could see he was having trouble with one engine."

"He made a come around and set the plane down at the end of the field. I moved my tractor over to one side of the field. He made a perfect landing, all wheels touching down at the same time. I guess I was about 150 ft from him when he went by. From the air the field must have looked real smooth. Of course, the pilot didn't know that right across the middle of the field was a drainage ditch about a foot and a half deep, the grass had grown up over it, so he couldn't see it. As I say, he went by me real close and I could see the pilot as he threw up his hand at me as he went by."

"About 50 ft further on, the plane's wheel dropped into the ditch and about all the damage it did was to break off the landing gear and bent the propellers when they hit the ground. The plane slid on for a good distance in the grass and stopped. I ran to it and when the pilot got out, he said *"What the hell happened?"* for the field still looked nice and smooth. I showed him the ditch. He asked me to go to a phone and call a number and tell them what happened and where - which I did."

Though Almond had not suffered any personal injury during what was a relatively good landing, the drop into the ditch caused one tyre on the Henschel to blow and the starboard-side wheel to break away. Furthermore, according to the USAAF accident report, "major damage" was incurred to the starboard wing outboard panel, right aileron, and wheel strut. "Major damage" was also recorded to the propellers.

Shortly afterwards, a guard from Sheriff S.K. Baker's office arrived and stayed in place until technicians and engineers arrived from Freeman Field. W.B. Bate Jr. continues: "In a matter of hours, several trucks and men came and they took the wings off the plane and loaded the plane and the wings on the trucks and I cut the fence to let them out on the road and they left with the Hs 129. Often, when I go by that field, I wonder what happened to my German Hs 129. The field is still there, but a road runs through it and there are two factories on part of it now. I remember that after they had gone with the plane, I picked up part of the landing gear they left behind. I think it was about half of a wheel rim."

Later dismantled, the aircraft was taken to No.803 Special Depot at Orchard Place but when this was required for other purposes during the Korean War, FE-4600 was put up for disposal as scrap.

In June 1951, the nose section was purchased from the scrapyard by Mr Earl Reinert who stored it at his home until it went on display at Mundelein, Illinois, where Reinert had set up the Victory Air Museum with Mr Paul Polidori. When Polidori was killed in a flying accident in 1985, the contents of the museum were dispersed and in May 1986, the cockpit was obtained by Mr Martin Mednis of Sydney, Australia, for display in his Adler Air Museum. It was during the course of Martin Mednis's refurbishment of the cockpit section, that various clues were discovered which have since led to the belief that FE-4600, alias EB-105, was originally W.Nr. 0385 captured at El Aouina airfield in Tunisia.

On 7 July 1943, W.Nr. 0385 - Blue "G" of 8.(Pz)/Sch.G 2 landed at Toubakeur as a result of being damaged by anti-aircraft fire and was listed as 20% damaged. When the Allies discovered the aircraft abandoned at El Aouina with its wings removed, presumably to facilitate transportation from Toubakeur to El Aouina, it was reported as being in an otherwise "fair" condition. However, no record has been found of any attempts to salvage or transport this, or any other, aircraft to the USA and, likewise, although the Progress Reports submitted by the Spartan School of Aeronautics provide considerable detail on the restoration of the Hs 129, no mention was made of its original identity. But when Martin Mednis began to strip the cockpit section prior to restoration, he discovered two scribbled numbers - "0388" on the inside of the upper, curved, nose panel and "0385" on the inside of the main cockpit section. The existence of the two numbers was confusing, but closer examination of the cockpit section revealed that when the aircraft was originally under construction, some engineering errors had been made which would have prohibited normal assembly. To rectify the situation and finish building the aircraft, it seems likely that some parts marked "0388" were used to complete W.Nr. 0385; in all probability, the original incorrect parts intended for 0385 were also later rectified and fitted to W.Nr. 0388. When the flak damage described in the German report and the details of the repairs carried out by the Americans is taken into consideration together with the existence of the number "0385" in the main cockpit shell, there is, therefore, reasonable evidence to suggest that Martin Mednis's Hs 129 cockpit section is part of 8.(Pz)/Sch.G 2's Blue "G", W.Nr. 0385.

Front page news: Extract from *The Gallatin Examiner*, 2 August 1946.

APPENDIX TWO

Camouflage, Markings and Manufacturer's Data

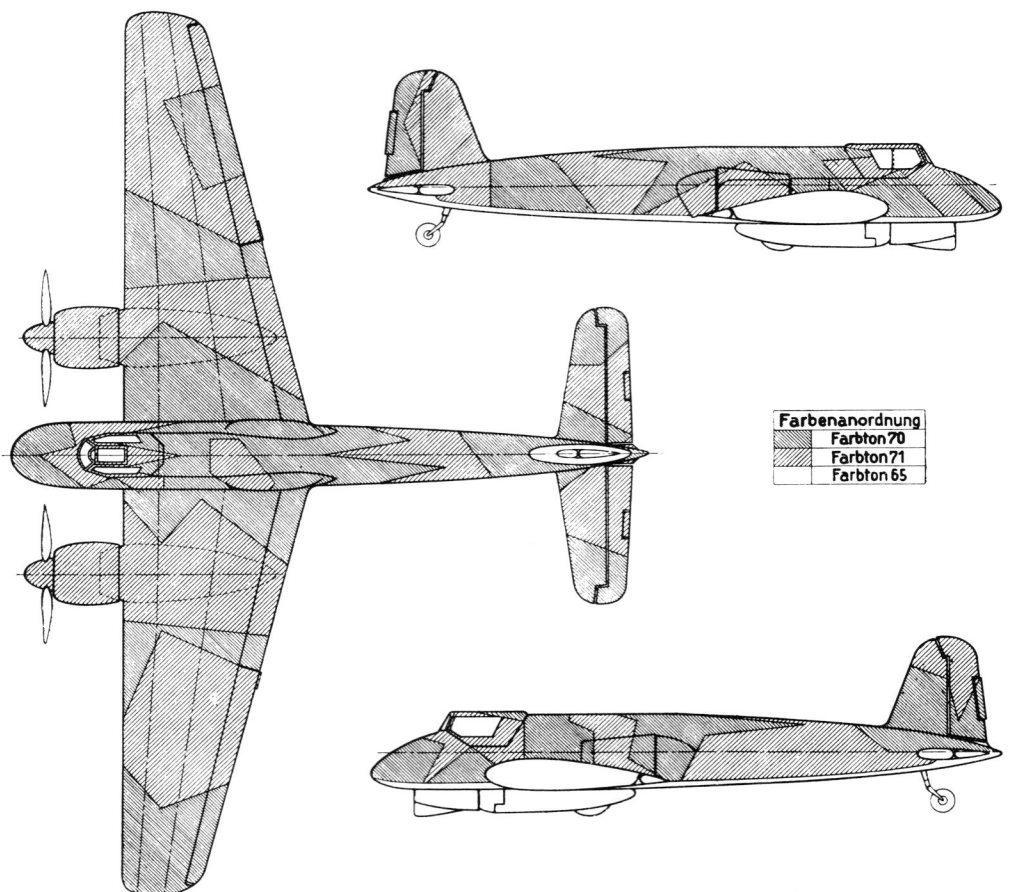

Diag. 1
standard RLM camouflage pattern taken from:
D.(Luft)T.2129 B-1 u. B-2
Teil 0
Allgemeine Angaben
Flugzeug-Handbuch
(Stand Januar 1944).

Colour Key:
70 Schwartzgrün
(Black Green)
71 Dunkelgrün
(Dark Green)
65 Hellblau
(Light Blue)

The documents illustrating this and the next four pages are reproduced from official RLM aircraft handbooks relating to the Henschel Hs 129 B-1 and B-2 as published in March 1944. They are reproduced here in their original German form.

Once aircraft had been accepted for operational service, the RLM required that a full set of maintenance manuals be produced by the manufacturers so that *Luftwaffe* ground crews could keep the aircraft serviceable. These Service Manuals *(Flugzeug Handbuch)* were divided into several standard parts numbered from 0 to 11, with each part dealing in detail on every different aspect of the aircraft. The formula for these publications is complex and space precludes going into any great detail here, but this subject will be discussed more fully in one of our future publications.

One of the most interesting Manuals was *Teil 0, Allgemeine Angaben* (Part 0, General Specifications) which provided an overview of the aircraft, including in many instances, a drawing showing the standard camouflage pattern with precise RLM colours as well as exact positions and dimensions of the national insignia (see diagram 1 & 3).

However, as most studies of Luftwaffe camouflage and markings have shown, although aircraft may have left the factory sporting the standard finish, once they reached the front it was not long before the ground crews were concerned with keeping the aircraft airworthy rather than debate about whether they had the right shade of green.

The Hs 129 was no exception. In fact, because the aircraft were working in close support of the army, the airfields were often very close to the front line. In addition, with the vastness of the Eastern Front, the units were constantly being moved from one makeshift airfield to another. This coupled with continuous operations in all weathers, meant that the machines suffered damage from exposure as well as combat.

The photographs in this book give ample testimony that the Hs 129 very rarely found itself in a hangar but was left out in the open in all weathers. The rough treatment obviously had a great effect on the original paintwork which was often overpainted with washable white winter paint which always left some residue after removal.

The colour illustrations in this work show a variety of individual aircraft camouflage schemes and unit markings which are described in detail with each illustration.

Diagram 2 indicates the placement of stencilling information showing exactly what and where information should be positioned. The DIN *(Deutsche Industrie Normen)* stencil references are clearly indicated, together with the size and type of lettering. The second set of stencil references, HsN, are believed to stand for *"Henschel Nummer"* and related to the Henschel Company's own standard. Whether or not, every aircraft carried all the necessary markings is doubtful so the reader and modeller need to undertake their own research into each specific aircraft and apply their findings accordingly.

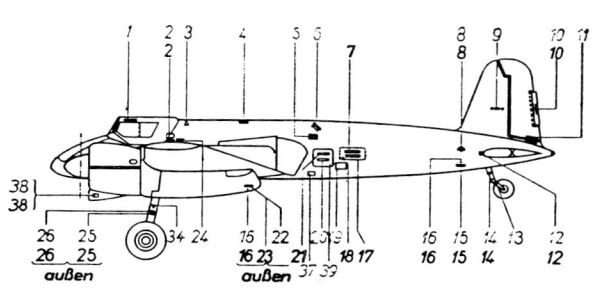
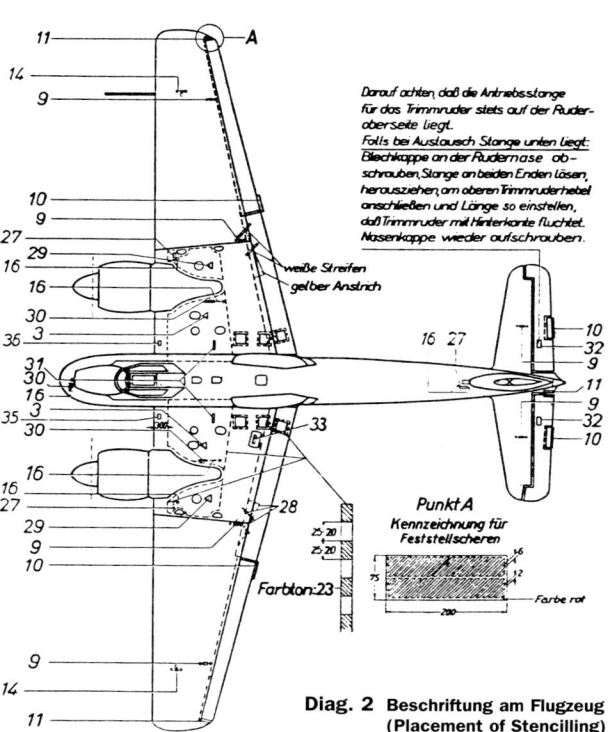

Diag. 2 Beschriftung am Flugzeug
(Placement of Stencilling)

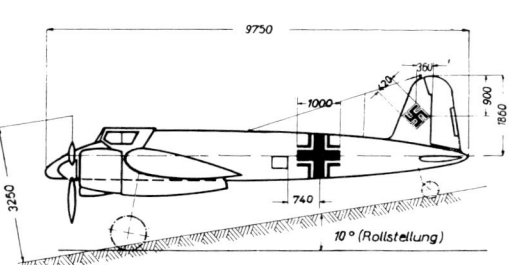

Diag. 3 Hauptmaße und Gewichte
(Main Dimensions and Weights)

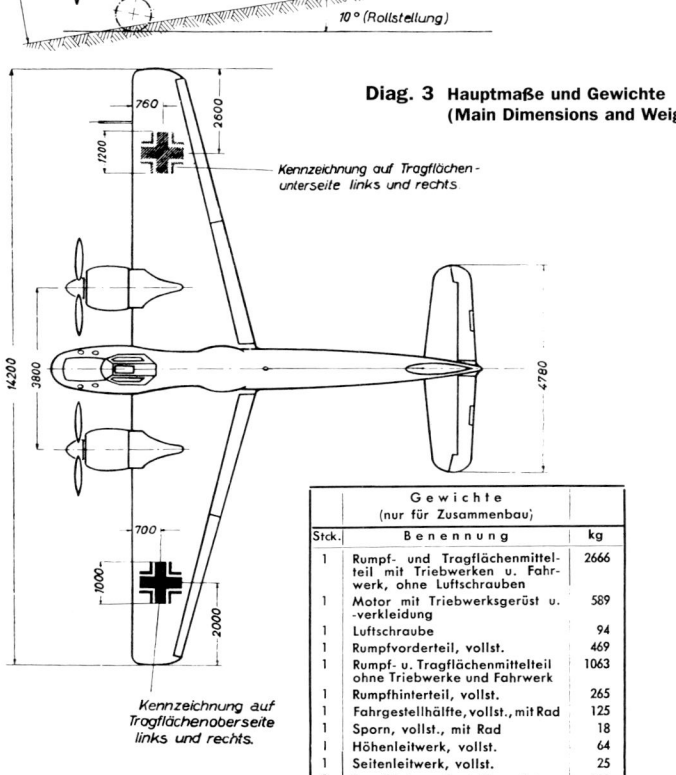

Beschriftung am Flugzeug

Nr.	Aufschrift	Schriftart
1	Haube öffnen! Nach Öffnen der Scheibe Hebel an der linken Kabinenseite ziehen!	Fette Mittelschrift 10 DIN 1451 rot
2	Druckölanlage „Fl-Drucköl"	Fette Mittelschrift 10 DIN 1451 rot
3	△ Kraftstoff-Kennzeichnung B 4	LgN 16 616
4	Akku	Fette Mittelschrift 16 DIN 1451 rot
5	Drücken für Leiter (nur bis W. Nr. 0290)	HsN 16 625.37
6	Handgriffklappe	HsN 16 625.36
7	Bordsack	Fette Mittelschrift 10 DIN 1451 weiß
8	Hier anheben	HsN 16 625.10
9	Einstellehre	HsN 16 625.45
10	Nicht anfassen	HsN 16 625.7
11	Kennzeichnung für Feststellscheren	Siehe Punkt A
12	Kennzeichnung für Höhenflossen-einstellung	Siehe Nivelliermeßblatt, Abb. 17
13	Reifendruck 3,5 atü	HsN 16 625.13
14	Verankerung	HsN 16 625.6
15	Hier Lagerjoch	HsN 16 625.11
16	Pfeil	HsN 16 625.2
17	Motorbezüge (Kofferraum RHT)	Fette Mittelschrift 12,5 DIN 1451 weiß
18	Preßluft	HsN 16 625.8
19	Rotes Kreuz	HsN 16 625.27
20	Handkurbel mit Verlängerung	Fette Mittelschrift 10 DIN 1451 weiß
21	Bordbuch, Schematasche	Fette Mittelschrift 10 DIN 1451 weiß
22	Werkzeugtasche	Fette Mittelschrift 10 DIN 1451 rot
23	Bezug für Laufrad	Fette Mittelschrift 10 DIN 1451 rot
24	Zerstörkörper	Fette Mittelschrift 10 DIN 1451 rot
25	Für Bremsen „Fl-D"	Fette Mittelschrift 10 DIN 1451 schwarz
26	Reifendruck 4 atü	Fette Mittelschrift 10 DIN 1451 schwarz
27	Hier aufbocken	HsN 16 625.5
28	Kennzeichnung für Landeklappen-einstellung	Siehe Zeichnung 129.502/512 Bl. 4
29	△ Schmierstoff-Kennzeichnung Aero Shell mittel	HsN 16 625.51
30	Hier aufheißen	HsN 16 625.17
31	Nur hier betreten	HsN 16 625.33
32	Siehe Text auf der Abbildung (bis W. Nr. 0188)	Fette Mittelschrift 8 DIN 1451 weiß
33	Bereitschaftsbüchse (Gasmaske) MP und Stahlhelm	Fette Mittelschrift 10 DIN 1451 weiß
34	Füllmarke für Stoßdämpfer (roter Strich)	Fette Mittelschrift 10 DIN 1451 schwarz
35	Preßluftanschluß für Druckspeicher (ab W. Nr. 0331)	Fette Mittelschrift 16 DIN 1451 weiß
36	Außenbordanschluß für Druckölanlage (ab W. Nr. 0331)	Fette Mittelschrift 16 DIN 1451 weiß
37	Ziehen für Leiter (ab W. Nr. 0291)	Fette Mittelschrift 10 DIN 1451 schwarz
38	Luftfilter nach jedem zweiten Start reinigen Bei Winterbetrieb wegen Vereisungsgefahr mit offener Nebeneinlaßklappe fliegen	Fette Mittelschrift 10 DIN 1451 schwarz
39	Endkappe für Re (ab W. Nr. 0331)	Fette Mittelschrift 10 DIN 1451 weiß

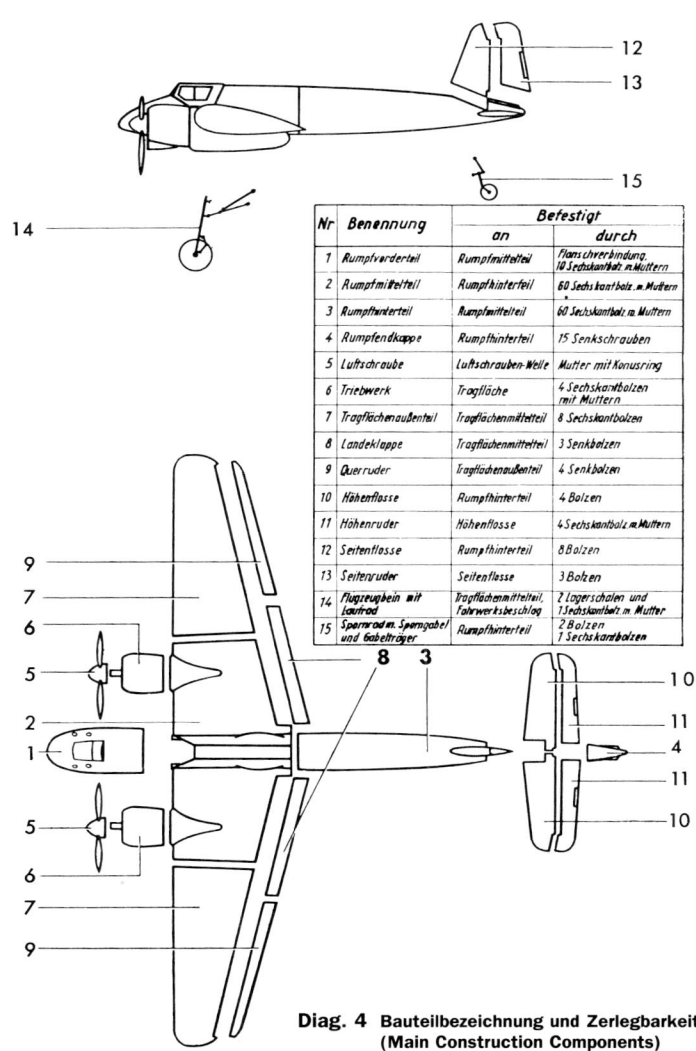

Diag. 4 Bauteilbezeichnung und Zerlegbarkeit
(Main Construction Components)

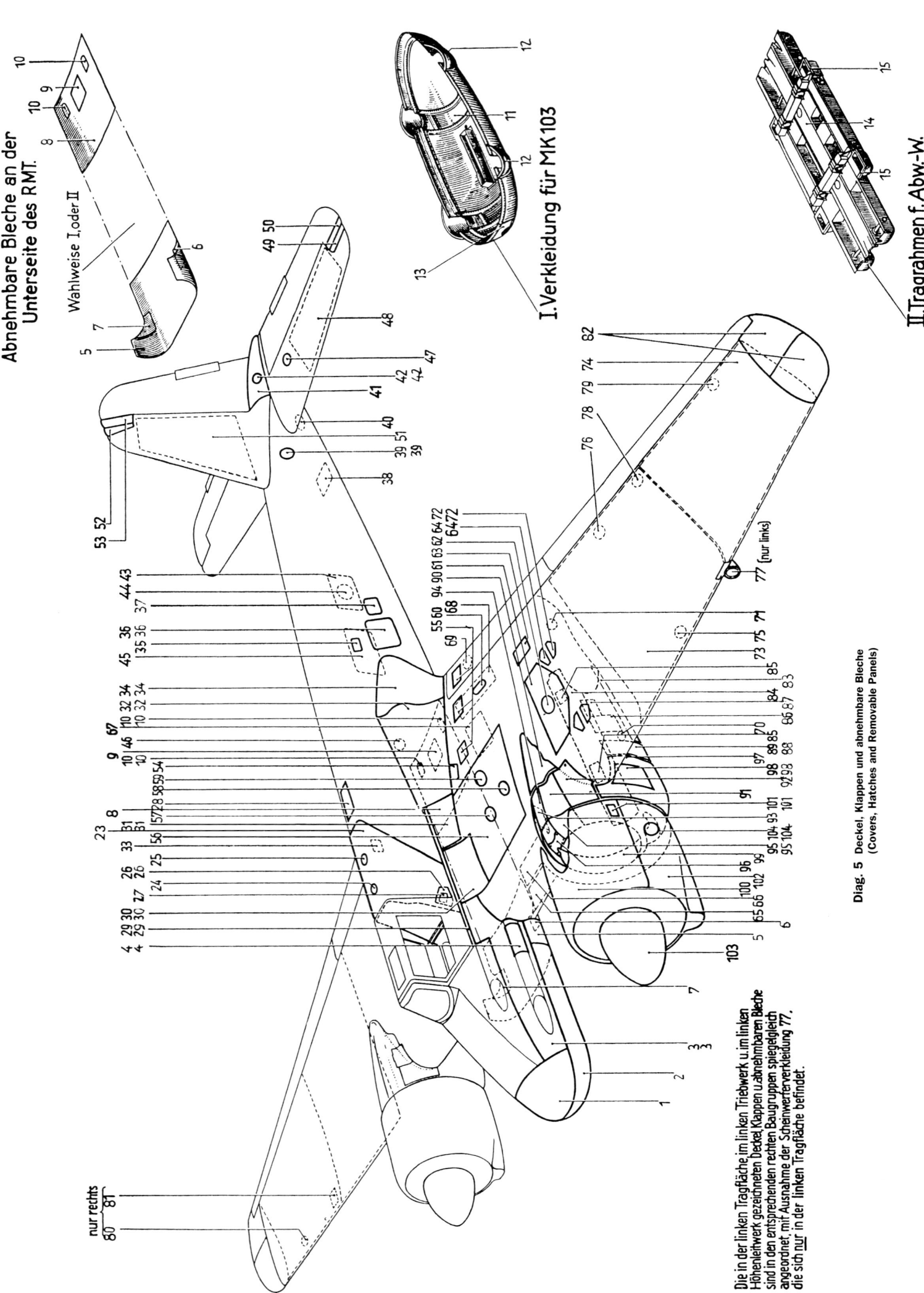

Diag. 5 Deckel, Klappen und abnehmbare Bleche (Covers, Hatches and Removable Panels)

Deckel, Klappen und abnehmbare Bleche
(Covers, Hatches and Removable Panels)

Nr.	Lage	Zweck	Befestigung durch
1	Rumpfvorderteil, vorn	Zugang zur vorderen Wand der Panzerkabine, Heißbeschlag, Heizaggregat	Schnellverschlüsse
2	Rumpfvorderteil, unten	Zugang zu den Befestigungsbolzen für Panzerplatte, zu den elektrischen Schalttafeln und den unteren Trennstellen zwischen RVT und RMT	Schnellverschlüsse
3	Rumpfvorderteil, links und rechts	Übergangsverkleidung: Zugang zu den Trennstellen zwischen RVT und RMT, zur Handpumpe und zum Umschalter für Druckölanlage, Fertigung und Zusammenbau	Schnellverschlüsse
4	Rumpfvorderteil, links und rechts	Seitenjustierung des MG 17	Linsensenkschrauben
5	Rumpfmittelteil, unten	Zugang zur unteren Aufhängung der Panzerkabine und zu den unteren Trennstellen zwischen RVT und RMT; Höhenjustierung für MG 17	Schnellverschlüsse
6	Rumpfmittelteil, unten links	Zugang zum Preßluftanschluß für Druckspeicher der Druckölanlage, Elt-Leitungen	Schnellverschlüsse
7	Rumpfmittelteil, unten rechts	Zugang zu den Außenbordanschlüssen für Druckölanlage, Elt-Leitungen	Schnellverschlüsse
8	Rumpfmittelteil, unten	Zugang zu den Einbauten im RMT und RHT	Flügelmuttern
9	Rumpfmittelteil, unten Mitte	Entleeren des Hülsenkastens	Schnellverschlüsse
10	Rumpfmittelteil, unten links und rechts	links: Blinddeckel; rechts: Zugang zum Anschluß des Zünderbatteriekastens ZBK 241/1	Schnellverschlüsse
11	Rumpfmittelteil, unten	Verkleidung für MK 103	Linsenschrauben
12	Rumpfmittelteil, unten links	Zugang zu den Verbindungsbolzen für Anschluß der MK 103 an den Rumpf	Scharnier
13	Rumpfmittelteil, unten	Anbaugründe	
14	Rumpfmittelteil, unten	Verkleidung für Tragrahmen der Abwurfwaffe	Verriegelung
15	Rumpfmittelteil, unten links	Zugang zu den Anschlußstellen für Tragrahmen der Abwurfwaffe	Verriegelung
23	Rumpfmittelteil, oben	Kraftstoffbehälteraus- und -einbau	Linsensenkschrauben
24	Rumpfmittelteil, oben	Zugang zum Füllkopf für den Kraftstoffbehälter	Schnellverschluß
25	Rumpfmittelteil, oben	Zugang zum Kraftstoffbehälterkopf (Anschluß der Leitungen)	Schnellverschluß
26	Rumpfmittelteil, links und rechts	Zugang zum Auffüllen der Druckölbehälter	Schnellverschluß
27	Rumpfmittelteil, links	Zugang zum Zerstörkörper	Scheibe
28	Rumpfmittelteil, oben	Zugang zur Batterie für Elt-Ausrüstung	Schnellverschluß
29	Rumpfmittelteil, links und rechts	Zugang zu den Haubenführungen	Linsensenkschrauben
30	Rumpfmittelteil, links und rechts	Wartung des MG 17	Schnellverschluß
31	Rumpfmittelteil, links und rechts	Wartung des MG 17	Schnellverschluß
32	Rumpfmittelteil, links und rechts	Wartung des MG 151	Schnellverschlüsse
33	Rumpfmittelteil, rechts	Zugang zur elektr. Schalttafel am Spant 3, RMT	Schnellverschluß
34	Rumpfhinterteil, links und rechts	Ein- und Ausbau des EDSK 151 B für MG 151	Linsensenkschrauben
35	Rumpfhinterteil, links	Handgriff zum Auslösen der Aufstiegleiter	Scharnier mit Federn
36	Rumpfhinterteil, links und rechts	Zugang zum Geräteblock der Funkanlage; rechts: auch ZBK 241/1	Schnellverschlüsse
37	Rumpfhinterteil, links	Zugang zum Sanitätspack	Schnellverschluß
38	Rumpfhinterteil, unten	Zugang zum Umlenkhebel für Höhensteuerung, Ein- und Ausbau des Sporns	Linsensenkschrauben
39	Rumpfhinterteil, links und rechts	Zugang zum Umlenkhebel für Höhensteuerung, Ein- und Ausbau des Sporns	Schnellverschlüsse
40	Rumpfhinterteil, unten	Prüfung der Steuerung im Rumpfhinterteil	Linsensenkschrauben
41	Rumpfhinterteil, Endkappe	Zugang zum Steuerungsgestänge im Rumpfhinterteil, zum unteren Seitenruderlager, zum mittleren Höhenruderlager, Leitwerksmontage	Linsensenkschrauben
42	Rumpfhinterteil, in Endkappe links und rechts	Zugang zum Hecklicht, Steuerungsanschluß am Seitenruder	Schnellverschlüsse
43	Rumpfhinterteil, rechts	Ein- und Ausbau des Mutterkompasses	Linsensenkschrauben
44	Rumpfhinterteil, rechts	Justierung des Mutterkompasses	Schnellverschluß
45	Rumpfhinterteil, rechts	Zugang zum Kofferraum, Preßluftanschluß	Schnellverschlüsse
46	Rumpfhinterteil, rechts	Außenbordanschluß für elektrisches Bordnetz	Schnellverschluß
47	Höhenflosse links und rechts, oben und unten	Anbau der Höhenflosse an den Rumpf, Zugang zum Bolzen für Höhenflossenverstellung	Schnellverschlüsse
48	Höhenflosse, Unterseite	Zugang zu den Einbauten der Höhenflosse zwecks Prüfung und Wartung	Linsensenkschrauben
49	Höhenflosse Aerodynam. Ausgleich	Fertigungsgründe	Linsensenkschrauben
50	Höhenruder, Aerodynam. Ausgleich	Einbau der Ausgleichsgewichte	Linsensenkschrauben
51	Seitenflosse, rechts	Zugang zu den Einbauten der Seitenflosse zwecks Prüfung und Wartung	Linsensenkschrauben
52	Seitenflosse, Aerodynam. Ausgleich	Fertigungsgründe	Linsensenkschrauben
53	Seitenruder, Aerodynam. Ausgleich	Einbau des Ausgleichsgewichtes	Linsensenkschrauben
54	Tragflächenmittelteil, links und rechts	Zugang zum Zuführungshals für MG 151	Gehalten durch Klappe 32
55	Tragflächenmittelteil, links und rechts	Auftrittklappen	Druckfedern
56	Tragflächenmittelteil, links und rechts	Kraftstoffbehälterein- und -ausbau	Linsensenkschrauben
57	Tragflächenmittelteil, links und rechts	Zugang zum elektrischen Vorratsgeber für Kraftstoff	Schnellverschlüsse
58	Tragflächenmittelteil, links und rechts	Zugang zum Füllkopf für den Kraftstoffbehälter	Schnellverschlüsse
59	Tragflächenmittelteil, links und rechts	Zugang zum Kraftstoffbehälterkopf (Anschluß der Leitungen)	Schnellverschlüsse
60	Tragflächenmittelteil, links und rechts	Zugang zur Gasmaske	Schnellverschlüsse
61	Tragflächenmittelteil, links und rechts	Schmierstoffbehälterein- und -ausbau	Linsensenkschrauben
62	Tragflächenmittelteil, links und rechts	Zugang zum Füllkopf für den Schmierstoffbehälter	Schnellverschlüsse
63	Tragflächenmittelteil, links und rechts	Zugang zur Aufhängung des Schmierstoffkühlers und zu den Trennstellen der Kühlerleitungen	Linsensenkschrauben
64	Tragflächenmittelteil, links und rechts	Zugang zu den Verbindungsbolzen zwischen Tragflächenmittel- und -außenteil	Schnellverschlüsse
65	Tragflächenmittelteil, links und rechts	Zugang zum Triebwerksbedienungsgestänge in der Tragflächennase	Schnellverschlüsse
66	Tragflächenmittelteil, links und rechts	Einsetzen und Herausnehmen des Vollgurtkastens für MG 17	Spezialverschluß
67	Tragflächenmittelteil, links und rechts	MG 17 Aus- und Einbau	Linsensenkschrauben
68	Tragflächenmittelteil, links und rechts	Einsetzen und Herausnehmen des Vollgurtkastens für MG 151	Spezialverschluß
69	Tragflächenmittelteil, Landeklappe, links und rechts	Links: Zugänglichkeit der Landeklappe für Einbau der Auftrittklappe 55, rechts: blind	Schnellverschlüsse
70	Tragflächenmittelteil, links und rechts	Zugang für Elt-Trennstellen, rechts: auch zu den Entwässerungsstutzen für Fahrtmesserleitungen	Schnellverschlüsse
71	Tragflächenmittelteil, links und rechts	Zugang für Elt-Trennstellen Bombennotzug	Schnellverschlüsse
72	Tragflächenaußenteil, links und rechts	Zugang zu den Verbindungsbolzen zwischen Tragflächenmittel- und -außenteil	Schnellverschlüsse
73	Tragflächenaußenteil, links und rechts	Zugang zu den Einbauten; Fertigungsgründe	Linsensenkschrauben
74	Tragflächenaußenteil, links und rechts	Zugang zu den Einbauten; Fertigungsgründe	Linsensenkschrauben
75	Tragflächenaußenteil, links und rechts	Zugang zu den Elt-Verbindungen für Abwurfwaffe	Schnellverschlüsse
76	Tragflächenaußenteil, links und rechts	Zugang zu den Elt-Verbindungen für Abwurfwaffe	Schnellverschlüsse
77	Tragflächenaußenteil, links	Scheinwerferaus- und -Einbau, Zugang zum Elt-Anschluß für Scheinwerfer	Linsensenkschrauben
78	Tragflächenaußenteil, links und rechts	Zugang zum Umlenkhebel für Querruder bei Querwand 6	Schnellverschlüsse
79	Tragflächenaußenteil, links und rechts	Rechts: Zugang zu den Schlauchverbindungen der Fahrt- und Höhenmesserleitung; Elt-Stecker für Staurohr links: blind	Schnellverschlüsse
80	Tragflächenaußenteil, rechts	Zugang zur Fahrt- und Höhenmesserleitung und Luftleitung für Staurohr	Schnellverschluß
81	Tragflächenaußenteil, rechts	Kameraein- und -ausbau	Schnellverschlüsse
82	Tragflächenaußenteil, links und rechts	Zugang zur Elt-Ausrüstung in den Tragflächenspitzen; Fertigungsgründe	Linsensenkschrauben
83	Fahrwerkskabine, äußere Klappe	Montage der Einbauten in der Fahrwerkskabine	Linsensenkschrauben
84	Fahrwerkskabine, innere Klappe	Verkleidung des eingezogenen Fahrbeins	Gummiseil und Fahrgestellbein
85	Fahrwerkskabine, innere Klappe	Fertigungsgründe: Zugang zu den Scharnieren der inneren Klappe	Linsensenkschrauben
86	Fahrwerkskabine	Zugang zur Anlaßgerätetafel	Schnellverschlüsse
87	Fahrwerkskabine	Zugang zum Schnellablaßventil des Schmierstoffbehälters	Schnellverschlüsse
88	Fahrwerkskabine	Auf- und Abbau des Fahrgestells, Zugang zu den Thermometeranschlüssen der Schmierstoffleitungen, zum Bedienungsgestänge für Einspritzpumpen, Bremsleitungen	Linsensenkschrauben
89	Fahrwerkskabine	Auf- und Abbau des Fahrgestells	Linsensenkschrauben
90	Übergang Motorraum-Tragflächenmittelteil	Zugang zum Elt-Trennstellengehäuse Übergangsverkleidung	Linsensenkschrauben
91	Motorraum, oben	Triebwerkswechsel, Zugang zu Triebwerksleitungen und -geräten	Linsensenkschrauben
92	Motorraum: linker Motor, linke Seite, rechter Motor, rechte Seite	Prüfung der oberen Triebwerksgerüstanschlüsse, Triebwerkswechsel	Schnellverschlüsse
93	Motorraum: linker Motor, rechte Seite, rechter Motor, linke Seite	Prüfung der oberen Triebwerksgerüstanschlüsse, Triebwerkswechsel	Schnellverschlüsse
94	Motorraum, oben	Zugang zu Triebwerksleitungen und -geräten	Schnellverschlüsse
95	Motorraum, oben	Zugang zu den Triebwerksgeräten, Aus- und Einbau des Stromerzeugers	Linsensenkschrauben
96	Motorraum, oben	Fertigungsgründe, Aus- und Einbau des Stromerzeugers	Linsensenkschrauben
97	Motorraum, unten	Triebwerkswechsel, Zugang zu Triebwerksleitungen und -geräten	Schnellverschlüsse
98	Motorraum, links und rechts	Prüfung der unteren Triebwerksgerüstanschlüsse, Zugang zu Triebwerksleitungen	Schnellverschlüsse
99	Motorraum	Zugang zu Triebwerksgeräten	Linsensenkschrauben
100	Motor, oben	Motorverkleidung	Spannverschlüsse
101	Motor, oben	Zugang zur Sicherung des Spannverschlusses der Motorverkleidung	Linsensenkschrauben
102	Motor, unten	Motorverkleidung	Spannverschlüsse
103	Luftschraube	Zugang zur Luftschraubennabe und zum Verstellgetriebe	Linsensenkschrauben
104	Motor, unten	Zugang zum Schmierstoffsumpf und Zündkerzen	Schnellverschlüsse

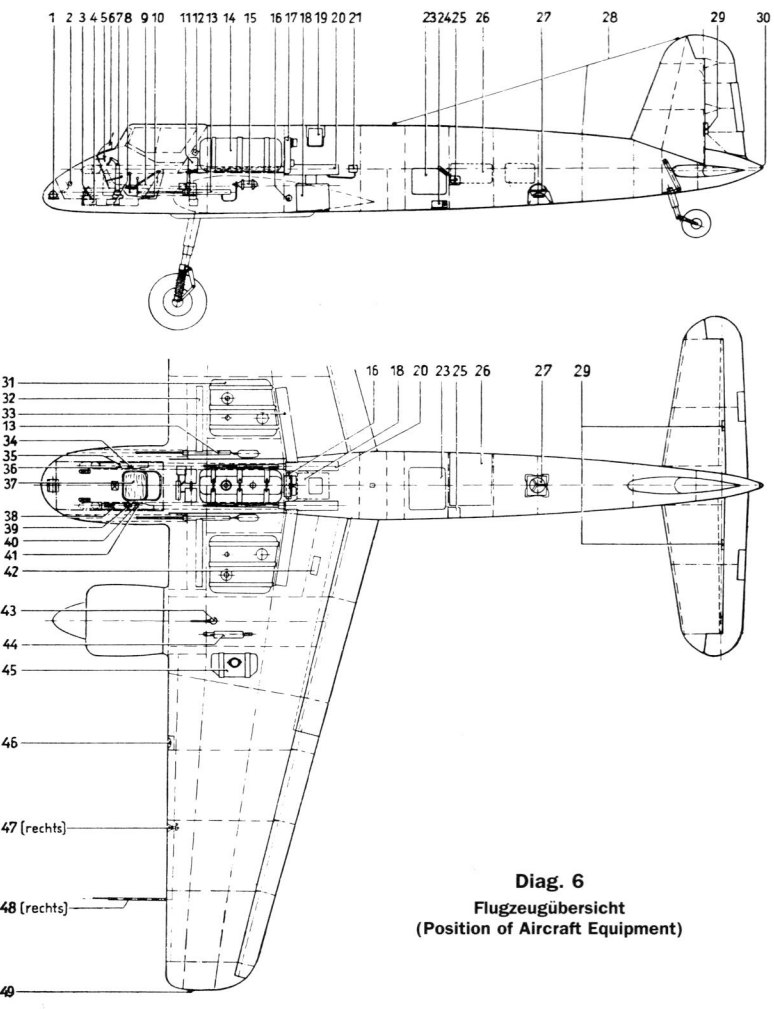

Diag. 6
Flugzeugübersicht
(Position of Aircraft Equipment)

Flugzeugübersicht

Nr.	Benennung	Einbauort
1	Lufterhitzer (ab W. Nr. 0331)	RVT, Stirnwand der P-Kabine
2	Boschhorn (bis W. Nr. 0300)	RVT, Führerraum
3	Seitensteuerpedal mit Bremsfußpumpe	RVT, Führerraum
4	Hauptschalttafel	RVT, unter der P-Kabine
5	Handgriff für Bombennotzug	RVT, Führergerätetafel
6	Revi	RVT, oben
7	Steuerknüppel für Höhen- und Quersteuerung	RVT, Führerraum
8	Waffenschalttafel	RVT, unter der P-Kabine
9	Führersitz	RVT, Führerraum
10	Führersitzverstellung	RVT, Führersitz
11	Drucköltbehälter für Druckölanlage	RMT, zwischen Spant 1 und 2
12	Zerstörkörper	RMT, linke Rumpfseitenwand
13	MG 17	RMT, links und rechts
14	Kraftstoffbehälter 200 l	RMT, zwischen Spant 1 und 2
15	Preßluftflasche für MG 17	RMT, MG 17 links und rechts
16	Arbeitszylinder für Landeklappe	RMT, Spant 3
17	Schalttafel RMT	RMT, Spant 3
18	Leergurtkasten für MG 151	RMT, Rumpfboden zwischen Spant 3 u. 4
19	Akku	RMT, Rumpfdecke zwischen Spant 3 u. 4
20	MG 151	RMT, links und rechts
21	Edukasten für MG 151	RMT, vor Spant 4 links und rechts
23	Gerät FuG 16 z	RHT, zwischen Spant 3 und 4
24	ZBK 241/1	RHT, Rumpfboden vor Spant 4
25	Sanitätskasten	RHT, linke Rumpfseitenwand
26	Kofferraum	RHT, rechts
27	Mutterkompaß	RHT, Spant 6
28	Antenne FuG 16 z	Außenbord RHT-Seitenflosse
29	Elektrische Trimmruderverstellgetriebe	Höhenruder- und Seitenrudernase
30	Hecklicht	Rumpfende
31	Kraftstoffbehälter 2×205 l	TMT, zwischen Querwand 1 a und 2, links und rechts
32	Vollgurtkasten für MG 17	TMT, Vorderholm
33	Vollgurtkasten für MG 151	TMT, Hinterholm
34	Handgriff: Notzug für Kühlerklappen	RVT, rechte Handhebelbrücke
35	Hebel für Landeklappenbetätigung	RVT, rechte Handhebelbrücke
36	Hebel für Fahrwerkbetätigung	RVT, rechte Handhebelbrücke
37	Sitzkissenfallschirm	RVT, Führersitz
38	Hebel für Brandhahnbetätigung	RVT, linke Handhebelbrücke
39	Gashebel	RVT, linke Handhebelbrücke
40	Gemischhebel	RVT, linke Handhebelbrücke
41	Hebel für 110%-Leistung	RVT, linke Handhebelbrücke
42	Bereitschaftsbüchse (Gasmaske)	TMT, links
43	Motorbrandlöscher	Fahrwerkskabine
44	SS-Arbeitszylinder für Fahrwerk	Fahrwerkskabine
45	Schmierstoffbehälter 2×35 l	TMT, zwischen Querwand 3 und 4, links und rechts
46	Scheinwerfer	linke Tragfläche
47	Robot	rechte Tragfläche
48	Staurohr	rechte Tragfläche
49	Flugzeugkennlicht (links rot, rechts grün)	linke und rechte Tragfläche

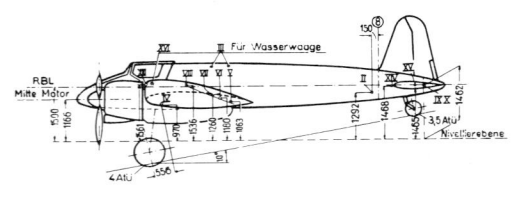

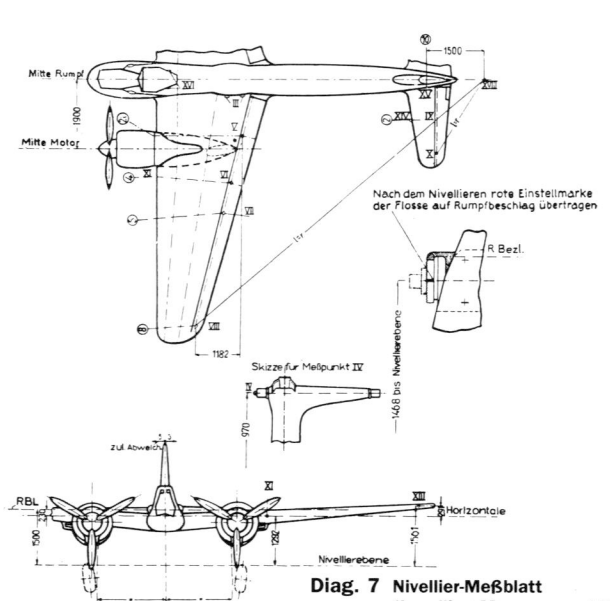

Diag. 7 Nivellier-Meßblatt
(Levelling Measurement Table)

Meß-punkt	Ort	Meß-punkt	Ort	Meß-punkt	Ort
II	Rumpfhinterteil	VII	Querruderlager Rippe 5	XIII	Vord. Flügelnasenpunkt Rippe 8
III	Flügelmittelteil	VIII	Querruderlager Rippe 8	XIV	Vord. Nasenpunkt Höhenflosse Rippe 2
IV	Fahrwerk Mitte Lagerzpf. (Innens.)	IX	Mittleres Höhenruderlager	XV	Höhenflosse-Lagerung Spant 10
V	Landeklappenlager Rippe 2 i	X	Äußeres Höhenruderlager	XVI	Obere Schußkanäle
VI	Landeklappenlager Rippe 4	XI	Vord. Flügelnasenpunkt Rippe 4	XVIII	Rumpf-Bezugslinie

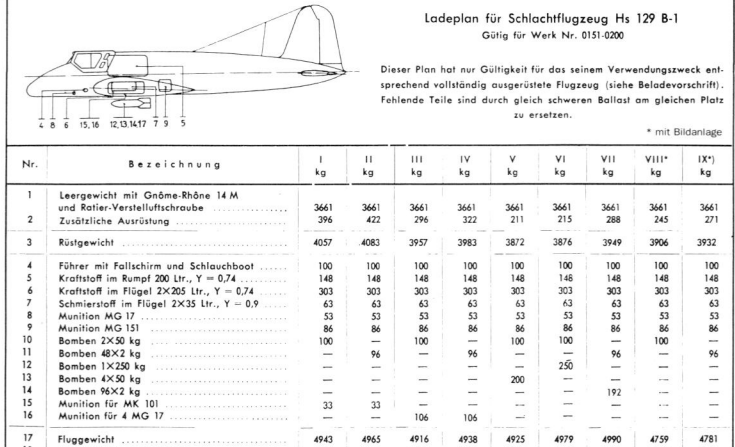

Ladeplan für Schlachtflugzeug Hs 129 B-1
Gültig für Werk Nr. 0151-0200

Dieser Plan hat nur Gültigkeit für das seinem Verwendungszweck entsprechend vollständig ausgerüstete Flugzeug (siehe Beladevorschrift). Fehlende Teile sind durch gleich schweren Ballast am gleichen Platz zu ersetzen.

* mit Bildanlage

Nr.	Bezeichnung	I kg	II kg	III kg	IV kg	V kg	VI kg	VII kg	VIII* kg	IX*) kg
1	Leergewicht mit Gnôme-Rhône 14 M und Ratier-Verstellluftschraube	3661	3661	3661	3661	3661	3661	3661	3661	3661
2	Zusätzliche Ausrüstung	396	422	296	322	211	215	288	245	271
3	Rüstgewicht	4057	4083	3957	3983	3872	3876	3949	3906	3932
4	Führer mit Fallschirm und Schlauchboot	100	100	100	100	100	100	100	100	100
5	Kraftstoff im Rumpf 200 Ltr., Y = 0,74	148	148	148	148	148	148	148	148	148
6	Kraftstoff im Flügel 2×205 Ltr., Y = 0,74	303	303	303	303	303	303	303	303	303
7	Schmierstoff im Flügel 2×35 Ltr., Y = 0,9	63	63	63	63	63	63	63	63	63
8	Munition MG 17	53	53	53	53	53	53	53	53	53
9	Munition MG 151	86	86	86	86	86	86	86	86	86
10	Bomben 2×50 kg	100	—	100	—	100	100	—	100	—
11	Bomben 48×2 kg	—	96	—	96	—	—	96	—	96
12	Bomben 1×250 kg	—	—	—	—	—	250	—	—	—
13	Bomben 4×50 kg	—	—	—	—	200	—	—	—	—
14	Bomben 96×2 kg	—	—	—	—	—	—	192	—	—
15	Munition für MK 101	33	33	—	—	—	—	—	—	—
16	Munition für 4 MG 17	—	—	106	106	—	—	—	—	—
17	Fluggewicht	4943	4965	4916	4938	4925	4979	4990	4759	4781
18	Abgerundetes Fluggewicht	4940	4970	4920	4940	4930	4980	4990	4760	4780
19	Höchstzulässiges Fluggewicht	5000 kg (H 4)								

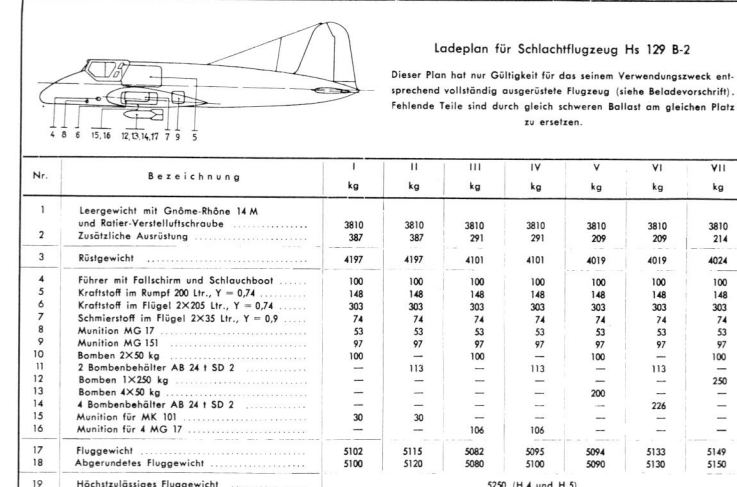

Ladeplan für Schlachtflugzeug Hs 129 B-2

Dieser Plan hat nur Gültigkeit für das seinem Verwendungszweck entsprechend vollständig ausgerüstete Flugzeug (siehe Beladevorschrift). Fehlende Teile sind durch gleich schweren Ballast am gleichen Platz zu ersetzen.

Nr.	Bezeichnung	I kg	II kg	III kg	IV kg	V kg	VI kg	VII kg
1	Leergewicht mit Gnôme-Rhône 14 M und Ratier-Verstellluftschraube	3810	3810	3810	3810	3810	3810	3810
2	Zusätzliche Ausrüstung	387	387	291	291	209	209	214
3	Rüstgewicht	4197	4197	4101	4101	4019	4019	4024
4	Führer mit Fallschirm und Schlauchboot	100	100	100	100	100	100	100
5	Kraftstoff im Rumpf 200 Ltr., Y = 0,74	148	148	148	148	148	148	148
6	Kraftstoff im Flügel 2×205 Ltr., Y = 0,74	303	303	303	303	303	303	303
7	Schmierstoff im Flügel 2×35 Ltr., Y = 0,9	74	74	74	74	74	74	74
8	Munition MG 17	53	53	53	53	53	53	53
9	Munition MG 151	97	97	97	97	97	97	97
10	Bomben 2×50 kg	100	—	100	—	100	—	—
11	2 Bombenbehälter AB 24 t SD 2	—	113	—	113	—	113	—
12	Bomben 1×250 kg	—	—	—	—	—	—	250
13	Bomben 4×50 kg	—	—	—	—	200	—	—
14	4 Bombenbehälter AB 24 t SD 2	—	—	—	—	—	226	—
15	Munition für MK 101	30	30	—	—	—	—	—
16	Munition für 4 MG 17	—	—	106	106	—	—	—
17	Fluggewicht	5102	5115	5082	5095	5094	5133	5149
18	Abgerundetes Fluggewicht	5100	5120	5080	5100	5090	5130	5150
19	Höchstzulässiges Fluggewicht	5250 kg (H 4 und H 5)						

APPENDIX THREE

Loss Lists

22 February Hs 129 B-2 W.Nr.0278 underwing code DQ+ZN 8.(Pz)/Sch.G 2. Suffered engine failure at Bou Flidja. 30% damage.

22 February Hs 129 B-2 W.Nr.0317 8.(Pz)/Sch.G 2. 20% Bomb damaged on El Aouina airfield.

24 February Hs 129 B-2 W.Nr.0295 8.(Pz)/Sch.G 2. Burst tyre on landing at Gabes-East. 35% damage.

24 February Hs 129 B-2 W.Nr.0413 Flugzeugleitstelle Lfl.Kdo.2. Oblt. Karl-Peter Bartel injured in emergency landing due to lack of fuel, SEW of Sernaglia. 80% damage.

10 March Hs 129 B-2 W.Nr.0437 Crashed at Henschel-Flzg.-Werke Johannisthal. Civilian pilot killed. 100% destroyed.

17 March Hs 129 B-2 W.Nr.0382 Flugzeugleitstelle Lfl.Kdo.2. Uffz Mörsch injured due to engine failure, Gallico. 100% destroyed.

17 March Hs 129 B-2 W.Nr.0394 Pz.Jg.Kdo.Weiss. Aircraft 100% destroyed by bomb damage on Zaporozhye-East airfield.

21 March Hs 129 B-2 W.Nr.0416 8.(Pz)/Sch.G 1. Damaged taxiing at Kharkov airfield. 15% damage.

22 March Hs 129 B-2 W.Nr.0316 Coded J, 8.(Pz)/Sch.G 2. Fw. Otto Kiefer crashed at Maknassy due to enemy ground fire, pilot injured. 100% destroyed.

22 March Hs 129 B-2 W.Nr.0340 Coded G, 8.(Pz)/Sch.G 2. Crashed at Mezzouna due to enemy ground fire. 100% destroyed.

22 March Hs 129 B-2 W.Nr.0343 8.(Pz)/Sch.G 2. Hit by AA fire over El Guettar. 15% damage.

22 March Hs 129 B-2 W.Nr.0387 8.(Pz)/Sch.G 2. Attacked by fighter(s) near Maknassy. 20% damage.

23 March Hs 129 B-2 W.Nr.0426 Erg.Zerst.Gr. Lt. Herbert Elend injured when aircraft struck the ground at Deblin-Garwolin due to pilot error. 100% destroyed.

26 March Hs 129 B-2 W.Nr.0422 Erg.Zerst.Gr. Aircraft rammed by Fw. 190 at Deblin-Irena airfield. 30% damage.

26 March Hs 129 B-2 W.Nr.0429 Erg.Zerst.Gr. Aircraft struck the ground at Glac-Morovina due to pilot error. 20% damage.

27 March Hs 129 B-2 W.Nr.0259 8.(Pz)/Sch.G 2. Uffz. Hans-Joachim Hesse killed when aircraft hit by AA fire 20km SW. of El Hamma. 100% destroyed. .

27 March Hs 129 B-2 W.Nr.0352 8.(Pz)/Sch.G 2. Hit by enemy ground fire at El Hamma. 65% damage.

27 March Hs 129 B-2 W.Nr.0388 8.(Pz)/Sch.G 2. Uffz. Karl Krauss injured in belly landing after aircraft hit by AA fire NE. of El Hamma. 100% destroyed.

05 April Hs 129 B-2 W.Nr.0377 8.(Pz)/Sch.G 1. Obgfr. Gerhard Sembritzki wounded by ground defences in Map Grid Qu.7526. Aircraft 100% destroyed.

05 April Hs 129 B-2 W.Nr.0380 8.(Pz)/Sch.G 2. 50% bomb damaged on Tunis airfield.

05 April Hs 129 B-2 W.Nr.0408 8.(Pz)/Sch.G 2. 45% bomb damaged on Tunis airfield.

07 April Hs 129 B-2 W.Nr.0385 Coded blue G, 8.(Pz)/Sch.G 2. Hit by AA fire at Toubakeur. 20% damage.

08 April Hs 129 B-2 W.Nr.0381 8.(Pz)/Sch.G 2. Hit by AA fire at Dar el Bay. 40% damage.

10 April Hs 129 B-2 W.Nr.0391 8.(Pz)/Sch.G 2. Ofw. Albert Busch missing after aircraft belly-landed in enemy territory having been hit by AA fire or as a result of air combat with a Spitfire 10km NE. of Qued Zarga. 100% destroyed.

12 April Hs 129 B-2 W.Nr.0423 Coded M, 4.(Pz)/Sch.G 1. Lt. Otto Mostböck killed. Aircraft crashed and burst into flames following engine failure at Stalino-North airfield. 100% destroyed.

15 April Hs 129 B-2 W.Nr.0347 Coded R, 8.(Pz)/Sch.G 1. Fw. Walter Thiel killed. Aircraft crashed at Werch railway station following air combat. 100% destroyed.

15 April Hs 129 B-2 W.Nr.0372 8.(Pz)/Sch.G 1. Fw. Günther Hilgendag injured in emergency landing as a result of being hit by AA fire N. of hill near Werch-Bakanskaja. 100% destroyed.

15 April Hs 129 B-2 W.Nr.0378 8.(Pz)/Sch.G 1. Engine failure at Kerch. 15% damage.

15 April Hs 129 B-2 W.Nr.0409 8.(Pz)/Sch.G 1. Hit by AA fire at Anapa. 40% damage.

16 April Hs 129 B 8.(Pz)/Sch.G 1. Fw. Ernst Beutter wounded by ground defences near Krymskaya. 100% destroyed.

16 April Hs 129 B-2 W.Nr.0435 8.(Pz)/Sch.G 1. Uffz. Hans Trenkel injured when aircraft hit by AA fire over Werch-Bakanskaja. 100% destroyed.

16 April Hs 129 B-1 W.Nr.0196 Erg.Sch.Gr. Uffz. Werner Wolf in emergency landing at Deblin-Irena due to engine failure. 50% damage.

17 April Hs 129 B-2 W.Nr.0421 4.(Pz)/Sch.G 1. Engine failure at Stalino. 50% damage

19 April Hs 129 B-2 W.Nr.0290 Erg.Sch.Gr. Engine failure at Deblin-Irena. 65% damage.

21 April Hs 129 B-0 W.Nr.0025 Coded 4M+ZD, 2./Erg.Sch.Gr. Uffz. Wolfgang Keller injured in crash due to accidental contact with the ground, SE. of Garbolin. 90% damage.

23 April Hs 129 B-2 W.Nr.0257 Erg.Sch.Gr. Emergency landing near Deblin due to engine failure. 20% damage.

23 April Hs 129 B-2 W.Nr.0330 Erg.Sch.Gr. Belly landing on Deblin-Irena airfield. 10% damage.

24 April Hs 129 B-0 W.Nr.0023 Erg.Sch.Gr. Uffz. Theodor Keller in emergency landing near Warsaw due to engine failure. 70% damage.

26 April Hs 129 B-2 W.Nr.0313 Flugzeugleitstelle Lfl.Kdo.2. Bombed on Bari airfield. 40% damage.

26 April Hs 129 B-2 W.Nr.0321 Flugzeugleitstelle Lfl.Kdo.2. Bombed on Bari airfield. 60% damage.

26 April Hs 129 B-2 W.Nr.0429 Flugzeugleitstelle Lfl.Kdo.2. Bombed on Bari airfield. 40% damage.

26 April Hs 129 B-2 W.Nr.140496 Flugzeugleitstelle Lfl.Kdo.2. Bombed on Bari airfield. 100% destroyed.

26 April Hs 129 B-2 W.Nr.140503 Flugzeugleitstelle Lfl.Kdo.2. Bombed on Bari airfield. 100% destroyed.

27 April Hs 129 B-2 W.Nr.0351 8.(Pz)/Sch.G 2. Hit by AA fire W. of Tunis. 100% destroyed.

02 May Hs 129 B-0 W.Nr.0027 2./Erg.Sch.Gr. Uffz. Karl Schröder injured in belly-landing due to pilot error at Deblin-Irena airfield. 40% damage.

02 May Hs 129 B-2 W.Nr.0204 Erg.Sch.Gr. Emergency landing near Bialystok due to lack of fuel. 80% damage.

03 May Hs 129 B-2 W.Nr.0392 8.(Pz)/Sch.G 1. Hit by ground fire in Map Grid Qu.75266. 100% destroyed.

04 May Hs 129 B-2 W.Nr.0289 Erg.Sch.Gr. Pilot error at Deblin-Irena resulted in 20% damage.

05 May Hs 129 B-2 W.Nr.0363 4.(Pz)/Sch.G 1. 30% damaged in belly-landing at Kerch due to technical fault.

05 May Hs 129 B-2 W.Nr.0398 8.(Pz)/Sch.G 1. Ofw. Günther Schlegel killed when aircraft crashed into the sea having been hit by AA fire in Map Grid Qu.7664. 100% destroyed.

05 May Hs 129 B-2 W.Nr.0434 8.(Pz)/Sch.G 1. Hit by AA fire in Map Grid Qu.76643. 100% destroyed.

05 May Hs 129 B-2 W.Nr.0386 8.(Pz)/Sch.G 2. Flg. Gert Borghardt killed. Aircraft hit by AA fire or in air combat N. of Mateur. 100% destroyed.

07 May Hs 129 B-2 W.Nr.140495 8.(Pz)/Sch.G 1. Collision during take-off on airfield at Anapa. 80% damage.

08 May Hs 129 B-2 W.Nr.0443 4.(Pz)/Sch.G 1. Hit by AA fire, Krymskaya. 100% destroyed.

09 May Hs 129 B-2 W.Nr.0300 8.(Pz)/Sch.G 1. Hit by ground fire at Kerch. 25% damage.

10 May Hs 129 B-2 W.Nr.140506 4.(Pz)/Sch.G 1. Shot down by ground fire at Chuguyev. 100% destroyed.

13 May Hs 129 B-2 W.Nr.0366 4.(Pz)/Sch.G 1. Emergency landing at Kerch due to technical fault. 50% damage.

13 May Hs 129 B-2 W.Nr.0417 4.(Pz)/Sch.G 1. Hit by AA fire N. of Kerch. 80% damage.

14 May Hs 129 B-2 W.Nr.0298 Coded Black C, 2./Erg.Sch.Gr. Fhr. Heinz Rehfeld killed by accidental contact with ground at Sarny near Deblin. 100% destroyed.

15 May Hs 129 B-1 W.Nr.0160 Erg.Sch.Gr. Emergency landing due to engine failure N. of Garwelin. 30% damage.

15 May Hs 129 B-2 W.Nr.0428 Sch.G 101. Lt. Erich Dettling injured in emergency landing near Mondesir due to engine failure. 70% damage.

20 May Hs 129 B-2 W.Nr.140724 II/Sch.G 101. Emergency landing near Mondesir due to engine fault. 10% damage.

27 May Hs 129 B-2 W.Nr.0364 Coded J, 8.(Pz)/Sch.G 1. Hit by ground defences in Map Grid Qu.76882. 100% destroyed.

27 May Hs 129 B-2 W.Nr.0373 Coded N+ – , 8.(Pz)/Sch.G 1. Hit by AA fire in Map Grid Qu.234. 100% destroyed.

27 May Hs 129 B-2 W.Nr.0412 8.(Pz)/Sch.G 1. Undercarriage damage on airfield at Kerch. 30% damage.

27 May Hs 129 B-2 W.Nr.0355 8.(Pz)/Sch.G 2. Bomb damaged on airfield at Decimomanu. 35% damage.

28 May Hs 129 B-2 W.Nr.0367 Sch.G 101. Damaged taking off from Orly. 60% damage.

29 May Hs 129 B-2 W.Nr.0404 Pz.Jg.St./JG 51. Lt Friedrich Seuken hit by AA fire W. of Krymskaya and posted missing. Aircraft 100% destroyed.

29 May Hs 129 B-2 W.Nr.0356 8.(Pz)/Sch.G 1. Aircraft hit by AA fire and attacked by fighters in Map Grid Qu.75234. 100% destroyed.

01 June Hs 129 B-2 W.Nr.140718 Coded Blue K, Pz.Jg.St./JG 51. Fw. Rainer Siebrecht killed. Aircraft 100% destroyed W. of Krymskaya. Reasons unknown.

01 June Hs 129 B-2 W.Nr.140507 Coded Blue A+, 4.(Pz)/Sch.G 2. Uffz. Ernst Menzel hit by AA fire and posted missing NW. of Krymskaya. 100% destroyed.

01 June Hs 129 B-2 W.Nr.140514 4.(Pz)/Sch.G 2. Hit by AA fire over Krymskaya. 40% damage.

01 June Hs 129 B-2 W.Nr.140715 4.(Pz)/Sch.G 2. Hit by AA fire Krymskaya. 60% damage.

07 June Hs 129A-0 W.Nr.3015 II/Sch.G 101. Uffz. Wolfgang Reinhold injured in emergency landing due to technical fault near Wissons. 40% damage.

18 June Hs 129 B-2 W.Nr.140763 Fl.Ü.G. 1. Emergency landing at Krakow-Proskurov. 25% damage.

20 June Hs 129 B-2 W.Nr.140726 II/Sch.G 101. Uffz. Rudolf Lorenz injured in crash due to engine failure near Choisy le Roi. 55% damage.

20 June Hs 129 B-2 W.Nr.140760 Fl.Ü.G. 1. Fw. Linberger injured at Krakow-Proskurov, reasons unknown. 100% destroyed.

05 July Hs 129 B-2 W.Nr.0272 Sch.G 101. Uffz. Fritz Turnwald killed in crash at Orly airfield due to engine failure. 100% destroyed.

07 July Hs 129 B-1 W.Nr.0197 Erg.Sch.Gr. Lt. Heinz L˘big killed. Pilot error at Deblin-Irena. 70% damage.

08 July Hs 129 B-2 W.Nr.0399 Pz.Jg.St./JG 51. Hit by ground fire in Map Grid Qu.61184. 20% damage.

08 July Hs 129 B-2 W.Nr.140750 4.(Pz)/Sch.G 1. Technical fault at Varvarovka. 30% damage.

08 July Hs 129 B-2 W.Nr.0448 8.(Pz)/Sch.G 1. Technical fault in Map Grid Qu.6538. 15% damage.

09 July Hs 129 B-2 W.Nr.0414 Coded G, 8.(Pz)/Sch.G 1. Obgfr. Gerhard Sembritzki killed. Aircraft hit by AA fire S. of Novenkoye and crashed in flames. 100% destroyed.

12 July Hs 129 B-2 W.Nr.0371 Pz.Jg.St./JG 51. Hit by AA fire in Map Grid Qu.61242. 60% damage.

12 July Hs 129 B-2 W.Nr.0397 Pz.Jg.St./JG 51. Hit by AA fire in Map Grid Qu.61187. 100% destroyed.

12 July Hs 129 B-2 W.Nr.0280 4.(Pz)/Sch.G 1. Hit by AA fire in Map Grid Qu.61242. 50% damage.

12 July Hs 129 B-2 W.Nr.140509 4.(Pz)/Sch.G 1. Lt. Ullrich Hadamzik hit by AA fire 500m E. of Yassnaya Polnaya and posted missing . 100% destroyed.

12 July Hs 129 B-2 W.Nr.140745 4.(Pz)/Sch.G 1. Hit by AA fire in Map Grid Qu.61218. 60% damage.

12 July Hs 129 B-2 W.Nr.140755 8.(Pz)/Sch.G 1. Hit by AA fire in Map Grid Qu.61564. 60% damage.

14 July Hs 129 B-2 W.Nr.0419 8.(Pz)/Sch.G 1. Hit by AA fire in Map Grid Qu.41255 and Lt Bäuerle posted missing. 100% destroyed.

15 July Hs 129 B-2 W.Nr.0331 Pz.Jg.St./JG 51. Hit by AA fire in Map Grid Qu.63537. 100% destroyed.

15 July Hs 129 B-2 W.Nr.0403 Pz.Jg.St./JG 51. Hit by AA fire at Orel-West. 20% damage.

15 July Hs 129 B-2 W.Nr.0427 Pz.Jg.St./JG 51. Hit by AA fire in Map Grid Qu.63584. 100% destroyed.

16 July Hs 129 B-2 W.Nr.0401 Pz.Jg.St./JG 51. Uffz. Siegfried Geffke shot down by enemy aircraft in Map Grid Qu.54648 and posted missing. 100% destroyed.

16 July Hs 129 B-2 W.Nr.140758 Pz.Jg.St./JG 51. Hit by AA fire in Map Grid Qu.54655. 100% destroyed.

16 July Hs 129 B-2 W.Nr.140508 8.(Pz)/Sch.G 1. Hit by AA fire in Map Grid Qu.54653. 100% destroyed.

17 July Hs 129 B-2 W.Nr.0365 4.(Pz)/Sch.G 1. Hit by AA fire in Map Grid Qu.63527. 100% destroyed.

17 July Hs 129 B-2 W.Nr.0438 4.(Pz)/Sch.G 1. 60% bomb damaged airfield at Orel-West.

17 July Hs 129 B-2 W.Nr.140500 4.(Pz)/Sch.G 2. Hit by AA fire in Map Grid Qu.54816. 60% damage.

17 July Hs 129 B-2 W.Nr.140739 Pz.Jg.St./JG 51. Technical fault in Map Grid Qu.53238. 50% damage.

19 July Hs 129 B-2 W.Nr.140769 Pz.Jg.St./JG 51. Shot down by enemy aircraft in Map Grid Qu.54671. 100% destroyed.

19 July Hs 129 B-2 W.Nr.140512 4.(Pz)/Sch.G 2. Major Matuschek killed. Aircraft hit by ground fire in Map Grid Qu.54847. 100% destroyed.

19 July Hs 129 B-2 W.Nr.141113 Henschel-Flzg.-Werke airfield at Schönefeld. Emergency landing due to technical fault. 90% damage.

20 July Hs 129 B-2 W.Nr.140751 Pz.Jg.St./JG 51. Technical fault in Map Grid Qu.64779. 100% destroyed.

20 July Hs 129 B-2 W.Nr.140822 Pz.Jg.St./JG 51. Fw. Fritz Buchmann killed. Aircraft hit by ground fire in Map Grid Qu.54793. 100% destroyed.

20 July Hs 129 B-2 W.Nr.0396 4.(Pz)/Sch.G 1. 100% destroyed on airfield at Poltava, reasons unknown.

20 July Hs 129 B-2 W.Nr.0374 8.(Pz)/Sch.G 1. Technical fault W. of Poltava 80% damage.

20 July Hs 129 B-2 W.Nr.0441 4.(Pz)/Sch.G 2. Hit by ground fire in Map Grid Qu.54729. 50% damage.

20 July Hs 129 B-2 W.Nr.140502 4.(Pz)/Sch.G 2. Pilot error at Orel-West. 20% damage.

20 July Hs 129 B-2 W.Nr.140747 4.(Pz)/Sch.G 2. Technical fault in Map Grid Qu. 647. 100% destroyed.

21 July Hs 129 B-2 W.Nr.0445 Pz.Jg.St./JG 51. Technical fault on airfield at Orel-West. 20% damage.

22 July Hs 129 B-2 W.Nr.140746 4.(Pz)/Sch.G 1. Uffz Sansl killed. Aircraft hit by AA fire in Map Grid Qu.63134. 100% destroyed.

23 July Hs 129 B-2 W.Nr.140752 Pz.Jg.St./JG 51. Pilot error at Orel-West. 20% damage.

23 July Hs 129 B-2 W.Nr.141127 Technical fault at Henschel-Flzg.-Werke airfield at Johannisthal. 30% damage.

23 July Hs 129 B-2 W.Nr.0436 4.(Pz)/Sch.G 1. Ofw Juschka hit by AA fire in Map Grid Qu.54651 and posted missing. 100% destroyed.

24 July Hs 129 B-2 W.Nr.0343 8.(Pz)/Sch.G 2. Lt. Hugo Diemer killed. Aircraft crashed near Monte Moneta during a transfer flight and burned on the ground. 100% destroyed.

25 July Hs 129 B-2 W.Nr.140823 4.(Pz)/Sch.G 1. Hit by AA fire in Map Grid Qu.64726. 100% destroyed.

25 July Hs 129 B-2 W.Nr.0375 8.(Pz)/Sch.G 1. Crashed during taxiing on airfield at Karachev. 40% damage.

25 July Hs 129 B-2 W.Nr.140425 8.(Pz)/Sch.G 1. Fw. Eduard Etzdorf injured, aircraft hit by enemy aircraft gun fire in Map Grid Qu.53474. 100% destroyed.

25 July Hs 129 B-2 W.Nr.0446 8.(Pz)/Sch.G 1. Hit by AA fire in Map Grid Qu.54725. 100% destroyed.

26 July Hs 129 B-2 W.Nr.140828 8./Rum.Sch.Gr. Damaged during take-off on airfield at Kramatorskaya. 15% damage.

27 July Hs 129 B-2 W.Nr.140740 2./Erg.Sch.Gr. Obfhr. Erich Sauckel injured, engine failure S. of Kurov near Pulawy. 85% damage.

28 July Hs 129 B-2 W.Nr.140519 4.(Pz)/Sch.G 1. Fw. Hinz killed. Aircraft hit by AA fire in Map Grid Qu.54721. 100% destroyed.

30 July Hs 129 B-2 W.Nr.0449 4.(Pz)/Sch.G 1. Fw. Schmidt hit by aircraft gunfire in Map Grid Qu.54718. 100% destroyed.

31 July Hs 129 B-2 W.Nr.140767 8.(Pz)/Sch.G 1. Hit by AA fire in Map Grid Qu.54864. 30% damage.

31 July Hs 129 B-2 W.Nr.140732 Sch.G 101. Oblt. Ernst Hessl killed when aircraft crashed due to pilot error W. of Ercardenville. 100% destroyed.

04 August Hs 129 B-2 W.Nr.0244 4.(Pz)/Sch.G 2. Blown up by own troops on airfield at Varvarovka. 100% destroyed.

04 August Hs 129 B-2 W.Nr.0450 Coded G, 4.(Pz)/Sch.G 2. Blown up by own troops on airfield at Varvarovka. 100% destroyed.

06 August Hs 129 B-2 W.Nr.140757 Pz.Jg.St./JG 51. Lt. Pfingsttag injured in crash. 100% destroyed.

07 August Hs 129 B-2 W.Nr.0440 Pz.Jg.St./JG 51. Lt. Franz Stelzl posted missing following low-level ground-attack. 100% destroyed.

07 August Hs 129 B-2 W.Nr.140816 4.(Pz)/Sch.G 2. Hit by AA fire near Bogadukhov. 100% destroyed.

07 August Hs 129 B-2 W.Nr.140806 8.(Pz)/Sch.G 2. Ofw. Willi Heisel hit by AA fire near Bogadukhov and posted missing. 100% destroyed.

08 August Hs 129 B-2 W.Nr.0238 Pz.Jg.St./JG 51. Damaged during landing due to engine failure. 75% damage.

08 August Hs 129 B-2 W.Nr.140493 4.(Pz)/Sch.G 2. Uffz. Wehinger killed. Aircraft suffered 80% damage near Golavanevsk, reasons unknown.

08 August Hs 129 B-2 W.Nr.0333 8.(Pz)/Sch.G 2. Lt. Friedrich Ott hit by AA fire and posted missing near Bogadukhov. 100% destroyed.

08 August Hs 129 B-2 W.Nr.0341 8.(Pz)/Sch.G 2. Uffz. Walter Bode suffered engine failure on airfield at Poltawa. 100% destroyed.

08 August Hs 129 B-2 W.Nr.0354 8.(Pz)/Sch.G 2. Fw. Alfred Wollner killed. Aircraft hit by AA fire E. of Sossnovka. 100% destroyed.

08 August Hs 129 B-2 W.Nr.140504 8.(Pz)/Sch.G 2. Hit by AA fire near Bogadukhov. 100% destroyed.

09 August Hs 129 B-2 W.Nr.0291 4.(Pz)/Sch.G 2. Hit by AA fire in Map Grid Qu.5189. 35% damage.

09 August Hs 129 B-2 W.Nr.0348 8.(Pz)/Sch.G 2. Lt. Gert Ganghofer posted missing. Aircraft either accidentally struck the ground or was hit by AA fire at Mirolyubovka. 100% destroyed.

10 August Hs 129 B-2 W.Nr.0312 8./Rum.Sch.Gr. Lt. Orth injured during landing on airfield at Mariupol-West due to technical fault. 30% damage.

12 August Hs 129 B-2 W.Nr.0216 Erg.Sch.Gr. Aircraft suffered undercarriage failure during landing on airfield at Deblin-Irena. 50% damage.

14 August Hs 129 B-2 W.Nr.140836 Erg.Sch.Gr. Emergency landing due to engine failure E. of Rzeszow. 70% damage.

15 August Hs 129 B-2 W.Nr.40815 4.(Pz)/Sch.G 2. Fw. Plathe killed. Aircraft crashed in Map Grid Qu.41816. 100% destroyed.

15 August Hs 129 B-2 W.Nr.140741 8./Rum.Sch.Gr. Bomb damaged on airfield at Kramatorskaya. 90% damage.

16 August Hs 129 B-2 W.Nr.140829 8./Rum.Sch.Gr. Bomb damaged on airfield at Kramatorskaya. 15% damage.

17 August Hs 129 B-2 W.Nr.140714 Pz.Jg.St./JG 51. Lt. Kurt Grobe posted missing, reasons unknown. 100% destroyed.

17 August Hs 129 B-2 W.Nr.140824 Pz.Jg.St./JG 51. Fw. Ernst Gerhards killed. Reported 100% destroyed, reasons unknown.

17 August Hs 129 B-2 W.Nr.140840 4.(Pz)/Sch.G 2. Damage taxiing on airfield at Bol. Rudka. 15% damage.

17 August Hs 129 B-2 W.Nr.140749 8./Rum.Sch.Gr. Bombed on Kramatorskaya airfield. 60% damage.

17 August Hs 129 B-2 W.Nr.140804 8./Rum.Sch.Gr. Hit by AA fire at Kramatorskaya. Extent of damage unkown.

17 August Hs 129 B-2 W.Nr.140817 8./Rum.Sch.Gr. Engine failure. 30% damage.

18 August Hs 129 B-2 W.Nr.140731 8./Rum.Sch.Gr. Bomb damaged on airfield at Kramatorskaya. 10% damage.

18 August Hs 129 B-2 W.Nr.140811 8./Rum.Sch.Gr. Hit by AA fire S. of Sissinski. 15% damage.

19 August Hs 129 B-2 W.Nr.140738 8./Rum.Sch.Gr. Crashed at Kramatorskaya. 90% damage.

19 August Hs 129 B-2 W.Nr.140742 8./Rum.Sch.Gr. Bombed on Kramatorskaya airfield. 20% damage.

19 August Hs 129 B-2 W.Nr.140743 8./Rum.Sch.Gr. Undercarriage damage on airfield at Kramatorskaya. 15% damage.

20 August Hs 129 B-2 W.Nr.140833 Führer der Pz.Jg.Staffeln. Aircraft flown by Lt. Wenzel hit by infantry fire in Map Grid Qu.41561. 100% destroyed.

21 August Hs 129 B-2 W.Nr.0429 4.(Pz)/Sch.G 2. Uffz. Gerhard Mix, hit by AA fire NE. of Krimchka. 100% destroyed.

23 August Hs ,129 B-2 W.Nr.140513 Coded Red H, 8.(Pz)/Sch.G 2. Fw. Karl Buchinger, hit by AA fire and posted missing. 100% destroyed.

24 August Hs 129 B-2 W.Nr.0376 4.(Pz)/Sch.G 2. Hit by AA fire in Map Grid Qu.88183. 40% damage.

24 August Hs 129 B-2 W.Nr.140497 4.(Pz)/Sch.G 2. Undercarriage defect on airfield at Zaporozhye. 30% damage.

28 August Hs 129 B-2 W.Nr.0393 8.(Pz)/Sch.G 1. Hit by AA fire in Map Grid Qu.42177. 100% destroyed.

02 September Hs 129 B-2 W.Nr.141111 4.(Pz)/Sch.G 2. Technical fault in Map Grid Qu.99195. 60% damage.

05 September Hs 129 B-2 W.Nr.0370 4.(Pz)/Sch.G 1. Bomb damaged on airfield at Zaporozhe-East. 100% destroyed.

05 September Hs 129 B-2 W.Nr.141230 8.(Pz)/Sch.G 1. Lt. Maximilian Becker, hit by AA fire and crashed in Map Grid Qu.22651C. 100% destroyed.

06 September Hs 129 B-1 W.Nr.0172 Coded Black G, 2./Erg.Sch.Gr. Uffz. Adolf Böckler killed. Aircraft accidentally struck ground due to pilot error at Rokitnia near Deblin. 100% destroyed.

08 September Hs 129 B-2 W.Nr.140802 8.(Pz)/Sch.G 1. Hit by AA fire in Map Grid Qu. 69435. 100% destroyed.

08 September Hs 129 B-2 W.Nr.140830 8./Rum.Sch.Gr. Lt. Hans Ort killed when shot down by tanks in Map Grid Qu.7951. 100% destroyed.

08 September Hs 129 B-2 W.Nr.140810 8./Rum.Sch.Gr. Belly landing at Bliznetsy. 20% damage.

09 September Hs 129 B-2 W.Nr.141126 4.(Pz)/Sch.G 1. Gefr. Willi Berbert hit by AA fire N. of Krasilovka. 100% destroyed.

10 September Hs 129 B-2 W.Nr.0379 Coded Red C, 8.(Pz)/Sch.G 2. Uffz. Heinz Heuschkel killed. Aircraft hit by AA fire on the SE. edge of Maryevka village. 100% destroyed.

14 September Hs 129 B-2 W.Nr.141116 8.(Pz)/Sch.G 1. Destroyed by ground fire in Map Grid Qu.68321. 100% destroyed.

14 September Hs 129 B-2 W.Nr.141235 8./Rum.Sch.Gr. Shot down by enemy aircraft in Map Grid Qu.6951. 100% destroyed.

14 September Hs 129 B-2 W.Nr.141240 8./Rum.Sch.Gr. Ofw. Ludwig Schmid hit by AA fire in Map Grid Qu.6928 and posted missing. 100% destroyed.

15 September Hs 129 B-2 W.Nr.0313 Erg.Sch.Gr.Deblin. Uffz. Artur Gersch injured, after aircraft accidentally hit the ground. 80% damage.

17 September Hs 129 B-2 W.Nr.140518 Pz.Jg.St./JG 51 Uffz. Hermann Saarmann killed. Aircraft attacked by fighter(s) NW. of Pologi. 100% destroyed.

17 September Hs 129 B-1 W.Nr.0196 Coded Black 2, 2./Erg.Sch.Gr. Uffz. Arno Ribinski crashed N. of Stenzyca near Deblin. 85% damage.

18 September Hs 129 B-2 W.Nr.0349 4.(Pz)/Sch.G 1. Lt. Werner Goetschke injured by ground defences at Borispol. 75% damage.

18 September Hs 129 B-2 W.Nr.140729 8./Rum.Sch.Gr. Hit by friendly AA fire in Map Grid Qu.5881. 40% damage.

19 September Hs 129 B-2 W.Nr.0442 4.(Pz)/Sch.G 1. Hit by ground defences in Map Grid Qu.11/15. 100% destroyed.

19 September Hs 129 B-2 W.Nr.140813 8./Rum.Sch.Gr. Shot down by enemy aircraft in Map Grid Qu.85584. 100% destroyed.

19 September Hs 129 B-2 W.Nr.141128 8./Rum.Sch.Gr. Shot down by enemy aircraft in Map Grid Qu.85584. 30% damage.

26 September Hs 129 B-2 W.Nr.140864 4.(Pz)/Sch.G 2. Lt. Lehmann suffered technical fault in Map Grid Qu.0353. 75% damage.

27 September Hs 129 B-2 W.Nr.141241 4.(Pz)/Sch.G 1. Uffz. Heinrich Michalcke injured in emergency landing due to ground fire in Map Grid Qu.0164, following which aircraft was blown up. 100% destroyed.

27 September Hs 129 B-2 W.Nr.141255 4.(Pz)/Sch.G 1. Emergency landing in Map Grid Qu.0164 due to being hit by AA fire, following which aircraft was blown up. 100% destroyed.

27 September Hs 129 B-0 W.Nr.0018 Sch.G 101. Collision with an obstruction during landing on airfield at Orly. 35% damage.

27 September Hs 129 B-2 W.Nr.0230 Sch.G 101. Uffz. Paul Frischmuth killed. Aircraft crashed near Juvisy. 100% destroyed.

29 September Hs 129 B-2 W.Nr.141247 Coded C, 8.(Pz)/Sch.G 1. Fw. Hilgendag injured, reasons unknown. 100% destroyed.

29 September Hs 129 B-2 W.Nr.141224 8./Rum.Sch.Gr. Undercarriage damage on airfield at Genichesk. 15% damage.

30 September Hs 129 B-2 W.Nr.140510 8.(Pz)/Sch.G 1. Hit by AA fire in Map Grid Qu. 49319. 100% destroyed.

01 October Hs 129 B-2 W.Nr.140724 II/Sch.G 101. Collision with obstruction during landing on airfield at Orly. 40% damage.

02 October Hs 129 B-2 W.Nr.0361 4.(Pz)/Sch.G 1. Hit by infantry fire in Map Grid Qu.0279. 100% destroyed.

03 October Hs 129 B-2 W.Nr.0420 II/Sch.G 101. Gefr. Josef Blei killed when aircraft crashed and caught fire near Orly. 100% destroyed.

04 October Hs 129 B-2 W.Nr.0350 8./Rum.Sch.Gr. Hit by AA fire in Map Grid Qu.5751. 30% damage.

06 October Hs 129 B-2 W.Nr.141250 Pz.Jg.St./JG 51. Hit by AA fire in Map Grid Qu.39267. 100% destroyed.

06 October Hs 129 B-2 W.Nr.0290 Erg.Sch.Gr. Emergency landing at Warthenau due to disorientation. 65% damage.

08 October Hs 129 B-2 W.Nr.141123 4.(Pz)/Sch.G 1. Uffz. Hans Grunwald killed. Aircraft hit by AA fire. Extent of damage unknown.

09 October Hs 129 B-2 W.Nr.141127 8./Rum.Sch.Gr. Crashed. 100% destroyed.

11 October Hs 129 B-2 W.Nr.141223 8./Rum.Sch.Gr. Hit by AA fire at Genischesk. 10% damage.

11 October Hs 129 B-2 W.Nr.141263 8./Rum.Sch.Gr. Hit by AA fire in Map Grid Qu.5732. 35% damage.

11 October Hs 129 B-2 W.Nr.141266 8./Rum.Sch.Gr. Hit by AA fire at Genischesk. 10% damage.

12 October Hs 129 B-2 W.Nr.141265 Coded M, 4.(Pz)/Sch.G 2. Fw. Georg Haeder, aircraft hit by ground fire in Map Grid Qu.01329. 100% destroyed.

14 October Hs 129 B-2 W.Nr.141279 8./Rum.Sch.Gr. Hit by ground fire in Map Grid Qu.5731. 10% damage.

15 October Hs 129 B-2 W.Nr.140819 8./Rum.Sch.Gr. Hit by ground fire in Map Grid Qu.5732. 30% damage.

15 October Hs 129 B-2 W.Nr.141277 8./Rum.Sch.Gr. Hit by ground fire in Map Grid Qu.5718. 25% damage.

15 October Hs 129 B-2 W.Nr.141288 8./Rum.Sch.Gr. Hit by ground fire in Map Grid Qu.5838. 25% damage.

16 October Hs 129 B-2 W.Nr.140870 13.(Pz)/Sch.G 9. Uffz. Wolfgang Röhr killed. Aircraft crashed 12km W. of Mishurin-Rog following attack by fighter(s). 100% destroyed.

16 October Hs 129 B-2 W.Nr.141275 8./Rum.Sch.Gr. Hit by enemy fire and overturned during emergency landing E. of Nikolayev. 50% damage.

18 October Hs 129 B-1 W.Nr.0159 Coded Black S, 2./Erg.Sch.Gr. Uffz. Johannes Skrebbas injured in emergency landing due to misorientation and lack of fuel at Wlodawa. 90% damage.

18 October Hs 129 B-2 W.Nr.0387 Coded Black G, 2./Erg.Sch.Gr. Fw. Georg Haas killed when aircraft accidentally hit the ground NE. of Trzcianka. 100% destroyed.

18 October Hs 129 B-2 W.Nr.140776 Erg.Sch.Gr. Emergency landing due to lack of fuel S. of Brest-Litowsk. 25% damage.

21 October Hs 129 B-2 W.Nr.141228 8./Rum.Sch.Gr. Hit by ground fire at Genichesk. 10% damage.

21 October Hs 129 B-2 W.Nr.141231 8./Rum.Sch.Gr. Hit by ground fire in Map Grid Qu.576. 20% damage.

22 October Hs 129 B-1 W.Nr.0168 Erg.Sch.Gr. Damaged during landing due to engine failure at Wieckovy. 50% damage.

23 October Hs 129 B-2 W.Nr.140759 Coded Red M, 13.(Pz)/Sch.G 9. Fw. Joachim Maciejewski posted missing in the area N. of Losowatka, probably hit it by AA fire. Aircraft reported 100% destroyed.

23 October Hs 129 B-2 W.Nr.140748 14.(Pz)/Sch.G 9. Uffz. Albert Frankenstein killed N. of Losovatka, probably hit it by AA fire. Aircraft reported 100% destroyed.

23 October Hs 129 B-2 W.Nr.141271 8./Rum.Sch.Gr. Hit by AA fire in Map Grid Qu.5718. 100% destroyed.

24 October Hs 129 B-2 W.Nr.140826 8./Rum.Sch.Gr. Hit by AA fire at Genichesk. 15% damage.

25 October Hs 129 B-2 W.Nr.140739 8./ Rum.Sch.Gr. Blown up by own troops following emergency landing in Map Grid Qu.47293. 100% destroyed.

25 October Hs 129 B-2 W.Nr.141239 8./Rum.Sch.Gr. Blown up by own troops following emergency landing E. of Kuibyshevo. 100% destroyed.

26 October Hs 129 B-2 W.Nr.141299 14.(Pz)/Sch.G 9. Lt. Hans Jentsch killed. Aircraft suffered direct hit from AA fire NW. of Wesseloye. 100% destroyed.

30 October Hs 129 B-2 W.Nr.141284 14.(Pz)/Sch.G 9 Uffz. Rudolf Petzold hit by AA fire 5km N. of Askania-Nova and posted missing. Aircraft 100% destroyed.

30 October Hs 129 B-2 W.Nr.140712 8./Rum.Sch.Gr. Blown up by own troops on airfield at Genichesk. 100% destroyed. .

30 October Hs 129 B-2 W.Nr.140716 8./Rum.Sch.Gr. Blown up by own troops on airfield at Chaplinka. 100% destroyed.

01 November Hs 129 B-2 W.Nr.141262 10.(Pz)/Sch.G 9. Hit by AA fire in Map Grid Qu.39764. 100% destroyed.

01 November Hs 129 B-2 W.Nr.141226 14.(Pz)/Sch.G 9. Oblt. Friedrich Wilhelm Quilitsch, posted missing following crash and fire 5km E. of Malaya-Myjachka. Aircraft 100% destroyed.

01 November Hs 129 B-2 W.Nr.0433 Coded Black G, 2./Erg.Sch.Gr. Fw. Johann Ketzer injured during collision on landing at airfield at Deblin-Ulez. 85% damage.

01 November Hs 129 B-2 W.Nr.141289 8./Rum.Sch.Gr. Hit by AA fire in Map Grid Qu.3767. 100% destroyed.

02 November Hs 129 B-2 W.Nr.140717 8./Rum.Sch.Gr. Hit by AA fire in Map Grid Qu.2766. 100% destroyed.

02 November Hs 129 B-2 W.Nr.141244 8./Rum.Sch.Gr. Hit by AA fire in Map Grid Qu.2762. 100% destroyed.

02 November Hs 129 B-2 W.Nr.141264 8./Rum.Sch.Gr. Hit by AA fire in Map Grid Qu.2676. 100% destroyed.

02 November Hs 129 B-2 W.Nr.141393 8./Rum.Sch.Gr. Hit by AA fire in Map Grid Qu.3754. 100% destroyed.

14 November Hs 129 B-2 W.Nr.141382 10.(Pz)/Sch.G 9. Damaged by infantry fire in Map Grid Qu.9179. 25% damage.

15 November Hs 129 B-2 W.Nr.140808 14.(Pz)/Sch.G 9. Melitopol Lt. Wilhelm Abt posted missing, reasons unkown. Aircraft reported 100% destroyed.

16 November Hs 129 B-2 W.Nr.141725 8./Rum.Sch.Gr. Aircraft hit by AA and overturned at Nikolayev during emergency landing. 50% damage.

19 November Hs 129 B-2 W.Nr.0325 Erg.Sch.Gr. Emergency landing S. of Kozienice due to engine failure. 65% damage.

21 November Hs 129 B-2 W.Nr.0233 8./Rum.Sch.Gr. Belly landing due to damaged undercarriage on airfield at Nikolayev-East. 25% damage.

21 November Hs 129 B-2 W.Nr.141266 8./Rum.Sch.Gr. Aircraft overturned upon landing on airfield at Apostolovo-South. 10% damage.

22 November Hs 129 B-2 W.Nr.141287 10.(Pz)/Sch.G 9. Emergency landing in Map Grid Qu.91843 having been hit by AA fire. 20% damage.

27 November Hs 129 B-2 W.Nr.141267 10.(Pz)/Sch.G 9. Hit by AA fire in Map Grid Qu.39312. 100% destroyed.

27 November Hs 129 B-2 W.Nr.141398 10.(Pz)/Sch.G 9. Hit by AA fire near Beresovka. 80% damage.

27 November Hs 129 B-2 W.Nr.141115 Coded E, 12.(Pz)/Sch.G 9. Uffz. Anton Meier unhurt. Aircraft hit by ground defences N. of Pandorovka. 100% destroyed.

27 November Hs 129 B-2 W.Nr.141259 Coded Red I, 13.(Pz)/Sch.G 9. Ofw. Albert Strenkert injured by enemy fighters at Miropol, 10km W. of the Krivoi Rog - Dnepropetrovsk railway line. Extent of damage unknown.

27 November Hs 129 B-2 W.Nr.141285 8./Rum.Sch.Gr. Emergency landing in Map Grid Qu.3858 following damage inflicted by enemy fire. 85% damage.

28 November Hs 129 B-2 W.Nr.140723 8./Rum.Sch.Gr. Engine failure. 30% damage.

29 November Hs 129 B-2 W.Nr.140720 8./Rum.Sch.Gr. Hit by AA fire in Map Grid Qu.3883. 10% damage.

29 November Hs 129 B-2 W.Nr.141224 8./Rum.Sch.Gr. Pilot error at Nikolayev-East airfield. 10% damage.

29 November Hs 129 B-2 W.Nr.141231 8./Rum.Sch.Gr. Hit by AA fire. 10% damage.

30 November Hs 129 B-2 W.Nr.141383 8./Rum.Sch.Gr. Hit by ground defences in Map Grid Qu.2746. 100% destroyed.

06 December Hs 129 B-2 W.Nr.0224 II/Sch.G 101 Belly landing due to pilot error on airfield at Orly. 20% damage.

07 December Hs 129 B-2 W.Nr.0300 8./Rum.Sch.Gr. Attacked by fighter(s) in Map Grid Qu.27411. 10% damage.

07 December Hs 129 B-2 W.Nr.0416 8./Rum.Sch.Gr. Crashed due to collision with an obstruction, Map Grid Qu.27453. 100% destroyed.

08 December Hs 129 B-2 W.Nr.141732 12.(Pz)/Sch.G 9 Hit by AA fire E. of Znamenka. 100% destroyed.

13 December Hs 129 B-2 W.Nr.141531 10.(Pz)/Sch.G 9 Oblt. Georg Dornemann injured, aircraft hit by enemy fire and crashed in Map Grid Qu.2968. 95% damage.

15 December Hs 129 B-2 W.Nr.0204 8./Rum.Sch.Gr. Hit by AA fire. 15% damage.

15 December Hs 129 B-2 W.Nr.140736 8./Rum.Sch.Gr. Hit by AA fire. 10% damage.

15 December Hs 129 B-2 W.Nr.141233 8./Rum.Sch.Gr. Hit by AA fire in Map Grid Qu.2746. 100% destroyed.

16 December Hs 129 B-2 W.Nr.0430 Sch.G 101. Undercarriage damaged during landing at Orly airfield. 10% damage.

20 December Hs 129 B-2 W.Nr.141129 8./Rum.Sch.Gr. Hit by own AA fire at Odessa. 10% damage.

28 December Hs 129 Fl.Ü.G. 1. Uffz. Helmut Schüttler crashed and killed at Strichovka. 100% destroyed.

1944

05 January Hs 129 B-2 W.Nr.141536 10.(Pz)/Sch.G 9. Uffz. Siegfried Lewerenz killed during emergency landing with burning engine 2km NE. of Malaya-Walitsa following which aircraft exploded. 100% destroyed.

06 January Hs 129 B-2 W.Nr.141270 14.(Pz)/Sch.G 9. Uffz. Philipp Himmelsbach killed taking off on an operational mission from Malaya-Viska airfield when bomb under right wing exploded. 100% destroyed.

08 January Hs 129 B-2 W.Nr.141293 12.(Pz)/Sch.G 9. Uffz. Werner Vosseler killed. Aircraft collided in the air with Hs 129 B-2 W.Nr. 141379 at Kalinovka. 100% destroyed.

08 January Hs 129 B-2 W.Nr.141379 12.(Pz)/Sch.G 9. Lt. Erhard Fuchs collided in the air with Hs 129 B-2 W.Nr. 141293 at Kalinovka. 100% destroyed.

09 January Hs 129 B-2 W.Nr.141249 12.(Pz)/Sch.G 9. Fw. Karl Hessel killed. Aircraft reported as 100% destroyed in Map Grid Qu. 70/2/2, reasons unknown.

11 January Hs 129 B-2 W.Nr.0281 Coded Red W, 13.(Pz)/Sch.G 9. Uffz Herbert Schreiter killed. Bombs exploded on take-off and aircraft crashed. 100% destroyed.

12 January Hs 129 B-2 W.Nr.141395 10.(Pz)/Sch.G 9. Obfhr. Egon Pfaff killed due S. of Losovaya. Aircraft broke-up and crashed. 100% destroyed.

12 January Hs 129 B-2 W.Nr.141380 14.(Pz)/Sch.G 9. Fw. Otto Steitz killed. Aircraft received direct AA hit at Brazlav-Odessa. 100% destroyed.

14 January Hs 129 B-2 W.Nr.0249 Sch.G 101. Swung off runway on landing at Orly airfield and tipped up on its nose. 15% damage.

14 January Hs 129 B-2 W.Nr.0439 Sch.G 101. Collided while landing at Orly airfield with Hs 129 B-2 W.Nr.0814. 10% damage.

14 January Hs 129 B-2 W.Nr.140814 Sch.G 101. Collided while landing at airfield Orly with Hs 129 B-2 W.Nr.0439. 15% damage.

16 January Hs 129 B-2 W.Nr.141392 10.(Pz)/Sch.G 9. Uffz. Gerd Logemann injured during emergency landing on Kalinovka airfield following enemy damage to the right hand engine, extent unknown.

24 January Hs 129 B-2 W.Nr.141583 IV(Pz)/Sch.G. Lt. Heinz Knieling killed. Aircraft crashed during ferry flight 1km E. of Ganorovka. 100% destroyed.

27 January Hs 129 B-2 W.Nr.141589 10.(Pz)/Sch.G 9. Lt. Horst Michel reported missing, aircraft 100% destroyed N. of Otcheretnya, reasons unknown.

21 February Hs 129 B-1 W.Nr.0191 Fl.Ü.G. 1. Bomb damaged on airfield at Diepholz. 80% damage.

14 March Hs 129 B-2 W.Nr.141711 13.(Pz)/SG 9. Fw. Helmut Fromm injured in crash 20km E. of Lyubashevka, 1km N. of Lyubashevka - Pervomaisk railway line due to sudden poor weather and icing. Extent of damage unknown.

19 March Hs 129 A-0 W.Nr.3012 SG 101. Uffz. Adolf Melkers injured in belly landing near Clermont-Ferrand due to engine failure. 80% damage.

20 March Hs 129 B-2 W.Nr.0430 SG 101. Undercarriage damaged while landing at Clermont-Ferrand airfield. 25% damage.

31 March Hs 129 B-2 W.Nr.141549 Coded D, 10.(Pz)/SG 9. Uffz. Otto Mehlig killed by direct hit from AA fire 2km SW. of Starobrodzkie. 100% destroyed.

05 April Hs 129 B-2 W.Nr.141731 Coded D, 10.(Pz)/SG 9. Ofw. Franz Birnbaum killed 1km NW. of Hobubica when aircraft was hit by enemy fire and crashed in flames. 100% destroyed.

14 April Hs 129 B-2 W.Nr.140862 13.(Pz)/SG 9. Swung off runway while landing at Otopeni. 10% damage.

14 April Hs 129 B-2 W.Nr.141848 13.(Pz)/SG 9. Uffz. Johannes Skrebbas reported killed 35km E. of the Nyierghaza, reasons unknown. 100% destroyed.

15 April Hs 129 B-2 W.Nr.141587 2./Fl.Ü.G. 1. Aircraft overturned, incurring 20% damage at Craiova.

25 April Hs 129 B-2 141863 Coded SR+JC 12.(Pz)/SG 9. Uffz. Werner Wolff killed. Aircraft received direct hit from AA guns S. of Grigoriopol. 100% destroyed.

26 April Hs 129 B-2 W.Nr.141717 10.(Pz)/SG 9. Uffz. Martin Moninger seriously injured during sortie NW. Carligul and died whilst being transported to the main airfield at Jassy. Extent of damage unknown.

28 April Hs 129 B-2 W.Nr.141570 10.(Pz)/SG 9. Lt. Lothar Kallerhof injured during test flight at Bacau due to failure of one engine. Damage extent unkown. (One eye-witness states that Kallerhoff was stunt flying on one engine and was unable to restart the dead engine at a critical moment).

30 April Hs 129 A-0 W.Nr.3004 SG 101. Bombed on airfield at Clermont-Ferrand. 100% destroyed.

30 April Hs 129 A-0 W.Nr.3010 SG 101. Bombed on airfield at Clermont-Ferrand. 65% damaged.

30 April Hs 129 A-0 W.Nr.3014 SG 101. Bombed on airfield at Clermont-Ferrand. 60% damaged.

30 April Hs 129 A-0 W.Nr.0031 SG 101. Bombed on airfield at Clermont-Ferrand. 55% damaged.

30 April Hs 129 A-0 W.Nr.0179 SG 101. Bombed on airfield at Clermont-Ferrand. 50% damaged.

30 April Hs 129 A-0 W.Nr.0235 SG 101. Bombed on airfield at Clermont-Ferrand. 75% damaged.

30 April Hs 129 A-0 W.Nr.0344 SG 101. Bombed on airfield at Clermont-Ferrand. 35% damaged.

30 April Hs 129 A-0 W.Nr.0431 SG 101. Bombed on airfield at Clermont-Ferrand. 100% destroyed.

30 April Hs 129 A-0 W.Nr.140721 SG 101. Bombed on airfield at Clermont-Ferrand. 60% damaged.

30 April Hs 129 A-0 W.Nr.140814 SG 101. Bombed on airfield at Clermont-Ferrand. 60% damaged.

11 May Hs 129 B-2 W.Nr.141237 Henschel-Flzg.-Werke aircraft. Emergency landing due to technical fault, near Bohnsdorf.

01 June Hs 129 B-2 W.Nr.141752 Coded C, 10.(Pz)/SG 9. Fj.Uffz. Ernst Berg attacked by fighter(s) SW. of Stanka and posted missing. Aircraft reported 100% destroyed.

02 June Hs 129 B-2 W.Nr.141850 14.(Pz)/SG 9. Flg. Bruno Nindler killed. Aircraft attacked by fighter(s) at Cucuteni, 15km W. of Jassy. 100% destroyed.

15 July Hs 129 B-2 W.Nr.141556 Coded B, 12.(Pz)/SG 9. N. of Krasne Ofw. Hans Kaschel posted missing as a result of engine damage and subsequent emergency landing. Observed baling out, probably uninjured, in partisan territory. 100% destroyed.

15 July Hs 129 B-2 W.Nr.141720 Coded F, 12.(Pz)/SG 9. Uffz. Walter Hetzel killed near Lojki when aircraft received direct hit from AA fire. 100% destroyed.

16 July Hs 129 B-2 W.Nr.141227. 30% damage at Cacoti, reasons unknown.

16 July Hs 129 B-2 W.Nr.141966 Coded G, 10.(Pz)/SG 9. Hptm. Rudolf-Heinz Ruffer killed following direct AA hit NE. of Volkasusanska. 100% destroyed.

16 July Hs 129 B-2 W.Nr.141973 Coded F, 10.(Pz)/SG 9. Uffz. Karl Bayerle killed following direct AA hit N. of Volkasusanska. 100% destroyed.

17 July Hs 129 B-2 W.Nr.141749 Coded J, 10.(Pz)/SG 9. Ofw. Helmut Corell killed following direct AA hit 6km S. of Sokal. 100% destroyed.

20 July Hs 129 B-2 W.Nr.141878 14.(Pz)/SG 9. Uffz. Karl Böttcher injured in emergency landing due to AA damage. Extent of damage unknown.

22 July Hs 129 B-2 W.Nr.141880 Coded K, 10.(Pz)/SG 9. Oblt. Hans-Werner Wenzel posted missing, aircraft hit by AA fire in Map Grid Qu.21865. 100% destroyed.

22 July Hs 129 B-2 W.Nr.141729 Fl.Ü.G. 1. Emergency landing in Arradeo, Rumania, due to technical fault. 10% damage.

25 July Hs 129 B-2 W.Nr.141837 Coded Red C, 13.(Pz)/SG 9. Uffz. Rolf Ruthmann wounded as result of being attacked by enemy fighters on take-off from airfield at Triciana near Rzeszow. Aircraft set on fire and belly-landed. Pilot died 27 July 1944 in Tarnow. Aircraft 100% destroyed.

27 July Hs 129 B-2 W.Nr.141872 Coded W, 10.(Pz)/SG 9. Ofw. Hermann Holtermann injured having been hit by AA fire near Deblin-Irena. 100% destroyed.

27 July Hs 129 B-2 W.Nr.141858 14.(Pz)/SG 9. Lt. Oskar Bressler injured in emergency landing at Przemsl due to AA damage. Extent of damage unknown.

31 July Hs 129 B-2 W.Nr.141713 Coded O, 12.(Pz)/SG 9. Fw. Walter Lippstreu killed. Aircraft received direct hit from AA guns NE. of Kaunas. 100% destroyed.

02 August Hs 129 B-2 W.Nr.141534 13.(Pz)/SG 9. Fw. Heinrich Fuhrmann attacked by fighter(s) 10km W. of Klimontov and posted missing. 100% destroyed.

02 August Hs 129 B-2 141839 13.(Pz)/SG 9. Uffz. Alfred Scherb attacked by fighter(s) 10km W. of Klimontov and posted missing. 100% destroyed.

II./SG 101 moved from Paris-Orly to Clermont-Ferrand during 10 and 11 March 1944. During the night of 29/30 April 1944, bombers from the RAF's 57, 97, 207 and 630 Squadrons attacked a repair works for BMW aero-engines situated south-east of Clermont-Ferrand airfield and, in the late morning of 30 April, the airfield was attacked by bomber and fighter aircraft of the USAAF. In the combined RAF/USAAF raids, the factory, various airfield installations, 10 Hs 129s, 12 Fw 190s, 7 Ar 96s, 5 Fw 58s and 5 other types were damaged or destroyed, including this Hs 129 B.

11 August Hs 129 B-2 W.Nr.142002 10.(Pz)/SG 9. Fw. Artur Neumann killed in crash due to technical fault NW. of Grabowiec. 100% destroyed.

18 September Hs 129 B-2 W.Nr.141371 Fl.Ü.G. 1. Fw. Alfred Schäfer belly landed at Birkenfeld/Würzburg due to engine failure. 10% damage.

06 October Hs 129 B-2 W.Nr.141869 14.(Pz)/SG 9. Oblt. Hans-Hermann Steinkamp injured in emergency landing in Map Grid Qu.7456 due to AA damage. Extent of damage unknown.

18 October Hs 129 B-2 W.Nr.141828 Coded Red B, 13.(Pz)/SG 9. Ofw. Ferdinand Bey posted missing after sustaining hits from light AA gun near Haselgrung. Fuselage fuel tank exploded in the air. Aircraft seen to burn in the air and the crash. 100% destroyed.

13 December Hs 129 B-2 W.Nr.141865 14.(Pz)/SG 9. Fw. Theodor Keller killed in Map Grid Qu.78667 14 Ost. Cause and damage unknown.

23 December Hs 129 B-2 W.Nr.141728 14.(Pz.)/SG 9. Damaged by gun fire from enemy aircraft. 15% damage.

1945

14 January Hs 129 B-2 W.Nr.140405 Coded White 1, 10.(Pz)/SG 9. Uffz. Franz Natzen, posted missing in area 01366, reasons unknown. Aircraft reported 100% destroyed.

14 January Hs 129 B-2 W.Nr.141738 Coded White 4, 10.(Pz)/SG 9. Ofw. Hans Fleddermann killed, aircraft hit by AA fire and crashed in flames 2km NW. of Motkowice. 100% destroyed.

14 January Hs 129 B-2 W.Nr.141759 Coded White 7, 10.(Pz)/SG 9. Destroyed by own troops following belly landing on airfield at Warzyn due to hits by AA fire. 100% destroyed.

14 January Hs 129 B-2 W.Nr.141970 Coded White 2, 10.(Pz)/SG 9. Damaged tail wheel during taxiing and subsequently blown up by own troops at Warzyn airfield. 100% destroyed.

19 January Hs 129 B-2 W.Nr.141741 Coded White 11, 10.(Pz)/SG 9. Belly landing due to ground defences 2km E. of Yerolchusz. 100% destroyed.

19 January Hs 129 B-2 W.Nr.14197 (sic) 13.(Pz)/SG 9. Ofw. Heinz Heger posted missing following fighter attack E. of Insterburg. 100% destroyed.

19 January Hs 129 B-2 W.Nr.141855 13.(Pz)/SG 9. Ofw. Wilhelm Piper injured in belly landing after being attacked by fighter(s) SE. of Insterburg. 100% destroyed.

20 January Hs 129 B-3 W.Nr.162044 13.(Pz)/SG 9. Damaged on landing at Inowraclaw airfield due to engine failure. Aircraft destroyed by own troops. 100% destroyed.

20 January Hs 129 B-2 W.Nr.141744 IV(Pz)/SG 9. Damaged on landing at Kreysing airfield due to engine failure. Aircraft destroyed by own troops. 100% destroyed.

21 January Hs 129 B-2 W.Nr.141969 Coded White 13, 10.(Pz)/SG 9. Fw. Georg Becker injured in crash due to engine failure. 70% damage.

21 January Hs 129 B-2 W.Nr.141976 13.(Pz)/SG 9. Aircraft destroyed by own troops on airfield at Kalich, due to unconfirmed technical fault. 100% destroyed.

22 January Hs 129 B-2 W.Nr.141582 Coded White 9, 10.(Pz)/SG 9. Fw. Horst Kurek posted missing. Shot down, probably by AA fire, in area 81562. Assumed 100% destroyed.

22 January Hs 129 B-2 W.Nr.140500 IV(Pz)/SG 9. Destroyed by own troops on Tonndorf airfield. 100% destroyed.

22 January Hs 129 B-2 W.Nr.140838 13.(Pz)/SG 9. Destroyed by own troops on Tonndorf airfield. 100% destroyed.

22 January Hs 129 B-2 W.Nr.140537 IV(Pz)/SG 9. Destroyed by own troops on Tonndorf airfield. 100% destroyed.

22 January Hs 129 B-2 W.Nr.141748 13.(Pz)/SG 9 Destroyed by own troops on Tonndorf airfield. 100% destroyed.

22 January Hs 129 B-2 W.Nr.141840 13.(Pz)/SG 9. Destroyed by own troops on Tonndorf airfield. 100% destroyed.

22 January Hs 129 B-2 W.Nr.141867 13.(Pz)/SG 9. Destroyed by own troops on Tonndorf airfield. 100% destroyed.

22 January Hs 129 B-2 W.Nr.141975 13.(Pz)/SG 9. Destroyed by own troops on Tonndorf airfield. 100% destroyed.

22 January Hs 129 B-2 W.Nr.141981 13.(Pz)/SG 9. Destroyed by own troops on Tonndorf airfield. 100% destroyed.

22 January Hs 129 B-2 W.Nr.141982 13.(Pz)/SG 9. Destroyed by own troops on Tonndorf airfield. 100% destroyed.

22 January Hs 129 B-2 W.Nr.142003 IV(Pz)/SG 9. Destroyed by own troops on Tonndorf airfield. 100% destroyed.

22 January Hs 129 B-3 W.Nr.162037 13.(Pz)/SG 9. Destroyed by own troops on Tonndorf airfield. 100% destroyed.

22 January Hs 129 B-3 W.Nr.162038 13.(Pz)/SG 9. Destroyed by own troops on Tonndorf airfield. 100% destroyed.

22 January Hs 129 B-3 W.Nr.162043 13.(Pz)/SG 9. Destroyed by own troops on Tonndorf airfield. 100% destroyed.

23 January Hs 129 B-3 W.Nr.162041 IV(Pz)/SG 9. Destroyed by own troops on Kleineichen airfield. 100% destroyed.

23 January Hs 129 B-2 W.Nr.141561 14.(Pz)/SG 9. Hit by enemy fire at Kamenez - St. Peter. 15% damage.

24 January Hs 129 B-2 W.Nr.141989 Coded White 3, 10.(Pz)/SG 9. Belly landing due to ground defences 4km W. of Krappitz. 10% damage.

24 January Hs 129 B-2 W.Nr.142084 Coded White O, 10.(Pz)/SG 9. Emergency landing on Roszweide airfield due to engine damage. 5% damage.

27 January Hs 129 B-2 W.Nr.141707 Coded White Q, 10.(Pz)/SG 9. Belly landing due to engine failure 1.5km E. of Roszweide airfield. 10% damage.

08 February Hs 129 B-2 W.Nr.141875 Coded White 3, 10.(Pz)/SG 9. Uffz. Herbert Heyrowsky killed during an anti-tank sortie from Weidengut, aircraft suffered direct AA hit 300m NW. of Märzdorf. 100% destroyed.

08 February Hs 129 B-2 W.Nr.141965 10.(Pz)/SG 9. Belly landing at Heidersdorf as a result of ground fire. 10% damage.

11 February Hs 129 B-2 W.Nr.141547 10.(Pz)/SG 9. Damaged in landing on airfield at Schweidnitz due to pilot error. 60% damage.

12 February Hs 129 B-2 W.Nr.141722 10.(Pz)/SG 9. Fw. Otto Ritz hit by AA fire in Jauer area and posted missing. 100% destroyed.

13 February Hs 129 B-2 W.Nr.140765 10.(Pz)/SG 9. Damaged in landing at airfield at Weidengut due to poor visibility. 80% damage.

17 February Hs 129 B-2 W.Nr.141691 Coded White 1, 10.(Pz)/SG 9. Belly landing 700m N. of Teha near Prag due to engine failure. 10% damage.

19 February Hs 129 B-2 W.Nr.141683 10.(Pz)/SG 9. Aircraft sustained 90% damage in Map Grid Qu.61261, reasons unknown.

06 March Hs 129 B-2 W.Nr.141584 10.(Pz)/SG 9. Bomb damaged on airfield at Weidengut. 70% damage.

06 March Hs 129 B-3 W.Nr.162046 10.(Pz)/SG 9. Bomb damaged on airfield at Weidengut. 60% damage.

16 March Hs 129 B-2 W.Nr.140743 10.(Pz)/SG 9. Emergency landing NW. of Rüben having been hit by AA fire. 90% damage.

16 March Hs 129 B-2 W.Nr.142004 10.(Pz)/SG 9. Belly landing SW. of Katcher due to engine failure. 10% damage.

22 March Hs 129 B-2 W.Nr.141251 10.(Pz)/SG 9. Hit by AA fire N. of Glenztal. 25% damage.

23 March Hs 129 B-2 141968 10.(Pz)/SG 9. Bomb damaged on airfield at Schweidnitz. 90% damage.

1946

24 July Hs 129 B-1/R2 FE-4600 USAF Lt. Kenneth Almond in emergency landing due to lack of fuel at Gallatin, Tennessee, USA. Major damage to propeller, right wing outboard panel, right aileron, right wheel, tyre and oleo.

APPENDIX FOUR

Technical and Weapons Specifications

TECHNICAL DATA

	Hs 129 B-0	Hs 129 B-1	Hs 129 B-2
Powerplant	2 x Gnôme et Rhône 14 M 04/05 (B-0, B-1, B-2)		
Length	9.75m (B-0, B-1, B-2)		
Height	3.25m (B-0, B-1, B-2)		
Wingspan	14.20m (B-0, B-1, B-2)		
Tail Span	4.78m (B-0, B-1, B-2)		
Wing Area	29.00m² (B-0, B-1, B-2)		
Empty Weight	3675kg	3661kg	3810kg
Take-Off Weight	3839kg	4057kg	4197kg
Max Take-Off Weight	5000kg	5000kg	5250kg
Rate of Climb			8.25m/s
Range	750km		680km

HS 129 B-2 FLIGHT PERFORMANCE

Max. indicated airspeed (km/h)	600	580	550	520
At given altitude (m)	**1000**	**2000**	**3000**	**4000**
Altitude (m)	300	2000		
Manifold Pressure (atm/kPA)	1.10/112	1.10/112		
RPM (ot/min RPM)	2350	2350		
Fuel Consumption (lit./h)	310	330		
True Airspeed	325	350		
Endurance	1.75	1.66		
Range	565	570		

TOTAL PRODUCTION: 859

PRODUCTION TABLE (HS 129 B-1, B-2, B-3.)

	1941	1942	1943	1944
January	–	3	24	30
February	–	3	27	25
March	–	6	30	35
April	–	31	33	35
May	–	18	36	35
June	–	18	40	27
July	–	20	40	18
August	–	24	40	18
September	–	15	40	17
October	–	33	40	–
November	–	24	40	–
December	1	24	24	–
Total	1	219	414	225

Comments on Scale and General Arrangement Drawings

During the preparation of this book every effort has been made to produce the most accurate scale drawings of all the main variants of the Hs 129. The lack of a complete surviving example of this aircraft has meant that research information has been based on material and documents to hand. Although a large quantity of information has been collected the bulk of the technical data has been collated from original maintenance manuals. However, this information does not constitute detailed manufacturing working drawings as these documents are mainly concerned with maintaining the actual aircraft. A similar document today would be a car manual. With the aid of these manuals and close study of available photographs, every effort has been made to achieve accuracy.

The Publishers would be pleased to hear from anyone having access to authentic works drawings or geometries so that corrections can be incorporated and used in planned future publications. However, we feel confident that the drawings appearing in this book are the most accurate to be found anywhere up to this time.

WEAPONS SPECIFICATIONS

	MK 101	MK 103	BK 7.5	SG 113A
Calibre	30 mm	30 mm	75 mm	77/44 mm
Muzzle Velocity	860 metres/second	860 metres/second	730 metres/second	650 metres/second
Shot Weight	0.33 kg	0.33 kg	6.8 kg	1.93 kg
Charge Weight	0.106 kg	0.106 kg	2.45 kg	–
Weight of Round	0.78 kg	0.78 kg	11.6 kg	–
Muzzle Energy	12.5 tonnes	12.5 tonnes	185 tonnes	–
Firing Method	Mechanical	Electrical	Electrical	Electrical
Length of Barrel	1350 mm	1350 mm	3,100 mm	1,600 mm
Weight of Barrel	40 kg	23 kg	450 kg	–
Gas Pressure	3,300 kg/sq.cm	3,300 kg/sq.cm	2,800 kg/sq.cm	1,700 kg/sq.cm
Rate of Fire	260 shots/min.	420 shots/min.	30 rnds/min.	Single shot weapon
Weight of Weapon loaded	180 kg	140 kg	595 kg	53.3 kg empty/65.8 kg
Wt of Weapon Installed	–	–	700 kg	–
Wt of Counterweight	–	–	–	10.9 kg
Magazine Capacity	–	–	12 rounds	–
Barrel Recoil	–	–	915 mm	–
Type of Brake	–	–	Hydraulic Fluid	–
Type of Feed	Magazine with 6 rounds, later a drum containing 30 rounds	Belt fed from ammunition tank containing 30 rounds	Rotary Magazine	–

Shell magazine 7.5cm BK, swung down.
1. Beladeeinrichtung

Cockpit Instruments for 7.5cm BK.
1. Sicherungsschalter
2. Gruppenwahlschalterhebel
3. Abzugshebel
4. Sprengschalter
5. Revi-Verdunker

Instruments/devices in cockpit

Geräte im Führerraum
1 Ferntrennschalter
2 Schalter für Bildgerät
  bei B-1: Kraftstoffbehälterpumpe
  bei B-2: 2a = Tragflächen Behälterpumpe
           2 = Rumpf
  Wendezeiger
  Heizdüse
  Positionslampe
  Scheinwerfer
3 Druckknopfschalter für Kleinbildkammer
4 Hebel für Gemisch
5 Hebel für 110% Leistung
6 Hebel für Normalgas
7 Spannhebel für Normalgas
8 Hebel für Brandhähne
9 Hebel für Führerraumheizung
10 Schweigeknopf für Fahrwerk
11 Schalter für Gerätelampen, Motor und Führerraum (Raumlampe)
12 Verdunkler
13 Feuerlöscher
14 Netzausschalter
15 Schaltkasten für Trimmruder-Verstellanlage
16 Handhebel für Führerhaube
17 Zündschalter
18 Verdunkler für Gerätelampen an den Handhebelbrücken
19 Schaltkasten für Luftschraube
20 Vierlampengerät für Fahrwerk
21 Borduhr
22 Fahrtmesser
23 Höhenmesser
24 Betriebsdatentafel
25 Schauzeichen für Staurohr-Heizung
26 Haubennotwurf
27 Führertochterkompaß
28 Wendezeiger
29 Doppelladedruckmesser
30 ZSK 244 A
31 Notwurf für Bomben und Abwurfbehälter (B-2)
32 Schalter für FuG 16 Z, Heizung, Umformer und Zielflug
33 Frequenzschalter und Anschlußdose FuG 16 Z
34 Hebel und Einführungsloch für Drucköl-Handpumpe (Fahrwerksnotbetätigung)
35 Bedienungsgerät FuG 16 Z
36 Hebel für Landeklappe
37 Hebel für Fahrwerk
38 Sicherung für Fahrwerkshebel
39 Notbetätigung für Kühlerklappen
40 Kontrollampe für Führerraumheizung

Geräte am linken Motor:
41 Drehzahlmesser
42 Kraftstoff-Reststandswarnung
43 Kraftstoff-Vorratsanzeiger
44 Schmierstofftemperaturmesser
45 Kraft- und Schmierstoffdruckmesser
46 Druckmesser für Drucköllanlage

Geräte am rechten Motor:
47 Drehzahlmesser
48 Kraftstoff-Reststandswarnung
49 Kraftstoff-Vorratsanzeige
50 Schmierstofftemperaturmesser
51 Kraft- und Schmierstoffdruckmesser

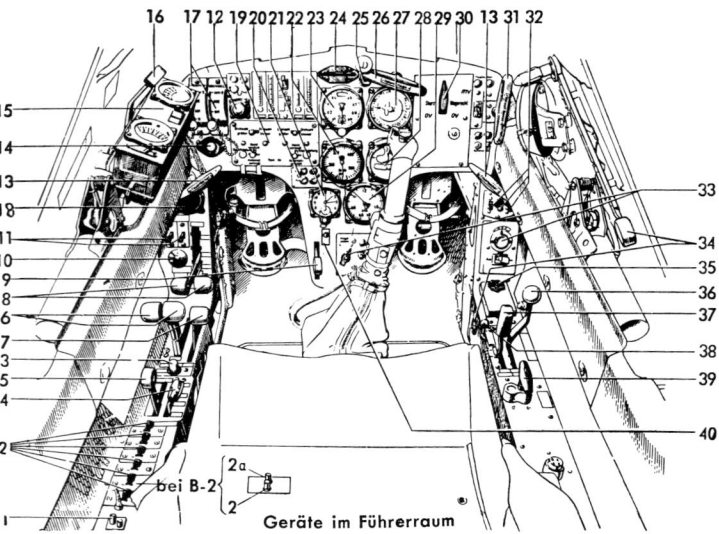

Geräte im Führerraum

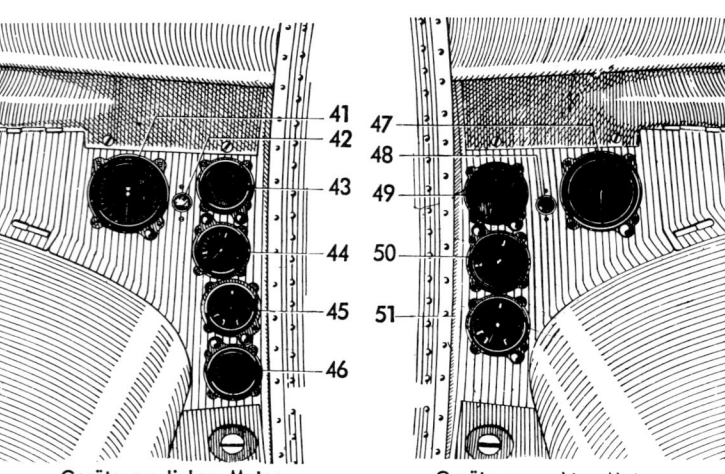

Geräte am linken Motor   Geräte am rechten Motor

1. Long range cut off switch
2. Switch for camera
   for B-1: fuel tank pump
   for B-2: 2a = wing tank pump
            2 = fuselage
   Artificial Horizon
   Heating Nozzle
   Position Light
   Landing Lamp
3. Press Switch for Gun Camera Bay
4. Mixture Lever
5. Lever for 110% Power (Emergency Boost)
6. Throttle Levers
7. Fuel Lever
8. Fuel Shut-Off Levers (Slow Running)
9. Cockpit Heating Lever
10. Undercarriage Selector Switch
11. Switch for Instrument Lamp, Motor and Cockpit (Cockpit Light)
12. Dimmer Switch
13. Fire Extinguisher
14. Master Cut-Off for Electrics
15. Switch Box for Rudder Trim Adjustment Indicator
16. Handle for Cockpit Locking
17. Magneto Switches
18. Dimmer Switch for Instrument Lights on the Hand Lever Framework
19. Switch Box for Airscrew Controls
20. Undercarriage Position Triple Lamp Indicator
21. Chronometer
22. Air Speed Indicator
23. Altimeter
24. Data Card Holder
25. Pitot Head Heating Indicator
26. Cockpit Canopy Emergency Release Lever
27. Repeater Compass
28. Artificial Horizon
29. Twin Manifold Pressure Gauge
30. ZSK 244 A (arming selector panel)
31. Emergency Release for Bomb and External Fuel Tank (B-2)
32. Heating Transformer Switch for FuG 16 Z
33. Frequency Switch and Selector for FuG 16 Z
34. Handle and Viewing Hole for Oil Pressure Hand Pump (Undercarriage Emergency Lowering)
35. Auxiliary Indicator for FuG 16 Z
36. Landing Flaps Lever
37. Undercarriage Lever
38. Safety Switch for Undercarriage Operating Lever
39. Emergency Operating Handle for Cooling Gills
40. Control Light for Cockpit Heating

Instrumentation for left motor:
41. RPM Gauge
42. Fuel Contents Gauge
43. Fuel Flow Gauge
44. Lubricating Oil Temperature Gauge
45. Fuel and Oil Pressure Gauge
46. Pressure Gauge for Pressurised Oil System

Instrumentation for right motor:
47. RPM Gauge
48. Fuel Contents Gauge
49. Fuel Flow Gauge
50. Lubricating Oil Temperature Gauge
51. Fuel and Oil Pressure Gauge

Gnôme-Rhône 14M Engine
(see photographs on page 33)

A
1. Ring Guidance for Rotary Lubrication
2. Front Ignition Line
3. Regulating Valve Balance Equaliser for Bearing Support for Rotary Lever
4. Quick Fastener for Valve Cover
5. Lubrication Return to Transmission from Controls
6. Lubrication Return to Driving Gear

B
1. Motor Lifting Bolts
2. Pressurised Lubrication Regulating Valve, 1.5kg/cm^2
3. Lubricating Injection Line for Starting Lubrication Pressure
4. Cable Harness
5. Fuel Pump Connection
6. Pressure Connection Regulating Valve for Fuel Pump Fuel Pressure
7. Not Shown
8. Fuel Lever
9. Carburettor Twin Adaptor
10. Pressurised Lubrication Connection
11. Lubrication Inlet Connection
12. Lubrication Pump
13. Lubricating Pressure Rotary Switch Lever
14. Lubricating Pressure Regulating Valve, 5kg/cm^2

C
1. Pressure Inlet Tube with Air Filter
2. Magneto
3. Overdrive for Electrical Coil
4. Connection Point for Lubrication Return from Tank
5. Pressure Connection for Fuel Pump
6. Return Line of the Lubricating Pump to the Sump
7. Oscillation Activated Self-Starter
8. Regulating Screw
9. Lever for Ignition Equipment
10. Quick Stop Cut Out Lever
11. Starting Pressure Lever
12. Mixture Adjustment Lever
13. Fuel Inlet
14. Fuel Filter
15. Carburettor
16. Fuel Pump Connection
17. Rear Ignition Line
18. Exhaust Gas Outlet Connection

APPENDIX FIVE

Logbooks and Award Citations

Vorläufiges Besitzzeugnis

Der Führer
und Oberste Befehlshaber
der Wehrmacht

hat

dem ___Hauptmann Franz Oswald___

das Ritterkreuz
des Eisernen Kreuzes

am ___24. Oktober 1944___ verliehen

Hauptquartier d.Ob.d.L. , den ___29. Oktober 1944___

Der Chef der Personellen Rüstung und
National-Sozialistischen Führung der Luftwaffe
I.A.

Oberst

Lfd. Nr. des Fluges	Führer	Begleiter	Muster	D.	Zweck des Fluges	Abflug Start-Ort	Landung Land-Ort	Tag	Start	Landung	Flugdauer	Kilometer	A
										Flug 345,39 h		39652	
795	Oehl	÷	Hs 129	B 3	Üb.Schiessen 7,5cm	Jürgenfelde	Jürgenfelde	17.10.44	10.25	10.50	25'	140	
796	"	"	"	T	Feindflug	"	"	18.10.	10.10	11.20	70'	350	March
797	"	"	"	E	"	"	"	20.10.	11.40	12.10	30'	150	R.F.
798	"	"	"	E	"	"	"	-	15.00	15.50	50'	450	
799	"	"	"	1410	"	"	"	21.10.	13.35	14.05	30'	150	
800	"	"	"	"	Verlegung	"	Gerdauen	-	15.40	16.00	20'	100	
801	"	"	"	"	"	Gerdauen	Schippenbeil	23.10.	16.00	16.10	10'	50	
802	"	"	"	B 3	L-Schiessen	Schippenbeil	"	24.10.	14.55	15.30	35'	175	
803	"	"	"	T 2	Ü. Einsatz	"	"	6.1.45	12.30	13.15	45'	220	
804	"	"	"	T	Feindflug	"	"	19.1.	8.25	9.25	60'	300	
805	"	"	"	"	Verlegungsfl.	"	Hohensalza	"	11.30	12.45	75'	375	
806	"	"	"	"	Feindflug	Hohensalza	"	20.1.	10.25	11.30	65'	350	
807	"	"	"	"	"	"	"	"	13.45	14.50	65'	340	
808	"	"	"	"	Verlegung	"	Kalisch	"	14.55	15.20	25'	140	
809	"	"	"	"	"	Kalisch	Posen-Kreising	"	16.05	16.30	25'	140	
810	"	"	"	"	"	Posen-Kreising	Tonndorf	21.1.	8.20	8.30	10'	50	
811	"	"	"	"	Kurierflug	Tonndorf	Kreising	"	9.05	9.15	10'	50	
812	"	"	"	"	"	Kreising	Tonndorf	"	9.25	9.35	10'	50	
										357.99		43048	

Lfd. Nr. des Fluges	Führer	Begleiter	Muster	D.	Zweck des Fluges	Abflug Start-Ort	Landung Land-Ort	Tag	Start	Landung	Flugdauer	Kilometer	A
								1945.		Flug 357,00 h		43042	
813	Oehl	÷	Hs 129	T	Feindflug	Tonndorf	Tonndorf	21.1.	12.35	13.50	75'	375	
814	"	"	"	B 3	Überführ. Flg	Perleberg	Finsterwalde	4.2.	10.30	11.25	55'	280	
815	"	"	"	"	"	Finsterwalde	Weidengut o/s	4.2.	14.05	15.15	70'	350	
816	"	"	"	"	Feindflug	Weidengut	Liegnitz	5.2.	10.15	11.05	50'	250	
817	"	"	"	"	Überführg. flg	Liegnitz	Freiwaldau	5.2.	13.10	13.35	25'	140	
819	"	"	Fw 190	6	Umschulstart	Perleberg	Perleberg	16.2.	14.31	14.49	18'		
820	"	"	"	"	Platzflug	"	"	"	14.52	15.05	13'		
821	"	"	"	"	"	"	"	"	15.08	15.14	6'		
822	"	"	"	"	"	"	"	"	15.16	15.23	7'		
823	"	"	"	1	"	"	"	17.2.	13.42	13.50	8'		
824	"	"	"	"	"	"	"	"	13.11	13.15	4'		
825	"	"	"	"	"	"	"	"	13.20	13.23	3'		
826	"	"	"	"	"	"	"	"	13.26	13.30	4'		
827	"	"	"	"	"	"	"	"	13.32	13.36	4'		
828	"	"	"	"	"	"	"	"	13.39	13.43	4'		
829	"	"	"	3	"	"	"	18.2.	11.07	11.11	4'		
830	"	"	"	"	"	"	"	"	11.19	11.24	5'		
831	"	"	"	"	Erfliegen	"	"	"	11.51	12.23	32'		

Pages from Jupp Oehl's Flugbuch showing his activities between October 1944 and February 1945. Entry number 795 for 17 October shows Oehl flying firing trials with the 7.5 cm BK-equipped Hs 129 B-3. Entry number 816 reveals that Oehl flew an operational sortie in an Hs 129 B-3 from Weidengut over Silesia on the morning of 5 February 1945 whilst with 13.(Pz)/SG 9, shortly before the Staffel moved to Perleberg for Fw 190 conversion training.

Verleihungsurkunde

Im Namen des
Oberbefehlshabers der Luftwaffe

verleihe ich dem

Oberleutnant

Franz Oswald

die

Frontflug-Spange für Jäger

in Gold

Im Feld, den 8. August 1942

SCHLACHTGESCHWADER 1

Major und Geschwaderkommodore

Besitzeugnis

Dem

Oberleutnant Franz Oswald
(Name, Dienstgrad)

8./(Pz) S.G. 2
(Truppenteil, Dienststelle)

ist auf Grund

seiner am 18. Januar 1943 erlittenen

ein maligen Verwundung oder Beschädigung

das

Verwundetenabzeichen

in Schwarz

verliehen worden.

Gefechtsstand, den 20. Jan. 1943

Generalmajor
und Fliegerführer Tunis
(Dienstgrad und Dienststelle)

Above:
The citation of the Frontflug-Spange in Gold for Oberleutnant Franz Oswald dated 8 August 1942 and signed by Major Hubertus Hitschhold, Kommodore of Sch.G 1. The award was made in recognition of 110 operational sorties. Note that the style of central motif – an upward-pointing arrow – is that for fighter-pilots despite the fact that a special design for Schlachtflieger, featuring a downward-pointing arrow, was available at this time. After 12 April 1944, a new clasp was instituted for the Schlachtflieger incorporating a central motif of two crossed swords.

Above right:
Oberleutnant Franz Oswald was awarded the wound badge in Black on 20 January 1943 whilst flying with 8.(Pz)/Sch.G 2 in Tunisia. The citation has been signed by Generalmajor Martin Harlinghausen, the Fliegerführer Tunis.

Right:
Oberleutnant Oswald's award document for the Deutsches Kreuz in Gold, dated 4 June 1943 and signed by Göring.

Page 331:
The preliminary certificate notifying Hauptmann Franz Oswald of the award of the Ritterkreuz on 24 October 1944 in recognition of his 300 missions and the destruction of 50 enemy tanks.

IM NAMEN DES FÜHRERS
UND OBERSTEN BEFEHLSHABERS
DER WEHRMACHT
VERLEIHE ICH
DEM

OBERLEUTNANT

FRANZ OSWALD

DAS DEUTSCHE KREUZ
IN GOLD

HAUPTQUARTIER, DEN 4. JUNI 1943

DER REICHSMINISTER
DER LUFTFAHRT
UND OBERBEFEHLSHABER
DER LUFTWAFFE

Göring

REICHSMARSCHALL

DIE ERFOLGTE VERLEIHUNG
WIRD BEGLAUBIGT:

GENERALOBERST

Glossary

Brillantenträger	Holder of the Diamonds to the Knight's Cross
Deutsches Kreuz	German Cross
Dipl.Ing.	Diploma Engineer
Ergänzungsgruppe	Replacement Group
Ergänzungsjagdgruppe	Fighter Replacement Group
Ergänzungs Schlachtgruppe	Ground Attack Replacement Group
Ergänzungs Zerstörergruppe	Destroyer Replacement Group
Erprobungskommando	Test Unit
Erprobungsstelle(n)	Testing and Evaluation Centre
Fliegerführer	Air Commander
Fliegerkorps	Flying Corps
Flugzeugbau	Aircraft Manufacturer
Flugzeugwerke	Aircraft Works / Factory
Frontflugspange	Mission Clasp
Frontreparaturbetriebe	Front Repair Station
Führer der Panzerjäger	Commander of Anti-Tank Forces
Gen.Ing.	Engineer General
General der Jagdflieger	General of Fighter Arm
General der Nahkampfflieger	General of Close Support Arm
General der Schlachtflieger	General of Ground Attack Arm
Generalstab	General Staff
Geschwader	Wing
Geschwaderkommodore	Commander of a Wing
Gruppe	Group
Gruppenkommandeur	Group Commander
Heimatreparaturbetriebe	Home Repair Station
IAK: Istrebitel'nyy aviatsionnyy korpus	lit. Soviet "Fighter Air Corps"
IAP: Istrebitel'nyy aviatsionnyy polk	it. Soviet "Fighter Air Regiment"
Infantriesturmabzeichen	Infantry Assault Badge
Inspizient	Inspector
Jabo	Jagd-Bomber - Fighter-Bomber
Jägerstab	Fighter Staff
Kampfgeschwader	Bomber Wing
Lehrgeschwader	Operational Demonstration Wing
Luftflotte	Air Fleet
Luftwaffenführungstab	Air Force Command Staff
Oberbefehlshaber der Luftwaffe	Commander in Chief of the Air Force
OKL (Oberkommando der Luftwaffe)	Luftwaffe High Command
Panzerarmee	Tank Army
Panzerfliegerstaffel	Anti-Tank Squadron
Panzerjagdkommando	Anti-Tank Command
Panzerjäger	Anti-Tank Pilot or Aircraft
Panzerjagdflieger	Anti-Tank Pilot
Panzerjägerstaffel(n)	Anti-Tank Squadron(s)
Reichsluftfahrtministerium (RLM)	German Air Ministry
Ritterkreuz	Knight's Cross
Ritterkreuzträger	Knight's Cross Holder
Rotte	Element of Two Aircraft
Rottenführer	Two Aircraft Element Flight Leader
Schlachtflieger	Ground Attack Pilot
Schlachtfliegerstaffel(n)	Ground Attack Squadron(s)
Schlachtflugzeug	Ground Attack Aircraft
Schlachtgeschwader(n)	Ground Attack Wing(s)
Schlachtfliegergruppe(n)	Ground Attack Group(s)
Schnellkampfgeschwader	Fast Bomber Wing
Schutzstaffel(n)	Escort Squadron(s)
Schwarm	Element of Four Aircraft
Stab	Staff
Staffel	Squadron
Staffelführer	Squadron Commander (acting)
Staffelkapitän	Squadron Commander
Storkampfstaffeln	Harassment Squadron
Stosstruppen	Storm Troops or Shock Troops
Stuka (Sturzkampfflugzeug)	Dive-Bomber
Technisches Amt	Technical Office of RLM
Werk	Works or Factory
Werkschar	Factory Defence Force

Table of Comparative Ranks

Luftwaffe	RAF	USAAF
Reichsmarschall	-	-
Generalfeldmarschall	Marshal of the RAF	General (Five Star)
Generaloberst	Air Chief Marshal	General (Four Star)
General	Air Marshal	Lieutenant-General
Generalleutnant	Air-Vice Marshal	Major-General
Generalmajor	Air-Commodore	Brigadier-General
Oberst	Group Captain	Colonel
Oberstleutnant	Wing Commander	Lieutenant-Colonel
Major	Squadron Leader	Major
Hauptmann	Flight Lieutenant	Captain
Oberleutnant	Flying Officer	First Lieutenant
Leutnant	Pilot Officer	Second Lieutenant
Stabsfeldwebel	Warrant Officer	Flight Officer
Oberfeldwebel	Flight Sergeant	Master Sergeant
Feldwebel	Sergeant	Technical Sergeant
Unteroffizier	Corporal	Corporal
Hauptgefreiter	-	-
Obergefreiter	Leading Aircraftman	-
Gefreiter	Aircraftman First Class	Private First Class
Flieger	Aircraftman Second Class	Private Second Class

Note: The Luftwaffe also applied three Officer Candidate grades, commencing with Fahnenjunker (prefixed to the normal NCO rank - eg Fhj.Ofw.) and continuing through Fähnrich and Oberfähnrich (used as rank designations in their own right).

(Thanks to Nick Beale)

Selected Bibliography

Aders, G and Held, W. *Stukas, Jagdbomber, Schlachtflieger* (Motorbuch Verlag, Stuttgart, 1986)

Avram, V. *Aviation de Asalt - G8* (Modelism International SRL, Bucharest, 1994)

Brütting, G. *Das Waren die deustchen Stuka-Asse, 1939-45* (Motorbuch Verlag, Stuttgart, 1976)

Butler, P.H. *War Prizes* (Midland Counties Publications, Leicester, 1994)

Carell, P. *Hitler's War on Russia, Vol.1 - Hitler Moves East* (George Harrap and Co. Ltd., London 1964)

Carell, P. *Hitler's War on Russia, Vol.2 - Scorched Earth* (George Harrap and Co. Ltd., London 1970)

Deichmann, General der Flieger a.D., P. *German Air Force Operations in Support of the Army* (Arno Press, New York, 1962)

Ehrengardt, C-J. *Normandie-Nieman* (Heimdal, Bayeux, 1986)

Ericson, J. *The Road to Berlin* (Grafton Books, London, 1985)

Goodenough, S. *Great Land, Sea and Air Battles of World War II - War Maps* (Peerage Books, London, 1988)

Gray, P. and Thetford, O. *German Aircraft of the First World War* (Putnam and Co. Ltd., London, 1962)

Green, W. *Warplanes of the Third Reich* (Macdonald and Janes, London, 1976)

Gunston, W. (Editor) *Aviation - The Story of Flight* (Sundial Publications, London 1978)

Irving, D. *The Rise and Fall of the Luftwaffe - The Life of Erhard Milch* (Purnell, London, 1973)

Muller, R. *The German Air War in Russia* (The National and Aviation Publishing Co. of America, Inc., Maryland, 1992)

Obermaier, E. *Die Ritterkreuzträger der Luftwaffe 1939-1945, Band II - Stuka und Schlachtflieger* (Verlag Dieter Hoffmann, Mainz, 1976)

Pegg, M. *Luftwaffe Ground-Attack Units, 1939-1945* (Osprey Publishing, London, 1977)

Perrett, B. *A History of Blitzkrieg* (The Berkley Publishing Group, New York, 1989)

Plocher, Generalmajor H. *The German Air Force Versus Russia, 1943* (Arno Press, New York, 1967)

Price, A. *Luftwaffe Handbook, 1939-1945* (Ian Allen, Surrey, 1986)

Rosch, B. *Luftwaffe Codes, Markings and Units, 1939-45* (Schiffer Publishing, PA, 1995)

Rudel, Hans-Ulrich. *Stuka Pilot* (Euphorian Books, London, 1952)

Scheibert, H. *Die Träger des Deutschen Kreuzes in Gold, Band II* (Podzun-Pallas Verlag GmbH, Friedberg, no date)

Shores, C., Ring, H. and Hess, W.N., *Tunisien 42/43 - Luftkämpfe über Fels und Wüste* (Motorbuch Verlag, Stuttgart, 1981)

Smith, J.R. and Kay, A. *German Aircraft of the Second World War* (Putnam, London, 1972)

Smith, J.R. *The Henschel Hs 129* (Profile Publications Ltd., Leatherhead, 1966)

Speer, A. *Inside the Third Reich* (Sphere Books, London, 1971)

Statura, P., Bernad, D., and Haladej, D. *Henschel Hs 129* (MBI, Prague, 1993)

Vasco, J. *Bombsights over England* (JAC Publications, Norwich, 1990)

Weeks, J. *Men Against Tanks - A History of Anti-Tank Warfare* (Purnell Book Services Ltd., London, 1979)

Willmott, N. and Pimlott, J. *Strategy and Tactics of War* (Marshall Cavendish Books Ltd., London, 1979)

Young, Brigadier P. (Editor) *Atlas of the Second World War* (Military Book Society, London, 1973)

Zeimke, E. *Stalingrad to Berlin - The German Campaign in Russia, 1942-1945* (Dorset, Washington DC, 1968)

The Rise and Fall of the German Air Force, 1933-1945 (Arms and Armour Press, London, 1983)

Another view of Hs 129 B-1 (see also page 231) coded 'KG+GI' which was fitted with the Rüstsatz II comprising four 7.9 mm MG 17 machine guns.

Source Notes

The documentary material used in the research for this work, was gathered from various archive venues throughout Europe and the USA. The following represents a sample listing of those documents used, with the exception of private correspondence in possession of the author.

Airfields

PRO/AIR40/1206 Rumanian Air Force, Strength and Order of Battle, 21.10.1943.

PRO/AIR40/1250 Rumanian Air Force 1943-1945, List of Airfields.

PRO/AIR40/1965-1988 inclusive. These are Allied intercepts of ULTRA traffic, arranged in alphabetical order by airfield, giving unit movements, orders etc.

AIR40/1995 Airfields in Sardinia

AIR40/1998 Airfields in Tunisia

FLGHFN.CDK, April 1993 Airfield Directory: Russia and Eastern Europe 1938-1945

Aircraft

- Air Ministry Tactical Bulletin No.20, May 1943: "German Ground Attack Aircraft - The Hs 129"
- Air Ministry Weekly Intelligence Summaries (Various issues, but particularly Nos.174, 178 and 184).
- PRO/AIR40/2165 A.I.2(g) Reports, July 1942-May 1943
- A.I.1(b) HQ, RAFME: Intelligence HQ RAF Middle East: Details and Performance of Enemy Aircraft, Sheet 27, dated 3.5.1943 "Hs 129"
- A.I.2(g) Crashed Enemy Aircraft Report No.174, dated 13.01.1943.
- A.I.2(g) Crash Report No.168, dated 15.12.1942..
- A.I.2(g) Crash Report No.180, dated 11.02.1943.
- A.I.2(g) Crash Report No.184, dated 25.02.1943.
- A.I.2(g) Crashed Enemy Aircraft Report No.245, dated 27.07.1944
- A.I.2(g) Report No.2106, 02.09.1942.
- A.I.2(g) Report No.2117, 05.10.1943.
- A.I.2(g) Report No.2145, dated 08.01.1943., "Hs 129: Résumé of All Available Information"
- A.I.2(g) Report No.2174, dated 19.05.1943.
- Ministry of Aircraft Production, Directorate of Technical Development, Foreign Aircraft Bulletin No.9, February 1943: "Henschel 129 Ground Attack Aircraft"
- Headquarters Ninth Air Force, Assistant Chief of Staff, A-2 Technical Section, Report No.30 dated 13.07.1943 : "Consolidated Report on Hs 129 B-2".
- Hs 129 B-1, B-2 and B-3 Servicing and Maintenance Handbooks.
- Royal Aircraft Establishment, Farnborough: Report E.A.49/1, July 1944.
- CSDIC File No.253, 20.12.1944.
- Correspondence from files of Commanding General, AAF Material Command, Engineering Division, Technical Data Laboratory, Wright Field, Dayton, Ohio, 1944.

Operations

- PRO/AIR20/7700 AHB Translations No.VIII/14. Study prepared by the German Air - Historical Branch (8. Abteilung), dated 01.12.1944.: "Development of Ground Attack Arm and the Principals Governing its Operations up to the End of 1944."
- PRO/AIR27/868 No.111 Squadron, RAF, Operations Record Book
- PRO/AIR27/1395 No.225 Squadron, RAF, Operations Record Book
- PRO/AIR40/233 A.I.3(b) Report, "The German "Tank-Buster". Experiences with the Hs 129 in Russia."
- PRO/AIR40/1324 GAF Training Units and Schools
- PRO/AIR40/1864 CSDIC Reports
- PRO/AIR40/1998 Airfields in Tunisia
- PRO/AIR40/2010 GAF in Mediterranean, November 1942-February 1943

- PRO/AIR40/2011 GAF in Mediterranean, June 1943-August 1943
- PRO/AIR40/2151 GAF in Mediterranean. Aircraft Types, Units, Orders and Intentions
- PRO/AIR40/2158 A.I.2(g) Report: "Enemy Aircraft Found in the Middle East since the Commencement of the Offensive, October 1942. List No.8, 17.02.1943".
- PRO/AIR40/2248 GAF Flying Training Establishments
- PRO/AIR40/2347 "Y" Service, Middle East, 1942-1943
- Schönefelder Feldpost, Nr.3/4, August 1944: "1,500 Sowjetpanzer abgeschossen - Erfolgsmeldung einer Hs 129 Schlachtflieger Gruppe".
- ADI(K) 324/1945 GAF Schlachtflieger
- ADI(K) 470/1944 II./SG 101
- ADI(K) 598/1944 SG 151
- CSDIC, CMF, a.446, F.N.805 01.10.1944: "Order of Battle of German Air Force in Rumania."
- Headquarters North East African Air Forces A-2 Section (Capture Intelligence) Technical Report No.134, 07.06.1943.
- Headquarters Mediterranean Allied Air Forces Intelligencer Section: "Technical Air Intelligence in the Mediterranean Theatre, 1941-1944".
- Kriegstagbuch, Luftflotte 2.
- "Operations by II./Schlachtgeschwader 1 in the Period October 1942-September 1943" by Major a.D. Frank Neubert (Karlsruhe Collection)
- "Kampführung der Luftflotte 4 nach dem rümanischen Verrat".
- "Verlegungen in rümanischen Raum un Rückführung der Verbände nach Ungern in der Zeit zwischen 22-27.09.1944".
- "Planung für die Panzerbekampfung an der Ostfront im Winter 1943/44", Luftwaffenfüfungstab Ia, 01.08.1943.
- Hs 129/Reiseberich (629/1) Schönefeld, 14.04.1944
- Hs 129/Reiseberich (634/1) Schönefeld, 28.04.1944
- OKL/US National Archives and Records Service Microcopy No. T321, Rolls 17 and 19, "Kriegstagbücher Luftflottenkommando 6, March and April 1945".
- Appendices to Air Staff Post Hostilities Intelligence Requirement: "Fighter Operations of the German Air Force", Section IVC, USAFE, Office of Assistant Chief of Staff A-2:
Appendix XX: "Chief Missions of the Ground Attack Units in Operations, Types of Missions and Attacks and Escorts for Ground Attack Units" by Generalmajor Hitschhold, 20.09.1945-04.10.1945
Appendix XXI: "Principals for the Control of Operations of Ground Attack Units" By Generalmajor Hitschhold, 02.10.1945.
Appendix XXII: "Tactical Execution of Ground Attack Missions (Fw 190)" by Generalmajor Hitschhold and Major i.G. Jacob, 15.10.1945
Appendix XXIII: "Command Principals for Operations of Day Ground Attack Units" by Generalmajor Hitschhold, 05.10.1945.
Appendix XXIV: "Organisation of Ground Attack Units" by Generalmajor Hitschhold, 20.10.1945
Appendix XXV: "Mistakes and Omissions in the GAF Ground Attack Arm" by Generalmajor Hitschhold, 24.10.1945
- "Historique du Normandie Neiman 1942-1945", SHAA G/851.
- "Journal de marche Normandie-Neiman, 20.10.1944-20.06.1945", G8011.
- "Schlachtflieger, Panzerjagd und Störflugzeuge im Jahre 1943" by Ernst Kupfer (USAFHRC Ref. K113.3019-3)
- "Einsatz von Schlachtfliegern" by Bruno Meyer, (USAFHRC Ref. K113.3019-3)

Personal Accounts
- "Hello Bacau! Die geschichte der 10.(Pz)/SG 9 vom 10.12.1943 - Kriegsende." Unpublished manuscript by Obstlt.a.D. Walter Krause.
- "Ritterkreuz für Hauptmann Rudolf-Heinz Ruffer - Als ersten Hs 129-Flieger verliehen im Abwehrkampf gegen die Sowjets gefallen." "Schönefelder Feldpost", the house magazine of the Henschel Flugzeugwerke, Berlin-Schönefeld, Nr.3/4 August 1944.
- Flugbuch Franz Oswald
- Flugbuch Anton Maier
- Flugbuch Hans-Günther Marufka
- Flugbuch Jupp Öhl
- Personal correspondence Franz Oswald to Oswald family, 11.05.1942-04.02.1945
- Letter Georg Dornemann to author via Hans Obert, 10.04.1989
- Letter Heinz Heger to Franz Oswald, 19.04.1947
- Letters Walter Krause to author, 25.01.1989-26.10.1992
- Letters Franz Oswald to author, 17.09.1987-18.07.1996

- Letters Willi Tholen to author, 28.03.1989-10.07.1996
- Letter Willi Scholl to author, 20.08.1991
- Letters Gebhard Weber to author, 10.08.1988-20.07.1996
- *""Fliegende Pak" am Kuban-Brückenkopf"* by Uffz. Gerhard Henning, Bericht Nr.1771/He/36, Luftwaffen-Kriegsberichter-Kompanie (mot.)1, 18.04.1943.
- *"Fliegerhorst - Fliegerschicksal!"* by Lt.Dr. N. Scharnagl, Bericht Nr.1813/Scha/21, Luftwaffen-Kriegsberichter-Kompanie (mot.)1, Mitte Mai 1943
- *"Das Deutsche Kreuz in Gold"* by Fhj.-Fw. Rupprecht Radebach, Bericht 494/Ra/10, Luftwaffen-Kriegsberichter-Abteilung beim Luftflotten-Kommando 6 (10.Zug), 14.09.1944.
- *"Aus dem Tagebuch eines Panzerschlachtfliegers"* by Fhj.-Fw. Rupprecht Radebach, Bericht 462/Ra/8, Luftwaffen-Kriegsberichter-Abteilung beim Luftflotten-Kommando 6 (10.Zug), 27.08.1944.
- *"Der Panzerjäger Toni Maier"* by Gefr. Peter W. Boehr, Bericht Nr. 495/Roe/66, Luftwaffen-Kriegsberichter-Abteilung beim Luftflotten-Kommando 6 (13.Zug), September 1944.
- *"Da unten stimmt etwas nicht!"* by Fhj.-Fw. Rupprecht Radebach Bericht 469/Ra/9, Luftwaffen-Kriegsberichter-Abteilung beim Luftflotten-Kommando 6 (10.Zug), 09.08.1944.
- *"Waffenkameradschaft schlug dem Feind!"* by Gefr. Peter W. Boehr, Bericht Nr. 488/Roe/65, Luftwaffen-Kriegsberichter-Abteilung beim Luftflotten-Kommando 6 (13.Zug), 21.09.1944.
- WO208/4120: CSDIC SRGG 1232(C), 18.05.1945
- WO208/4129: CSDIC SRA 3763, 23.02.1943

Production, Factories, Work Force
- ADI(K) 234/45 Henschel Werk II at Johannisthal.
- PRO/AIR34/272 RAF Photo-Reconnaissance of Henschel factory at Johannisthal.
- ADI(K) 316/1942 "French Aero-Engine Factories".
- ADI(K) 264/1943 "Aero-Engine Factories - France".
- ADI(K) 1/1944 "Aero-Engine Factories - Paris Area."
- FD5638/45 Henschel Flugzeug Werke Jahresbuch, 1942.
- FD5638/45 Henschel Flugzeug Werke Jahresbuch, 1943.
- Henschel Flugzeug Werke Technischer Berichte, 30.06.1940-31.12.1944
- Correspondence between Henschel Flugzeug Werke and RLM GL/C, 1944
- Verbatim reports of the Generalluftzeugmeister Staff Conferences under Chairmanship of Erhard Milch, March 1942 - June 1944

Weapons
- PRO/AIR40/2158 New German Aircraft Ammunition.
- PRO/AIR40/2158 Enemy Munitions. 20 mm Solothurn A.P. Shot (Tungsten carbide Core).
- ADI(K) 230/1945 75 mm Cannon in Ju 88.
- Halstead Exploitation Centre Reports Nos.:
HEC 169: "Automatically Fired Shot Perpendicular to the Course of Flight, its Possibility of Being Used and Some Methods for its Technical Realisation" by Paul Hackemann.
HEC 15470: "Report on 37 mm Aircraft Gun. HFW booklet with photographs on 37 mm gun mounting in Hs 129 B-2."
UNT 94T: "Installation of 7.5 cm PAK in JU 88 and Hs 129 Aircraft", by P. Riecker.
UNT 165: "SG 113, Flak 18, 5 cm BK, 7.5 cm BK".
UNT 176: "SG 113 A and Special Equipment to be Fitted in Aircraft" by Dr. Grasse
UNT 180: "Automatic Weapons: Development and Data on MK 101, MK 103, BK 3.7, BK 5 and BK 7.5 etc."
UNT 227: "7.5 cm BK in Ju 88"
UNT 338T: "Installation of Automatic Gun 75 mm in Hs 129 and Particulars of its Feed Mechanism" by Dipl.Ing. Johannes Linke
- *"Panzerbeschuss aus der Hs 129 mit SG 113 A"*: Report by Institute für Waffenforschung.
- *"Panzerbekämpfung mit 3.7 cm und 7.5 cm Bordkanonen"*: Technisches Amt, GL/C, 08.03.1943
- A.I.2(g) Report 12.04.1943: "Developments in Armament and Protection found in German Aircraft Subsequent to 1st October and up to 31st March 1943.
- "Luftwaffe Attack Payloads"Antony Kay (Gruppe 66 *"Archiv"* Vol.4, No.13)
- Schwerpunkerprobungsberichte 14.08.1943 - 31.12.1944, Erprobungsstelle der Luftwaffe, Tarnewitz.

INDEX

PERSONALITIES

Abt, Lt. Wilhelm, 158
Aigner, Oblt. Rolf, 269, 276, 279, 280
Albert, Asp. Marcel, 266
Alexandrescu, Capt. Stefan, 220
Amarger, Lt. Maurice, 266
André, Asp. Jacques, 270
Bartel, Oblt., 251, 271, 289
Bayrle, Uffz. Karl, 252
Becker, Fw. Anton, 207
Berg, Fhj.Uffz. Ernst, 213
Bewermeyer, Fw. Konrad, 42
Bey, Ofw., 266
Bock, GFM Feodor von, 70
Böttcher, Uffz. Karl, 251
Bressler, Lt. Oskar, 251
Cara, Capt. Ioan, 220
Chamiev, Lt. von, 199
Christ, Obst., 173
Classen, Obgfr., 258-260
Corell, Ofw. Helmut, 252
Cuffant. Lt. Leon, 266
Czolbe, Fl.Stabs.Ing. Helmut, 234
Darjes, Hptm. Paul-Friedrich, 64, 84, 87
Dessloch, Gen.obst., 208
Dittrich, Ofw. Erhardt, 202, 203, 207
Dörffel, Major Georg, 153
Dörnbrack, Hptm. Werner, 121
Dornemann, Oblt. Georg, 149, 150, 176, 179-181, 188, 189, 193
Druschel, Major Alfred, 145, 147
Dvornikov, Leading Pilot M.S., 213
Eck, Hptm. Max, 70
Eggers, Oblt., 90, 144, 231, 232, 234, 235
Elbers, Uffz. Willi, 65
Enache, Adj. Ion, 221
Fiodorov, I.V., 159
Fleddermann, Ofw. Hans, 270
Fröhlich, Uffz. Gustav, 114
Frydag, Carl, 79
Fuchs, Lt. Erhard, 192
Fuller, Maj.Gen JFC, 19
Fülop, Lt. Henrik, 218
Galland, Generalleutnant Adolf, 23, 24, 55, 83, 111, 121-123, 169, 232
Gaumer, Dr., 236, 237
de Geoffre, Asp. Francois, 266
Georgescu, Adj. Constantin, 221
Gerhardt, Hptm. Dietrich, 95
Gheorghiu, General Emil, 221
Göring, Reichsmarschall Hermann, 27, 28, 55, 77, 79, 90, 169
Graf, Obst. Hermann, 183, 297, 298
Guderian, Heinz, 19
Hackemann, Dr. P., 235-237
Hainisch, Fhr., 280
Hanschke, Hptm., 173, 211
Harlinghausen, Obst. Martin, 111
Hartmann, Lt. Erich, 190
Heger, Ofw. Heinz, 271, 273
Henschel, Oskar, 27, 299, 300
Henze, Major Karl-Heinz, 203
Hertel, Gen.Ing. Walter, 55
Herrnberger, Fw. Helmut, 263
Hesse, Obgfr., 111, 112
Hessel, Oblt., 172
Hetzel, Uffz. Walter, 251
Hitler, Adolf, 28, 29, 77, 83, 110, 134
Hitschhold, Obstlt. Hubertus, 170, 232, 245
Holtermann, Ofw. Hermann, 252
Hormel, Walter, 210, 299, 300
Jech, Lt. Franzl, 199, 296
Jentsch, Oblt. Hans, 144, 158

Jeschonnek, Generalobst Hans, 23, 64, 79, 162
Jurck, Lt., 123
Kaempf, Wilhelm, 65
Kaschel, Ofw. Hans, 251
Katzberg, Fw. Alfred, 72
Kent, Oblt. Eduard, 84-87, 95, 186
Kiefer, Fw. Otto, 111
Koch, Dipl.Ing. Erich, 27
König, Oblt., 174
Korten, Gen.obst. Günther, 162
Kozedub, Ivan, 213
Krause, Oblt. Fritz, 119
Krause, Oblt. Walter, 174, 176, 181, 188-191, 199, 202, 253, 261, 266, 268, 274, 275, 277, 279, 280, 296, 298-300
Krauspe, Oblt., 172
Krebs, Major Helmuth, 172
Kupfer, Obstlt.Dr. Ernst, 158, 162-165, 169, 170
Lammel, Uffz. Heinz, 72
Langemann, Major, 172
Laurent, Asp. Joseph, 266
Lehmann, Oblt., 262, 289
Leonida, Lt. Sotropa, 220
Lelanz, Obgfr., 116
Liadskiy, Capt. T.S., 273
Lidell-Hart, Capt.Sir Basil, 19
Lippstreu, Fw. Walter, 251
Logemann, Uffz. Gerd, 192
Lossberg, Obst. Viktor von, 165
Maier, Uffz. Anton, 71
Maksimov, Lt., 159
Manstein, Erich von, 19, 94, 135, 188
Marchi, Asp. Robert, 266
Marinescu, Adj. Dumitru, 221, 223
Marufka, Hptm. Hans-Günther, 210, 213
Matuschek, Major, 130, 152
Matras, Cne. Pierre, 266
Matzen, Uffz. Franz, 270
Meinardus, Hptm., 232
Meyer, Hptm. Bruno, 21, 64, 70, 72, 90, 102, 103, 106, 107, 112, 123, 130, 131, 136, 139, 144-149, 152-154, 159, 165, 174, 180, 182, 202, 210, 211, 276
Michalczak, Fw. Heinrich, 199, 205, 207, 257, 258-260, 269, 277
Michel, Lt. Horst, 194
Mierienkov, Lt. V.A., 213
Milch, GFM Erhard, 27, 28, 55, 58, 59, 79, 162, 164, 165
Mladin, Adj. Constantin, 223
Moninger, Uffz., 213
Montgomery, Field Marshall, 102
Munteanu, Lt. Lazar, 221
Nagy, Major von, 218
Neubert, Hptm. Frank, 94, 95
Neumann, Fw. Artur, 261, 262
Nicolaus, Dipl.Ing. Friedrich, 27, 28, 39, 76, 79, 232-235, 296-300
Obleser, Oblt. Friedrich, 261
Orth, Lt. Dieter, 221, 232
Ossenbühn, Ob.stabs.ing., 244
Oswald, Hptm. Franz, 33, 84, 85, 87, 88, 110-125, 137, 154, 159, 160, 165, 160, 165, 170, 175, 180, 182, 183, 186, 190, 205, 206, 211, 232, 244, 245, 251-253, 266, 288, 294
Otani, Major-General, 218
Pasewaldt, Obst. Georg, 231
Petersen, Obst. Edgar, 78, 234

Petz, Lt., 119
Petzold, Uffz. Rudolf, 158
Pfaff, Obfhr. Egon, 192
Piper, Ofw. Wilhelm, 273
Plümer, Lt. Arnold, 88, 89, 211
de la Poype, Asp. Roland, 266
Pokryshkin, Alexandre I., 252
Popescu, Adj. Vasile, 221
Preiner, Franzl, 296
Puscas, Adj. Sef Stefan, 221
Quilitsch, Oblt. Friedrich-Wilhelm, 158
Rada, Lt. Ion, 221
Raufelder, Uffz. Walter, 242, 244
Reidenbach, Gen.Ing. Gottfried, 78
Reitberger, Ofw. Hans, 221
Reuss, Gen.major Franz, 266
Richter, Oblt., 172
Richthofen, Gen.obst. Wolfram von, 65, 79
Ritter, Lt., 64
Ritz, Fw. Otto, 185, 188, 191, 192, 199, 202, 254-257, 264, 276
Risso, Asp. Joseph, 266
Rommel, GFM. Erwin, 102, 107, 110
Rudel, Obst. Hans-Ulrich, 183
Ruffer, Oblt. Rudolf-Heinz, 135, 137, 139-141, 158, 175, 199, 202, 203, 210, 211, 252
Ruthmann, Uffz. Rolf, 251
Sarbu, Adj. Petre, 221
Saur, Karl-Otto, 58
Schinkel, Hptm., 198
Scholz, Uffz., 194, 231-235
Scholtz, Capt. Miklos, 218
Schönthoner, Uffz. Georg, 296
Schwetzke, Dr. R., 236, 237
Seidemann, General Hans, 123, 147, 192, 198, 199, 203, 264
Serescu, Lt. Nocotae, 220
Seuken, Oblt., 139
Shishkin, Lt., 159
Siems, Fw. Otto, 116
Speer, Albert, 77
Steinhoff, Oblt. Siegfried, 64, 65
Steinkamp, Lt Hans-Hermann, 84, 158, 193, 262, 263, 266, 280
Tholen, Uffz. Willi, 38, 44, 93, 96, 296
Vasiliu, Lt.Comm.Dutu, 221
Vorwald, Obst.i.G.Dipl.Ing. Wolfgang., 78
Vosseler, Uffz. Werner, 192
Weber, Lt. Gebhard, 33, 139, 181, 183-185, 193, 194, 205, 253, 260-262, 276, 277, 289, 294
Weiss, Major Otto, 32, 64, 65, 130, 180, 210
Wenzel, Lt.Hans-Werner, 190, 198, 199, 205, 211, 252
Wörl, Lt., 232
Wultsch, Uffz. Karl, 88
Zabava, Adj. Theodor, 221
Ziehm, Oblt., 280

COMMANDS AND UNITS

(German)

Legion Condor, 19, 23
Luftflotte 1, 102
Luftflotte 2, 116, 121
Luftflotte 4, 65, 79, 149, 156, 208, 220, 221, 226, 250, 279
Luftflotte 6, 150, 156, 174, 250, 251, 270, 289
Luftflotte 10, 289

I. Fliegerkorps, 153, 159, 160, 213, 266
IV. Fliegerkorps, 65, 70
VIII. Fliegerkorps, 65, 70, 79, 147, 154, 189, 192, 194, 198, 205, 253, 264, 266, 268, 274, 278
1. Fliegerdivision, 150
4. Fliegerdivision, 266, 289
Fliegerführer Afrika, 103, 122
Fliegerführer Tunisia, 111
Panzerjagdkommando Weiss, 130, 180
Führer der Panzerjäger, 130, 131, 144, 154, 159, 170, 190
Einsatzstab Banat, 264
Erprobungskommando 26, 158, 234, 244, 245, 266, 288
Erprobungskommando Hs 129, 32, 64
Erprobungskommando 210, 77
Erprobungskdo Ju 88 (Pz.Jä.), 131
Erg.Sta.II/Lehrgeschwader 2, 42, 64
Erg.Jagd.Gr.Ost, 64
Ergänzungs-Schlachtgruppe, 172, 173, 211
3./Ergänzungszerstörergruppe, 102, 172
II./Jagdgeschwader 2, 118

Jagdgeschwader 51
II.Gruppe, 114, 166, 280
13.(Pz.) Staffel, 90, 91, 94, 95, 97, 135, 139, 144, 145, 150, 154-156, 170, 231, 235
Jagdgeschwader 52, 183, 185, 190, 198, 261, 276, 277, 296-298, 300
II./Jagdgeschwader 53, 118
8./Jagdgeschwader 77, 122
III./Kampfgeschwader 51, 131

II.(Sch.)/LG 2
  20, 21, 23, 32, 38, 64, 75
5.Staffel, 64
10.Staffel, 64
Nahaufklärungsgeschwader 14, 300
Schlachtfliegergruppe 10, 20
Schlachtfliegergruppe 20, 20
Schlachtfliegergruppe 30, 20
Schlachtfliegergruppe 40, 20
Schlachtfliegergruppe 50, 20

Schlachtgeschwader 1
I.Gruppe, 64, 145, 147, 153
II. Gruppe, 64, 70-72, 79, 83, 84, 89-91, 94, 95, 232
4.Staffel, 64, 65, 70, 83, 93-95, 97, 130, 131, 138, 139, 145, 150, 155, 156, 170, 180
5.Staffel, 64, 65, 70-72, 84, 86, 88, 110-114, 116
6.Staffel, 64, 84, 88
7.Staffel, 64, 97, 130
8.Staffel, 64, 97, 130, 131, 135, 138, 150, 154, 158, 170

Schlachtgeschwader 2
II.Gruppe, 121
4.(Pz) Staffel, 102, 103, 107, 130, 131, 150, 152, 153, 170, 221, 232
7.Staffel, 130
8.(Pz) Staffel, 116, 121-123, 130, 131, 150, 154, 155, 170, 175
10.(Pz)/Schlachtgeschwader 3, 207

Schlachtgeschwader 9
I. Gruppe, 139, 189, 289
IV.(Pz) Gruppe, 89, 134, 158, 191, 194, 208, 210, 211, 253, 288
10.(Pz) Staffel, 170, 175, 176, 181, 183, 188-192, 194, 198, 199, 202, 203, 205, 207, 210, 211, 242, 252, 253, 256, 257, 260, 264, 266, 268-270, 274, 276-280, 289, 296, 297, 300
11.(Pz) Staffel, 158, 170, 234

12.(Pz) Staffel, 170, 188, 189, 192, 210, 251, 262, 266, 270, 289
13.(Pz) Staffel, 170, 175, 183, 205, 206, 210, 244, 251, 252, 266, 270, 273, 288, 294
14.(Pz) Staffel, 158, 170, 176, 193, 205, 226, 251, 262, 264, 266, 279, 280, 289
SG 10, 266
I./Schlachtgeschwader 77, 176, 203
Schlachtgeschwader 101
II.Gruppe, 172
Schlachtgeschwader 151
III.Gruppe, 173, 174
14.(Pz) Staffel, 173
Schlachtgeschwader 152
I.Gruppe, 173
1.Staffel, 173
2.Staffel, 173
3.(Pz) Staffel, 173
4.(Pz) Staffel, 173
Staffel 92, 130
III./Schnellkampfgeschwader 10, 118, 121, 169
Stukageschwader 1, 131
Stukageschwader 2, 131, 162
Stukageschwader 3, 117
III./Zerstörergeschwader 2, 121
Zerstörerschule 2, 172

(Rumanian)
Grupul 8 Asalt
41st Escadrila, 220
42nd Escadrila, 220, 221
60th Escadrila, 220
Esadrila 41 Asalt, 226

(Hungarian)
5/1. Experimental Night Fighter Sqdn., 218

(American)
14th Fighter Group, 116
58th Fighter Squadron, 114

(British)
111 Squadron, 116
152 Squadron, 116
225 Squadron, 116

(Russian)
9th Fighter Aviation Division, 251
16th Guards IAP, 252
90th Guards ShAP, 273
288 IAP, 213
812 IAP, 159
240th Fighter Regiment, 213
Normandie-Niemen Fighter Regiment, 151, 266, 270

(Misc. Ground)
Panzerarmee Afrika, 102, 103, 108
II. SS Panzerkorps, 144
1. SS Pz.Gren.Div. "LAH", 144-147

AIRCRAFT VARIANTS

(German)
AEG C IV, 16
AEG J I, 16
Ar 68, 20
DFS 230, 92, 93
Dornier Do 17, 27
Focke-Wulf Fw 57, 77
Focke-Wulf Fw 58, 236
Focke-Wulf Fw 189, 26, 29, 220, 221, 236
Focke-Wulf Fw 190, 55, 97, 118, 121, 122, 130, 131, 145, 147-149, 158, 165, 169, 170, 184, 234, 245, 278, 279
Halberstadt CL II, 16
Hannover CL IV, 16

Hannover CL IIIa, 16
Heinkel He 46, 20
Heinkel He 51, 19, 20
Henschel Hs 123, 20-23, 64, 71, 130
Junkers J I, 16
Junkers 52/3m, 19, 221
Junkers Ju 87, 20, 21, 47, 93, 117, 118, 122, 130, 131, 134, 164, 169, 170, 184, 220, 234, 278
Junkers Ju 88, 27, 52, 80, 130, 134, 164, 165, 169, 184, 220, 282
Me Bf 109, 20, 21, 23, 47, 97, 112, 118, 122, 220, 282-285
Me Bf 110, 29, 47, 77, 130, 131

(Russian)
P-39 Airacobra, 251, 252
Il-2, 151, 273, 274
I-16, 130
LaGG-3, 151
MiG-3, 151
Yak-1, 151
Yak-9, 151

WEAPONS AND EQUIPMENT

AB 23, 117, 118
AB 50, 253
BK 5, 232
BK 7.5, 165, 231, 232, 285 *et passim*
Flak 18, 79, 80, 131, 163, 232
Flak C/41, 232
Flammenwerfereinbau, 235
FuG 7a, 264
FuG 101, 236
MG 17, 26, 29, 44, 45, 230, 231
MG 131, 231, 236
MG 151, 29, 44, 45, 230
MK 101, 29, 45, 52, 77, 78, 82 *et passim*, 102, 103, 145, 181
MK 103, 78, 145, 165, 169, 181, 203, 205, 230-232
Pak 38, 79, 80
Pak 40, 80, 282 *et passim*
Revi C/12 C gun sight, 50
Revi C/12 D gun sight, 50
SD 2 anti-personnel bomb, 47, 89, 117
SC 10 10kg bomb, 89
SC 50 50kg bomb, 47
SC 250 250kg bomb, 89, 118
SD 50 bomb, 117, 118, 220
SG 113A Mortar, 234-244
WK 28/35 Nebelwerfer, 234
ZFR 3 B gun sight, 294

ENGINES

Argus As 410, 28, 29, 32, 33, 38, 39, 57
Gnôme-Rhône 14M, 33, 38, 39, 41, 55, 57, 58, 103, 107, 230, 279
Issota-Fraschini Delta, 41, 230

TANKS

(American)
Sherman, 113
(British)
Churchill, 113
Crusader, 106
Valentine, 112
(Russian)
T-34 (Tech.Descp.), 74, 75, 151, 181
KV 1 (Tech.Descp.), 74
KV 2 (Tech.Descp.), 74
SU-152, 151